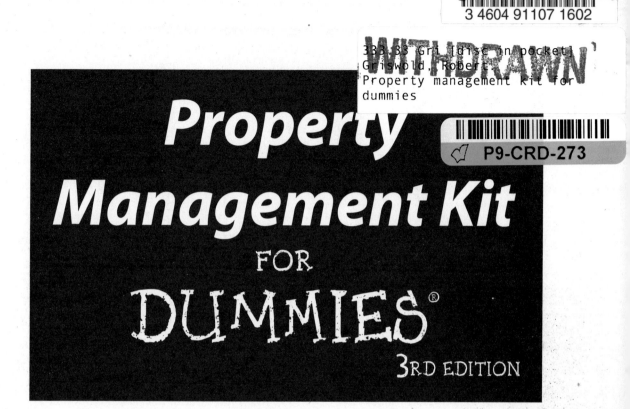

Property Management Kit

FOR

DUMMIES®

3RD EDITION

by Robert S. Griswold, BS, MBA, MSBA

Coauthor of *Real Estate Investing For Dummies*

WILEY

John Wiley & Sons, Inc.

Property Management Kit For Dummies®, 3rd Edition

Published by
John Wiley & Sons, Inc.
111 River St.
Hoboken, NJ 07030-5774
www.wiley.com

Copyright © 2013 by John Wiley & Sons, Inc., Hoboken, New Jersey

Published by John Wiley & Sons, Inc., Hoboken, New Jersey

Published simultaneously in Canada

For general information on our other products and services, please contact our Customer Care Department within the U.S. at 877-762-2974, outside the U.S. at 317-572-3993, or fax 317-572-4002.

For technical support, please visit www.wiley.com/techsupport.

Wiley publishes in a variety of print and electronic formats and by print-on-demand. Some material included with standard print versions of this book may not be included in e-books or in print-on-demand. If this book refers to media such as a CD or DVD that is not included in the version you purchased, you may download this material at http://booksupport.wiley.com. For more information about Wiley products, visit www.wiley.com.

Library of Congress Control Number: 2012956400

ISBN 978-1-118-44377-4 (pbk); ISBN 978-1-118-46108-2 (ebk); ISBN 978-1-118-46109-9 (ebk); ISBN 978-1-118-46110-5 (ebk)

Manufactured in the United States of America

10 9 8 7 6 5 4 3

WILEY

About the Author

Robert S. Griswold is the coauthor of *Real Estate Investing For Dummies* with Eric Tyson. He earned a bachelor's degree and two master's degrees in real estate and related fields from the University of Southern California's Marshall School of Business. His professional real estate management and investing credentials include the CRE (Counselor of Real Estate), CPM (Certified Property Manager), ARM (Accredited Residential Manager), CCIM (Certified Commercial Investment Member), PCAM (Professional Community Association Manager), CCAM (Certified Community Association Manager), and GRI (Graduate, Realtor Institute).

Robert is a hands-on property manager with more than 35 years of practical experience, having managed more than 800 properties representing more than 50,000 rental units. He owns and runs Griswold Real Estate Management, Inc., a property management firm with offices in southern California and southern Nevada.

Since 1995, Robert has been the real estate expert for NBC San Diego, a network-owned and number one–rated station. Every Saturday, he provided impromptu answers to viewers' real estate questions live on the air during *NBC News This Weekend.*

Once a week for nearly 15 years, Robert hosted a live, call-in, real estate news and information talk show called *Real Estate Today! with Robert Griswold,* heard throughout southern California on Clear Channel's AM 600 KOGO radio station and around the world on the show's website at www.retodayradio.com. He has twice been named the #1 Radio or Television Real Estate Journalist in the Country by the National Association of Real Estate Editors (NAREE) in its annual Journalism Awards Program. The first award was for *Real Estate Today! with Robert Griswold,* and the second was for his work for NBC News.

Robert is the lead columnist for the syndicated "Rental Roundtable" landlord-tenant Q & A column at www.rentalroundtable.com, which is also featured in the *San Diego Union-Tribune* and the *San Francisco Chronicle.* He also writes a nationally syndicated column, "Rental Forum," at www.inman.com.

He's a nationally recognized real estate litigation expert, having been retained on more than 1,750 real estate legal matters and serving more than 200 times as a court-appointed receiver, referee, or bankruptcy custodian.

Robert is a member of the national faculty of the Institute of Real Estate Management (IREM) and a National Apartment Association (NAA) and California Department of Real Estate Certified Instructor. He's a licensed California and Nevada real estate broker, a Realtor, and an active member of the NAA, the California Apartment Association, and his local apartment association, the San Diego County Apartment Association. Since 2005 he has served as a planning commissioner for the City of San Diego.

In his spare time (?!), he enjoys travel (especially cruising!) and watching his children excel in all aspects of life, including academics (University of San Diego, University of California at Irvine, Point Loma Nazarene University, and Stanford) and sports, especially soccer. Robert wishes he had more opportunities but savors those precious times when he, his wife, Carol, and their four young adults (Sheri, Stephen, Kimberly, and Michael) can travel together, enjoy the holidays, or even have an old-fashioned family game night. Above all, he tries to retain his sense of humor and truly enjoy what he's doing!

Dedication

I dedicate this book to my best friend and wife, Carol, with whom I celebrated 30 years of marriage in 2012. Carol played a key role in, and deserves much of the credit for, successfully raising our four children, but I also appreciate her 30+ years of love, friendship, support, patience, and persistence in attempting to bring the proper balance to my life, which starts with putting God first in everything I do. Of course, life's always exciting and has real meaning thanks to my four great children, who have become incredible young adults — Sheri, Stephen, Kimberly, and Michael. I also want to express my appreciation to my mom, Carol, for her unconditional love and infinite encouragement. I'm also grateful to my father, Westcott Griswold (who passed away just after I finished writing the second edition of this book), for the positive role model he was in his work ethic and love for his family and friends. We all miss him. Most of all, I want to praise and thank God for the wonderful gifts and incredible opportunities He has given me.

Author's Acknowledgments

This book was made possible through the efforts of some very fine people at John Wiley & Sons, Inc. Mark Butler initially believed in my concept for the first edition of *Property Management For Dummies.* Lindsay Lefevere was very supportive of my efforts to include a CD-ROM with forms for the second edition and has continued to strive for excellence in this third edition.

My project editor, Jennifer Tebbe, really understood the rental housing industry after serving as the copy editor for the second edition. She was helpful and supportive throughout, and this new edition is the most comprehensive book in the field and a fantastic resource for rental owners and property managers. My thanks also go to copy editor Todd Lothery for a masterful job. I'd also like to thank technical editor Kathleen Harmon, who helped make sure that the information was accurate and that my advice hit the mark.

My interest in real estate can be traced back to my father and mentor, attorney Westcott Griswold, who advised me to excel in real estate, not law; and my friend and first real estate professor at USC, Dr. Rocky Tarantello. Thank you!

I was blessed to formally begin my real estate management career working with two of the most savvy, knowledgeable, and ethical men in real estate — thank you, Rod Stone and George Fermanian, for starting me on the right track. In my property management days, I met many fine people, and two of the best are my friends, property manager Wade Walker and attorney Steve Kellman. I also want to thank attorney Kathy Belville-Ilaqua for her review and sage advice on fair housing materials covered in the new edition.

I'll always be thankful to Carl Larsen, homes editor of the *San Diego Union-Tribune,* who started me in my writing career when he gave me a shot with the first "Rental Roundtable" column while his lovely wife, Sharon Larsen, assisted in creating my original book proposal.

Finally, I'd like to thank all my NBC news viewers, "Rental Roundtable" and "Rental Forum" readers, and radio listeners who've educated me with their interesting and thought-provoking questions on literally every aspect of real estate management.

Publisher's Acknowledgments

We're proud of this book; please send us your comments at `http://dummies.custhelp.com`. For other comments, please contact our Customer Care Department within the U.S. at 877-762-2974, outside the U.S. at 317-572-3993, or fax 317-572-4002.

Some of the people who helped bring this book to market include the following:

Acquisitions, Editorial, and Vertical Websites

Project Editor: Jennifer Tebbe

(Previous Edition: Chad Sievers)

Executive Editor: Lindsay Sandman Lefevere

Copy Editor: Todd Lothery

(Previous Edition: Jennifer Tebbe)

Assistant Editor: David Lutton

Editorial Program Coordinator: Joe Niesen

Technical Editor: Kathleen Harmon

Vertical Websites: Josh Frank, Laura Moss-Hollister

Editorial Manager: Christine Meloy Beck

Editorial Assistants: Rachelle S. Amick, Alexa Koschier

Cover Photo: © Marcus Lindström/ iStockphoto.com, © rysick/iStockphoto.com, © Maciej Maksymowicz/iStockphoto.com, © Alexander Mirokhin/iStockphoto.com

Cartoons: Rich Tennant (`www.the5thwave.com`)

Composition Services

Project Coordinator: Sheree Montgomery

Layout and Graphics: Melanee Habig, Joyce Haughey

Proofreader: ConText Editorial Services, Inc.

Indexer: BIM Indexing & Proofreading Services

Publishing and Editorial for Consumer Dummies

Kathleen Nebenhaus, Vice President and Executive Publisher

David Palmer, Associate Publisher

Kristin Ferguson-Wagstaffe, Product Development Director

Publishing for Technology Dummies

Andy Cummings, Vice President and Publisher

Composition Services

Debbie Stailey, Director of Composition Services

Contents at a Glance

Table of Contents

Part V: Money, Money, Money! *327*

Introduction

Welcome to *Property Management Kit For Dummies,* 3rd Edition. You can discover many of life's lessons by doing some on-the-job trial and error. But that doesn't apply to property management — the mistakes are too costly, and the legal ramifications too severe. This book gives you proven strategies to make rental property ownership and management both profitable and pleasant.

About This Book

Many landlord-tenant relationships are strained, but they don't have to be. A rental property owner who knows how to properly manage his property and responds promptly to the legitimate concerns of his tenants will be rewarded with good people who stick around. The key is properly maintaining your property and constantly investing in upgrades and improvements. By doing this, you can be successful in meeting your long-term financial goals and realize that being a landlord is an excellent primary or secondary source of income.

This book is based on hands-on experience and lessons from my own real-life examples. Unlike many landlords and property managers, I believe that your tenants are your customers, not your enemies, and as such, you should treat them with respect. You may find investing in rental real estate to be a key piece of your overall investment strategy, but not everyone is cut out to be a property manager. I want to make sure you understand not only the basics of the rental housing business but also some of the tricks that can make you glad you're a real estate investor.

Although this book is overflowing with useful advice and information, it's presented in a light, easy-to-access format. It explains how to wear many hats in the property management business: advertiser/promoter (in seeking tenants), host (in showing the property), handyman (in keeping up with and arranging for repairs), bookkeeper (in maintaining records), and even counselor (in dealing with tenants and their problems). Just as important, this book helps you maintain your sense of humor — and your sanity — as you deal with these challenges and more.

I wrote this book in essentially chronological order — from your first entry into the world of rental property ownership and the corresponding steps to prepare and promote your property to showing your rental and selecting the right tenants. As a result, reading the book cover to cover makes sense, but feel free to read the sections that are most relevant to you at any given time.

Skip around and read about those areas that are giving you problems, and I'm confident that you'll find some new solutions to try.

To make your life easier, I've included many of the forms you need to be successful in managing your rental — whether you're just starting out with a single-family rental home or condo, you have a handful of rental units, or you possess a whole portfolio of rental properties. If you're reading this book in print, these forms are available on the accompanying CD; if you're reading a digital version of this book, simply click the link in the table of contents to access the forms. Either way, feel free to print them out, have your local legal counsel review them, and start putting them to use.

Conventions Used in This Book

The Institute of Real Estate Management (IREM) and the National Apartment Association (NAA) are invaluable resources for rental property managers and owners. Because I mention them often, I refer to them by their acronyms.

I also employ the following conventions to help you navigate the text:

- ✔ *Italics* highlight new, somewhat technical terms and emphasize words when I'm making a point.

- ✔ **Boldface** indicates key words in bulleted lists and the action steps in numbered lists.

- ✔ Monofont highlights websites and e-mail addresses.

What You're Not to Read

Managing rental property takes time, so you may want to read just the essential information to help you find success. In that case, feel free to skip the following:

- ✔ **Sidebars:** These gray-shaded boxes are full of fun bits or humorous stories that are quite interesting (if I do say so myself), but they're not essential for you to understand the topic at hand.

- ✔ **Text with True Story icons:** These passages contain some of my real-life experiences to help keep you from making my mistakes.

Foolish Assumptions

When writing this book, I assumed that you're likely reading this book because you're one of the following:

✔ An unintentional property owner — someone who, through a series of circumstances, suddenly and unexpectedly came upon an opportunity to own property. Perhaps you inherited a house from a relative and, not wanting it to sit idle, you decided to rent it out. Or maybe you transferred to a job in another city and because you've been unable to sell your home, you've been forced to rent the property to help cover the mortgage and operating expenses. Many property owners find themselves in the rental housing business almost by accident, so if you count yourself in this group, you're not alone.

✔ One of those people who has made a conscious decision to become a rental property owner. Perhaps, like many rental owners with a plan, you needed to buy a new, larger home and decided to keep your existing home as a rental property. Or maybe while you were looking to own your own place, you found a great duplex and decided to live in one unit and rent out the other. In a world where people seem to have more and more demands on their time, many aspects of rental property ownership are very appealing, like the capacity to supplement a retirement plan with additional income or the proven opportunity to build wealth. The key to achieving this success is finding a way to make money while still retaining control over your life.

✔ Someone who already works in the rental housing industry. Maybe you're just starting out or maybe you've been in the field for some time. Either way, you want to find out more about your chosen profession. Good for you. The rental housing industry has so much variety that you'll always be discovering new things and appreciating that every day is a new challenge. Yes, there is some repetition (you must collect the rent every month), but unlike many jobs, no two days ever seem to be the same. That's what attracts so many professionals to the field of property management (and keeps them there).

As an owner, real estate offers one of the best opportunities to develop a steady stream of residual income that you earn whether you're sleeping, participating in your favorite leisure activity, enjoying your retirement, or relaxing on vacation. Whatever the circumstances, the bottom line is the same: You hope to generate sufficient income from the property to cover the debt service, pay for all operating expenses, and possibly provide some cash flow, along with tax benefits, appreciation, and equity buildup. The key to your success is knowing how to manage people and time. And this book has plenty to offer you on that front.

How This Book Is Organized

I've divided this book into six parts. The chapters within each part cover specific topic areas in more detail, so you can easily and quickly skim a topic of interest or troubleshoot the source of your latest headache! Each part addresses a major area of rental housing management. Following is a brief summary of what I cover.

Part I: So You Want to Be a Landlord?

Managing rental property isn't everyone's cup of tea. The chapters in this part assist you in evaluating your skills and personality to see whether you have what it takes to manage rental units — or whether you should call in the property management cavalry. If a management company is the answer to your prayers, I show you how to select one, what to expect, and how much it'll cost. Finally, when the day of your escrow closing arrives and the ink is dry, flip here to find out what your immediate priorities are as you take over your new rental property.

Part II: Renting Your Property

The most important aspect of rental housing is keeping the unit occupied with paying tenants who don't destroy it or terrorize the neighbors. In this part, you figure out how to prepare the property for rent, set the rents and security deposits, develop a comprehensive (yet cost-effective) marketing and advertising campaign, and show your rental unit to prospective tenants. Because all tenants look great on paper, I also fill you in on some tricks and techniques for establishing good tenant selection criteria.

Part III: The Brass Tacks of Managing Rentals

This part takes you from moving in your new tenants to moving them out — and everything in between. You get some strategies for collecting and increasing rent, retaining tenants, and dealing with those few tenants who give you a headache whenever your paths cross. Minimizing vacancies and retaining tenants is the key to success as a rental owner. But when your tenants complain incessantly, decide to repaint in nontraditional colors, or stop paying the rent, the real challenge of managing rental housing begins. In this part, you discover techniques for dealing with these issues and more.

Part IV: Techniques and Tools for Managing the Property

Assembling the right team of professionals — from employees to contractors — is one of the main ways to find success as a landlord. Another way involves maintenance, which can be one of the largest controllable expenses most rental owners face. In this part, I also shed light on how to meet the minimum standards required for your property to be habitable and the pros and cons of different alternatives for handling maintenance.

Last but most certainly not least, because landlords and property managers are sued more than any other business entity, you definitely want to review the issues of crime, fire protection, environmental hazards, and the safety and security of your rentals — and I help you do that here, too.

Part V: Money, Money, Money!

Having the proper insurance for your properties and property management activities can be a complex topic, so in this part, I guide you through the ins and outs of insurance. Taxes are another inevitability of life in the rental property business, so here's where you find basic info on property taxes, the way rental property income is taxed, and some of the tax advantages of owning rental property. With all that money going out for insurance and taxes, you also want to know just how much cash flow your rental empire is generating, so I provide you with some basics on rental accounting and record-keeping.

Every seasoned rental owner should look for additional sources of income beyond rent, including the opportunities of lease options, which I cover in this part. The effect of government-subsidized housing programs continues to play an important role in many communities, so here you find info on the advantages and disadvantages of working with public rental assistance programs. Niche rental markets — like those catering to students and pet owners — are also worthy of your consideration, and I let you know how you can use them to your advantage.

Part VI: The Part of Tens

Here, in a concise and lively set of condensed chapters, are the tips to make the difference between success and foreclosure. In this part, I address the benefits of owning rental properties and provide tips to rent your vacancy today. I also suggest you check out the CD for a bonus Part of Tens chapter on ten common management mistakes and how to avoid them.

Property management and rental housing laws are dynamic, with something new arising every day. So because I'm just that nice of a guy, I also offer an appendix to help you navigate them. Count on the invaluable resources in this appendix to keep you current and improve your management skills.

Icons Used in This Book

Scattered throughout the book are icons to guide you along your way and highlight some of the suggestions, solutions, and cautions of property management.

This icon points your page-turnin' fingers to files or forms you can use in your day-to-day property management.

Remember these important points of information, and you'll have great success as a rental property owner.

Keep your sights on the bull's-eye for important advice and critical insight into the best practices in property management.

Focus on this icon for real-life anecdotes from my many years of experience and mistakes. When you've managed more than 50,000 rental units in 30 years, you see some interesting situations. Now, I share them with you.

This icon highlights the land mines that both novice and experienced rental property owners need to avoid.

Where to Go from Here

Like any great resource book, you must read it! This book is designed for experienced or seasoned landlords, as well as rookies who still think all tenants are nice and prompt with rent payments and should be invited over for Thanksgiving supper.

Whether you're contemplating rental real estate, looking to fine-tune your proven landlord secrets, or facing total financial ruin at the hands of the Tenant from Hell, this book offers chapter after chapter of solid rental property management advice, especially for the small rental property owner. It explains how to attract qualified prospects; select and screen tenants; maintain the rental rate; handle security deposits, rental contracts, broken water pipes, late rents, tenants who overstay (and don't pay), and more. Find the topic you want to know more about and start reading right there. ***Remember:*** Everything is manageable and workable — if you know what you're doing!

Property Management Kit For Dummies, 3rd Edition, helps you protect your investment and maintain your sense of humor, as well as your sanity, as you deal with one of the most unpredictable professions in life — property management. Consider this book your Property Management Bible, written just for you.

Part I

So You Want to Be a Landlord?

The 5th Wave
By Rich Tennant

"Well, you've just gone over the line in breaking the no pets, no smokers clause in the rental agreement, Mr. Crawford."

In this part . . .

Managing rental property isn't for the faint of heart, but it can be very rewarding for the right person. The chapters in this part guide you through the process of figuring out whether you have what it takes to manage rental property or whether you're better off leaving it to a pro — someone you hire to do the dirty work for you. I also fill you in on what you need to know if you're taking over ownership of a rental property, including how to deal with the current tenants and inform them of your policies and procedures. This is the part for you if you're just starting to think about purchasing a rental property but aren't quite sure what that entails.

Chapter 1

Property Management 101

In This Chapter

▶ Looking at the pros and cons of property management

▶ Exploring the different types of real estate

▶ Surveying the steps involved in renting your property

▶ Walking through the day-to-day details of property management

The key to long-term success and wealth-building through real estate ownership lies in the foundation you acquire as a hands-on property manager. For instance, some people start out managing rental properties owned by someone else and gain a great deal of experience that they can use for their portfolio.

There are many positive reasons for becoming a rental property owner or manager, and just as many ways of doing so. Perhaps you've saved up the down payment to purchase your first small rental unit and hope to see your investment grow over the years as a nice retirement nest egg or a supplement to your current income. Maybe you want to invest in a medium-sized apartment building and build some equity as well as rental income to supplement or replace your current income. Perhaps you've inherited Aunt Gertrude's run-down cottage and need to find a good tenant who'll care for it and pay the rent on time. Maybe you've recently closed on your new primary residence, only to find that selling your existing home isn't as easy as the real estate agent promised. Or perhaps you've had to move across the country to find a suitable job but want to return to your home in the future.

Whether you plan to become a full- or part-time property manager, you need to know what you're doing — legally and financially. This chapter serves as a jumping-off point into the rental property world. Here you can find useful info, tips, and checklists suitable for novice or seasoned rental property managers. So get ready for some practical advice from the tenant trenches to help you handle situations when they arise!

Understanding What Property Management Really Is

Property managers provide consumers with a product known as *shelter*. In other words, as a property manager, you supply tenants with a place to live in exchange for the payment of rent. Although property management doesn't seem that complex, you can avoid the many mistakes unprepared property managers make by knowing what you're getting into.

The following sections give you a quick overview of the pros and cons of property management. Chapter 2 provides more in-depth analysis of these advantages and disadvantages to help you determine whether renting your property is the right choice for you.

Considering the benefits

Property management can be a rewarding and fun venture. I can't imagine my life without some aspect of property management in it (why else would I have written this book, right?). Following are some of the reasons why I get such a kick out of this business:

- **Experience with real estate investment:** As you manage rental property, you have the opportunity to observe and begin to understand investing cycles, which is an essential skill for becoming a successful real estate investor. Of course, some real estate investors succeed without ever being hands-on property managers because they hire others to handle the task for them. However, I believe rental property owners should gain that real estate investment expertise by actively working as property managers for several years, either for themselves or others.

- **Interaction with different people:** If you're a people person, you'll find that property management is a great opportunity to meet all types of people. Not everyone you encounter is someone you want to make your close friend, but you'll certainly have the chance to work with a smorgasbord of personalities.

- **Skill development:** Property management requires diverse skills because you must handle so many different tasks (such as marketing, advertising, leasing, screening, and maintenance). But it also allows you to grow those skills beyond the basics through patience and passion. For example, you may begin by advertising your rental unit in a basic way and move to analyzing an entire ad campaign. Pay attention to how unrelated products are presented for sale and apply those concepts to rental housing. Most of the best marketing ideas are already out there, and you just need to adapt them to your rental property.

✔ **Variety:** Personally, I enjoy the variety of tasks and challenges found in property management. Sure, some aspects of it are repetitious. Rent is due every month, and all properties require ongoing care and maintenance. But for the most part, every day in property management is something new.

Confronting the icky parts

You can't expect all aspects of property management to be fun. Just like your primary job, some days run smoothly, and others are filled with problems. Here are a few of the bad aspects of the property manager gig:

✔ **Difficult tenants:** Despite the great people you meet, property management has its fill of difficult and challenging personalities, including people who're downright mean and unpleasant. You have to be prepared for adversarial and confrontational relationships with others. Collecting the rent from a delinquent tenant, listening to questionable excuses, or demanding a contractor come back and do the job properly requires patience, persistence, and a fair but firm approach.

✔ **Long hours:** Because you're dealing with housing, you don't know when you're going to be needed. It may be 3 p.m. or 3 a.m. Like me, you can expect to be constantly on call — even when you're on vacation, at the movies, or in the middle of a family holiday dinner — to deal with issues that only the rental owner or property manager can handle. Fortunately, you can minimize these inconveniences by planning carefully and hiring competent and reliable employees and vendors who can prevent many unexpected emergencies through good management and maintenance. However, owning and managing rental property remains a 24/7, year-round commitment.

✔ **Need for emergency capital:** One of my favorite sayings and goals in life is "No surprises," but owning rental properties can lead to situations in which unanticipated expenses arise at any time. Tenants suddenly stop paying rent at the same time the roof leaks and the water heater goes out in the middle of the night! Having a nice nest egg, a rainy-day fund, or at least a decent unsecured credit line at reasonable rates can be very helpful, as most rental property owners experience a squeeze on their cash flow at times.

✔ **Potential liability:** After more than 30 years in property management, my opinion is that most tenants are good people just looking for a decent, quiet place to call home. But some "professional tenants" look for any mistakes you make or even set traps for you to fall into that can lead to claims for free rent or even litigation. You need to stay on top of all the legal requirements for landlords in your area and make sure you always comply with all laws and disclosures. If you're not willing or able to keep up with ever-changing legal requirements and health and safety issues, or if you're sloppy with your record-keeping, you may learn some expensive lessons!

Renters drive rental property management

The Census Bureau reports that more than one-third of the U.S. population, or 94 million people, are renters occupying nearly 39 million rental units, including more than 13 million single-family home rental properties. The number of renters has increased in the last few years with the economic challenges in most areas of the country. Also, the limited availability of credit has made it more difficult to become a home-owner, and the overall percentage of home-ownership has fallen from a high of 69 percent in 2006 down to 65 percent in late 2012.

Individual property owners dominate the rental housing industry. According to the National Multi Housing Council, individuals own nearly 85 percent of the small rental properties with 2 to 4 units and nearly 60 percent of the residential income properties with 5 to 49 units. In comparison, one of the most popular ways for individuals to invest in real estate is through real estate investment trusts (REITs), which have exploded in the market with the acquisition of billions of dollars of high-profile rental real estate assets. Yet, in spite of the significant publicity they've received in the real estate media, REITs actually own less than 10 percent of all residential rental housing units in the United States.

The good news is that these negatives can be found in many other careers or professions that don't offer the benefits and satisfaction you can get from property management. So in my opinion, the pros outweigh the cons.

Examining the Types of Real Estate Available

Before you run out and purchase a rental property, you need to have a good idea of the different types you can own. Most real estate investors specialize in properties with specific uses. Investment properties fall into classifications such as residential, commercial, industrial, and retail.

For the purpose of this book, I focus only on residential real estate because the majority of rental real estate is housing, and the basic concepts are easy to understand and master. (After you master the basic concepts of residential real estate, you may want to consider other types of property management.) The best practices I present throughout this book are applicable for these types of residential rental properties:

- ✓ **Single-family houses and condominiums or townhomes:** Most real estate investors start with a rental home, condo, or townhome because these properties are generally the easiest ones to gain experience on. They may be located in a common interest development (CID) or community association where all the common areas are the association's responsibility.

- ✓ **Duplexes, triplexes, and four-plexes or subdivided houses:** This category includes properties with two to four units. Often these properties are the first choice for real estate investors who plan to live in one of the units or want to take the next step up from investing in a single-family rental home or condo. These properties qualify for favorable financing terms, so they're perfect for the new investor or an investor buying in higher-priced urban markets.

- ✓ **Medium-sized multi-family apartment buildings:** These buildings usually have between 5 and 30 units and are best run with on-site management and regularly scheduled maintenance and contractor visits.

- ✓ **Large, multi-family apartment buildings:** These properties are larger buildings that can have 30 or more rental units in a single location, with an on-site manager or maintenance staff. Owning one of these properties is the goal for many real estate investors who look forward to being able to hire a professional property manager and just check their bank account for their regular cash distributions. (I reveal what to look for in a good professional property manager in Chapter 3.)

No matter what type of residential real estate you're involved with, you need to understand the basics of property management. You must market or staff a property differently depending on its size and location, but many of the fundamentals are the same, regardless.

Over the course of your tenure as a property manager, you'll probably manage several different types of properties. That's just one of the challenging yet fulfilling aspects of the job. For example, you may start out managing single-family rental homes or condos and then see your investments or career progress to larger rental properties. Sometimes people in the rental housing business start out as on-site employees for large rental properties, learn the ropes, and later apply that knowledge to become the Donald Trump of rental houses in their area.

Owning and managing all types of rental property can be lucrative, and I suggest you jump in where you have your first opportunity, because no rules mandate your starting position.

Factors that influence real estate as an investment

Almost everyone has heard the adage that the top three keys to success in real estate are location, location, location. This adage is more than just a cliché. Unlike a stock investment, you can't easily liquidate real estate and reinvest in another opportunity in a different geographic area. Real estate success is closely correlated to a property's location.

Real estate is also a very cyclical business that's subject to the Economics 101 concepts of supply and demand. During economic business expansions, the demand for real estate is strong, enabling owners to raise rents. With the higher rents, real estate developers can build new properties, which causes the supply of real estate to catch up with the demand and forces rent increases to slow or disappear. When the business economy begins to slow, the demand declines, and once again you have an abundance of rental real estate. This cycle typically repeats every seven to ten years but can go longer.

One of the best reasons for investing in residential real estate (versus commercial or retail properties) is that it tends to be the most stable sector of the real estate market, a fact that was proven again in the economic downturn that began in the mid-2000s. Virtually all types of real estate income properties saw significant decreases in value during that downturn, but residential real estate fared better than any other category and rebounded first when the market began to improve.

Thanks to very generous tax laws, for many years (prior to the major income tax law changes in 1986) real estate investors really didn't have to worry about the cash flow generated from their properties. An owner's ability to generate tax losses that could be offset against earned income, plus other creative tax strategies, outweighed the common-sense goal of generating more income than expense. Positive cash flow was just an added benefit.

The bottom line: After you purchase your property, you can't effectively control or change its location. Nor can you really influence the overall business economy or real estate cycles.

Seem perplexing? Many so-called "investing gurus" try to sell you their DVDs, but if you're looking for honest advice on the proper way to find, evaluate, and invest in residential real estate, I suggest you read *Real Estate Investing For Dummies,* 2nd Edition (Wiley), which I coauthored with Eric Tyson.

Renting Your Property

One of the first and most important lessons I learned when I started in property management more than 30 years ago is that vacant real estate isn't a very good investment. You need to fill those vacancies and keep them filled with tenants who pay on time. Just try looking in the mirror and telling yourself that all the rent came in last month. I bet you can't do it without smiling!

Of course, renting your property and retaining your tenants doesn't just magically happen; it requires a plan and a lot of work. But you want to work smart and not just hard. In the following sections, I cover some of the best practices for preparing your rental units, setting your rents, attracting qualified prospects, and closing the sale.

Chapter 4 expands on where it all begins: the acquisition of the rental property. Part II then helps you position your new rental property within the rental market and discover how to find good tenants.

Preparing the property

Before you can rent your property, you have to make sure it's ready for a tenant to move in. However, you can't simply put a For Rent sign up and expect to rent to the first caller. You need to spend some time properly preparing the property. And by "some time," I mean a lot.

Relax! Tear up that application to those cable shows that completely renovate your fixer-upper for free, because you *can* prepare your property yourself. Just remember to focus on the inside as well as the outside. Chapter 5 shows you the best way to determine what to upgrade and renovate to meet the needs of your target market of prospective renters. I also explain how to ensure that your property's *curb appeal,* or its exterior appearance, makes your potential new tenants want to see the inside of it and not keep driving by to the next property on their list.

During this stage, you really get to test your decorating skills on a budget because you don't want to over-improve the property. But if you're too tight and try to get by with anything less than your best effort, be ready for the majority of those individuals showing interest in your rental unit to be the least-qualified prospective tenants. The moral of the story? Don't be cheap, but do be practical!

To get the great tenants, you need to guarantee your rental property compares favorably to other properties in your area and makes that important positive first impression. This impression starts on the exterior, with a neat and well-maintained appearance, and continues with a clean and inviting interior, with the features and amenities expected by prospective tenants in your area.

Properly preparing the unit also often requires the use of outside vendors or contractors. What you don't contract out — tasks such as basic cleaning, maintenance, and painting — you need to do yourself. You also need to know how to perform a careful inspection to make sure the unit is ready to show. I give you details about how to accomplish all these tasks in Chapter 5.

Knowing how much to charge

Understanding what you can charge your tenants is far from arbitrary. Setting the rent in particular can be tricky — especially if you've just spent hours investing your time and sweat into renovating and scouring your rental unit to make it sparkle.

In such cases, you may overestimate the market value of your unit because you have so much personally invested. But your prospects aren't likely to be impressed that you laid the tile. Instead, they'll quickly point out that the carpet color doesn't match their furniture, but if you lower the rent $300 per month, they'll consider taking the unit off your hands, almost as if they're doing you a favor. You may be able to structure some mutually beneficial rental concessions, but don't be a pushover.

Many rental property owners are simply too nice. Maybe you're someone who has trouble bargaining and holding out for the top fair-value dollar, kind of like my mother-in-law, a sweet but overly generous woman — especially when it came to yard sales. My wife and I are glad no one ever offered Rita 50 cents for our car!

In addition to setting the rent, you need to make the following decisions before a tenant moves in:

✔ **The amount of the security deposit:** Setting security deposits is a function of not only market conditions but also limitations on the amount you can charge and whether that amount's fully refundable. These restrictions are set by your state laws. Determining whether you want to pay your tenants interest on the deposits you hold is also subject to law, but certain advantages can warrant doing so even where not required (especially for long-term tenants).

The best way to decide on all the details of the security deposit is to conduct market surveys to see what others are doing. If everyone else has security deposits set at approximately half of a month's rent, requiring your new tenants to come up with a security deposit of two full months' rent upon move-in is difficult.

✔ **The type of rental contract:** Another important decision that has lasting consequences is deciding whether a lease or month-to-month rental agreement is best for your property. Such conclusions are often reached after conducting a market survey and understanding the pros and cons of each type of contract.

Check out Chapter 6 for more info on determining how much to charge, setting deposits, and figuring out what type of rental contract to use.

Capturing prospects' interest

A successful property manager needs to understand the role of marketing in creating demand and meeting the needs of local renters. Fortunately, your marketing and advertising possibilities have increased dramatically with the advent of the Internet and social media. You (or perhaps your teenage children) can develop a fantastic website with digital photos and floor plans. Just make sure you follow all the fair housing laws as you work to generate rental traffic.

In Chapter 7, I review the various electronic and nonelectronic options available for promoting your rental property and attracting prospective tenants.

Turning interest into property visits

The ways to attract potential tenants are endless, but the fundamentals of getting them to visit your property are centered around your ability to answer their questions on the phone. You need to understand how to qualify your prospects both for what you want in a stable, long-term resident and what they need to call your rental property their home for years.

Converting your e-mails or phone calls to actual property visits is the next essential step to creating maximum interest in your rental unit. Chapter 8 explains how to get prospective tenants to view your property.

The way in which you show your property to prospects is important. Avoid walking from room to room, stating the obvious. Instead, point out certain benefits of your unit's unique or special features. Just don't oversell the product and talk fast, like a late-night cable infomercial. Ultimately, the best technique for showing your property is letting the property itself make the right impression, as I explain in Chapter 9.

The best result you can expect to achieve at the property-viewing stage is convincing the prospect to complete your rental application and put down a holding deposit. What the prospect can expect from you at this time is the receipt of any mandatory disclosures.

Picking your tenants and signing the deal

Property management isn't exactly like an online dating game, but you do want to gather information (while following all fair housing laws to the letter) and select a tenant who meets or exceeds your minimum written rental qualification standards. Tenant selection is probably the one single step in the rental process that can make or break you as a property manager, and I devote a lot of detail to this important topic in Chapter 10.

With tenant selection, what seems to be a fairly straightforward process can actually be tricky because of the various limitations on the questions you can ask and the information you can request from interested applicants. Follow the same procedure for everyone to comply with fair housing laws, and determine how you're going to verify each prospect's rental application. Be sure to select tenants based on objective criteria and then properly communicate your decision to both approved tenants and unsuccessful applicants.

Getting Your Hands Dirty: Managing the Property

You never hear from your tenants, yet the check seems to come in the mail each month. Managing your rental unit seems easy — just like you pushed a button! But after a year of progressively busting out with pride at your exceptional property management skills, you decide to drive by the property . . . only to find that your retirement plans and financial nest egg are candidates for a remake of *Animal House!*

In the next sections, I present the practical, in-the-trenches part of property management that can help you get familiar with every day-to-day eventuality related to the operational side of property management and the life cycle of a tenancy.

Moving tenants in and out

Coordinating the move-in of a new tenant is one of your most pleasant tasks because this time is your best opportunity to ensure your tenant starts out on the right foot by explaining your rental rules and guidelines. Chapter 11 helps ensure your move-in process runs smoothly.

But all good things must come to an end. That end should start with you making sure that the move-out date is mutually agreed upon in writing and that the tenant understands your expectations, policies, and procedures through a tenant move-out information letter. I share more about how to make the move-out process as painless as possible for all involved in Chapter 15.

Collecting rent

You can greatly improve your chances of making the rent collection process a positive experience by emphasizing your rent collection policy when your tenant first moves in and by asking all the who, what, when, where, and how questions of rent payments.

But no matter how carefully you screen your tenants and how thoroughly you explain your rent collection policy, sometimes the inevitable happens and your tenant is unable to pay the full rent when it's due. What do you do? Start by issuing reasonable but firm policies when the tenant moves in and enforcing your grace period and late-period policies. Then, when your tenant doesn't pay the rent or doesn't live up to his responsibilities under the rental contract, you're prepared to take the appropriate legal action to regain possession of your property as quickly as possible. Chapter 12 provides more in-depth info to help you collect rent.

Keeping the good tenants

Turnover is your number one nemesis as a rental property owner. Although it's inevitable, your ability to renew your leases and provide incentives for your tenants to stay and pay can be significant in controlling your expenses and maximizing your rental income. That's why keeping your tenants, particularly your good tenants, is a smart move. After tenants have lived at your property for a while, you can quickly determine which ones are the better ones by asking yourself a few questions:

- ✔ Who pays the rent on time?
- ✔ Who quickly lets you know when the unit needs maintenance?
- ✔ Who takes care of the property, perhaps by cleaning up outside debris and planting flowers?

One of the best ways to ensure your good tenants stay with you is to develop a tenant-retention program where you offer them incentives. This action shows that you appreciate them. Chapter 13 offers more on the importance of developing a good landlord-tenant relationship from the perspective of your tenants. It also reveals your tenants' most important needs: good communication, timely maintenance, respect for their privacy, consistent policies, and a good value for their rental dollar.

Dealing with troublesome tenants

Despite your best tenant-screening efforts, you're going to make the wrong decision at some point and allow a problem tenant to move in or have a good tenant who turns sour. But you can lessen the number of these incidents by getting to know some of the problems you may encounter and how to deal with them early on:

- ✔ **Late or missed rent payments:** The timely payment of rent is the life-blood of real estate investing because you can't pay your mortgage or expenses without it. A written rent collection policy is a valuable tool to minimize these problems.

- ✔ **Loud tenants:** It only takes one boisterous tenant to disrupt the tranquility of the whole neighborhood and destroy your tenants' right to "quiet enjoyment." Developing and implementing rental policies and rules can avoid your problem tenant chasing the good tenants away.

Chapter 14 gives you some additional tools to effectively deal with these problem tenants. I also describe the best way to handle common tenant problems and the pros and cons of alternatives to an eviction. But because avoiding eviction doesn't always work, I make sure you have everything you need to know to go to court, present a winning case, and collect your judgment. Life is full of unexpected events, so I also include suggestions on how to cope with tenants who fall into bankruptcy, refuse to leave, insist on leaving early or want someone else to take their place, have personal relationships that deteriorate during their tenancy, pass away at your property, or don't allow you access to properly maintain the property.

Maintaining the property

Are you familiar with the saying, "To own is to maintain"? When you have only a few rental units or are just starting out, you often do much of the maintenance work on your units yourself. But as you acquire more properties or advance in your primary career, you need to explore the benefits and consequences of using employees. If you own a larger property, having an on-site employee who's responsible for its day-to-day management is absolutely mandatory.

To keep your property in tip-top shape, you also need to work with outside vendors and suppliers who are pros within their industry. Always keep in mind that you get what you pay for and that maintenance can be one of the largest expenses faced by most landlords. Part IV helps you navigate the nitty-gritty, hands-on aspects of managing employees and contractors and maintaining your property.

Protecting your investment

Like many property managers, you probably consider your property an investment. If you continuously lose money, having the property isn't worth the hassle or the expense, right? Not to worry. Although you can't predict bad weather or crime, you can safeguard the value of your investment by

- **Being aware of environmental hazards that can occur:** Minimize your risk and be prepared for natural or environmental hazards such as storms, fire, carbon monoxide gas, or mold. See Chapter 18 for details.

- **Buying the necessary insurance:** You can't avoid buying insurance, so I make sure you know enough to be dangerous when your insurance agent says you need coverage for snowstorms at your duplex in Phoenix. Chapter 19 covers the types of insurance you need to consider.

- **Increasing your cash flow:** Sometimes, recouping all the costs for your property isn't easy, so you may need to find ways to get more cash in your hands. As you discover in Chapter 21, a wide assortment of options awaits, including government-subsidized housing programs, special niche housing markets, and different lease options.

- **Keeping detailed records:** You're going to be so successful as a rental owner and manager that I need to make sure you have good record-keeping and financial reporting so you can keep track of all the money you make. Chapter 20 reveals some simple ways to handle filing.

- **Paying your taxes:** Property taxes are a reality of life almost everywhere. Chapter 19 makes sure you know how they're calculated and what you can do to minimize your tax payments by appealing your property's assessed value when market conditions decline.

Chapter 2

Do You Have What It Takes to Manage Your Own Rental Property?

*R*eal estate is a great source of income, whether you're looking for steady, supplemental retirement income or a secure financial future. Most residential rental property owners want to become financially independent, and real estate is a proven investment strategy for achieving that goal. But after you sign your name on the dotted line and officially enter the world of rental property ownership, you face some tough decisions. One of the very first concerns is who handles the day-to-day management of your rental property. You have units to lease, rents to collect, tenant complaints to respond to, and a whole host of property management issues to deal with. So you need to determine whether you have what it takes to manage your own rental property or whether you should hire and oversee a professional property management firm.

Owning investment real estate and managing rental units are two separate functions, and although nearly everyone can invest in real estate, managing it takes time, special skills, and the right personality. In this chapter, I highlight the importance of relationships with people, because property management is really people management. I also give you the lowdown on some of the advantages of owning rental property and help you assess whether you have what it takes to manage your own property.

Understanding That Managing Rental Property Is a People Business

Some rental property owners find themselves managing their own properties without even knowing what management requires. Managing the physical aspects of your properties (the buildings) and keeping track of your income and expenses are fairly straightforward tasks. However, many rental property owners' most difficult lesson is the management of people.

Rental management requires you to deal with many more people than you may think. In addition to your tenants, you interact with rental prospects, contractors, suppliers, neighbors, and government employees. People, not the property, create most rental management problems. An unpredictable aspect always exists in any relationship with people.

As with most businesses, the ability to work with people is one of the most important skills in being a successful property manager. If you enjoy interacting with people and are adept at working with them, you're off to a good start toward becoming a prosperous property manager.

Identifying the Types of Real Estate Owners

Rental property management has been around for hundreds of years, ever since property owners first realized they could earn income on their land and buildings by renting them to tenants. These days, the title of *landlord* is no longer bestowed only on the landed gentry. There are as many different ways that people become property owners as there are types of rental properties. Although the nature of the business has changed over the centuries, today you can classify rental property owners in two categories: the inadvertent rental property owner and the long-term investment rental property owner. No matter which category you find yourself in, one thing is constant: The key to your success is sound management.

The inadvertent rental property owner

Many property owners find they're in the rental housing business almost by accident. Although solid reasons to invest in and own rental real estate exist, many owners begin their real estate careers by chance or through circumstances beyond their control. For example:

✔ Some people inherit a house from a relative and don't want it to sit empty.

✔ Others transfer to a job in another city and can't sell their old home, so they're forced to rent the property because they want some income to help cover the mortgage and operating expenses.

✔ Some folks looking to own their own place find a great duplex where they can live in one unit and rent out the other one.

✔ Other owners are *upside down* on their mortgage (owe more than the house is worth) and can't sell their property for enough money so they rent it (while finding more modest accommodations themselves) until the market improves for sellers. (Note that this scenario also applies to some couples going through a divorce.)

Whatever the circumstances, the bottom line is the same: The property owner hopes to generate sufficient income from the property to cover the debt service and all operating expenses and to possibly even provide some cash flow, along with appreciation and equity buildup.

The long-term investment rental property owner

Despite lower values nationwide due to a weak economy in recent years, real estate remains one of the best, most reliable, and most consistent investments in terms of long-term return on investment. Of course, the popularity of real estate with many current landlords started with the tremendous increase in the value of real estate in the decade from the mid-90s to mid-2000s. Many individuals found that real estate investing is a key element of their diversified investment portfolio. And why not? Real estate is a cornerstone of the American dream. Many people strive for years to own their first home and then realize the tremendous investment opportunity offered by income-producing rental real estate.

In today's world, more and more demands are placed on your time, so many aspects of rental property ownership are appealing. People want to supplement their current retirement plans (which are predominantly invested in cyclical stocks, bonds, and mutual funds) with additional sources of cash flow, and real estate has a proven track record as one of the greatest wealth builders of all time. Most folks find that generating a stable income without having to punch a time clock and not being limited to earning an income only for time spent working for someone else is an attractive option. Even most professionals, such as lawyers and accountants, are constrained in their income to their billable hours. The more hours they work, the more money they usually make. And time-wise, people are limited in the actual number of hours they can work, which limits their income potential, so having ways to generate income outside of their main job is beneficial.

The long-term investment category allows you to accumulate more wealth in your lifetime than you can with just one source of income. Real estate investments provide additional cash flow and significant asset value over time. So what are you waiting for? The time to begin your real estate ownership and management career is now. The sooner you start, the sooner you can achieve your personal and financial goals. The key is to make money while still retaining control over your life. Real estate offers one of the best opportunities to develop a steady stream of residual income that you earn whether you're sleeping, engaging in your favorite leisure activity, vacationing, or enjoying your retirement.

Recognizing the Advantages of Owning Rental Property

A great advantage to building wealth through real estate is the ability to use other people's money. You'll likely purchase a rental property with the help of financing from a lender, and then your tenants provide the monthly funds for the debt service payments and for ongoing operating expenses and capital improvements.

The wide availability and low cost of real estate financing over the past few years make real estate investing a viable and realistic option for virtually everyone. Even when commercial lender real estate loans were difficult to obtain during the financial crisis of the late 2000s, many deals still went through, thanks to seller financing.

Most people purchase real estate using leverage gained by borrowing from the seller or a lender. *Leverage* is when you purchase real estate with financing, and it usually consists of a cash down payment from the buyer and a loan or other people's money. Here are the two types of leverage:

- ✔ **Positive leverage:** With this type of leverage you can earn a return on both your cash investment and on the entire value of the real estate. The ability to control significant real estate assets with only a small cash investment is one of the best reasons to invest in real estate. For example, you may purchase a $100,000 rental home with $20,000 in cash and a bank loan for $80,000. If the home value doubles in the next decade and you sell this home for $200,000, you've turned your $20,000 cash investment into a $100,000 profit.

- ✔ **Negative leverage:** Real estate enjoyed a long run of steady appreciation from the mid-1990s through 2007, but you must remember that real estate doesn't always appreciate and can even decline, as it has in most areas since 2007. Negative leverage can wipe out your entire investment with just a 20 percent decline in the market value of your rental property. So if you buy a rental home for $200,000, with $40,000 in cash and

$160,000 from your bank, only to see the economy falter or the local real estate market sour, you may have to sell your rental home for less than your acquisition price. If you sell the home for only $160,000 after the costs of sale, you may have just enough to pay off your bank, and your cash down payment of $40,000 simply evaporates. Negative leverage is, unfortunately, the experience of many investors and homeowners who purchased real estate in the early to mid-2000s using little or no cash down payments and now find that their mortgage balance exceeds the current value of their property.

Although you can actually purchase some rental properties without a down payment, remember that you get what you pay for. The rental properties that are the best performers (high-occupancy units with stable, long-term tenants paying full-market-value rents and reasonable operating expenses) in the long run generally aren't available with creative financing.

Despite the downturn in real estate nationally, people with an incredible amount of capital are seeking to acquire rental real estate in many markets. Though opportunities exist for the patient and persistent investor, finding really good, well-located rental properties is competitive and challenging in many urban markets.

Limited exceptions do exist where you can reposition a poorly performing property in an essentially good neighborhood. Although these opportunities exist in some (generally rural) areas of the country, they're only for the most experienced real estate investors and property managers with a high tolerance for risk. Don't invest in no-down-payment rental properties outside of your own area or in a neighborhood you don't know extremely well. If you do, you'll likely be the next seller offering the property and may even be willing to pay someone to take it off your hands!

Rental real estate also offers you the opportunity to pay off your mortgage by using your tenants' money. If you're prudent in purchasing a well-located property in a stable area, you should have enough income to pay all the operating expenses, utilities, maintenance, taxes, insurance, and your debt service. Each month your property becomes more valuable while your tenant essentially pays all your expenses, including principal and interest payments on your loan.

Your lender and tenant aren't the only ones who can help you with the purchase of your rental investment property. Even the government is willing to offer its money to help your cash flow and encourage more investment in real estate. The government allows rental property owners to take a *deduction* (or offset to income) for depreciation on their income taxes each year. *Depreciation* isn't an actual out-of-pocket cash expense but an accounting concept that provides you with an allowance for expected wear and tear. Depreciation deductions basically reduce the taxable income from rental properties and give you more cash flow during your ownership. See Chapter 19 for an explanation of how depreciation can defer income taxes until you sell your rental property.

Over time, you may find that your rental income collections grow faster than your operating expenses. That's why many economists feel real estate is a superior investment, because historically, real estate has been a very effective hedge against inflation. And after your tenants have finished paying your mortgage for you, you suddenly find that you have a *positive* cash flow — in other words, you're making a profit.

Eyeing the Unique Characteristics of a Good Manager

Good management equals good financial results. Having tenants who pay on time, stay for several years, and treat the property and their neighbors with respect is the key to profitable landlording. However, finding those individuals is easier said than done. One of the greatest deterrents to financial independence through real estate investments is the fear of management and dealing with tenants. That's why management is so important, but what exactly makes a good manager? The next several sections take a closer look at the many different aspects of managing your own rental properties.

Realizing that good management makes a difference

To get a firm grasp on managing your rental property, you need to understand what good management really is. Good management entails having a well-maintained rental property that's occupied with a paying tenant on a long-term lease who treats the property like her own. As with many things in life, managing well is much easier said than done, but by doing your homework in advance and understanding what it takes to be a good manager, you can reduce those beginner's mistakes.

Who hasn't heard or even personally experienced horror stories about a greedy or downright unpleasant landlord who took advantage of his tenants? The image of rental property owners and managers as overbearing, stingy, and snoopy has become part of the culture. Of course, you've probably also heard about tenants who don't pay their rent, damage the rental property, and harass the neighbors and the owner. Virtually all these horror stories are true, but it isn't a coincidence or bad luck that they happen to the same landlords again and again.

Bad management can bring down a rental property investment — pure and simple. If you choose the wrong tenant or fail to address certain maintenance issues, your real estate investment may turn into a costly nightmare. You can be financially devastated when you have a mortgage to pay and your new tenant gives you a rubber check for the security deposit and first month's rent. And to make matters even more challenging, you may find that your occupant has skipped town after trashing your rental unit.

Fortunately, you can master good property management skills. Where to start? Well, aside from this book, I encourage you to look into professional organizations that have qualified staff who can present educational offerings for property owners and managers. Here are three of the better organizations out there:

- The Institute of Real Estate Management (IREM) at www.irem.org
- The National Apartment Association (NAA) at www.naahq.org
- The National Association of Residential Property Managers (NARPM) at www.narpm.org

Separating your personal style from sound management

Owning and maintaining your home is good experience for many aspects of rental property management. For example, you may be very handy fixing that leaky faucet or painting cabinets. However, owning a home doesn't give you all the skills needed to become a successful rental property owner. The main difference you need to remember is that a rental property is an investment — nothing more, nothing less. Although in a perfect world you'd find your rental property personally appealing, ultimately it's just an income-producing investment.

At your home, you're in full control of making sure you have money to pay the debt service on the property. And you take a very serious interest in addressing small maintenance problems while they're still low-cost items. As a home-owner, you also probably have experience at trying to live on a budget.

When managing rental property, you must be able to put your personal tastes and style aside in favor of what keeps your tenants happy and your costs reasonable. Because you don't live at your rental property, you need to make sure the furnishings and the property's condition appeal to the broadest number of potential renters — even if you'd rather decorate it like the Palace of Versailles. You also have to be practical and think about the long-term implications of your management decisions. For example, you may prefer drapes for window coverings in your own home, but vertical blinds are more practical for a rental property. Although they may not be as luxurious as drapes, blinds are more durable and much easier to clean.

Home business opportunity

Many people who manage their own rental properties value the aspect of being their own boss. They often run their business from a home office. Many people today are looking for an opportunity to work at home, and rental management can provide the second income with flexible hours.

You may also expand your real estate holdings to the point that you outgrow your home office or prefer to have a separate business location. The advent of private postal service centers can also combine the best of a home office with the image of a professional operation. And many rental properties offer you the opportunity to live and have a small separate management office on-site.

Managing your time

For most rental property owners, managing their rental units is a part-time job. They handle tenant calls, collect the rent, show the units, and even perform most maintenance in the early evenings or on weekends. However, managing your time is an important part of managing your rental properties. Time management is really about evaluating how much time you have and then looking for ways to streamline tasks so that you make the best use of your time.

Although rental management can be a part-time job, don't be fooled. It takes a lot of time, patience, and hard work to be successful. At first, most people assume they're equipped to handle any and all property issues. They may even find they can manage two or three units without any problems or time conflicts. They enjoy managing their rental properties and appreciate the cost savings. However, as their portfolio grows, the need to be very efficient in handling management activities becomes essential. The challenge of being a landlord is finding the time required for this second job.

The good news is that the time required to be a landlord is in your control. If you acquire sound properties and master the skills of marketing (see Chapter 7) and tenant screening and selection (see Chapter 10), you can greatly reduce the amount of time you spend managing your rental property. You also have to work smart or you may find that your time is better spent in areas other than management, because time is money.

Delegating management activities

As a landlord, you may look at all the tasks you have to do and get a bit overwhelmed. However, dealing with some responsibilities yourself and delegating some to other people can make your job much easier. To manage your property to the best of your ability, look at your personal skill set to determine which tasks you can do and which ones you need to delegate.

Throughout this book, I tell you various ways that you can delegate certain management activities and responsibilities to your very own personal team of experts, composed of the following:

- ✓ **A property manager:** Ultimately, you can delegate all the management activities to a professional property manager. However, having a property manager doesn't mean you're totally off the hook. Depending on the arrangement with your property manager, you may still find yourself providing the oversight. (Turn to Chapter 3 for more on using a property manager.)

- ✓ **A maintenance professional:** The skills required to successfully manage your own rental properties are different from the skills you need to handle your own property maintenance. Most rental property owners find that using trusted and reasonably priced contractors is the best alternative. You may not have the requisite skills, equipment, or time to do the work properly and quickly. Although doing the work yourself may seem more cost-effective, you'll quickly lose any savings if the rental unit sits vacant for additional time. (Flip to Chapter 16 for help finding the right maintenance personnel.)

A client once hired me to manage a large, 100-unit rental property with nearly 30 vacant units. The rental market was actually pretty good, and together we knew we could rent the units after they'd been painted and cleaned. The owner had always managed the property personally and used only in-house maintenance personnel for all work, including painting. The owner wanted to have the in-house maintenance person paint two units per week, but that would take nearly four months until all the units were rent-ready. I was able to demonstrate that hiring an outside contractor to paint and having the in-house maintenance folks focus only on cleaning the units would get all 30 units rent-ready in less than a month. Even though the painting contractor was an expense the owner didn't want to incur, hiring the contractor was the better way to go because we were able to rent the units quickly and more than cover the additional costs. Sometimes the cheapest way isn't the best way to solve a problem.

- ✓ **An accountant:** Many owners don't have the patience or discipline to keep accurate accounting records that are so important at tax time, so they prefer to have a bookkeeper take care of the record-keeping and help them manage their bills. See Chapter 20 for more information on accounting.

- ✓ **A legal expert:** Some landlords may look forward to their day in court, but most find the experience unrewarding and problematic. Using a local landlord-tenant attorney is an excellent idea when you have legal issues that may end up in court.

✔ **A prescreened applicant source:** Some owners use a rental locator service or certain real estate brokers who seem to always have a steady stream of potential renters coming into the area to provide prescreened rental applicants. Your level of delegation on this matter may very well depend on whether you own one or ten rental units.

Knowing that your style is unique

The most important fact to remember is that no one will ever manage your rental property like you will. Accept that fact and then determine whether you're cut out for property management. Remember, property management isn't just a question of style. Ultimately, it comes down to sound, responsible practices.

You're motivated more than anyone else to watch out for your real estate investments. Only you would work through the night painting your rental unit for the new tenant move-in in the morning. Who else would spend a Hawaii vacation looking through the local newspaper classifieds or local rental ad books for creative ad ideas?

Be honest with yourself. Know your strengths and weaknesses as a property manager. You may find that you're able to do the job but that you wind up with frazzled nerves and doubts. If you aren't truly excited and challenged by handling your own property management tasks, then you probably won't have success in the long run managing your own property and you may need to delegate (see the preceding section).

Being Honest with Yourself about Your Skills and Experience

One of the first steps in determining whether to manage your rental property on your own or to delegate some or all of the duties is to analyze your own skills and experience. Many successful property owners find that they're better suited to deal-making, so they leave the day-to-day management for someone else.

This decision is a personal one, but you can make it more easily by thinking about some of the specifics of managing property. Property management requires basic skills, including marketing management, accounting, and people skills. You don't need a college degree or a lot of experience to get started, and you're sure to pick up all kinds of ideas about how to do things better along the way.

Examine your own personality. Are you a people person? Serving as a landlord is a labor of love; you must love people, you must love working with your hands, and you must love solving problems. Most of all, you must be able to do all this without getting much back in the way of appreciation.

Whether you're confident you have what it takes to be a good rental property manager or you're still not sure, take stock of yourself and your abilities by answering the following questions. Interview yourself as though you were a job applicant. Ask the tough questions and, more important, answer honestly:

- Are you a people person who enjoys working with others?
- Can you keep your emotions in check and out of your business decisions?
- Are you a patient and reasonably tolerant person?
- Do you have the temperament to handle problems and respond to complaints and service requests in a positive and rational manner?
- Are you well organized in your daily routine?
- Do you have strong time-management skills?
- Are you computer literate?
- Are you meticulous with your paperwork?
- Can you write well enough to communicate effectively?
- Do you have basic accounting skills?
- Do you have maintenance and repair abilities?
- Are you willing to work and take phone calls on evenings and weekends?
- Do you have sales skills? Can you be creative in attracting rental applicants?
- Are you a good negotiator?
- Are you willing to commit the time and effort required to determine the right rent for your rental unit?
- Will you be persistent in collecting the rent?
- Are you familiar with or willing to find out about the laws affecting property management in your area?
- Are you able and willing to visit your rental property regularly?
- Are you willing to consistently and fairly enforce all property rules and rental policies?
- Are you interested in finding out more about property management?
- Are you willing to make the commitment to being your own property manager?

Ideally, you answered *yes* to each question. This assessment isn't scientific, of course, but it does raise some important issues, particularly the level of commitment that you need to succeed as a rental property manager.

You need to be fair, firm, and friendly to all rental prospects and tenants. Treat everyone impartially and remain patient and calm under stress. Be determined and unemotional in enforcing rent collection and your policies and rules. And maintain a positive attitude through it all. Not as simple as it looks, is it?

Even if you didn't answer with an enthusiastic *yes* to all the questions in this section, you may still make a good rental property manager if you're prepared to be flexible and learn from your property management experiences. The really good property managers graduated from the school of hard knocks.

If your assessment revealed that your skills may be better served doing something other than managing your own property, turn to Chapter 3 for some alternatives. Owning rental property can still be a great investment, even if you don't manage it yourself.

If you're impatient or easily manipulated, you aren't suited to being a property manager. Conveying a professional demeanor to your tenants is important. You want them to see you as someone who'll take responsibility for the unit's condition. You must also insist that tenants live up to their part of the deal, pay their rent regularly, and refrain from causing unreasonable damage to your property. If you don't like confrontation, managing your own rental may not be the wisest choice.

Chapter 3

Managing Your Property Yourself or Hiring a Pro

In This Chapter

▶ Assessing the pros and cons of property self-management

▶ Understanding the benefits of working with a pro

▶ Knowing what to look for in a property management firm

*T*he late-night TV real estate gurus can make real estate investing sound so simple. But a prime location at the right price isn't all you need. The other key to success in real estate is having a well-managed property.

Initially, you may try to manage your rental property yourself, particularly if you have a single-family rental home or condo or even a small, multifamily rental property such as a duplex, triplex, or fourplex. That's why I spend time in this chapter guiding you through the pros and cons of managing your own property (as opposed to hiring a pro to do it for you).

If you're like most owners, though, at some point you'll consider hiring a professional property management firm, which is why I also give you some tools for evaluating property management companies, from the services they offer to the fees they charge. I explain the importance of the big three traits to look for — experience, qualifications, and credentials — and reveal some of the common tricks management companies use to generate additional income that aren't in your best interest.

Deciding how your rental property is managed is one of the most important decisions you make as a rental property owner, so take the time to look at all your options.

Managing Your Rental Yourself

With your first rental, you probably do all the work yourself — painting, cleaning, making repairs, advertising, showing the units, screening the applicants, collecting rent, and paying bills. This scenario certainly has its advantages, but it has its disadvantages, too. Use the information in the following sections to help you decide whether you want to go it alone or hire a pro. (If you decide the latter, check out the later "Exploring Professional Management" section for the scoop on working with a professional management company.)

The advantages

If you have the right traits for managing property (see Chapter 2 to help determine whether you do), if you have the time, and if you live reasonably close to your property, you should definitely manage it yourself. Here are some advantages of keeping direct control of the management of your rental property:

- ✔ **You save on a monthly management fee.** If you purchase a single-family rental home or condo as an investment property, you most likely won't be able to generate enough money to pay for a professional property manager and make a profit — at least not right away.

- ✔ **You save on maintenance costs.** *You* decide who does the repair work and who mows the lawn. Doing your own maintenance or yard work is usually a good idea; if you hire someone else to do it for you, the cost can devour your monthly cash flow in a hurry.

- ✔ **No one cares as much about your investment as you do.** *You* are always going to be the one who's most dedicated to achieve the best results from your rental investment efforts. Property managers are professionals, but their retirement and future wealth aren't riding on the success of your investment.

 Even if you hire someone to manage your property, you're better off choosing the maintenance contractors yourself than turning over the decision — and your money — to a professional property management firm. So develop a list of reliable and insured fix-it and landscape personnel who do good work and charge reasonable rates.

The drawbacks

If you're just starting in the world of property management, you may be thinking of it as a part-time venture — something you'll do in addition to your day job. If that sounds like you, be sure to check out the following list of the cons of self-managing rental property:

- ✔ **You can damage your day job.** If you're a higher-income, full-time professional, rushing off on weekdays to handle some minor crisis at your rental unit is not only impractical but can also be downright damaging to your career. Most employers have little tolerance for a second job, particularly one that often has unpredictable and unscheduled demands.

✔ **You can spend far too much time.** If you earn your living from something other than managing your rental property, managing that property may not be worth your valuable time. Rental management can take up more time than you anticipate, especially if you buy additional properties. Remember, property management often requires working in the evenings and on weekends, when most prospective tenants want to see your vacant rental units and when current tenants are home to allow access for repairs.

✔ **You run the risk of increased liability.** If you're just a part-time property manager, you may not keep abreast of the latest laws or issues affecting the rental housing industry. Just one lawsuit over a situation that you handled improperly can quickly turn your dream of retiring early into the year's next big horror flick.

As a jobholder, look at your annual income and figure out approximately what you earn per hour. Then do the same for the cash you're saving by managing your own property. Unless your management efforts produce significant cash savings compared to your job, you may be better off hiring a property manager. The same guideline holds true even if you're an independent business owner or self-employed. Your schedule may be more flexible than the typical fixed workday of a 9-to-5 employee. But if you earn $50 an hour as a consultant, devoting hours of your productive work time to managing rental units, which may amount to a savings of only $25 an hour, may not make sense. Also, remember that the management fee is a deductible expense.

The distance factor

If you own rental property in another city or state, you may initially consider managing your unit from afar. As long as your tenants have lengthy tenancies, faithfully mail their rent checks, and make only a few maintenance demands, this arrangement can work — but it's a fragile one. One major problem, or a few minor ones, can turn the job of managing the property into a nightmare.

Many real estate investors are attracted to the prospects of higher returns by purchasing out-of-state rental properties. But even with lower acquisition costs and supposedly decent rents, many of these investment opportunities are too thin to allow for hiring a local professional property manager. Consequently, long-distance property management becomes tempting. My strong advice is to think twice about handling your own rental property maintenance from hundreds of miles away. You, or someone you trust, need to be in the immediate area to routinely inspect and maintain a rental property, especially when an unexpected vacancy, roof leak, or broken pipe demands urgent attention.

Exploring Professional Management

Property management companies typically accept responsibility for all operations of the property, including rental unit preparation, marketing, setting rents, tenant selection, rent collection, maintenance, and accounting.

Many rental property owners who are just starting out drift blindly into self-management by default because they assume they can't afford a management company. Others simply don't want to give up part of their profit — "Why pay someone to manage my rental property when I can keep the money myself?" is a common refrain. Other owners would really prefer to hire a professional management company, but they've heard so many horror stories that they don't know whom to trust. Many of their concerns are real; some property managers mismanage properties and lack any semblance of ethics.

Luckily, you can avoid hiring the wrong management company by following my advice on how to choose a good property manager. The following sections touch on some important points for you to consider if you're contemplating using a professional management company.

Eyeing the pros and cons of using a pro

The pros of using management firms are many. Namely, these firms

✔ Have the expertise and experience to manage rental property.

✔ Stay up to date on federal, state, and local laws — plus liability issues such as mold and fair housing policies — so you don't have to.

✔ Are fair, firm, and friendly with tenants.

✔ Have screening procedures and can typically screen tenants more objectively than you can.

✔ Handle property management issues throughout the day and have staffing for after-hour emergencies.

✔ Have contacts and preferential pricing with many qualified, licensed, and insured suppliers and vendors who can quickly and efficiently get work done.

✔ Handle all bookkeeping, including rent collection.

✔ Have well-established rent collection policies and procedures to follow when tenants' rent is late.

✔ Have an online presence, with websites that provide detailed information and photos of all their available rental properties.

✔ Handle all aspects of hiring employees so you don't have to process time sheets, calculate and submit payroll, generate paychecks, or oversee all the legal requirements that come from having employees.

✔ Can be excellent sources for purchasing additional properties because they're often the first to know when their current clients want to sell.

Of course, management companies have numerous downsides as well:

✔ Using a management company for small rental properties that you've recently acquired may not be cost-effective because the management fees can run up to 10 percent or more of your gross income, including leasing fees.

✔ Some smaller companies may not be technologically advanced and aren't able to offer online services such as rental applications to prospective tenants and ACH (Automated Clearing House), electronic rent payments, or maintenance requests to current tenants.

✔ Some companies may have in-house maintenance that charges markups or surcharges on supplies and materials, as well as increased labor costs.

✔ They often don't have the same care, consideration, and concern that you have for the rental property.

✔ They often charge extra (a *leasing fee*) to fill vacancies or take longer to fill the spots if they have several other vacancies they're dealing with at the same time.

✔ Some companies require tenants to drive to their offices to apply for the rental, to pay rent, or to request maintenance, which can be a disadvantage if the company isn't located close to the rental property.

✔ They may not be as diligent in collecting delinquent rent, particularly if the management contract provides that they keep all late fees and other administrative charges.

✔ Some companies may try to falsely impress you with low maintenance expenses when they're really not spending enough on repairs and maintenance to properly maintain the property.

✔ Management companies affiliated with "for sale" real estate brokerages may be more interested in a large real estate commission from a sale and may not provide the best property management services.

Understanding what a good property manager does

Professional property managers normally handle a wide range of duties. If you hire a full-service management company, you typically get the following services:

- ✔ Performance of rental market surveys and advice on setting the rental rate
- ✔ Preparation, advertisement, and showing of the rental unit
- ✔ Tenant screening, selection, and help with moving
- ✔ Preparation of leases or rental agreements and all legal forms
- ✔ Property physical and/or visual drive-by inspection as agreed
- ✔ Rent collection, bank deposits, and paying bills (including the mortgage, property taxes, and insurance, if the owner doesn't pay directly)
- ✔ Preparation of regular accounting reports
- ✔ Quality repair and maintenance of the rental unit
- ✔ Timely response to tenant complaints
- ✔ Enforcement of the rules and regulations and compliance with laws

 Although I usually recommend full-service management, you can pay for just the items that tickle your taste buds instead of shelling out for the full-course menu by working with more limited or a la carte management services. For example, maybe you just need help with the rental of your property and are willing to pay a leasing fee. Or perhaps you want a property manager who charges only a small fee to cover the basic service and not much more.

Telling the good from the bad

A good management company may be able to operate your rental properties better and more efficiently than you can on your own. Its superior knowledge and experience can result in lower costs, higher rents, better residents, and a well-maintained property. A good management company more than pays for its costs, allowing you more time to take up additional properties or other pursuits. Of course, a poor management company can cut into your profits with its fees, improper maintenance, or poor-quality tenants who run your property into the ground. A bad property manager can leave you in worse shape than if you'd never hired one in the first place.

The right property manager can make a big difference in the cash flow your rental unit generates because he finds good replacement tenants quickly or makes sure that maintenance is done in a timely manner without breaking your budget. You need a property manager who's committed to helping you get the optimum results from your rentals. The following sections help identify what to think about when searching for a management company and what to ask potential managers so you can find the right fit.

 A good property manager always remembers that the rental property belongs to the owner, not to the property manager. That means he should seek your input so the two of you can work together to formulate a property management plan that achieves your personal investment goals.

Finding the right management company for you

You want to find a property management company that suits you. Size isn't the only determining factor in whether a property manager can deliver quality service. Some management companies specialize in large rental projects, whereas small operations may focus on individual home rentals and apartment complexes with only a few units. Don't assume that a big company managing mega-complexes will do the best job for your duplex or that a small company has the credentials, experience, and knowledge you need for your larger property. Try to find property managers who are active in the area and specialize in your kind of rental unit.

Keep the following in mind to help you select the management company that best fits you and your property:

- ✔ **Make sure the firm you hire manages property exclusively.** This guideline is particularly important when selecting a management company for a single-family home, condo, or very small rental property. Many traditional real estate sales offices (as opposed to property management firms) offer property management services; however, property management is often a *loss leader* (meaning it costs more for the real estate office to manage your property than it's charging you for that service because it's hoping to get your business later on, when you're ready to sell the property). Many property managers in real estate sales offices don't have the same credentials, experience, and expertise as employees of property management firms. The skills required to represent clients in *selling* property are entirely different from the skills required to *manage* property. You can always hire a firm that sells only real estate when the time comes to dispose of your rental property.

- ✔ **Verify that the property manager and the management company have current licenses that are in good standing.** You can call or use the Internet to double-check. Most states require property managers to have a real estate license and/or a property manager's license. Simply holding a license doesn't ensure exceptional services, but it does show that the property manager is motivated enough to comply with state law.

The recent significant rise in unemployment has led to increases in the number of unlicensed individuals offering their services as property managers. Often, they may be managing properties that they partially own themselves and are exempt from state licensing laws, but they're breaking the law in most states if they manage a rental property of which they aren't an owner. Working with one of these people can lead to serious liability for you if there's ever a problem and it turns out you used an unlicensed property manager. Always, always make sure the property manager you're considering has a current license, designations/certifications, and proper insurance coverage.

- ✔ **Examine the property manager's credentials.** IREM provides professional designations and certifications, including the Certified Property Manager (CPM) designation and the Accredited Residential Manager

(ARM) certification. A very select group of management firms have earned the Accredited Management Organization (AMO) accreditation. These designations and certifications signify excellence and dedication. Pop in the CD or, if you're viewing this book in an electronic format, head to the link in the table of contents for more information, plus details on NAA designations.

✔ **Confirm that the company is properly insured.** The company should carry insurance for general liability, automobile liability, workers' compensation, and professional liability. The company is your agent and will collect your rents and security deposits, so it should also have a fidelity bond to protect you in case an employee embezzles or mishandles your money. Look for a company that has separate accounting for each property managed.

Many property managers use a single master trust bank account for all properties. Although this is legal in most states, avoid this practice because, typically, the number one violation encountered during audits of property managers by state oversight agencies is related to shortages and other misuse of the master trust bank account.

✔ **Check references, particularly the company's other clients.** Don't sign a management contract until you feel confident that the company you hire has a sound track record. Checking with the company's chosen referrals isn't enough. Ask for a list of all its current and past clients, and contact the ones with rental properties similar in size and type to your own. Make certain the rental owners you contact have been with the company long enough to have a meaningful opinion on the quality of the service and are truly unbiased.

I must caution here that online business rating or reference sites can be deceiving. Some very good companies may have a few disgruntled former tenants, or a few planted recommendations can lead you to a false sense of confidence that you've found the best management company or disqualify a good one.

Knowing what to ask a prospective management company

The quality of your property management company directly affects the success of your real estate investments and your peace of mind. Visit the company's office armed with the following questions:

✔ Can you give me a list of exactly what management services you provide and a breakdown of management fees/costs?

✔ Is your firm an Accredited Management Organization (AMO) recognized by IREM?

✔ Is your firm an active member in good standing with a local affiliate of the NAA, and does it hold any NAA designations?

✔ Are your legally required state and/or local licenses current and without any history of violations?

✔ Do you carry errors and omissions coverage of at least $500,000, plus general liability coverage of at least $2 million?

✔ Do you have a $500,000 fidelity bond and a forgery and alterations policy of at least $25,000 for all employees?

✔ Do you have separate bank trust accounts for each client rather than a single master trust bank account containing multiple owners' funds?

✔ Can you communicate via e-mail with your clients, your contractors/suppliers, and your tenants to be responsive and efficient, providing excellent customer service?

✔ Can you explain your methods of advertising or generating interest in my rental property and of selecting tenants in compliance with all fair housing laws?

✔ How do you screen prospective tenants? Do you use an outside firm? Who pays for the service and how much is it?

✔ Do all funds that you collect from applicant screening fees, tenant late charges, and other administrative charges go directly to the owner and not the manager?

✔ Do you provide 24/7 on-call maintenance services with a live person answering the calls who also has e-mail capability?

✔ Whether you provide maintenance in-house or use an affiliated firm, do you only charge the actual cost of labor and materials, without any surcharges, markups, administrative fees, or other such add-ons?

✔ Do you pass along any volume-purchasing discounts fully and directly to clients for appliances, carpeting, and other items, without any markups?

✔ If allowed by law, do you give all employees screenings that include thorough background checks by an independent employment screening consultant, plus drug and alcohol testing by a certified lab?

✔ Can I contact several of your current and former clients with rental properties that are similar in type, size, and location to mine?

If at all possible, also try to secure a meeting with the person who would have control of the hands-on management of your property so you can ask these questions:

✔ How many years have you been in the property management business? Do you exclusively manage real estate?

✔ What are your qualifications? Do you hold IREM's distinguished Certified Property Manager (CPM) designation or Accredited Residential Manager (ARM) certification? Do you hold National Association of Residential Property Managers (NARPM) designations such as Residential Management Professional (RMP) or Master Property Manager (MPM)?

✔ How many other properties do you manage? Where are these properties located?

Watch those repair bills!

Most management contracts contain clauses that allow property management companies to perform emergency repairs up to a specified dollar amount without advance approval from the owner. Of course, this clause allows the company to take care of problems that occur unexpectedly. When you're in the early stages of working with a new management company, make sure you closely monitor its expenses. Even though it may have the legal right to use funds up to a certain amount, the company should always keep you informed as the owner. "No surprises" is one of my favorite sayings!

Repairs serve as a profit center for many management companies. They may offer very low property management fees, knowing that they'll make it up through markups on repairs, and often the repairs aren't even necessary. Look for a property management firm that doesn't mark up materials, supplies, or maintenance labor or one whose costs for such work you consider fair and equitable.

When you hire outside property managers, treat them as valued members of your management team, but be sure they know that you're the team manager and they understand your long-term goals. If you're looking for appreciation and preservation of your rental property's value, make sure the company keeps your property in great condition and looks for stable, long-term tenants rather than just premium rent from short-term rentals. Of course, the manager should ask before spending significant amounts of your money, and he should keep you informed on a regular basis.

Compensating your property manager

Management companies are compensated in a variety of ways, and the type of fees and typical compensation vary widely throughout the country. In addition to a percentage or flat monthly fee, a firm may charge extra for leasing fees, copies, postage, reports, court appearances, coordinating maintenance, getting bids, supervising capital improvements, and so on. Ask about these extra fees and make sure you fully understand the compensation of your property manager, but never evaluate the management company based on the management fee alone.

Discovering how property management companies charge

The typical professional management fees for single-family homes or individual rental condominiums are 10 percent of the collected income with an additional fee earned each time the unit is rented. The rental fee can be a flat fee that ranges from $250 to $500 or a percentage of the monthly rental rate, such as 50 to 100 percent. If the rental home or condo has a high rental value, then the management fee is often lower, in the 7 to 10 percent range.

When a property manager considers how much to charge you, she typically looks at the following pieces of information:

✔ **The amount of time required to manage the property:** An experienced property management company owner knows the average number of hours the property manager, the accounting staff, and other support personnel will spend each month on managing your property. She then calculates a management fee schedule that should generate the fees necessary to provide the proper company resources to effectively manage your rental units. If you have larger rental properties, management fees don't typically include the services of any on-site manager, superintendent, or caretaker; these individuals are paid separately.

✔ **The size, location, condition, and expected rental collections of the property:** Generally, the larger the rental property, the lower the management fee as a percentage of collected income. Fees vary by geographic area and by the income potential of the rental unit, with a higher-end rental property commanding a lower percentage management fee. For certain properties that may be more difficult to manage, the company may have higher management fees or additional charges for certain types of services or for a certain period of time. Management companies may also propose charging a minimum monthly management fee or a percentage fee (opting for whichever of the two is greater). For example, a property that's in poor physical condition and needs extensive repairs and renovations requires the property manager to spend extra time supervising the improvements. This additional time is worthy of additional compensation to the property manager.

Try to find a company with a management fee that's a percentage of the collected income; this kind of fee is a strong motivator to the company to keep rents at market rate and collect them on time. Never pay a management fee based on the potential income of a rental unit, only on actual collected income.

Structuring compensation as a win-win for you and your property manager

Your management company's compensation can be affected by more than just the standard considerations mentioned in the preceding section. Knowing how to look beyond the basics can help you save money in the long run and make your choice of management company work for you and your investment.

Always make sure that your property manager is compensated in a way that incentivizes or motivates him to keep your rental property occupied with a stable, long-term tenant who treats your rental property as her home, respects her neighbors, and pays a market rent in a timely manner. For example, structure the compensation so the company has an incentive to get the property *leased-up* (meaning all your vacant units are filled) as soon as possible.

When analyzing your property manager's compensation rate, keep these tidbits in mind:

- ✔ **Watch out for management fees that seem too low.** The old adages *You get what you pay for* and *If it's too good to be true, it probably is* come to mind. Management fees that seem too low are a good indication that the property managers are spread too thin and may not properly manage your property. Poor management can result in unhappy tenants, which leads to higher turnover and longer periods of vacancy without rental income.

- ✔ **Understand that leasing fees are often justified and usually not negotiated.** The most time-intensive portion of property management is tenant turnover. When one tenant leaves, the property manager must make the unit rent-ready. Then she must advertise, show the property, and screen the prospective tenants. Leasing fees may vary, but you can usually expect either a flat fee of several hundred dollars or a percentage of the rent, such as half or all the monthly rental rate.

Making sense of management agreements

The management agreement is a pivotal document; it spells out the obligations of the property management company to you, the client. Be sure to study the fine print; doing so is tedious but necessary in order to avoid unpleasant surprises. Even the management agreements available through state and national real estate organizations can contain clauses that are clearly one-sided in favor of the management company.

For example, many management agreements call for the property manager to collect and keep all the income from applicant screening fees, late charges, or returned check charges. Of course, property managers justify this policy on the basis that they incur additional time and costs when handling such situations. But these fees should belong to you because you want to give the property manager a financial incentive to fill your unit with a tenant who pays rent on time and cares for the property. A management fee based on actual rents collected is a better arrangement.

Read on to find out what other nuggets may be hidden in the fine print of your management agreement and how to protect your investment:

- ✔ **The "no management fee charged when the unit is vacant between tenants" line:** Although this seems like an arrangement that saves you money, especially when rental revenues aren't coming in, the property manager can rush to fill the vacancy without properly screening tenants — and a destructive tenant can be worse than no tenant in the long run.

✔ **The "hold harmless" clause:** This clause protects the property manager from liability for his own errors in judgment or the mistakes of the workers the firm sends to your rental unit. One solution is to include a "reasonable care" provision so the property manager is motivated to be diligent in his management and avoid workers he knows have had problems in the past. Your agreement should also mention such obvious requirements as informing you of what's happening with your rental property.

✔ **The long-term management contract request:** Some property management companies request long-term management contracts that can't be canceled or can only be canceled for cause. Avoid signing any contract that can't be canceled by either party with or without cause upon a 30-day written notice. A company that knows it's only as good as its most recent month's performance will stay motivated to treat your property with the time and attention needed to get top results. But the company can make a reasonable argument that it needs a minimum term in order to amortize the significant time and cost of taking over a property. So, rather than agree to a long-term, non-cancelable agreement, I suggest you negotiate an early termination fee that's waived after a certain number of months.

✔ **The confusing language trick:** If the property manager won't agree to reasonable clarifications of the contract language or a complete list of the services provided for his fee, he may not go out of his way to help you later. Consider this refusal a warning sign and find a property management company willing to accept your reasonable terms.

✔ **The "I'll use my own agreement that suits my best interests" maneuver:** Many property managers use their own proprietary agreements written strictly in the best interests of the property management company. Be sure to have your attorney review this agreement very early in the discussions with your potential property manager.

Make sure that the management agreement addresses all your concerns. You need to know how much the manager can spend without your authorization, what weekly or monthly reporting the company provides, when your property expenses will be paid, and who's responsible for payment of critical items such as mortgages, insurance, and property taxes. Leave nothing to chance.

I include a sample Residential Management Agreement from IREM on the CD (you can access it through the link in the table of contents if you're viewing an electronic version of this book). Use it to better familiarize yourself with such contracts. And remember, ultimately you can propose that your property manager sign *your* agreement — after your attorney reviews it, of course.

Being aware of the tax consequences

As a rental property owner, you're running a business and must file Schedule E with your federal tax return. The tax laws allow your rental housing business to deduct all operating expenses, including the costs of advertising, maintenance, payroll, insurance, property taxes, and management fees, whether paid to yourself or a property management firm. *Note:* Federal and state tax codes change from year to year, so discuss your personal tax situation with your accountant or tax preparer in advance.

Although your expenses are deductible, they erode the net income from your property. If your annual expenses are greater than your rent revenues, you may find that you can use those losses to help ease the tax burden from your full-time job or other sources of income unrelated to your rental property. But a loss is a loss, and trying to keep your rental property in the black is still a good idea, even if you have to pay some taxes on the income.

The IRS's passive loss rule states that all real estate rental activities must be treated as passive, with an exception that some taxpayers are allowed up to a $25,000 deduction. However, real estate investors who can be classified as *real estate professionals* are permitted to deduct all their rental real estate losses from their ordinary income, such as current employment income (wages, commissions), interest, short-term capital gains, and nonqualified dividends. See Chapter 19 for more information on whether you meet the stringent IRS requirements to qualify as a real estate professional.

Even though federal real estate taxation laws consider most real estate activities passive rather than active investments, definite tax advantages exist for owners who are actively involved in the management of their rental properties. The definition of *actively involved* allows you to hire a property management firm and still take advantage of the tax write-offs available for rental income property, as long as you're involved in setting the rents and policies for the property.

Chapter 4

Taking Over the Property

- -

In This Chapter

▶ Getting copies of important documents before the deal is final

▶ Helping existing tenants through the transition process

- -

Somewhere during the process of thinking about investing in rental property, you may have considered acquiring a property already occupied by tenants. Or maybe you just found out that your dear old Aunt Beatrice left you an occupied rental property in her will. On the surface, these opportunities seem positive because you don't have to advertise and select tenants yourself — at least not right off the bat. But just how positive an experience you have taking over an occupied rental property depends on the quality of your tenants. Some real estate investors prefer to acquire vacant properties so they can renovate the units and select their own tenants.

This chapter focuses on some of the important issues involved in taking over rental property, whether you're purchasing a property or you've inadvertently become the proud owner of one. Here you find out how to begin the all-important task of implementing your own policies and procedures with the existing tenants, who may be living under an entirely different set of rules. The proper procedures for taking over a rental property actually begin before you're legally the new owner. Ensuring your transition goes smoothly requires some know-how, and in this chapter I give you exactly that.

For more information on rental property acquisitions, proper due diligence steps, and property inspections, plus ideas on how to hold title to your rental properties, check out *Real Estate Investing For Dummies,* 2nd Edition, by Eric Tyson and yours truly (Wiley).

Knowing What to Get Upfront

If you're thinking about buying a rental property, you need to start by thoroughly investigating all aspects of it and its current tenants, if any. After all, no one is going to represent your interests as well as you. During the *due diligence period,* which is when your escrow and purchase are pending, put on your Sherlock Holmes cap and ask lots of questions. (*Escrow* is an account for funds and documents held by a neutral third party in a real estate transfer until all the conditions have been met, per the written instructions of the seller and buyer.) Don't be shy. Talk to the tenants, the neighbors, the local government officials, and the property's contractors or suppliers to be sure you know what you're getting. Search the web for public information such as code violations, police reports, and sexual predator tenants. When in this situation, remember my favorite motto: *No surprises.*

Most sellers are honest and don't intentionally withhold information or fail to disclose important facts. However, the old adage *buyer beware* rings particularly true in the purchase of rental real estate. Resolving questions and issues now through regular communication with your seller eliminates some very unpleasant and possibly contentious disagreements with your tenants in the future.

The due diligence period may be your best or only opportunity to seek adjustments if the seller misrepresents any important issues. When you sign your name on the dotted line, the deal's done. You can't go back and ask the seller where the tenant's security deposit is. So even though taking over your new property can be chaotic, don't fall into the trap of just verbally verifying the facts. Confirm all information in writing and begin setting up a detailed filing system for your new property.

In the following sections, I cover some items you must make sure you have in writing *before* the deal is final. On the accompanying CD I include a Property Takeover Checklist for both small and large properties (click the link in the table of contents if you're reading a digital version of this book).

A list of personal property included in the sale

Take an inventory of all the personal property included in the sale. This list may include appliances, equipment, and supplies owned by the seller.

Don't assume anything is included in the sale unless you have it in writing, and be sure to verify that all items indicated are actually physically at the property before you close the deal. A significant dispute can occur if a misunderstanding arises about who owns the appliances in the rental unit. For example, if the seller says all the refrigerators belong to the property owner (as opposed to the tenants), you want to verify that in writing with each tenant. Otherwise, you run the risk of a serious dispute or loss in future years as tenants take appliances when they leave, claiming that fancy fridge belongs to them.

Some ingenious tenants have been known to sell the new appliances in their rental unit and replace them with used appliances when a change in the property's ownership or management occurs, so be sure to keep a list of all your appliances' serial numbers.

A copy of all tenant files

Make sure you have all the appropriate paperwork in the tenant files. These documents include rental applications, current and past rental contracts, move-in inspection checklists, full payment history and any rent increase documents, all legal notices, maintenance work orders, current contact information, a tenant complaint or communication log, and correspondence sent to or received from each and every tenant.

A seller-verified rent roll and list of all tenant security deposits

A *rent roll* is a listing of all rental units with information on the tenants' names, move-in dates, current and market rents, and security deposits. Be sure you get a written seller statement that no undisclosed verbal agreements or concessions have been made with any tenant regarding any aspect of the tenancy, including rent or security deposits. Ensure that where interest must be paid on security deposit balances, you collect the deposits (plus all accrued interest to date) at closing.

When acquiring an occupied rental property, be sure you follow state or local laws in properly handling the tenant's security deposit. Most state laws require the seller and/or purchaser of a rental property to advise the tenants *in writing* of the status of their security deposit. These laws usually give the seller the right to return the deposit to the tenant or transfer the deposit to the new owner. Here's why you want the latter to happen:

- ✔ If the seller refunds the security deposits, you have to collect them from tenants already in possession of the rental units. Avoid this scenario by strongly urging the seller to give you a credit for the full amount of the security deposits on hand in escrow, and have each tenant agree *in writing* to the amount of the security deposit transferred during the sale. Close the loop by sending each tenant a letter confirming her security deposit amount.

- ✔ If the seller transfers the security deposits to the buyer — rather than returning the deposits to the tenants — make sure you receive in cash (or as a credit in escrow) an amount equal to all the security deposits held (plus all accrued interest owed to the tenants, if any). Of course, remember that if you do just get a credit in escrow, you must be able to refund the remaining balances (after taking proper deductions) of any tenant security deposits when the individuals move out.

For more information on state laws concerning security deposits, check out the accompanying CD. Or, if you're reading a digital version of this book, head to the link in the table of contents.

Without written proof to the contrary, dishonest tenants may later claim they had a verbal agreement with the former owner or manager for a monthly rent credit or discount for maintaining the grounds, or that they were promised new carpeting or another significant unit upgrade. If this scenario happens to you, offer to get the former owner or manager on the phone to verify the tenant's story. In my experience, when you offer to verify the story, the tenant typically begins to backpedal, and the truth comes out. But to avoid any surprises, obtain a written statement from each tenant indicating that no such verbal agreements exist.

A copy of all required governmental licenses and permits

Rental property owners in many areas are now required to have business licenses or permits. Contact the appropriate government entity in writing and make sure to notify it of the change in ownership and/or billing address.

These governmental entities often impose stiff penalties if you fail to indicate the change in ownership in a timely manner. They inevitably find out about the change because they monitor the local recording of deeds and receive notification of changes in billing responsibility from local utility companies.

Make sure you have current copies of all state and local rental laws and ordinances that affect your rental property. Pop in the CD or click the link in the table of contents for access to resources for state landlord-tenant laws.

A copy of all the latest utility bills

Get copies of all account information and verification that all payments are current for every utility that provides services to the rental property. These utilities may include electricity, natural gas, water/sewer, trash collection, telephone, cable, and Internet access. Prior to the close of escrow, contact each utility company and arrange for the transfer of utilities or change in billing responsibility as of the estimated escrow closing date. If provided with sufficient advance notice, many utility companies can arrange for the final meter reading and/or billing cutoff to coincide with the close of escrow, which prevents the need to prorate any of the utility billings between the owners.

Let me reiterate: Verifying the accuracy of all utility bills is extremely important. One of my expert witness cases involved a water utility improperly charging a property owner for sewer charges related to a water meter used only for irrigation. (Some water utilities allow for irrigation-only meters that are exempt from sewer charges because the water never enters the sewer system.) In this case, the water company had been collecting sewer fees for many years until the discrepancy was brought to its attention. The property owner did receive lower billings in the future, but state law protected the company from refunding any overcharges beyond the previous 12 months. The owner paid thousands of dollars in overpayments for a very expensive management lesson.

A copy of every service agreement or contract

Make sure you obtain copies of all service agreements and/or contracts. These documents may include agreements with maintenance landscapers or gardeners; pest control services; heating, ventilating, and air conditioning (HVAC) companies; boiler maintenance services; laundry services; elevator, swimming pool, or spa servicing; and other providers. Review all current contracts and meet with service providers that the current owner uses. If contracts bind you to continue service, ensure such provisions are legal and in your best interest.

If you plan to terminate the services of a particular contractor or service provider, the seller may be willing to voluntarily send a written conditional notice of termination indicating that, should the property sell as planned, the provider's services will no longer be needed as of the close of escrow. You're then free to make your own plans for services and can even renegotiate with the current company for better terms. Of course, if you find the seller already had favorable pricing from the provider, you may be able to negotiate the same terms.

A copy of the seller's current insurance policy

One of the most important things you do when taking over your new rental property is to secure insurance coverage. You need to make sure you have the proper insurance policy in place at the time that you legally become the new owner. Although the seller's policy won't protect you in any way, request a copy of his existing policy or declaration of coverage because this information can be very helpful to your insurance agent when analyzing the property to determine the proper coverage you need.

When you receive the current insurance information, take steps to verify the accuracy of all records. If certain representations about the types and amounts of coverage are made verbally but not given in writing, then you need to protect yourself by sending written documentation to the seller and all agents to confirm any information you've received. This step can be important in preventing future disputes about the representations made by the seller or any of the agents.

A final walk-through can save you headaches

Before you close escrow, take a final walk-through to make sure the property hasn't been damaged prior to closing. I was an expert witness in a case where the new buyers learned this lesson the hard way because they didn't visit the rental home before closing.

After the sale was complete, the new buyers excitedly went to see their new property, which had sat vacant for nearly a week during escrow. They were shocked to find the home completely flooded and severely contaminated with mold. The buyers sued the seller, claiming that someone had intentionally or inadvertently left the water supply line valve to the refrigerator ice maker open, allowing water to cover the entire first floor. The buyers were unable to prove that the damage occurred while the seller still owned the property, so the seller's insurance company denied the claim.

Ultimately, the buyers' insurance company agreed to pay for some of the damage, but not before the buyers went through more than two years of expensive and emotionally draining litigation and lost rent as the property sat vacant the entire time. The buyers could've avoided this mess if they had simply inspected the property just before the close of escrow and stopped the sale until the damage was addressed.

 Always seek the advice of a professional insurance agent when obtaining insurance coverage. To avoid the unpleasant surprise of very high premiums, be sure to have your agent run a *loss history* on your new property before you close escrow to determine whether any losses have been claimed. You may find that the property has had significant claims in the past, which affects your ability to find reasonably priced insurance coverage. The loss history can also show some of the problems that have occurred at the property, including several small instances that can indicate a larger problem (such as plumbing leaks). Finally, you should ensure that no claims have been paid by the current insurer for repair or replacement work that hasn't been done.

 Although you may trust your insurance agent implicitly, don't allow your escrow to close until you have written documentation confirming that your insurance coverage is in force. A property can suffer a catastrophic loss or liability claim hours after it changes hands, before the new owner's insurance coverage is in place.

Working with the Current Tenants during the Transition

If you're like most rental property owners and you're acquiring property that's already occupied, the tenants are probably well aware of the pending ownership change. But that doesn't mean they're excited about it. Tenants are typically full of apprehension when their rental unit changes ownership, not because they think you'll be an unreasonable landlord but because of the uncertainty of change. So begin your relationship with your tenants on a positive note by following the steps I outline in the next sections.

Meeting with the tenants in person

When you first acquire your new rental property, contact your tenants in person and reassure them that you intend to treat them with respect and have a cordial yet businesslike relationship. Deal with your tenants' questions honestly and directly. Often, the first question they ask is whether they'll be allowed to stay. Other common concerns are the potential for a rent increase, the status of their security deposit, the proper maintenance or condition of their rental unit, and the continuation of certain policies, such as allowing pets. Anticipate these concerns and prepare your responses. You'll lose credibility and damage your relationship with the tenant if you later decide to implement changes that you didn't acknowledge upfront.

Give your tenants a letter of introduction during this brief in-person meeting. This letter should provide your contact information and explain your rent collection policies, the status of tenants' security deposits, and the proper procedures for requesting maintenance and repairs.

Inspecting the rental unit

Although you likely had a brief chance to view the unit's interior during the due diligence period before escrow closed, walking through again with the tenant can be helpful. However, know your state laws. In most states, tenants don't have to let you enter their units unless you have a legal reason and have given proper advance notice. If you set a voluntary appointment, the tenant knows you're coming and can prepare. If conducting a periodic unit interior inspection (perhaps annually) is legal in your state, set that expectation with your tenants at the outset and include it in their lease.

Don't just knock on the door and expect to walk through your tenant's rental unit. But if you're already at the property delivering your letter of introduction (see the preceding section for more on this), you can schedule a mutually convenient time to meet. Some tenants are glad to meet with you right then, but don't necessarily count on that. Giving your tenants time to think about any issues they'd like to discuss is beneficial for you both.

The former owner of the property may have had a policy of documenting the unit's condition at the time the tenant took possession of it. If so, you may want to compare those notes to the notes you make when you walk through the unit. If proper documentation of the unit's move-in condition wasn't made, consider preparing such information during your walk-through. This info allows you to establish some sort of baseline for the unit's condition to use when the tenant moves out, which then helps you determine the proper amount of the security deposit to return.

Using a new lease or rental agreement

When taking over an occupied rental property, you always want to transfer the tenants to your own lease or rental agreement eventually. The sooner you begin to convert your new property to your rental contracts, the better. If your policies are markedly stricter, you may find the transition period difficult. For a single-family rental or a small rental property, implementing your own rental agreement as soon as legally allowed is relatively easy. However, with larger rental properties, you may want to gradually transition to a new contract upon tenant turnover. Regardless, establish uniform policies for all your tenants to avoid any possible fair housing violations (find out more about fair housing in Chapter 10).

Your tenants already have one of the following:

- ✔ A valid written lease
- ✔ An expired written lease that has become a month-to-month rental agreement
- ✔ A written month-to-month rental agreement
- ✔ A written rental agreement for a period of less than a month
- ✔ A verbal agreement

Although you may want to make some changes in the terms or policies of your tenants' current leases or rental agreements, when you acquire an occupied rental property, your legal and business relationship is already established by whatever agreement the tenants had with the former owner. Wait until the contract's expiration to change the terms — or provide the tenant with proper legal notice of any proposed changes.

Consider the potential impact of making significant changes in the rental rates or policies immediately after you acquire the property. For example, although you may have strong feelings against allowing pets on the property, your tenants may have pets already. Although you legally have the right to implement your no-pet policy upon lease renewal or upon giving proper legal notice, you're almost guaranteed a vacant rental unit if you do so. Impose your policies over a reasonable time frame, but be sure you're aware of the potential financial consequences in the short run.

Do unto others' pets

One of the most common and emotional complaints I've received concerns a new owner implementing a no-pets policy in a rental property that previously allowed pets. Though exceptions exist for service animals under the Americans with Disabilities Act and fair housing laws, the elimination of pets affects a lot of tenants. Nothing fosters resentment and animosity as much as telling dedicated pet owners that they need to get rid of a member of their family. Though in most circumstances a new owner can implement a no-pets policy as the leases expire, I believe implementing such a policy on existing tenants is inherently unreasonable. Better to apply such a policy to new tenants only. Doing so is a good way to implement other new policy changes — about parking, late charges, or anything that may be unfair to your current tenants. As a rental property owner and manager, you really need to have empathy for your tenants and practice the golden rule.

The tenant information the seller provided you during escrow may be outdated. One quick way to update your records is to have the tenants voluntarily complete your rental application form. In many states, you may not have a strong legal argument for requiring existing tenants to provide this information; however, many tenants will understand your reasoning and not mind. Other tenants may be reluctant to complete an entirely new rental application. Even if you receive initial resistance, seek this updated information prior to renewing any lease. You need to be able to properly determine the financial qualifications of your tenants, particularly if you anticipate future rent increases.

Evaluating the current rent

When you acquire a rental property, part of your research is to establish its fair market rental value. This accurate calculation should play a role in your decision to buy. If a tenant's current rent is below market value, one of your toughest decisions is how to handle rent increases.

As the new owner, you often have higher mortgage payments and expenses to make necessary repairs and upgrades to the property than the last owner did. Some tenants get very upset and antagonistic about any rent increase, however, and you won't be able to appease them. If tenants simply can't afford an increase, work with them and give them ample time to relocate. Other tenants often welcome the improvements that accompany the purchase of their building by a new owner and will accept the necessary increase.

Fortunately, the majority of tenants just expect to be treated fairly and honestly. They understand you may have higher expenses and will reluctantly accept a rent increase as long as two basic conditions are met:

- ✔ **You don't raise the rent beyond the current market rent for a comparable rental unit in the area.** Give tenants documented information on comparable rentals in your area to show them you're not asking for an unreasonable rent.

- ✔ **You're willing to make basic repairs to the rental unit.** Don't ask tenants to shell out extra cash without proving you're committed to maintaining and even improving the property. But tenants don't appreciate all improvements equally. A new roof may not mean much if their unit didn't leak, but a new boiler or water heater could mean better water pressure or more consistent hot water, which all tenants will notice.

Most tenants just want to be sure they're receiving some of the benefit of paying higher rent. So if you ask for more rent, be willing to reinvest a portion of the rent increase into the property with cost-effective improvements that conserve energy and/or increase tenant desirability. Clean the carpet, repaint the unit's interior, or send in a maintenance person for a few hours to repair the miscellaneous items that need attention. Of course, if you have a very good and stable tenant, you may want to consider more significant upgrades. Replacing the carpet, installing a new appliance or countertops, or adding a ceiling fan and microwave oven may be an incentive for your golden tenant to sign a new lease at a higher rental rate.

Although tempting, be wary of making significant renovation or repairs to the property before the close of escrow. If the sale of the property doesn't go through as planned, you may have spent considerable sums to upgrade the seller's property without any recourse.

Buying unoccupied rental property

The takeover procedure for an unoccupied rental property or one that has some vacant rental units isn't much different from the procedure for taking over an occupied property. You may actually prefer a vacant property so you can quickly implement a plan to upgrade and get the property rent-ready as soon as possible. If you want an occupied rental property vacant upon the change of ownership, make the vacancy of the unit a condition for the close of escrow. *Remember:* After you own the property, every day a unit sits vacant is lost income you'll never recoup, so work diligently during the escrow time frame to make as much progress as possible.

Begin your marketing and advertising of the rental property near the close of escrow and the completion of renovation. Time is of the essence if you want to minimize any lost rent.

Part II
Renting Your Property

The 5th Wave   By Rich Tennant

"And I suppose you think this will attract prospective tenants?"

In this part . . .

The chapters in this part guide you through the process of actually renting your property — everything from getting your rental unit ready to setting the rent and advertising. I also give you some great tips for showing your property to prospective tenants and fill you in on the importance of good tenant screening policies. So if you have a vacancy on your hands — or you will soon — read on.

Chapter 5

Getting Your Rental Property Ready for Prospective Tenants

In This Chapter

▶ Examining and assessing the exterior and interior of your rental property

▶ Cleaning, repairing, and upgrading your property

▶ Working with professionals to prep your rental unit

*P*roperly preparing your vacant rental property for its new tenants is critical to your overall success as a rental property manager. Because vacant rental units don't generate rental income, you need to fill your vacancies with good, stable, rent-paying tenants as quickly as possible. How, you ask? By making sure the interior, exterior, and grounds of your vacant units are clean and in rent-ready condition when you show them to prospective tenants.

In this chapter, I show you how to look critically at the exterior and interior of your property to formulate a plan for preparing the unit. I also help you figure out what needs to happen when and whether you're better off hiring outside contractors to assist you in your preparation efforts.

Viewing Your Rental Property from a Prospective Tenant's Shoes

First impressions are huge, which is why you want to make sure your prospect's first impression of your property is a positive one. If the property's exterior and grounds don't look nice, your prospect won't even bother to see the interior — where you've just installed new appliances and high-quality carpeting. Similarly, a prospective tenant's positive first impression of your property's exterior soon disappears if its interior isn't just as sharp and well-maintained.

Ideally, your vacating tenant will be cooperative and allow you access to the rental unit so you can determine what items need to be cleaned, repaired, replaced, or even upgraded. If the tenant doesn't let you in voluntarily, review the rental unit maintenance records to find out the age and condition of the flooring and appliances so you have some idea of the type of work that may be necessary.

After you do get access, as you walk through the unit, take lots of notes on its condition and what needs attention in order to get it ready to rent again. Your notes are the foundation for a detailed plan to help you attract several qualified prospects who want to lease the unit at the rate you're seeking. The next sections help you put that plan into place.

Paying attention to the exterior and common areas

A poor first impression of your unit's exterior is hard to reverse, regardless of how great the inside may look. That's why you want to make a great first impression. To do so, you need to think about *curb appeal,* or how your property looks to a prospective tenant when she first visits.

To attract tenants who'll treat your property properly and stay for years, keep the following suggestions in mind:

- ✔ **Start at the street and carefully critique your property as if you were entering a contest for the best-looking property in your area.** First impressions are critical, and one of the key areas that all prospective tenants see is the front entry. Make sure the entryway is clean, well-kept, and well-lit. Clean the front door or apply a new coat of paint or stain. Buy a new welcome mat. Remove or replace a broken screen door or mailbox. Also, check the driveways and walkways and make sure they're as neat and tidy as possible.

- ✔ **Be sure your grounds and exterior areas are sparkling clean and the landscaping is well-maintained.** Believe it or not, you can renovate your grounds inexpensively by picking up trash and junk, removing weeds, watering the grass, and using the right fertilizer. A nice green lawn and shade trees enhance any property. Additionally, the use of flowering shrubs or perennial flowers is a great way to boost curb appeal and bring color to your property that will catch a prospect's eye. Savvy rental property owners know that landscaping is one of the most cost-effective ways to significantly upgrade a unit.

- ✔ **Check all patios, balconies, and entryways.** They should be clean, and the railings should be solid, secure, and firmly attached. You want to be sure that the entryways are unobstructed by landscaping and other items and that there are no tripping hazards.

✔ **Make sure the building structure is presentable and inviting.** Although major architectural changes are often cost-prohibitive, you can do a lot with a little paint, landscaping, and cleanup. These items generally don't cost much compared to the positive benefits you gain. Some specific exterior improvements to consider are ground-level or hanging planters, brass house numbers with night lighting, awnings, and freshly painted fence or house trim. Examples of exterior and landscaping renovations that can completely change a property's curb appeal and even reposition tired rental properties include seasonal flowering plants, new shrubs to replace the ones that have become sparse and woody, low-voltage landscape lighting, motion sensor lights, and new electrical fixtures.

Making sure the interior is up to snuff

The most qualified, stable renters always have choices, no matter how good or bad the rental market. You're in competition for these excellent tenants, and you need to make sure your unit stands out from the rest.

Don't show your unit until it's completely rent-ready. Prospective tenants often have a hard time seeing a unit's potential. If you show them a dirty unit, they'll *always* think of it that way. Although you may lose a couple of potential showing days by taking time to prepare the unit, you benefit in the long run by signing a more conscientious tenant. Trust me when I say that tenants who are more careful in the selection of their new rental home are planning to stay longer, and this is exactly the type of tenant you want.

Curb appeal in a community association

If you own a rental unit in a *community interest development* (CID), commonly referred to as a *community association* or *homeowners' association* (HOA), the responsibility for the maintenance and repair of the common areas typically falls to the association. Contact the association or its property manager about any common area concerns you have. The association has a vested interest in ensuring the proper maintenance of the premises and maintaining a sense of desirability for owners and tenants, but it may require some persuasion to take action.

Community associations are nonprofit entities run by volunteer boards of directors who are often reluctant to assess their owners and spend money to upgrade or modernize aging properties. Rarely do you find an association with plentiful reserves and well-maintained property unless it has strong leaders willing to make beneficial upgrades a priority. So I encourage you to get involved as a member of the association and use your expertise to demonstrate to the other owners (many may be owner-occupants) that proper maintenance can actually reduce long-term operating costs and maintain higher property values, which is a concern to all owners.

Forget second chances when it comes to showing a rental

Early in my property management career, I learned a valuable lesson about the importance of cleanliness and first impressions. I'd just arrived at a rental property for a management inspection and was speaking to the on-site manager when a prospective tenant entered the rental office and asked to see a vacant unit. She was a local college student out apartment hunting with her mother. I told my manager to go ahead and show the unit and explained that I'd just follow along if they didn't mind.

Together we left the rental office. The property grounds were very well-maintained, and the on-site manager did a great job getting to know the prospect's needs and determining the right unit to show. With the manager's help, the prospect and her mother asked to see an upstairs unit, away from the street.

Everything was going great . . . until we got to the actual unit. A dirty, cobweb-filled entryway led us to an interior (that hadn't been tidied in at least a week!) where we could see a large tree branch hanging precariously over the balcony rail. Before seeing the unit, the prospective tenant and her mother had been very positive, even discussing how soon she could get approved and move in. Afterward, they stopped asking questions, barely answered any, and became very noncommittal.

Learn from my mistake: Remember that the unit's cleanliness is paramount, and *never* show a rental unit without having gone through it yourself just prior to the showing.

When preparing a rental unit for a new tenant, don't overlook or forget a single item. I recommend using an inspection checklist to guide you through the process and assist you with final inspection. Here's a list of what to go over in preparation for your new tenant:

- ✔ **When you have legal possession, remove any personal possessions and trash left behind by the previous tenant.** Be sure that you follow any state or local laws providing the former tenant an opportunity to reclaim any abandoned personal property.

- ✔ **Check all plumbing (toilets, faucets, and pipes) for proper operation.** Make sure nothing leaks, the plumbing has the proper pressure, and everything drains adequately.

- ✔ **Test all appliances for proper operation.** Run the dishwasher through a full cycle and look for leaks. Be sure the oven's drip pan, broiler pan, and racks are included and spotless. If you have a free-standing oven or range, be sure the anti-tip bracket is installed. It's also a good idea to pull out each appliance, vacuum the refrigerator coils, wipe down the entire appliance till it shines, and scrub the floor upon which it sits as well as the adjacent walls and cabinet surfaces.

✔ **Try out all hardware.** Rekey or change the locks and make sure they're operational. Pay attention to all latches and catches, doorknobs and pulls, doorstops, and sliding doors.

✔ **Check all windows, window or insect screens, and window coverings.** Verify that they're clean, unbroken, secure, and properly operational. Test all window locks to be sure they work as well. Check for broken window seals, scratches on doors and window frames, and condensation stains.

Window treatments can make your rental property look great, and your tenant will value attractive and functional window coverings. A wide range of affordable window treatments are available; explore all your options to determine what's most desirable in your local area. Choose window coverings that are durable and easy to maintain and that appeal to your prospective tenants. I recommend vertical blinds or drapes because they're much easier to maintain and clean than mini blinds. But don't be too cost-conscious — I suggest you splurge for a little more quality here, especially in the primary common rooms where tenants spend most of their time.

✔ **Inspect all walls, ceilings, and baseboards.** Confirm that the paint and/or wall coverings provide proper coverage, without holes, cuts, scratches, nail pops, or bad seams.

✔ **Examine all floor coverings.** Make sure floors are clean and in good condition. All flooring should be properly installed, without bad seams.

✔ **Check all bathrooms.** Thoroughly clean the toilet, tub, tile grout, shower, sink, mirrors, and cabinets. Check the toilet paper holder and towel bars to be sure they're securely mounted and clean. Put a paper sanitary ring around each toilet seat and a new roll of toilet paper in each bathroom.

✔ **Look over all closets and storage areas.** Clean rods, closet dowels, hooks, shelves, lights, floors, and walls. Ensure that all doors open and close properly.

✔ **Examine all counters, cabinets, doors, moldings, thresholds, and metal strips.** Verify that they're clean, fully operational, and present no hazards.

✔ **Test smoke and carbon monoxide detectors, lighting, and electrical outlets, including all ground fault circuit interrupters (GFCI, also referred to as GFI) and circuit breakers, for proper operation.** Make sure all electrical components work at move-in; it's then the tenant's responsibility to notify you of any problems during the tenancy.

✔ **Check the fireplace.** If your unit has a fireplace, clean out ashes and debris. Have the chimney flue and vent cap inspected periodically, based on the amount of usage.

✔ **Inspect the heating and air conditioning unit(s) for proper operation.** Be sure the thermostat, filters, vents, and registers are all in working order. You may find that your local natural gas utility company offers complimentary inspections of all gas heating and cooking appliances. Contact a professional if necessary.

✔ **Perform a final walk-through of the entire unit for appearance and cleanliness.** Be sure to recheck the unit every few days because dust can settle quickly in a vacant unit. I've also seen an unpleasant surprise in the form of dead pests or insects that took their time expiring from recent pest control efforts. Nothing stops a good conversation with a great prospective tenant faster than stumbling upon a dead bug on the middle of the kitchen floor!

For a sample Interior Unit Inspection Checklist, pop in the CD or click the link in the table of contents.

Preparing Your Rental Unit the Right Way

You may think you're saving time and money by allowing a new tenant to lease a rental unit that hasn't been properly prepared. After all, if Bob doesn't mind that the unit isn't rent-ready, why should you? Unfortunately, this strategy isn't as problem-free as it seems on the surface. In fact, it's a big mistake. Why? Because the kind of tenant that a unit that hasn't been properly prepared attracts is someone who has lower standards and may even be desperate. New tenants who accept a dirty and poorly maintained rental unit surely won't make any extra effort to leave the property in good condition when they depart.

Know that cheaper isn't always the wise choice. Weigh the cost of frequent replacement against the cost of a more durable product when making renovation decisions. Cleanliness is essential. If you rent a dirty unit, new tenants will rightfully assume your standards are low and show a lack of care during their tenancy.

One of the best ways to maximize your rental income is to develop a system to improve your efficiency by completing your rent-ready process in minimum time. But you may be so overwhelmed by the amount of work you need to get done in the amount of time you have that you don't stop to consider the order you should do it in. I recommend you stick to the following order to maximize your time and efficiency:

1. General cleaning

2. Maintenance (which includes inspecting safety items, making repairs, and installing upgrades)

3. Painting

4. Final cleaning

5. Carpet or floor covering cleaning

Though you can't begin turning the rental before the tenants vacate, now's the time to walk through the unit and come up with your plan for getting it ready to rent again.

General cleaning

As soon as old tenants move out, clean the vacant rental unit. During this initial cleaning, you should

- ✔ Remove all trash left behind by the former tenants, including anything remaining in drawers, cabinets, and closets.
- ✔ Wipe down countertops and shelves.
- ✔ Sweep or vacuum the floors.
- ✔ Wash the windows, window coverings, and doors.
- ✔ Clean out the storage areas, including the attic, basement, or garage, as applicable.

Maintenance

Maintenance is more than just fixing something that's broken. A comprehensive maintenance approach also includes inspections of all safety items before renting your property to make sure they're in place and working as intended. While you'll routinely handle basic repairs, you should also look for opportunities to perform preventive maintenance to improve the performance and life span of your building systems. You also need to evaluate whether renovations and upgrades are cost-effective.

The following sections help you figure out which safety items you need to check and which maintenance tasks require a closer eye. They also help you determine whether renovating or upgrading your property is worthwhile, and if so, what direction you should go in with your changes.

 Inspecting everything in your rental property while it's vacant is important. Properly completing this inspection doesn't mean you need to be a certified repair technician; you just need to ensure that the interior unit systems are operational for the standard day-to-day usage you expect from your new tenants. If you aren't certain what to look for or if anything seems awry, be sure to contact a repair professional who's qualified for the building system that needs inspecting.

Inspecting safety items

Although tenants need to take an active role in and have the ultimate responsibility for their own safety, you need to check all safety items upon unit turnover. The most basic items found in virtually every rental unit include door locks, window locks, and smoke detectors. Be sure the following items are in place and working before the new tenant takes occupancy:

✔ **A small fire extinguisher:** Even if it isn't required by code, I recommend that each rental unit have a fire extinguisher. Although there's always the potential liability that the tenant won't use the fire extinguisher properly, most lifesaving professionals advise it's worth having because quickly using a fire extinguisher can keep a fire from spreading. Of course, the tenant should first ensure that someone has contacted 911 or the appropriate agency before attempting to put out the fire.

✔ **Adequate locking mechanisms:** Many local and state building codes have specific requirements concerning the types and specifications of door lock sets. Recent trends in legislation are requiring that all windows that open and are accessible from the ground have proper window locks. Window or insect screens should be in place and in good condition. The primary purpose of window screens is to keep the elements and insects out; however, screens can also have some value as a crime deterrent.

✔ **Smoke and carbon monoxide detectors:** These items are inexpensive and extremely important to your tenants' safety. Check with your local fire department for its code requirements; some departments expect detectors to be electrically hard-wired, and others may still allow battery-operated units. Contact your local fire safety or building officials for the latest info on fire and safety codes. Many of the rules have changed in recent years, particularly regarding the number and locations of required smoke detectors. Consider complying with any recommendations, even if the action isn't required in existing rental units. For example, carbon monoxide detectors are just becoming a requirement in many areas.

Make sure your records clearly indicate that you tested all the detectors and found them to be operating properly before your new tenant moved in. Afterward, the tenant must not disconnect or disable them in any way. The tenant is also responsible for replacing the batteries and regularly testing the detectors and alerting you in writing if they don't operate properly.

✔ **Other important items:** Your rental unit preparation work should also include testing of the ground-fault circuit interrupters (GFCI or GFI) in kitchens and baths, plus any other safety items, such as radon detectors, if you have them.

If the municipality in which your rental property is located requires that tenants always have access to the roof, then check with local agencies about possibly restricting that access for tenant safety. You may be able to install panic hardware that meets the code requirements of access but sounds an alarm if the door to the roof is opened.

Although not required, if you're ever sued, having written confirmation that all safety items were operating as intended at move-in can be helpful.

Be sure the house number or address is clearly marked on the exterior of your rental unit with at least 6-inch characters so locating the property from the street is easy. This simple measure can be a huge help to lifesaving personnel in an emergency.

Performing turnover maintenance

The majority of the items requiring maintenance in your vacant unit are minor, such as sticking closet doors, loose door knobs and towel bars, and burnt-out light bulbs. But be sure to carefully and regularly evaluate the current condition of all systems and equipment, including plumbing, electrical, appliances, and heating, ventilating, and air conditioning (HVAC). Keep the following in mind:

- **Carefully inspect all plumbing fixtures.** Look for leaky faucets, clogged aerators, or running toilets, and check that all drains work adequately. Test the angle stops or shut-off valves for all toilets, washers, dishwashers, and faucets, including under each sink, and look for signs of leakage. Even small leaks can be a major problem if not detected and repaired quickly. Though leaks in drains are difficult to detect because they're not pressurized, look for telltale signs of water on the ceilings of downstairs units from drain leaks of upstairs units.

- **Inspect and test the electrical components.** Make sure the circuit breakers or fuses are all in place and operating properly. Replace burnt-out light bulbs and check light switches and outlets. If possible, verify that the cable or satellite television and telephone lines are working, too.

- **Inspect each appliance and make sure it's operating properly.** Stoves and ovens contain modular parts, and you can replace the burner drip pans and control knobs very easily because replacement parts are readily available for most major appliances. Run the dishwasher through a cycle and look carefully for any signs of leaks around the gasket or underneath, near the pump housing.

- **Conserve energy by turning off the water heater, furnace, and air conditioning units at the breaker and setting the refrigerator/ freezer to low.** Your turnover work should also include the cleaning or replacement of all filters. This simple, low-cost item greatly improves energy-efficiency and lowers the wear on the equipment. Keep records indicating the date the filters were changed (you can write in felt pen right on the filter) and be sure to remind your tenants when they should be changed again.

  Tenants are becoming increasingly aware of the importance of conservation and energy efficiency. If you install water-saving fixtures, pilot-less ignition gas stoves and water heaters or tankless water heaters, weatherproofing, insulated windows and doors, and energy-efficient appliances, you'll have a competitive advantage in the rental marketplace. Be sure to emphasize your "green" efforts in promoting your rental property.

✔ **Check the pool/spa.** If your property has a pool or spa, have a professional evaluate its condition and provide a written report documenting the findings, including the state of the equipment and the water quality. This evaluation establishes a baseline that can often head off any tenant complaints down the road.

✔ **Perform maintenance that will minimize the likelihood of pests.** Caulk all cracks around the windows, foundations, drains, and pipes that may allow pests to enter the unit. Almost every rental property has the need for pest control at some point. An occasional cockroach or ants in search of water or food are commonplace, and consumer products are available to handle these limited situations. However, use professional exterminators to treat more significant problems and talk to your exterminator about establishing a regular schedule for follow-ups to be sure your unit stays pest-free.

The recent increase in bedbug infestations can be a real problem for landlords, so you should seriously consider a pre-occupancy inspection or certification that the property is "bedbug-free" when your tenant takes occupancy. That doesn't mean you shouldn't aggressively respond to eradicate any future infestations, but it does provide a baseline that the bedbugs weren't present at the time the tenant moved in. For more info about bedbugs, flip to Chapter 18.

Considering renovations and upgrades

Almost every rental unit has the potential for renovation or upgrades, giving you the opportunity to create real value in your units. The trick is evaluating the cost of the renovation or upgrade versus the rent increase you can get out of a particular improvement *before* you start renovating. You need to be sure you'll get your money back from your investment. The following sections help you figure out how much to renovate, what features prospective renters like to see, and what you need to do to stay within the law.

Determining whether to renovate: What's your return?

When you're considering making renovations and upgrades, you need to understand what they can and can't do for you. Many times renovations and property upgrades result in increased net income and higher property value. However, sometimes the renovations may not justify the investment.

To consider the *payback* of a proposed improvement, calculate the total installed cost of the upgrade and divide that number by the monthly increase in rental income. For example, if you install a dishwasher for $400 and consequently increase your monthly rent by $25, the payback is 16 months. Whether 16 months is an acceptable payback and worth the initial investment of $400 is determined by each owner. Just remember that you're not only increasing your monthly gross income but also generating increased property value as a result of higher net income. The higher income makes your property worth more to a buyer when you look to sell it.

Every real estate investor has different expectations, but generally, any payback of less than 24 months is good, especially when you look at the increase in property value that accompanies increased net income. See *Real Estate Investing For Dummies,* 2nd Edition (Wiley), by me and coauthor Eric Tyson for more discussion of ways to increase the value of your rental property.

Not everyone appreciates or values the same features in a rental unit as you. This is a rental property, and as the old saying goes, "Beauty is in the eye of the beholder." The features and amenities that appeal to you may not be worth the extra investment from the perspective of your target tenant market. For example, although you prefer expensive travertine floor tiles in your own home, you may find that more durable flooring products can tolerate the heavier wear and tear of rental units much better. Although cleanliness has universal appeal, some features such as ceiling fans and microwaves appeal more to some prospective tenants than others.

Eyeing what prospective renters want

Some tenants value certain improvements more than others. So the main question is this: What features and improvements do most prospective renters want (which in turn can give you more money in terms of a higher rent)? You can't come up with an exact answer to what amount of increased rent a particular upgrade will generate. For example, a new granite countertop in the kitchen or new light fixtures in the dining room have a different impact on each prospective tenant; some are willing to pay more for those amenities, and others aren't.

Feeling a bit confused about what direction to take to figure out the features prospective renters want? Never fear! The following tips can guide you:

> ✔ **Keep in mind what features and strengths your prospective renters will find in competitive rental units.** Look for outmoded or outdated features in your own unit. Perhaps most of your competition offers dishwashers, but you don't have one in your unit. You may want to install a dishwasher so that you remain competitive. But don't forget that you'll lose cabinet space, so this is an example of how you need to really evaluate all aspects of potential upgrades and not just the cost. Or maybe your unit has a very old dining room light fixture that you can easily replace with a modern light fixture or ceiling fan with a light kit. Another simple upgrade is to replace your old electrical switches and outlets for a more modern look. New hardware or refinishing the face of the kitchen cabinets is also a low-cost upgrade. Many older cabinets are of good quality, and only the doors need a face-lift. Pay particular attention to those items that are quick, easy, and inexpensive to replace but that can really improve the overall look of your unit.

✔ **When upgrading or replacing your current appliances, always compare energy-efficiency ratings and standardize the brand and model wherever possible.** One advantage of upgrading your appliances is energy efficiency. Though your tenant may be the one paying the rent, remember that "green" sells, and you can easily demonstrate that your unit will cost your tenant less each month in utilities with new energy-efficient appliances.

The advice to standardize the brands and models of appliances in your rental units is particularly true for certain appliances that have modular components that you can easily replace to give the appliances a new look and extended life. Stoves, ranges, ovens, refrigerators, and washers and dryers fit into this category. When other appliances such as microwaves, dishwashers, and garbage disposals fail, it's simply more cost-effective to replace the units. So for this latter category of appliances, you want to take advantage of appliance vendors who have certain models on closeout or special pricing. Bonus: Tenants generally don't pay that much attention to the brand of the garbage disposal, so you may as well take advantage of any specials. Buying a discontinued brand or model of a stove, however, may save you money upfront but cost you much more in the long run, when you're unable to find replacement parts.

If you have an older property, renovating may be more difficult because of some of the hazardous materials used in your unit's original construction. Hazardous materials such as asbestos or lead-based paint aren't cheap to remove. Often, you're better off just leaving the materials in place as long as they haven't been disturbed. Consult with hazardous materials removal experts before determining the extent of the renovation and the proper methods to ensure that all hazardous materials are safely maintained. Also, check with your local building code enforcement or health department for requirements regarding the proper handling and disposal of hazardous materials. The Environmental Protection Agency (EPA) has also implemented a lead-safe certified renovator program, and you should only use contractors that are on the approved EPA list. See www.epa.gov/lead to find a lead-safe certified firm near you. For more information on environmental hazards, see Chapter 9.

Obtaining the appropriate permits

When you're considering renovations or upgrades, make sure you get the appropriate building permits or licenses as required in your area. You don't need to be a code expert, but having a general understanding of both local housing codes and state housing laws is important. Evaluate your property and ensure that the planned work meets current building codes. Every state and many local municipalities have building codes that dictate the minimum standards to which all buildings must comply. Often, they have housing, fire, and health and safety codes as well. Reviewing rental housing industry publications can alert you to significant changes in these codes.

If inspectors find that your property isn't in compliance with the proper codes, you may receive violation notices and potentially expensive fines.

Building codes are regularly updated and changed, and typically, properties aren't required to meet the new code requirements unless the properties are renovated and new building permits are obtained. Be sure you or your contractors are aware of the code requirements and incorporate the necessary code-compliance measures in your renovations to ensure the safety of your tenants and to protect yourself from violations and fines.

Painting

The next step in getting your vacant rental unit ready is painting. The keys to success here are preparation and knowing what to paint when. Follow these steps to turn your unit into a rental work of art:

1. **Select and purchase the paint you want to use.**

   Remember, standardized colors are best so you can easily and affordably touch up your rental unit instead of having to completely repaint it. One coat of a high-quality flat white latex paint is usually sufficient, so use this standard to help determine the quantity you need to buy. *Note:* You may require more gallons if you're changing the paint color to a much lighter shade than the current version. Try and use the same brand of paint because colors can vary by brand. If you're changing from a flat to a semigloss finish, you may be able to do so in one coat. If you're painting a flat finish over a gloss, you'll likely need to prepare the surface so that the new paint adheres.

    Plan to use a semigloss paint in kitchens and baths for easy cleanup and resistance to moisture. Although this type of paint may cost more, you save in the long run because purchasing higher-quality paint means you don't have to repaint the entire unit when it inevitably turns over.

2. **Take everything off the surfaces you're painting.**

   Remove all nails, screws, picture anchors, and other similar items. Detach all door hardware, air vent covers, and electrical cover plates, too.

3. **Strip all dirt from the painting surfaces.**

   Make sure to clean the walls in particular. Treat grease, crayons, water stains, and other blemishes with products designed for that specific purpose.

4. **Check that walls are properly patched.**

   You may also need to do some scraping and sanding to ensure your new coat of paint adheres properly.

5. **Start painting.**

   Paint the unit in its entirety (yes, I mean walls, doors, door and window frames, baseboards, closets and closet dowels, and ceilings), unless you've recently painted the whole unit and only need to touch up one or two walls. Lucky you!

If you have acoustic ceilings, be aware that these present special problems, particularly if they contain asbestos. Always consult with a professional painter or licensed acoustic contractor before attempting to patch or paint an acoustic ceiling, and note that spraying paint is better than using a roller.

Don't paint damaged surfaces and/or those surfaces showing signs of moisture without determining the source of the problem and correcting it. Wet or moisture-damaged drywall indicates either plumbing leaks or water intrusion into the property's interior. The sooner you identify the culprit and make the necessary repairs, the better. If, after you resolve the problem and the surface is dry, a slight stain remains, try lightly spraying the area with a bleach mist to see whether the stain disappears. If not, you must paint.

6. **Replace everything you removed from your painting surfaces after the paint has dried.**

   Reinstall all the switch plates and outlet covers, replacing any that are damaged or covered with paint.

7. **Clean up any lingering mess.**

   Remove any paint that has strayed or splattered onto the floor, windows, countertops, cabinets, appliances, and woodwork. Don't use sinks or bathtubs for paint cleanup.

Final cleaning

Cleanliness sells. And the only people you want as renters are the ones who only accept dirt in their home as a temporary condition. For many rental property owners, the thought of cleaning up after someone else is too much to bear. Luckily, many local cleaning services do a great job for a very reasonable price. *Remember:* You don't have to do everything yourself.

However, if you decide to clean the unit yourself, keep the following pointers in mind:

- ✔ **Pay particular attention to the kitchens and baths.** A dirty or grimy kitchen or bathroom can be a real turnoff to potential tenants. Be sure you clean and re-grout the tile, completely caulk around all countertops and bathroom fixtures, and clean the single dirtiest spot in most rental properties — the shower door track. For a final touch, install a new toilet seat and place a paper sanitary ring around the toilet to indicate it's been professionally sanitized.

✔ **Focus on smell.** If a rental unit doesn't smell clean, it won't matter how diligently you've cleaned it. Rental property owners often overlook the importance of the sense of smell. Consequently, you can have a real advantage over the competition for an amazingly small investment by recognizing this underappreciated sense's value. Here are a few ideas:

- Use a pine oil or lemon disinfectant and cleanser to neutralize any bad odors from prior tenants.

- Place baking soda in the refrigerator and drains, and grind a lemon in the garbage disposal to suppress any bad odors.

- Put a cinnamon stick in a shallow pan of water and place it in the oven on low heat.

- Go to your favorite big box discount store to find many affordably priced liquid potpourris available in a variety of scents.

- Avoid certain fragrances that may be offensive to your prospective tenants. Too much use of scents may actually be distracting; your prospect may think you're attempting to cover up a bad smell that will return. Remember that two of the most difficult scents to eradicate are cat urine and smoking, and because they permeate the carpet and wall finishes, air fresheners will only work temporarily. Consult with a professional for a better solution.

In a short time, your rental unit will be filled with pleasant scents that remind your prospective tenants of Mom and apple pie. Why? Because this is a time when you want to go with something with mass appeal rather than your personal favorite scent — essence of yak.

Carpet or floor covering cleaning

Cleaning the carpet or floor covering is the last step in preparing your rental unit for new tenants. You can clean most floor coverings, such as linoleum or sheet vinyl, during the final cleaning stage; however, you should let outside contractors with professional truck-mounted steam cleaning equipment handle carpet cleaning. The cost of professional carpet cleaning is very competitive, and you can't achieve the same results with the non-truck-mounted equipment that's readily available for rent at your local grocery or hardware store.

Unless they're obviously damaged, thoroughly clean your floor coverings before deciding to make replacements. The best choice in floor covering material is determined by your tenant profile, your prospective tenants' expectations, and the competition in your area. Linoleum or sheet vinyl is very competitively priced, and the range of materials available is impressive. The most common problem with sheet vinyl is that any damage requires complete replacement. Some owners avoid sheet vinyl and prefer individual floor tiles that they can replace as needed; however, these tiles quickly trap dirt at the seams and can look unsightly. Be sure to select neutral colors and basic patterns.

If the carpets are too dated, severely worn, or badly stained and damaged, replace them. Carpeting is a decorator item, and you should take care to select colors and styles designed for use in rental property. I recommend selecting a standard carpet style in a couple of basic colors for all your properties. Although sculptured carpet works well for some units, a nonsculptured carpet with short *knap,* or fibers, available in one or two neutral colors has the broadest appeal. If you own a lot of rental units and have proper storage space, purchasing your standard carpet by the roll can offer significant savings. You can use the extra carpeting to patch or even replace a full room if needed. However, be aware that each roll of even the same carpet style and color can be different because the manufacturer's dye lot may vary slightly each time the carpet is produced.

Many rental property owners make the mistake of purchasing a higher grade of carpeting and trying to save money on the carpet pad. But the carpet pad can make all the difference in the world. Consider using a higher grade of rebond padding with a medium-grade carpet for competitively priced, yet excellent, results.

Using Outside Contractors

Determining how to handle the required turnover work in vacant rental units is one of the toughest decisions rental property owners have to make. Owners of large apartment buildings have maintenance personnel on staff and many contractors ready to assist them as needed. They routinely handle vacant units and just need to schedule the work. But owners of small rental properties are typically on their own to either handle the work personally or locate contractors to quickly prepare the vacant units.

Even if you're inclined to do your own turnover preparation work, understand that certain maintenance functions requiring specialized or licensed training are best handled by outside contractors. For example, it would be unwise for you to act as an exterminator or a contractor dealing with environmental hazards, or to attempt to recharge the coolant in an air-conditioning unit. Specific regulations are in place, and unique knowledge and licensing is required in these areas.

Your skill level, time constraints, and opportunity cost may help determine whether you do some chores yourself or hire a pro. For example, cleaning, painting, and light maintenance may be items that you feel qualified to handle, that you can complete promptly, and that you believe won't cause you to forgo significant income in other areas. When in doubt, let others do what they do best while you focus on what *you* do best: managing your rental property investment.

Every day your unit sits vacant costs you rental income you can never recover. Painting a single-family rental home yourself may take you six days working in the evenings and on weekends. If the rental market is strong and the daily rental rate is $50 per day, you're actually losing money you could've had if you'd hired professional painters for one day's work at $300.

Regardless of how much work you choose to handle yourself, you need to have a list of competent and competitively priced service companies and suppliers on hand for those times when you need a quick response. Your local affiliate of the NAA, IREM, or National Association of Residential Property Managers (NARPM) can often provide names of service companies. Carefully check references and the status of any bonds or licenses with the appropriate governmental agency and ensure the company has the proper insurance in place prior to commencing any work on your property. (Flip to Chapter 16 for more on the ins and outs of working with contractors.) If services exceed $600 in a calendar year and the vendor isn't a corporation or limited liability company (LLC), you need to file Form 1099 with the Internal Revenue Service.

Chapter 6

The Big Three of Property Management: Rent, Security Deposits, and Rental Contracts

In This Chapter

▶ Determining the appropriate rent for your rental unit

▶ Setting and using security deposits wisely

▶ Selecting the type of rental contract to use

*B*efore you begin to advertise and show your rental unit, you need to set your rent, determine the appropriate security deposit, and have a rental contract ready to go. Not sure where to start? Don't worry.

This chapter gives you some tips on figuring out what to ask for rent and deciding on your security deposit. It also guides you through the advantages and disadvantages of leases and month-to-month rental agreements and recommends how to get the benefits of each.

Setting the Rent

Setting the rent is an important decision because your net income from your rental property is determined by the amount of rent you charge. Although you may be tempted to pull numbers out of thin air, resist that urge. If your rent is too high, you'll have difficulty renting your vacant unit. If it's too low, you'll have plenty of prospective tenants but not enough money to cover your costs and generate a return on your investment. Finding the optimum price takes time and effort, which is why it's one of the most critical steps in being a successful rental property owner.

You can use two common methods for determining how much rent to charge — return on investment and market analysis. This section takes a close look at these two options and helps you figure out which method is best for you.

Knowing how much money you need to break even is important for evaluating the potential return on your real estate investment. But the reality is that the amount you need or want to collect in rent is subject to market conditions, the desirability of your property, and your abilities as a rental property owner.

If you currently own a rental property, you probably already know how much rental income is necessary to cover your mortgage and other basic operating expenses. If you're looking to buy a rental property, determine your minimum income needs *before* the deal is final. If you purchase a property that already has tenants on a long-term lease, you don't need to address the issue of rent immediately, because the tenants' rent is set through the end of their lease. If they're not on a lease or have an expired lease, then they're most likely on a month-to-month rental agreement — which only requires you to give sufficient written notice of a rent increase. (For more information on working with existing tenants, see Chapter 4).

Whichever category you're in, you need to determine market rents so you can calculate the appropriate rent when it comes time to renew a lease or consider increasing rents to market level.

Examining the return on your investment

The first step in determining your rent based on the return on your investment is to calculate your costs of owning and operating the property. Estimate costs for your mortgage, taxes, insurance, maintenance, leasing, management, and profit on invested funds. For example, if your annual expenses per rental unit are $12,000 for such fixed expenses as mortgage, insurance, and property tax payments and $7,000 for other variable operating expenses, plus you want a 10 percent ($5,000) annual return on your original cash investment of $50,000, you need to generate a total rent of $24,000 per year, or $2,000 per month. (Of course, this simple calculation doesn't account for appreciation, increasing equity, or other tax advantages of real estate, but it's a place to start.)

Although you may have calculated that you need $2,000 per month to achieve your estimated break-even point (including your 10 percent profit), if comparable rental units are readily available for $1,750, you may not be able to fully achieve your financial goals at this time. With most real estate investments, initial returns often don't match original projections. In many areas of the country with higher-priced income properties, your rent in the beginning years may not cover your carrying costs for the property. Yet in the long run, rents often increase at a greater rate than your expenses, thereby improving the return on your investment. Plus, cash flow is just one of several reasons you may be investing in real estate.

To avoid surprises, use a conservative budget that anticipates rental income at $50 to $100 per month *below* the full market rent for a comparable rental unit and also provides for a vacancy allowance of one full month each year. In my experience, some tenants don't fulfill their lease obligations, leaving you with a vacancy even if you had a 12-month lease.

For example, if you feel that the comparable monthly rent for your property is $1,600, estimate your rental income as no more than $1,500 per month. Then anticipate receiving this amount for 11 months rather than 12. After allowing for one month of vacancy, your gross rental income projection falls from $18,000 annually to $16,500. Yes, this is a very conservative way to calculate your cash flow from your pending real estate purchase, but even if you purchase the property using more aggressive numbers, this is a good, less-than-ideal-case scenario that gives you an idea of the range.

Many new rental property owners make a major mistake by overestimating the potential income from their property. They develop unrealistic operating budgets or projections by using above-market rents, not allowing for rental discounts, and anticipating virtually no vacancy or bad debt. This is often the result of overly optimistic information provided by the seller or their real estate agent. I've seen many income property sales fliers show estimated income and expense projections for potential buyers that simply aren't accurate.

In addition to overestimating potential rental income, some rental property owners make the mistake of factoring property taxes based on the taxes the prior owner paid rather than on their purchase. Sellers and real estate agents often use historical taxes in their cash flow analysis, attempting to create the illusion that the net income from the property is greater than it actually is. When reality strikes, owners are faced with negative cash flow and the possibility of losing their rental property. Avoid this situation by playing it safe and staying conservative with your estimated income.

Setting the rent is particularly critical if you own single-family or condo units and other small rental properties because the rent loss from an extended vacancy or one bad tenant can seriously jeopardize your entire investment. If you're among this group, be conservative in setting your rents, cautious in screening tenants, and aggressive in keeping your properties in excellent condition to attract good, long-term tenants who pay on time. When analyzing these types of investments, pay particular attention to any major items needing replacement in the near future, such as the roof, pavement, and mechanical equipment used for heating and cooling.

Regarding condominiums, look carefully at the financial health of the governing association. Lots of good deals appear to exist in condo or townhouse communities because of short sales or foreclosures. But a downside is that the owners of these units aren't paying their mortgages, property taxes, or association dues and assessments. The governing association may not be collecting sufficient revenue to cover the expenses in the short term and may not be allocating the necessary funds for long-term capital items that will need attention in the years to come. The association may defer current operational and maintenance expenses, which negatively affects the aesthetics of the community. The budget shortfalls will likely result in special assessments to be paid by the paying homeowners until all the distressed units have been resold. Investing in such associations can dramatically affect your investment.

Conducting a market analysis of rents in your area

You can determine the amount of rent to charge by calculating a desired return on your investment and setting the rent accordingly (see the preceding section), but typically, the best way to set your rent is to conduct a market survey of comparable rental properties in your area. Why? The answer is simple: Most rental markets have a limit to what prospective renters will pay for a comparable unit, and tenants don't care how much you paid for the unit or how much you spend in operating and capital improvement costs.

Following are two schools of thought about performing a rent survey to determine the proper asking rent for your units:

- ✔ **Pose as a prospective renter and ask all the typical questions a prospect may ask.** The owner or manager will give you only the information that a prospective tenant needs about the property.

- ✔ **Be honest and tell the owner you're a rental property owner doing market analysis.** This is the method I recommend, particularly if you have a small rental property. Most rental owners will cooperate and share the information you need. They may even be willing to give you additional important information you can't get otherwise, such as the length of time their units have been vacant, the number and types of phone calls they've received to date, the actual occupancy rate for the properties, and the feedback from their own research into rental rates and vacancies in the local market. This behavior is especially true if they've recently rented their properties and are no longer competing with you for prospective tenants.

Keep in mind that the owners of competing large apartment communities probably won't provide you with any information about their current occupancy rate. This number is important, however, because it indicates overall demand for rental units in the market. Over the years, I've discovered some creative ways to determine vacancy levels:

- • Talk with the mail carrier who delivers to the complex; she can tell you whether it's completely full or relatively vacant.

- • Ask a common vendor, such as a carpet-cleaning firm or exterminator, that services your property and the large apartment complex for the inside information you need.

• Drive through the property at night to see how many parking spaces are being used or apartments appear to be occupied or lighted.

To determine the rents in your market, do your homework and locate comparable rental properties. *Comparable properties* are those that your tenants are most likely to have also considered when looking for a rental unit. They may be located right in the neighborhood or all the way across town. For example, many of your rental prospects may work at the hospital located 6 blocks west of your property, but they're just as likely to choose a rental within 6 blocks of the hospital in another direction. So your comparable properties can be 12 blocks or more away. Don't assume your comparable properties are solely in your own neighborhood.

If your property is a single-family home or condo unit in a large housing development or community with identical or similar floor plans, you may find that your primary competition is the same (or a similar) model. Determine the current rental rates of occupied and vacant units that are now on the market (especially helpful are those just recently rented) and you'll get a good range of rents to consider. However, every property is unique, and many aspects of each property can make the rent higher or lower than other nearby properties.

After you determine which rental units are comparable, finding out the current market rent is easy. Begin by checking the For Rent signs in your area and calling for the asking rent and other details. The local or regional newspaper usually has ads listing the units for rent in the area. Although calling about ads gives you some good general information, you need to see the properties in person to truly determine whether they're comparable to yours.

Be careful to distinguish between the asking rents quoted on signs or by phone. Many landlords (especially those with single-family homes or condos) can be negotiated down from the asking rent pretty easily. Most owners of individual rental units can't afford vacancies for more than a couple of weeks and will quickly lower the rent if qualified prospects show interest in their properties, so you need to base your decisions on signed leases, not asking prices.

What you really need to know is what the market is willing to pay for a unit that's comparable to what you have to offer. In many communities the Multiple Listing Services (MLS) now post rentals and what rents were paid when they were occupied. This information is proprietary to subscribers but is becoming more available to the public. If you're unable to pull that data for your community, contact a Realtor or potential management company to get it for you. A Realtor may be willing to do so for a nominal fee.

Remember, rental rates can vary greatly from neighborhood to neighborhood and even from street to street because many factors affect rents, including the following:

✔ Landscaping

✔ Property features, such as location, age, and size

✔ Proximity to services and transportation

✔ Reputation of the neighborhood or property

✔ Traffic noise

✔ Views

As a result, determining the proper asking rent isn't scientific. Setting your rent a little too high at first is better than setting it too low because you can always reduce your asking rent slightly if you encounter too much resistance. Of course, be honest and make downward adjustments for aspects of your property that aren't as competitive or desirable as those of the comparable properties in your area.

Be willing to make necessary adjustments quickly. If you get no response — or even lots of responses but no confirmed rentals — you need to adjust something. It may be the curb appeal or condition of your property, or the rent level. You need to step back and take a hard look at all aspects of your property, your marketing and advertising, and your rental rates.

When estimating the proper market rent for your unit, be careful not to make adjustments based strictly on your personal preferences. Remember, you're probably *not* representative of your target market. The rental value of a particular property is subjective and can vary dramatically from one person to another. For example, you may prefer upstairs units and believe they should be priced higher than comparable downstairs units. Although many prospective renters may agree with you, just as many prospects may similarly value a downstairs unit because they may not want to climb stairs.

To access a sample Market Survey form for comparing and contrasting your rental property with other comparable properties to determine an appropriate rental rate, simply pop in the CD or click the link in the table of contents.

You really need to visit the properties to experience what your prospective renters see, hear, smell, and feel in order to conduct an accurate market survey. It takes time and energy, but it's well worth it.

The following sections break down some additional items to think about when conducting your market analysis.

Considering rental concessions in determining your rent

When you contact other rental property owners or managers to determine an *effective rent,* the actual net rent after all concessions and discounts, for your property, be prepared to receive a rent quote but don't expect to hear about rental concessions. A *rental concession* is basically a discount given to entice a prospective tenant to sign a rental contract. Landlords tend to give concessions in softer real estate markets where the demand for apartments has slowed, so identifying potential concessions is important in your comparison because you need to know what the net or actual collected rent is. If you don't, you may overprice your rental units.

To find out the actual effective rents with concessions included, I recommend you contact rental property owners or managers after they've rented their units and concluded marketing efforts. When their properties are occupied, they're more likely to cooperate and give you accurate, complete information regarding their agreed-upon terms.

Calculate the effective rental rate by dividing the total rent by the length of the rental period. *Note:* Various concessions may affect the total rent. For example, say a competitive property in your area recently rented at $1,200 per month on a one-year lease, but the first month's rent was waived. Then the total rent paid in 12 months is $1,200 per month for only 11 months, or $13,200. To find the effective rent, you divide the total rent of $13,200 by the 12 months of the lease: $1,100 per month.

Without knowing about the rental concession, you may mistakenly think the comparable unit rented at $1,200 per month. As a result, you may set your asking rent too high or be hesitant to offer your own rental concessions to stay competitive with what you think is a higher price. Just remember that every day your unit sits vacant because your rental rate is higher than the competition's is money lost.

You can calculate your daily lost rent by dividing the monthly rent by 30 days. So, with an asking rent of $1,200 per month, you're losing $40 every day that your property sits vacant, and you'll never recoup that lost income unless you can rent your property for a higher rent than $1,200 per month. This calculation can be helpful as you consider offers at a lower rent or a request for a concession from prospective tenants.

Deciding whether to market your rental property using gross rents or net rents

After completing your analysis of your local rental market and taking into consideration any concessions, you need to set your final asking price. You can do so by formulating a marketing strategy to ensure you get the best price for your rental property.

Here are your options:

- ✔ Quote a higher gross asking rent, which is similar to the "suggested retail price" that stores use, and then offer rental concessions to attract the attention of your target market.
- ✔ Go with a lower effective asking rent that is the net of the rental concessions prevalent in the market.

Dealing with potential rent control issues

Most areas of the country don't impose limits on the rental rate you set for your property. Rent control is currently only found in Washington, D.C., and specific cities or counties in a handful of states: California, Maryland, New Jersey, and New York. If you own a rent-controlled property, you need to obtain a current copy of the ordinance and fully understand the implications of local rent control when setting your asking rent. You also need to know how you can implement future rent increases because rent control limitations may influence your initial asking rents.

If you're limited to only nominal future rent increases, make sure you get the maximum rent possible for a new tenant because this base rent will be a factor in your rental income for the entire duration of the tenancy. In other words, if you lower your rent by $100 to quickly rent your property, you'll likely be negatively affecting your income stream for many years.

If you like to negotiate and can sell the special offer, the gross rent method is for you. Some prospective tenants are attracted by rental concessions; at least that's the impression I get when prospects call about a property and the first thing they ask is, "What's your special?" Be sure to watch out for tenants who are just looking for the special discount off the rent upfront because they likely aren't the long-term quality tenants you want (and need) to be a successful rental property owner. These renters may be out looking for another deal as soon as they're able and tend to treat the property with less care.

Have you heard about the great bargains available on air travel, hotel rooms, and cruise vacations booked at the last minute? Well, the concepts of inventory management and lost revenue also apply to the rental housing industry. Units that sit vacant for too long are usually overpriced, and each day that passes with your property vacant is more lost rent you can never collect. Either reevaluate your asking rent or concessions or see what you can do to make your rental unit superior to the competition to secure those long-term tenants.

Not into wheeling and dealing? Perhaps you prefer telling your prospective renters that, unlike all the other landlords offering gimmicks and special deals, you're all about cutting the hype and offering them the best net monthly rental rate. In my experience, many tenants find a lower, straightforward rental rate quote more attractive, especially if they plan on staying for a long time.

Regardless of which marketing strategy you take, avoid the temptation to set your rent based on the number of occupants your unit can hold. Some landlords have a policy that the base rental rate is for a certain number of tenants and then charge more for each additional tenant in the unit. This practice is sometimes called *per head* rent. However, the U.S. Department of Housing and Urban Development considers such policies violations of the Fair Housing Act. The only exception is if you can show a legitimate *business necessity,* or verifiable increased cost to maintain your rental property, such as higher water or sewage bills. If you think you can prove a business necessity, check with your legal expert before setting rents. Otherwise, take my advice and avoid these turbulent waters.

Ultimately, your marketing strategy is often influenced by what's most commonly done in your local market, but don't be afraid to incorporate your personal style.

Coming Up with a Fair Security Deposit

As an owner of rental property, you need to make sure the security deposit you collect adequately protects you from tenant damage or default. The *security deposit* serves as the protection you need before turning your real estate asset (the rental unit) over to a tenant. It needs to be large enough to motivate the tenant to leave the property in good condition, plus serve as an accessible resource to cover the tenant's unpaid rent or reimburse the costs to repair any damage. If you set the deposit too high, many qualified tenants may not be able to afford the move-in costs, resulting in fewer applicants.

State laws typically limit the amount of the security deposit you can collect and regulate its return, along with any lawful deductions. If you collect the first month's rent upon move-in, this money is *not* considered part of the security deposit. Some states specifically allow certain small rental owners to be exempt from these rules. Pop in the CD or click the link in the table of contents for more information on state laws about security deposits (including the maximum amounts you can request and the time limits to return deposits).

The next several sections help you determine the right amount for your security deposit.

Figuring what you can legally charge

Many states limit the security deposit to the equivalent of one or two months' rent. The limit varies in each state depending on certain factors, such as whether the rental is furnished, whether the tenant is on a lease or a month-to-month rental agreement, whether the tenant has pets or a water bed, and whether the tenant is a senior citizen. As you'll quickly discover, the laws affecting rental properties vary widely from state to state (and sometimes even from city to city), so you need to always check with a resource that applies to the specific jurisdiction where your property is located. One size does *not* fit all when it comes to rental property laws and regulations.

In most rental markets, the security deposits are well below the maximum allowed by law. While staying within the legal limits, I recommend you collect as large of a security deposit as the market can bear. A security deposit is rarely an adequate insurance policy against the damage caused by poor tenant selection. The better job you do in selecting tenants, the less you'll need to dip into your security deposits for repairs and replacements at the end of their lease.

Security deposits are more than just money you hold for protection against unpaid rent or damage caused by your tenant. Although the actual cash amount may be relatively small compared to the overall value of your property, the deposit is a psychological tool that's often your best insurance policy for getting your unit back in decent condition.

When trying to determine how much to charge for your security deposit, make sure you avoid the following potentially costly mistakes:

- ✔ **Don't lower the deposit or waive a deposit payment.** If the funds required to move in are too high, collect a reasonable portion of the deposit prior to move-in and allow the tenant, in writing, to pay the balance of the deposit in installments. This type of written agreement usually indicates that any funds that the tenant pays are first applied to the deposit and then applied to the rent. Don't allow the tenant to miss or delay payment of any subsequent security deposit installments. Take legal action immediately if the tenant misses any security deposit payments or fails to pay the rent in full.

  For single-family homes, I strongly advise getting as large a security deposit as possible. Aside from the inherent increased value of the rental home itself, you likely have tremendous value in the grounds, landscaping, and pool or spa (if applicable) — meaning tenants can damage much more of your valued property. Rental homeowners also tend to inspect or visit their property less frequently, and it takes only a few weeks of inadequate watering or shoddy landscaping maintenance to find that you've suffered significant damage. See Chapter 17 for advice on ways to convince tenants that landscaping or pool/spa maintenance is best left to professional contractors.

- ✔ **Don't completely eliminate security deposits.** Property owners in *soft* or low-demand rental markets often offer free rent or "no security deposit" move-in specials. Prospective renters attracted by such offers typically aren't the types to become stable, long-term tenants who treat your property with respect and care about peaceful, harmonious living with their neighbors.

  Although staying competitive is important, I recommend avoiding free rent or "no deposit" specials whenever possible. One way to lower the upfront move-in or out-of-pocket costs for your prospective tenant while motivating him to properly take care of your property is to offer to pay his security deposit. This way you still receive the first month's rent when your tenant moves in, and he may receive a deposit refund if the property is in good condition at move-out. Essentially a form of free rent (because you're crediting the tenant, not keeping the money), this strategy reduces the total funds your incoming tenant must pay. Unlike a risky move-in special, you're offering the real benefit of the concession at the *end* of the lease, not the beginning. As a result, you're less likely to attract tenants who move from landlord to landlord in search of upfront freebies. You also have a better shot at creating a strong psychological and practical motivation for the tenant to fulfill the terms of his lease. Why? Because that security deposit cash comes in handy for covering the costs of moving to a new residence . . . after several good years at your property, of course.

Keeping security deposits separate from your other funds

Security deposits are liabilities from an accounting point of view because they legally belong to the tenant. You hold them in trust as protection in case the tenant damages the property or defaults in paying rent.

Because the funds don't belong to you, several states require you to hold security deposits in a separate bank trust account instead of mixing them in with other funds from your rental properties or personal resources. Some states even insist you provide your tenant with a written notice indicating the location of this bank trust account at the beginning of the tenancy.

Keeping the deposits separate from the rest of your funds means they're readily available whenever a tenant moves out and is potentially entitled to the return of some or all of her money. Doing so, even if not required in your area, can be a great way to avoid cash flow problems. Say a tenant fulfills all contractual obligations before move-out and deserves a deposit refund. If you commingled her deposit with your personal funds, you may find that your current cash availability can't cover a large deposit refund within the short time frame required by law in most areas. This situation can lead to legal action by the tenant and additional penalties and interest. The lesson? Always make sure you have available funds to cover the potential refund of all security deposits.

Avoiding nonrefundable deposits

A *nonrefundable security deposit,* which is allowed in some states, is a portion of the deposit that you, the property owner, retain no matter what the state law allows as a proper deduction. In other words, in some states, even if your tenants leave the rental unit in perfect condition, there's a nonrefundable cleaning fee. A nonrefundable security deposit may sound like a good idea, but it may also send a message to tenants that they already paid for cleaning, so why bother, or that they have to pay for the costs of preparing the property for the next tenant. My 30 years of experience with tenants leads me to question the benefits of nonrefundable security deposits in most instances because the incentive is gone for tenants to keep and maintain the property in the best condition.

Last month's rent

For many years, many rental property owners collected the first month's rent, the last month's rent, and a security deposit from new tenants, a method that has some disadvantages. I strongly recommend you collect the first month's rent, plus a security deposit equal to or greater than one month's rent, because collecting the last month's rent can create unnecessary problems.

If the rental rate increases during the tenancy and you've already collected a lesser amount as the last month's rent, upon move-out, the tenant (and often the court) will likely take the position that the last month's rent has already been paid in full, even though the rental rate has increased. When giving rent increases, many owners fail to also require the tenant to increase the amount held as the last month's rent. Plus, in some states, the designation of last month's rent limits your use of these funds to only that specific use. Thus, even if the unit is extensively damaged and the security deposit is fully exhausted, you can't use the last month's rent to cover those damages.

Make your security deposit an amount that's different from the monthly rental rate to minimize the chance that your tenant will presume that the deposit covers his last month's rent. Ideally, you can collect a deposit that's higher than the monthly rental rate. But even if you collect a deposit that's $25 to $50 less than the rent, you effectively eliminate a tenant's attempt to claim the deposit was for the last month's rent.

In fact, I recommend avoiding nonrefundable fees in general in favor of seeking a higher, fully refundable security deposit so you have funds to cover damage repairs and cleaning, if necessary. It's a good day as a rental owner or property manager if your tenant vacates and leaves the property in good condition, so I prefer to make the entire deposit refundable.

Approximately a dozen states have specific laws permitting rental property owners to have nonrefundable security deposits or fees. These fees cover the costs of services such as cleaning, repainting, and redecorating. Some states have very specific limitations on these deposits or fees and don't allow you to charge for any excessive costs incurred. On the other hand, several states don't have laws specifically prohibiting nonrefundable deposits and leave such decisions to the mutual agreement of the owner and the tenant.

Regardless of where you live, not using nonrefundable deposits allows you to avoid potentially time-consuming disputes with your tenants, such as what happens if the $150 nonrefundable cleaning deposit is insufficient to cover the $250 costs for cleaning a filthy rental property.

Paying interest on security deposits

Although the extremely low interest rate environment of the past several years has minimized this as an issue for both landlords and tenants, several states have laws requiring rental property owners to pay interest on a tenant's security deposit. You can find some basic information about security deposit interest on the CD, but check with your local affiliate of the National Apartment Association for the exact requirements in your area, because the laws differ dramatically from state to state.

The method of calculating interest varies greatly, with some states providing a formula tied to the Federal Reserve Board rates or flat percentage amounts. Most states require interest payments to be made annually and at termination of the tenancy.

No laws prevent you from voluntarily paying interest on deposits, and some owners offer to pay interest as a competitive advantage or an inducement to collect a larger security deposit. If you're able to get a much larger deposit (but still not above the maximum allowed in your state), I recommend paying a slightly above-market interest rate on the funds. A good tenant who's confident she'll leave the property in excellent condition can earn a higher return on her money. The additional peace of mind and readily available cash resource to cover excessive damage is certainly worth much more than the relatively small amount you'll pay in interest.

Increasing (or decreasing) deposits

If you have a long-term tenant and you've increased your rents significantly over time, you may want to consider increasing your security deposit amount. This move is legal as long as you comply with the normal requirements for any change in the rental agreement's terms.

For example, if you have a fixed-term lease in effect, you must wait until the lease expires or rolls over to a month-to-month rental agreement before increasing the deposit. If you have a month-to-month rental agreement, you can increase the deposit the same way you raise the rent, typically by giving the tenant a written notice 30 days in advance. Either way, remember that you're subject to the maximum security deposit amounts as set by state law, if any.

It may seem counterintuitive at first, but you may also find that you want to decrease your tenant's security deposit. For example, you may have a tenant who has been with you for a number of years, keeps the rental unit in immaculate condition, and pays her full rent like clockwork. But the market rents keep increasing, and you want to keep your rents at market level. Lowering the security deposit is a way to cushion the blow of the higher rent and improve your chances of retaining this solid tenant.

Choosing the Type of Rental Contract You Want

Another important decision you need to make before you begin advertising and showing your rental is whether you want to use a lease or a month-to-month rental agreement. The *rental contract,* whether a lease or a month-to-month rental agreement, is the primary document that specifies the terms and conditions of the agreement that binds the property owner and the tenant. It's a contract between the owner and the tenant for the possession and use of the property in exchange for the payment of rent. The following sections give you the lowdown on the two types of agreements.

Contemplating a lease

A *lease* is a fixed-term contract that obligates you and the tenant for a set period of time. Some owners like the commitment required from leases. Although leases can be of any length, the most common lease terms are for 6 months, 9 months, or 12 months. The majority of leases are written to automatically convert to a month-to-month rental agreement after the expiration of the initial term. However, some leases are for fixed terms, and the owner and tenant must agree to sign a new lease for the tenant to stay.

A lease is advantageous for tenants because it's usually written to lock the rent and all the other terms in place for the term of the lease, and it's potentially advantageous for you because you can theoretically count on having a tenant for a set period of time. It may also be advantageous for you in a soft market, where good residents are hard to find and the economic conditions are forecast to be weak for an extended period.

Rental property owners generally charge a lower rental rate for leases than for month-to-month rental agreements because tenants on a lease aren't associated with as high a risk of turnover as individuals on short-term agreements. Yet in 20 years of writing a nationally syndicated, landlord-tenant Q & A column, I've received hundreds of inquiries from tenants seeking suggestions for a compelling story or legal argument to break their long-term leases. This is the single most commonly asked question in the past 20 years! Whether they just wanted the lower upfront cost of a lease or their personal needs changed, all of them wanted out of their long-term commitments. So be cautious and don't offer more than a $10 to $20 per month discount for long-term leases, unless your local market conditions warrant a higher amount.

With a lease, you can't increase the rent or change other terms of the tenancy until the lease expires. Also, you can't terminate the tenancy before the lease expires unless the tenant doesn't pay her rent or violates another term of the lease. Should you wind up in court, you'll have the burden of proof, meaning you're the one who has to prove the tenant didn't live up to her part of the contract (which can be difficult for issues other than the payment of rent).

Although the lease legally binds both you and your tenant, the current landlord-tenant laws in virtually every state favor tenants. A tenant can walk away from a lease without difficulty, and in most states, the owner has the duty of mitigating or minimizing the potential damages. This legal mumbo jumbo means you must make a reasonable effort to re-rent the premises and can only charge for the costs of marketing the property and the rent incurred until the new tenant begins paying rent.

Eyeing a periodic rental agreement

Some owners prefer the flexibility of a month-to-month rental agreement over the rigidity of a lease. A *month-to-month rental agreement* is essentially a 30-day lease that automatically renews each month, unless the owner or tenant gives the other proper written notice (usually 30 days) to terminate the tenancy. Month-to-month rental agreements give you much more freedom than leases because you can increase the rent or change other terms of the tenancy on 30 days' notice. You can also easily modify them for short-term rentals by converting the rent payment period from monthly to weekly or biweekly.

Of course, month-to-month rental agreements have their downsides:

- ✔ Your tenants may be concerned about the possibility of changing rental rates or policies.

- ✔ Your tenants may worry about having to relocate on short notice, leaving you to wonder whether you're likely to have a tenant locked in for a certain lease term.

- ✔ Your tenants may not like moving and want to stay somewhere long term.

- ✔ Frequent rent increases may serve as an irritant to your tenants and stimulate them to move sooner than they had anticipated.

Although the month-to-month rental agreement does allow your tenants the right to move at any time merely by giving a 30-day written notice, the reality is that most tenants don't like to move and will often stay long term. The majority of tenants only move because of a job transfer or another significant reason, or because the rental owner doesn't properly maintain the property.

The wide variations in laws regarding notice requirements for changing or terminating month-to-month rental agreements clearly illustrate the importance of knowing your state and local landlord-tenant laws. Some states don't have any statutory requirements for giving notice; others mandate a time frame such as 10 or 15 days. The majority of states require 30 days' notice, some less under certain circumstances, but four states (California, Delaware, Georgia, and Hawaii) currently require property owners or managers to give more than a 30-day written notice when changing agreement terms or terminating a month-to-month tenancy. For example, in California, property owners with tenancies greater than one year must provide a 60-day termination notice, whereas the tenant only needs to provide 30 days' notice. Rent increases in California can also be subject to either 30 or 60 days' notice, depending on the amount and timing of the increase in conjunction with previous increases. Check out the accompanying CD for more information on state landlord-tenant laws and acquaint yourself with the laws in your particular area.

Get familiar with and respect the types of agreements typically offered in your local rental market. If competing properties are all offered on month-to-month rental agreements, you may find it difficult to attract plenty of well-qualified rental applicants if you insist on a 12-month lease.

Getting your contract in writing

Never allow a tenant to take possession of your rental property without fully executing your written rental contract. Some tenants refuse to sign documents so they can claim they had a verbal agreement that's much different from the one you had in mind.

For a sample standard Lease Agreement and Month-to-Month Rental Agreement, pop in the CD or click the link in the table of contents. Be sure to have an attorney who specializes in landlord-tenant law review these documents (and all other forms from this book) before using them in your area. In some states, special language must be included in these documents. For example, Florida requires language about radon, and many states require information that must be given to tenants concerning access to a sexual offender or child molester database.

Standard lease forms are great, but many don't allow you to add your own clauses. However, you can modify the terms of your rental agreement fairly easily with an Addendum to Lease or Rental Agreement. Perhaps you want to add the requirement that the tenant acknowledges receipt of the rules and regulations of the community or homeowners' association and is responsible for any fines or assessments resulting from his breach of the rules. You can easily incorporate this condition into the lease by using the addendum. *Remember:* Be careful about adding additional clauses or language to your lease or rental agreement without seeking the advice of an attorney.

Click the link in the table of contents or pop in the CD to access a sample Addendum to Lease or Rental Agreement you can use.

Although oral rental agreements of up to one year are binding, make sure all your leases or rental agreements are in writing, because so many issues surrounding those agreements involve monetary considerations. Memories fade and disputes can arise that are usually resolved in the tenant's favor should legal action be required and proof to the contrary can't be found in writing. Courts expect the property owner or manager to operate his rental housing business in a professional manner and to have clear documentation at all times.

Oral agreements create the potential for charges of discriminatory treatment. Always put all terms and conditions in writing, even if you intend to have only a short-term agreement or you know the tenant personally. Oral agreements often can't be substantiated and aren't always enforceable.

Seeking the best of a lease and a rental agreement

In my experience, the number one reason tenants insist on a lease is that the rent is locked in for a minimum period. But in most instances, especially in rental markets where rent increases aren't likely, owners want the flexibility and latitude afforded by the month-to-month rental agreement. If the tenant doesn't abide by the lease's terms, she can simply terminate the rental agreement without having to prove the breach in a court of law.

Despite this discrepancy in desires, it's possible to achieve both goals. I strongly recommend using a month-to-month rental agreement in conjunction with a Rental Rate Guarantee certificate (you can see a sample of what one looks like by popping in the CD or clicking the link in the table of contents). This method affords your tenant the benefits of a stable rental rate for a minimum period *without* restricting your ability to change other rules or even ask the tenant to leave in 30 days if problems arise.

If your local market conditions dictate a longer fixed-rent term than what's indicated on this certificate, you can make an even more significant impression on a great prospective tenant by using a black marker or felt pen to clearly cross out "six months" and fill in a longer term. Be sure to print this certificate onto specialty paper to give it a valuable look.

Chapter 7

FOR RENT: Generating Interest in Your Rental

. . . .

In This Chapter

▶ Knowing your target market and creating your marketing plan

▶ Seeing how advertising can increase your rental business

▶ Getting acquainted with fair housing laws

▶ Choosing where and how to advertise your rental properties

. . . .

*M*ore than almost any other single item, locating and renting to good-quality tenants makes your experience as a property manager enjoyable and profitable. But finding a good tenant can be a long process if you don't know how to do it. So in this chapter, I take you through the process from beginning to end — from creating a marketing plan (which helps you narrow your focus and set goals) to writing solid print ads to using the incredible resources of the web to broaden your reach for prospective tenants. Start here if you just found out one of your units will be vacant in a month or if you've already had a vacancy for twice that long. It's never too late to start advertising effectively, and in this chapter, I give you all the tools you need to do exactly that.

Developing a Marketing Plan

A *marketing plan* can be anything from a formal written outline of your marketing strategies to some general marketing ideas you keep in mind as you try to find renters for your property. If you own only 1 or 2 properties or 20 or 30 rental units in multiple locations, you may not think you need a marketing plan. Developing one may seem like an unnecessary use of your time and energy. But the basic concepts of a marketing plan are important for *all* rental property owners, regardless of the number of units you own.

The key to success in owning and managing rental properties is to keep your units full with long-term paying tenants who treat your property and their neighbors respectfully. But first you need to determine the best way to attract and retain these highly desirable tenants. The following sections help you develop a marketing plan to do just that.

A good marketing plan consists of strategies for attracting prospective tenants and retaining your current tenants. Keeping your current tenants is so essential to your long-term success as a rental property owner that I devote Chapter 13 to figuring out how to make it happen.

Determining your target market

One of the first steps in developing a basic marketing plan is to determine the *target market* for your rental property. The target market consists of rental prospects who are most likely to decide that your rental unit meets their needs. Your target market can be relatively broad or fairly narrow, depending on your property's type, location, size, age/condition, rental rate, and features. If you have multiple rental properties, you may find that each property has a different target market or that the target markets overlap.

The likelihood of finding responsible renters is often a numbers game. The more prospective renters you're able to attract, the greater your opportunity to carefully evaluate their qualifications and select the most qualified applicant.

To identify your target market, make sure you carefully evaluate your rental unit by looking at the following features that make it unique:

- ✔ **Location:** What are some of the benefits of your property's location? Is it located near employment, medical services, shopping, schools, or other important neighborhood or regional facilities? Paying attention to your property's location may provide you with a target market that includes employees of certain companies, young families wanting to be close to good schools, or people who need to live near certain local facilities.

- ✔ **Size:** Larger units tend to be more attractive to families or roommates, whereas studio units are more suitable to single renters, independent seniors, or couples.

- ✔ **Age/condition:** Only newer properties will do for certain renters, whereas other renters prefer more classical or vintage properties with personality and character that can't be found elsewhere.

- ✔ **Rental rate:** Renters, like most people, would like to have the very best that money can buy, but in reality they need to find a property that meets their various criteria while still being in the price range they can afford.

- ✔ **Amenities:** A property that allows pets and has a large yard typically appeals to pet owners and/or renters with children. If your property has storage space or a garage, some hobbyists or empty nesters who are downsizing may be particularly interested in what you have to offer. Active renters will like that you have a pool and spa or tennis courts.

When you compare the attributes of your property to the needs of all prospective renters in your market, you'll probably discover that certain renters find that your unit meets their needs more than others. The term *target market* is appropriate to describe the group that you're out to attract. Certain words and images may be more likely to catch the attention of one group over another, such as "Located in the top-rated school district." You can use this knowledge to target specific audiences, but your rental efforts must never discourage, limit, or exclude *any* prospective renter from having an equal opportunity to qualify and rent from you.

If you don't attract and retain tenants, you can rest assured your competition will. You're competing with other owners and property managers for the best tenants, even if you only have a few rental units. In most rental markets, prospective tenants have many options, and the most responsible tenants are very selective because the rental unit they choose will be their home sweet home.

Thinking about what your renters stand to gain from your property

After you've established who your most likely rental prospects are, you need to shift your focus to incorporating the concept of a target market into your marketing plans. This time is when I usually think of the WIFM concept. *WIFM* stands for *what's in it for me,* and this theory represents the thought processes of virtually all consumers (including your potential tenants) when evaluating a purchase decision. (I discovered this important idea at the national faculty training sessions of the Institute of Real Estate Management.) The WIFM concept reminds you that, in general, people are most interested in the benefits they personally receive in any given relationship or business transaction.

When it comes to marketing and advertising your property, the important concept of WIFM can help you see the rental decision process through the eyes of your prospective tenants, making your goal of finding stable, long-term tenants more attainable. Unfortunately, rental property owners and managers are human, and they often fail to critically evaluate the advantages and disadvantages of the product they're selling — their rental housing unit. You have a competitive advantage if you understand the opportunities and challenges presented by your property and the specific unit that's available. You can also beat out the competition if you find ways to improve your property's weaknesses or narrow your marketing focus to those specific types of tenants who'll be attracted to your property.

Property owners often aren't part of their target market, so they may make incorrect assumptions about what prospective tenants value. If you have current tenants, you may want to ask them what they value most about renting in your building or why they chose to rent your unit over others in the marketplace. They live there. Others like them are your target market. The information they provide can be invaluable.

Looking at your property through your prospective tenants' eyes

I once had a rental property located near a major university. The property had several vacancies in the two-bedroom/one-bath units. Because I was wary of renting to large numbers of undergraduate students interested in only short-term leases for the school year, my marketing plan was to attract university faculty or graduate students whom I thought would have a roommate and be perfect for the two-bedroom units on a year-round basis. Although many prospective tenants looked at the units, my actual rentals were very slow, and the two-bedroom vacancies remained unacceptable. Clearly, I was trying to force the rental market and prospective renters to adapt to my perception of their needs.

When it became obvious that my efforts weren't having much success, I began carefully reviewing the comments of prospects. I found that my target faculty and graduate students preferred to live alone on a long-term lease so they could have a quiet place to work or study without roommates. With this new view of my prospects' needs, I quickly realized I could market my two-bedroom/one-bath units to my target market with a new approach.

Armed with this knowledge, I revised my marketing efforts by changing my advertising in the college newspaper to read, "One bedroom plus den." This move led to an increased interest in the property, a greater occupancy percentage, and more long-term leases. Just by changing the way I was advertising the units, I found that I was able to reach my original target market of faculty and graduate students who wanted to live off-campus.

Remember: While observing all fair housing laws, look at your property from the perspective of the most likely tenants. Then promote and accentuate the features of your property that are of greatest interest to that market. But always be careful not to discourage prospective tenants from renting your property.

Understanding the Importance of Good Advertising

Tenants rarely come looking for you. Your local newspaper may have a column for "Housing Wanted" (if so, lucky you!) or one of your current tenants may contact you inquiring on behalf of a friend who's looking for a rental unit. These scenarios are the exception, not the rule. The majority of your tenants come from the efforts you make to locate qualified rental prospects.

Advertising is how you let people know you have a vacant rental property available. If people don't know you have vacant units, they can't rent them. When advertising is done well, the money you spend on it is extremely worthwhile. But when it's done poorly, advertising can be another black hole for your precious resources. Advertising is more of an art than a science at times because what works for one particular property may not work for another.

The next few sections give you the lowdown on the role of advertising in renting your property and what you can do to get your property rented.

Review the information from your marketing plan about the most marketable features and attributes of your property and present it to prospects in your advertising.

Eyeing the different approaches

The key to success in any type of advertising is determining how you can reach your target audience. In the case of rental property advertising, you want to reach that very small, select group of qualified renters who'll be interested in your property when it's available to rent.

Although you can creatively and effectively advertise your property in many different ways, two of the fundamental differences between the advertising methods at your disposal are the precision with which you reach your target audience and the ultimate cost involved.

Consider these two different approaches:

- ✔ **Rifle approach:** This type of advertising is very specific and targets a narrow group of prospective renters. The best rifle approaches to advertising are word-of-mouth referrals and "For Rent" property signage. If your property is well located with great prospect signage visibility, this approach may work quite well. But if you rely solely on these approaches to find tenants, you may end up with vacant properties much longer than you want.

- ✔ **Shotgun approach:** This type of advertising blankets the market with information to renters and nonrenters, qualified and unqualified alike. Although their circulation numbers have been declining, many of the major daily newspapers in most metropolitan markets can still deliver impressive readership numbers — especially on weekends. However, they can't tell you how many of those readers are actually reading the rental property ads or looking for an apartment on the specific day your ad runs. The same applies to many non-targeted online ads, radio, and television. The rifle approach (if well executed) is often more productive and less costly than the shotgun alternative.

Many methods of advertising your property fall into the shotgun category; very few methods fall into the rifle category. Regardless of which method you choose, remember that advertising is, for the most part, a numbers game. Reach enough readers and you're bound to find a few who're looking for a property like yours on a given day. In an ideal world, you pay only for the ability to reach that limited number of qualified renters in your area who're looking for a property just like yours and who want it the day it's ready to rent. Of course, this ideal isn't reality, but it gives you a goal to strive for when you evaluate the different ways you can advertise.

Knowing which approach gives you the most bang for your buck

Creating interest in your property used to be as simple as putting up a sign or placing an ad in the local newspaper. Although the methods of informing potential renters in your area about your property may still include these tried-and-true techniques, the success and broad reach of the Internet means you have many other excellent options to consider. The target market for your property has a lot to do with which method of advertising works best for you.

One of the best ways to determine your property's most desirable features for your target market is to use the *what's in it for me* (WIFM) concept and ask your current renters what they like about where they live. You may also figure out from talking with the qualified *rental traffic* (all the people who look at your property, not just those who agree to rent) what they find of interest in your property. The key is remembering your property has different features that appeal to different prospective renters. Over a period of time, you can determine certain common factors that most prospects desire. Incorporate these selling points into your marketing and advertising efforts.

One size rarely fits all. When it comes to advertising a rental property, you need to employ a combination of both the shotgun and rifle approach (described in the preceding section) to be successful. Clearly, both methods have advantages. Referrals and property signs often give you good exposure to renters in your local area, whereas newspaper and Internet ads have the ability to let people relocating to your area know about your property as well. Check out Table 7-1 for the pros and cons of various advertising tactics.

Table 7-1   Pros and Cons of Different Advertising Tactics

Approach	Pros	Cons
Craigslist	Free; top source for tenants seeking rentals in some markets	Not in all areas, especially rural ones; must repost listing frequently
Community bulletin boards	Inexpensive	Narrow market
Direct mailings	Inexpensive	Low response rate
Drive-by radio transmitter	Very effective; inexpensive	Only targets prospects that are at your property
Fliers	Allow more details	Limited distribution
Internet	Ease of use; decreasing cost	Uncertain effectiveness for smaller properties

Approach	Pros	Cons
Local employers	Qualified prospects	Narrow market
Newspaper	Broad reach	Potentially expensive
Property signs	Very effective; inexpensive	Narrow market
Rental publications	Widely used by prospects	Expensive for small properties
Word-of-mouth	High credibility; inexpensive	Narrow market

Getting your property to rent itself

Before you spend money on advertising, take another look at your property with a critical eye or ask someone you know to critique it. You probably have a relative or friend with a sharp eye for finding little details that aren't quite right. So put these individuals to work helping you identify and correct those nagging items that detract from your rental unit. Even the best advertising campaign in the world can't overcome a poor physical appearance. Making sure your property looks good on the outside and the inside significantly improves your chances of finding just the right tenants.

The best advertisement for your rental unit is its curb appeal or exterior appearance. *Curb appeal* is the impression created when a prospective renter first sees the building from the street. The importance of a good first impression is well documented in business and clearly applies in rental housing, too. A property that has well-kept grounds with green grass, trimmed shrubs, beautiful flowers, and fresh paint is much more appealing to your prospects than a property that looks as though it has seen better days.

Curb appeal can be positive or negative. You can generate positive curb appeal by having litter-free grounds, well-manicured landscaping and lawns, well-maintained building surfaces, a clearly identifiable address, and clean windows. Any property amenities (such as a swimming pool and parking lots) should also be clean and well maintained.

You can rent properties with negative curb appeal, but finding a tenant often takes much longer. You may have fewer qualified prospects to choose from or you may have to lower the rent. Because time is money in the rental housing business, the lost revenue caused by poor or negative curb appeal is often much greater than the cost to repair or replace deficient items. Besides, a well-maintained and sharp-looking property often attracts the type of tenant who treats your property with care and respect — and pays a higher rent.

Properties rarely rent themselves, but a sparkling appearance goes a long way toward attracting the attention of good prospects. Keep in mind that poor curb appeal is the direct result of poor management. You have no excuse for poor curb appeal, and no one benefits from it. You can never regain your lost revenue, and your property value ultimately declines.

Being Aware of Fair Housing Laws

Whether you're the owner of a single rental unit or a small- to medium-size multiple unit property, you're subject to fair housing laws whenever you advertise. These laws prohibit advertising that indicates any preference, limitation, or discrimination based on race, color, ethnicity, religion, sex, familial status, or physical or mental disability. Consequently, any discrimination in rental housing advertising is illegal and can result in very severe penalties.

The 1988 federal Fair Housing Amendments Act also states that rental property owners and managers can't

- Target certain groups by advertising in select media only
- Imply a preferred type of tenant through the use of discriminatory language, locations, logos, or models in advertising
- Refuse to show, negotiate for, or rent housing
- Refuse to supply rental information or accept applications
- Make housing unavailable
- Determine discriminatory applicant qualification or selection criteria
- Set different rental rates, terms, conditions, or privileges for the rental of a dwelling
- Direct people to certain parts of a community, building, or floor
- Provide different housing services, facilities, or maintenance
- Enforce restrictions or different provisions in rental contracts
- Falsely deny that housing is available for viewing or rental
- Persuade owners to rent or deny anyone access to or membership in a facility or service related to the rental of housing
- Post discriminatory notices or statements or evict a tenant on the basis of protected class

Following fair housing regulations begins with advertising to all qualified prospects, continues throughout the screening and tenant selection process, and remains a key issue during the entire tenancy. If you plan to be in the rental housing business, make sure all your advertising, tenant screening and selection, and management and maintenance policies reflect both the intent and the letter of the law. Also, be aware that fair housing laws are constantly being redefined and expanded. Ignorance of the current law isn't an acceptable excuse if your policies and procedures are challenged.

Whenever you have the space available in your rental advertising, be sure to include the Equal Housing Opportunity logo. This logo may not be an option in certain ads, such as newspaper classifieds, but try to include it in all other advertising, like fliers, brochures, community bulletin boards, direct mailings, and web ads. You can download the logo for free at the website of the U.S. Department of Housing and Urban Development (HUD). Just go to www.hud.gov, type "Equal Housing Opportunity logo" into the search bar in the upper-right corner, and navigate to the logo home page. Then download to your heart's content!

If you have any questions about discriminatory housing practices, contact HUD's Office of Fair Housing and Equal Opportunity, which oversees the creation and enforcement of federal fair housing laws. Find it online at www.hud.gov/offices/fheo or call 800-669-9777. (If you're hearing impaired, call the TTY line at 800-927-9275.)

All rental property owners must comply with federal (and often state and local) fair housing laws. Know the laws for your area and make sure you don't violate them, even inadvertently. Check with local landlord-tenant legal experts, your local apartment association, or the NAA for more information about fair housing laws in your area. To contact the NAA, write to 4300 Wilson Boulevard, Suite 400, Alexandria, VA 22203, or call 703-518-6141. You can also visit the NAA online at www.naahq.org to find the location of the NAA's affiliated state or local association in your area.

To access a list of NAA affiliates, pop in the CD or click the link in the table of contents.

Analyzing Your Advertising Options

When it comes to advertising, you need to think like a tenant. Most rental property owners were renters at some point. You may have personal experience as a renter looking for the right place to live. Perhaps you found the search frustrating or maybe you developed a successful system for finding quality rental properties at a fair price. Your experience as a renter can be helpful as you place your ads. Just remember that your experience looking for an apartment 20 years ago, while in college, may be far different from the experience your prospect is having in today's market.

Many owners may remember that, when they began looking for their own rental years ago, they either drove around the area or sought out advertising specific to a particular geographic location. Although most prospective renters nowadays still practice these methods of researching their rental area of interest, many tenants have realized the advantages of online rental shopping. These renters ultimately go out to see each property that meets their needs but not before narrowing their search to just a few properties via the Internet.

Most renters dislike moving to an unfamiliar area. Although moving is enough of a disruption in your daily routine, adapting to a completely different neighborhood is even worse. Thus, the majority of renters relocate within the same geographic area, unless they're faced with a major change in employment, school, or another significant factor that requires a distant relocation.

The following sections outline the different ways you can reach your prospective tenants, from word-of-mouth to the Internet. Use more than one form of advertising and find your new tenant even quicker.

Talking the talk: Word-of-mouth referrals

Often the best source of new tenants is a referral from one of your property's neighbors, one of your other tenants, or possibly even the tenant who just vacated your unit. Many times, referrals also come from coworkers or friends. Word-of-mouth is often your most effective and least expensive method of finding new tenants, especially if people like your property or where it's located. They'll only refer others if they're happy. You need to earn their referral, but don't forget to ask for it.

In the long run, your best source for new tenant leads is other satisfied tenants. So keep your current tenants content and treat your departing tenants properly, with timely accounting and the return of any remaining security deposit balance. Tenants talk, and bad news travels faster than good news.

Many of your tenants or other people who own or rent in the area may have a family member or friend looking to relocate. Creating a sense of community in which your tenants have friends in the immediate area can lead to longer tenancies and lower tenant turnover. This combination translates directly into improved cash flow for you.

If your tenants or neighbors give you referrals, you may consider rewarding them or thanking them in a couple of different ways. Regardless of the kind of reward you give to referring tenants, the key is to make them feel appreciated for the referral. Here are some ways to reward your referring tenants:

✔ **Referral fee:** Typically, referral fees are $50 to $200 in cash or rent credit and are only paid after the new tenant has paid the full security deposit and the first month's rent and has actually taken occupancy. In a soft rental market, where the supply of vacant apartments exceeds the demand, some owners and property managers may even offer referral fees of up to 50 percent of the first month's rent. The market conditions in your area dictate the appropriate level of referral fee for your property. You can also offer a higher amount for multiple referrals.

Some owners give half of the referral fee upfront and the other half after the new tenant has lived in the unit for a specified number of months to ensure that the tenant plans to stay a while. In my experience, however, the referral fee is more effective if you pay the full amount immediately upon the new tenant taking occupancy. Although on some occasions the referred tenant doesn't stay for more than a month, this situation is usually nothing that the referring tenant can control, so he shouldn't be penalized.

As with all policies, be sure to offer your referral fees consistently and equally to all tenants to avoid any fair housing concerns.

✔ **Improvements or upgrades to the tenant's rental unit:** When cash or a rent credit is inappropriate (as in states where a real estate license is required for referrals), you can offer enhancements to the rental unit, such as installing a new ceiling fan, hanging new wallpaper, cleaning the carpet, or repainting the unit. Certain types of improvements may have a long life and stay with the unit after the current tenant leaves, making the unit more marketable and justifying a higher rental rate to a future tenant.

The psychological impact of giving an immediate reward for a referral can be very motivating. You can also adjust the amount of the referral fee for certain rental units that may be more difficult to rent or for certain times of the year when you have more trouble renting vacancies. For example, if you normally offer a $100 referral fee, you may want to consider offering a $200 fee for any referral given between Thanksgiving and the middle of January because this time of year is often very slow for rental traffic. (No one likes to move during the holidays or in inclement weather!)

If you're unable to give monetary rewards for referrals, don't forget the power of a thank-you call or a handwritten note. Getting a sincere "thanks" for a referral can be every bit as powerful as a rent concession.

Have any rental applicant referred by word-of-mouth fill out a tenant application and go through the same thorough background check as any other applicant. Any deviation in your normal application and tenant selection process can support later allegations that you favor certain incoming tenants. Always screen every referral carefully, but be particularly careful if the referring tenant has a poor payment history or has created other problems. Just as a referral from an excellent tenant often leads to another excellent tenant, a referral from a problem tenant often leads to another problem tenant.

Showcasing your site: Property signs

A property sign is the first step in most rental property advertising programs because it's one of the most economical ways to promote your vacancies. The use of a simple "For Rent" sign can be very effective and can generate great results for minimal cost. In certain areas with limited availability of rental units, a sign on the property is all you need to generate multiple qualified applicants. In the following sections, I explain how to determine whether property signs are an appropriate tactic in your area and, if so, how to make them work for you.

Weighing the weight of a sign on your marketing efforts

An advantage of the property sign is that callers already know the area and have seen your building's exterior. Consequently, the attractiveness and aesthetic qualities or curb appeal of a property are essential. The property must look good from the street or else rental prospects won't even bother to stop and see its interior.

A disadvantage of signs is that they announce to the world that you have a vacant rental unit. In some areas, this proclamation can lead to vandalism or the unwanted use of your property for parties or criminal activity. For this reason, many rental property owners post rental signs while the unit is still occupied by the outgoing tenant and then remove the signs when the unit is empty. Depending on your tenant and her level of cooperation, you may also want to indicate on the sign that the current tenant shouldn't be disturbed.

Making your signage stand out from the competition

If you choose to put up a property sign, do so as soon as you find out you have an upcoming vacancy, unless your property's curb appeal is poor or signs aren't allowed. Be sure to use signs that are in perfect condition, with large, crisp lettering that's easy to read. The condition of the sign reflects the image of your property — whether good or bad. A well-maintained sign provides a good first impression. A faded, worn out, or tacky sign is worse than no sign at all. Consider the following when developing and placing your signage:

- ✔ **Visibility:** Make sure your signage is clearly visible from the street and the lettering is large enough to read. Ideally, place a two-sided sign perpendicular to the street so passing vehicles can view it more easily. Also, pay attention to weather conditions. Make sure your sign can withstand seasonal winds and driving rain and won't get buried in snow.

  Drive by your property from both directions at the usual speed of traffic and make sure your sign can be seen and understood easily. The main objective of property signs is to get the driver's attention with the words "For Rent" or a similar basic message. You want the driver to pull over and write down the details and the phone number.

- ✔ **Content:** Don't get carried away or put so much info on the sign that it can't easily be read from the street. Include the phone number and date of availability in a very clear spot. You can also add the number of bedrooms and bathrooms and any special features. Clearly indicate your rental rate on the sign because you need to make sure prospective tenants know what to expect. Including the rental rate can even prescreen tenants who aren't financially qualified.

On the other hand, when the property's exterior doesn't do justice to the actual rental unit, you're better off *not* including the rental rate on your property sign. Because you're usually not there to show the unit at the time the prospect sees the sign, she may think the rent is either too high or too low and immediately decide not to call. The value of some rental units can't be appreciated until a prospect has seen the unit's interior.

✔ **Location:** Place your signage in a prominent location. Property signs don't work as well if your unit isn't on a busy street or if your sign isn't easily noticeable from a main road. Property signs on dead-end streets or cul-de-sacs are still worthwhile, but don't expect the kind of response you'd get if your sign were on a major thoroughfare or arterial roadway.

If your property is on a side street that's relatively close to a major road, you may be able to obtain the cooperation of the owner of a nearby property with a high-visibility location, unless such signage placement is prohibited by local law. Approach the owner about the possibility of placing a rental sign for your property on his land — either on a temporary basis only when you have vacancies or on a more formal ongoing basis (with a formal contract drafted by an attorney, outlining rights and terms and a financial incentive for the owner). Typically, you can expect to pay the landowner $25 to $100 per month to put your sign on his property, depending on the size and location of the sign.

Any off-site rental sign should clearly indicate the location of your property. Make sure the property where you place your sign is comparable to your property in terms of curb appeal. A property that's vastly superior to yours can actually deter potential renters. Naturally, a property that has poor curb appeal discourages prospects from any further inquiry into your property, even if your property is in much better condition. As with all signs, first impressions are very important and leave a lasting image in the minds of your prospective renters.

Broadening your horizons: The Internet

The Internet can be a useful tool to augment more conventional advertising methods (such as newspaper ads and fliers). But how can you effectively and efficiently reach your target market of prospective renters? The following sections take on this challenge and help you figure out how to incorporate the Internet into your own customized marketing strategy for attracting rental prospects.

Craigslist

Craigslist has become the favorite online advertising option of all segments of the rental housing industry, from the major Real Estate Investment Trusts (REITs) with multiple large rental properties to the novice rental property owner with just a single family home or condo to fill. Craigslist is effective because it's free, and your target market of prospective tenants is very likely to be aware of it. But that doesn't mean you'll have guaranteed success without finding out the best way to take advantage of the benefits and know the limitations of Craigslist.

Craigslist is offered in all 50 states and is further organized with separate lists for most major cities within each state. Many of the largest metropolitan areas or population centers are broken down into geographic sublists for specific areas. You need to find the area that serves your rental property and click the Housing heading. There you'll find dozens (if not hundreds) of listings of available rental properties, all posted in chronological order.

To post your listing, simply set up an account, click the Post to Classifieds link, and follow the submenus until you get to a blank posting description page. Be sure to fill in all the pertinent information such as the address, the cross streets, and whether pets are allowed.

Of course, you also need to master the fine art of catching the eye of your prospect in just a few words. I recommend clearly indicating the neighborhood or part of town that your property is located in upfront because most renters tend to have a specific area in mind for where they want to live. It can also be a good idea to indicate any limitations you have for the property, such as no pets or the date the unit will be available. You want to generate interest in your unit, but you don't need to spend time with prospects whose needs you aren't able to fulfill.

Craigslist is great for using digital photos to enhance your listing. In fact, many prospects won't even waste time contacting you unless you have photos of your property (not generic images of a "similar property"). Your posting should include wide-angle photos of your property's exterior and select photos of some of the main rooms in the house. Having separate pictures of each generic bedroom of a large, four-bedroom house may be too much, but including photos of the kitchen, master bedroom, and bathroom is a good start. You also want to include the dimensions of the major rooms because many prospects need to know right upfront whether their furniture will fit in your rental unit.

The first time you use Craigslist to post your upcoming vacancy, you may still have renters in place and may not be able to get the photos you want for your online posting. But be sure to grab your digital camera and use the first opportunity you have to take a number of photos of every portion of the property. You can then download and store these photos on your computer and use them for your ads. You can also use some of the more detailed photos if you have prospects that are interested in some specific aspect of your home. For example, maybe they're looking for a fenced yard for their favorite dog. Multiple photos of every angle of the yard won't be of interest to all your prospects, but having the photos when the need arises can be helpful.

If you don't get much action from a posted ad, change it up a bit when you repost it. Revisit your plan, ask who your target market is, and see whether you're touching on your target market's needs in your ad.

Listings on Craigslist can get buried or lost very quickly because of the site's extreme popularity. Also, listings automatically expire, usually within seven days. While still obeying all the rules of Craigslist, you need to make sure you repost your listing frequently so that you stay near the top of the listings because many prospects have limited patience for scrolling through page after page with 100 listings per page.

Online advertising

The opportunities to promote your rental vacancy online have exploded over the past several years to boast a number of choices, both locally and nationally. Although this list is dynamic, with new firms and mergers among competitors, here are some of the more popular and successful online advertising sites:

- ✔ Apartamentos Para Rentar: www.pararentar.com
- ✔ Apartment Finder: www.apartmentfinder.com
- ✔ Apartment Guide: www.apartmentguide.com
- ✔ Apartment Search by CORT: www.apartmentsearch.com
- ✔ Apartments.com: www.apartments.com
- ✔ For Rent: www.forrent.com
- ✔ Move.com: www.move.com
- ✔ Rent.com: www.rent.com
- ✔ RentalHomesPlus: www.rentalhomesplus.com
- ✔ Rentals.com: www.rentals.com

The online rental info you can offer is unlimited. Of course, you need to make sure you get the basics out there before trying anything flashy:

- ✔ **General geographic location of the unit:** Prospects want to know whether your property is near the places they frequent the most or whether it's in a safe part of town. (Just remember to make no such claim of safety or security in your ads; prospective tenants can make that determination from the address, from their visits to the property, or by checking with local law enforcement, which is always the best source.) In many cities, the name of your neighborhood makes an immediate impression on your prospect, which can be good or bad for you, depending on the reputation of the particular neighborhood. So if the name of the area may give a negative impression, leave it out.

- ✔ **Number of bedrooms and bathrooms:** This number is often a major determining factor for many renters. Always let prospects know what to expect from your property. Remember that, depending on your target market, a bedroom may actually be used as an office or a den.

- ✔ **Major features or amenities:** Inquiring minds want to know what makes your rental property better than all the others in the area.

- ✔ **Monthly rent:** Listing your monthly rent in your ad lets prospective renters know your requirements right upfront. Most prospects scan through rental ads trying to eliminate the ones that aren't worth calling about. Generally, prospects will disqualify any ad that doesn't give them enough information to determine their level of interest.

- ✔ **Telephone number and e-mail address where you can be reached:** If prospective tenants don't know how to reach you, then you definitely won't receive any inquiries about your unit.

- ✔ **Who pays for the utilities:** This bit of info can be a key factor for renters on tight budgets.

- ✔ **Whether the unit is furnished:** Some renters may not want to hassle with providing their own furniture; others may not want to use a recliner or dresser that's been around the block a few times.

- ✔ **Address of the property:** Include the address unless the rental unit doesn't have excellent curb appeal.

With a digital camera, you can place photos of your property online. If you have a wide-angle digital camera, you can even put interior photos online, which is helpful if the property is currently occupied and you can't or don't want to bother the current tenant by showing the place. Be critical of the quality of your photos. A shot of a dark, empty corner of a room isn't very enticing. If that's the best you can do, hire a professional or simply don't post photos. And don't get carried away with too many similar photos because they can slow down access and frustrate your prospects. You can also provide floor plans, detailed directions, and links to online maps.

If you're really computer savvy or know someone who is, you can provide a narrative soundtrack that augments your online info; just include some music. Keep in mind, though, that music can be annoying to many website viewers. The last thing you want to do is run off potential tenants with your favorite Barry Manilow song, so either choose something more generic or include a muting option.

Property website

Technology has progressed so quickly that now, even the owners of one single-family home or condo rental property can develop and publish their own website featuring their rental unit. These sites can be just a basic listing of the property address, the rent, and main features, but they're much more persuasive if they include some photos of the exterior and interior (preferably with a wide-angle lens) and even floor plans. The more information you can provide, the better, but be aware that, just like with any advertising, too much clutter or superfluous information can be a distraction.

Most major rental property owners and managers have websites for their properties, and I suggest you review several of them for ideas. Another source for ideas of great ways to present your property is the online listings of major rental advertising publications. You'll see that they start with the most important information near the top and always include contact information, like a phone number or e-mail address.

You may prefer to have someone who's a technical wiz set up your website, but with a little practice, most people can create a basic website on their own. I recommend using WordPress. This site used to be just for bloggers, but now it's the most popular software for creating individual websites. You can find it at www.wordpress.org.

After you create your website, you need to find a host service for it. I recommend you seriously consider using WordPress's web-hosting service. It offers a very basic free package, but you'll need the upgrades that include a domain name, mapping, online hosting, custom design tools, and VideoPress, which allows you to upload and play videos right from your WordPress website. WordPress has an intuitive interface that guides you through all the steps, or you can look for a copy of *WordPress Web Design For Dummies,* by Lisa Sabin-Wilson (Wiley), for even more information.

Social media outlets

Social media is a game-changer and is here to stay, but the question is, should you incorporate social media into your rental management marketing plan? Though the opportunities for larger rental property owners are apparent, and managers are implementing strategies to tap the power of social media, the effectiveness and efficiency for the small to medium rental property owner is still being determined.

There are many anecdotal stories about landlords and property managers who've found tenants through social media. They have Facebook pages, YouTube videos, and LinkedIn sites for their property management company, and they use Twitter to tweet several times per day, with catchy lingo to entice prospects. But using social media can be quite time-consuming, and it's questionable whether it's worth it for the average rental property owner with just a few rental properties.

You can determine how much of your scarce resources of time and money you should invest in social media marketing by how many qualified prospects you attract. It may make you feel good to "connect" with a lot of wonderful people and tell them about your property, but at the end of the day, you need to focus only on those methods that are the most cost- and time-effective in filling your vacant units with quality, long-term tenants.

Following are some points to consider about a few of the most popular social media sites so you can start deciding whether to include them in your marketing strategy:

✔ **Facebook:** This social networking site has become a phenomenon like nothing before it. It's international in its reach and has more than 1 billion users, many of whom spend time each day communicating on the site via a mobile device. Facebook even tops Google for weekly traffic, with users sharing virtually all aspects of their work and personal lives with friends and strangers, and occasionally talking about their living arrangements. This is the ultimate shotgun approach. You have no idea whether you're reaching anyone who may be looking for a new home.

Facebook has a lot of clutter, so even if you happen to see someone looking for a new place to call home, the odds of actually reaching that person aren't likely, even with an ad.

✔ **YouTube:** YouTube is a video-hosting service and the second largest search engine in the world after Google, which actually owns YouTube. This is another social media venue that has evolved tremendously over the past several years, and scores of companies use it to promote their products. However, like much of the content on the Internet, the key for rental property owner and managers is the ability to direct your prospective tenants to your specific video among the millions of popular videos, like the latest talking baby spoof.

If used properly, YouTube can be a great resource for the creative and talented rental property owner. You can provide links to your YouTube videos in all your different advertising options. However, if you take videos the way I do (my family has complained for years about my rapid and erratic panning or the dreaded ten minutes of the ground or inside of the camera bag), then you should seek the assistance of a qualified amateur or a professional. In your household, that may be anyone under 18.

✔ **Twitter:** This online social networking service allows users to send and read short, text-based messages of up to 140 characters. Proficient users have developed their own lingo and abbreviations to communicate very effectively within the platform's limitations.

At this time, Twitter is primarily useful in communicating breaking news or rental housing industry information, or communicating with people or companies. Currently, the use of Twitter doesn't seem to be effective for the advertising of vacant rental units, but some users have sought roommates or put the word out that they're looking for a new place to live. So Twitter, though not likely to be a cornerstone of your marketing program, can be a way to stay connected with your peers in the industry.

✔ **LinkedIn:** This site is currently the world's largest professional network, with nearly 200 million members around the world. Like Twitter, LinkedIn is a social networking site that may not have much to offer for the owner of just one or a few rental properties. But it can be a way for owners of rental management companies to promote their services and properties and to connect with potential on-site and corporate office employees, as it has established a solid reputation for those seeking new work opportunities.

Reading all about it: Newspapers

For many years, the most commonly used medium for advertising rental properties was hard-copy newspaper classified ads. Although the newspaper industry is declining, newspapers are still a viable method of reaching prospective renters because all major metropolitan newspapers have online editions and still take ads for rental properties. In many suburban and rural areas, the local newspaper still can be an effective tool in marketing your rental property vacancy.

Online metropolitan or local newspaper ads can be very effective if you follow these basic advertising rules:

- ✔ Attract the reader's attention.
- ✔ Keep the reader's interest.
- ✔ Generate a desire to find out more about your property.
- ✔ Convince the reader to contact you for more information.

Important considerations when using newspaper advertising include where to advertise, the size of your ad, what to include in the ad, and the schedule on which your ad should run. I cover each of these issues in the following sections.

Which newspaper should you advertise in?

In most metropolitan areas, you have at least one major regional newspaper and one or more neighborhood newspapers. The regional newspaper will certainly have an online version with rental ads.

Local or neighborhood newspapers are often more reasonably priced and can reach the renters already in the area. Some local or neighborhood newspapers even offer free ads. So do you advertise in the local weekly throwaway or the regional major daily? Unfortunately, there's no right answer to this question. You really need to try each newspaper and see which one works best for a particular property.

The key to effective advertising isn't the overall number of calls you receive but the number of dollars per qualified renter you spend on advertising. Effective advertising in most major metropolitan areas typically costs $20 to $50 per qualified prospect. So if your Sunday newspaper ad (the day of the week that usually has the highest circulation) costs $100, you want to receive inquiries from two to five qualified prospects every time the ad runs. Of course, you can expect to receive additional inquiries from unqualified prospects, but you can measure the effectiveness of your ad by noting how *few* unqualified prospects call in response to it.

Many of the larger newspapers have online editions or relationships with Internet firms that specialize in advertising rental properties. For example, the *Chicago Tribune* partners with Apartments.com so it can offer you a print ad in its newspaper and an online ad that can generate calls from around the nation.

How big should your newspaper ad be?

Newspapers typically offer two different types of rental housing ads: display and classified. Display ads are much more effective and eye-catching; they're also significantly more expensive and beyond the needs and budgets of most small-time rental property owners. Usually, only the owners or managers of large apartment buildings use display ads on a regular basis.

Owners or property management companies with multiple properties in a certain geographic area also use display ads because they're able to combine several of their properties into one large display ad, making the ad more cost-effective. If you're a small rental property owner, unless you have multiple properties with vacancies in the same general geographic area, use the classified rental housing section of your newspaper.

Wondering how to make a less flashy classified ad stand out to prospective tenants? The trick is to develop an ad that's efficient but doesn't place a higher priority on low cost while sacrificing the ability to attract and keep a prospect's attention. Your ad needs to be easily readable. One of the best ways to achieve readability is through the use of *white space,* the blank space that makes your ad stand out from the others, many of which are so crammed with information that readers instinctively skip them. Some newspapers also sell *black space;* the principle is the same, but the background is black and the letters are white.

Consider yourself lucky if a prospective renter spends more than just a few seconds looking at your ad. If you can't attract and keep his attention in those brief seconds, he'll move on to the next ad. So when it comes to writing your ad, provide as much information as possible while also keeping the ad readable. But know that the ad's overall size needs to be kept to a minimum or you risk a major shock to your advertising budget.

Most renters actually prefer to rent from small-time rental property owners, which is why classified ads can be very effective. Classified ads need to be directed to a specific target market and should stress the particular advantages of a property from the tenant's point of view.

What should you include in your newspaper ad?

Effective newspaper ads (like the ones shown in Figure 7-1) provide the basic facts (see the earlier section on what to include in an Internet ad for more on these), plus a *hook,* which is a call to action that helps your ad stand out from the rest. The hook can be monetary or an improvement to the property — basically anything that makes your ad grab the prospect's attention. Offering a tenant the opportunity to select new tile floor covering in the kitchen or entryway or providing a ceiling fan as an extra bonus are both excellent hooks.

Figure 7-1:
Good newspaper ads like these can help you find the right tenant quickly.

#1 Rated Schools!

Hidden Valley executive home. 4 bedrooms, 3 baths, 2250 sq. ft., 3-car garage pool/spa, fenced yard, lush landscaping, a/c, washer/dryer, f/p, gardener incl, pets welcome. $1,995/mo. Avail. 7/1. 423 Sycamore Lane. 555-1212

Cherry Hills Close to Everything

Lg. 1 & 2 BR townhouse apts, on bus route. Walk to schools, stores, medical center. Tennis, pool, spa, no pets. Owner-paid utilities. Furnished units avail. From $575. Maple Grove Apts. 575 Watson Rd. Mention ad for free credit check. Daily 9-6. Call (800) 555-1212

Courtesy of Robert S. Griswold

Even in tight rental markets, providing an incentive for the prospect to immediately call on your ad is smart. For example, you can offer to waive the fee for his credit report if he calls the day the ad runs. The credit report typically costs you less than $25, but this kind of offer makes your ad much more interesting to most cost-conscious renters.

Although leaving out some information saves you money in the cost of a classified ad, don't forget that incomplete information leads to qualified prospects skipping over your ad or many unqualified prospects calling and asking you every question under the sun.

Be careful with abbreviations in newspaper ads. Although abbreviating some words can stretch your advertising dollar without cutting into your message, the use of abbreviations often discourages prospects from reading your ad. If prospects can't understand your ad, it won't generate the phone calls you want. And if your ad doesn't generate phone calls, you've wasted your time and money. I recommend using basic abbreviations only if most rental property advertisers in your area commonly use them.

To address or not to address

Opinions differ on including a rental property's address in a newspaper ad, but I generally recommend including it. This information gives prospects the exact location of your property and helps them independently determine whether it's one they're interested in renting. The only situations in which you shouldn't indicate the address in the ad are when the curb appeal isn't up to your high standards or when the unit's exterior appearance is deceptive and gives the impression that the unit is small or undesirable in light of the rent.

If you include directions with your address, make sure they're correct and easily understandable.

Ask someone who's not familiar with your property or the area to proofread your ad to make sure the landmarks, cross streets, or directions make sense. If prospects can't find your property, you can safely assume they're not going to be interested in renting it. Although a more direct route to your property that goes past the local landfill may exist, have your prospects take the next freeway off-ramp and backtrack somewhat to your property to avoid any unpleasant areas of town. This first impression can be very important. The advertising and presentation of your property is marketing, and when it's done properly, it'll make your job as a rental property owner much easier.

How often or on which days should your newspaper ad run?

Although the Saturday or Sunday editions of many major metro papers have the most rental ads, running your ad on these days can be quite expensive. Newspapers often have specials that encourage you to run your ad for longer periods, which gives you more exposure.

Be sure to change your ad weekly, at least. Prospective tenants often skim ads for several weeks when they're beginning to look for a new rental unit. If they see the same ad for more than a week, they may assume your unit is undesirable. This advice is also true if you have many properties and run the same ad each week. Potential tenants may incorrectly think it's for the same unit every time.

Some newspapers offer discounts if you run the same ad for consecutive days, but doing so can be expensive. Instead, run a larger ad on the primary rental housing advertising day and then run a reference ad the rest of the week to lower your overall cost. For example, if the Sunday edition of your local newspaper is the primary day for rental housing ads, place a large ad on that day. Then on Monday through Saturday, run a small, two-line ad that simply states something like, "Kensington — 2bd/2ba available soon. See last Sunday's ad." Also, be careful not to run ads on off days just because it's cheaper. The marketplace has a rhythm, and people are used to looking for apartments on certain days. You may get a great rate, but it will be on a day that no one reads the ad.

When your ad first appears, be sure to check the newspaper yourself to confirm it's listed in the proper classification and is worded exactly the way you wrote it. Newspaper ad reps are very skilled at taking down complicated ads with abbreviations, but mistakes can and do occur. Nothing's worse than not receiving any phone calls because your ad was placed in the wrong section or because the phone number was listed incorrectly.

Checking your ad for accuracy may be relatively simple if you regularly subscribe to the newspaper. However, if you don't subscribe to it, be sure to have your newspaper ad rep send you a *tear sheet,* a sample of the page on which your ad ran. If the newspaper makes a mistake in your ad, be sure to notify it at once and ask for a corrected ad to run at no charge.

Some newspapers offer special ads for guaranteed results. For example, if your property doesn't rent after your ad has run for a week, a paper may give you up to an additional week of ads for free. Check with your newspaper sales rep for planned special sections featuring rental housing articles and news features. These special sections are written with the renters in mind and can increase your ad visibility to prospective tenants.

If your rental unit is located near a military installation, be sure to run an ad in a military newspaper. The military also has housing referral offices at many bases, and all branches require transferees to register with the housing referral office. Contact this office with your information. This is also true for university and college papers. Some have become known for their editorials and have a far-reaching community readership.

Papering the neighborhood: Fliers

Distributing and posting fliers informs the neighbors that you have a rental unit available, which can be helpful to them because they may know someone who wants to live close by. You can use fliers to direct people to more information (including maps and additional photographs) on a website. See the earlier section, "Broadening your horizons: The Internet," for the scoop on using the Net to advertise your property.

Fliers allow you a lot more space in which to describe your rental unit. You can go into detail and list many of the features that aren't cost-effective to list in a newspaper ad.

The cost to reproduce fliers is nominal, running about $5 for 500 black-and-white fliers on white paper stock. For an extra $5, consider printing your flier on colored paper. If you really want to stand out, you'll need to pay about $25 for 500 full-color fliers. The extra money is well worth it. Although keeping your costs low is always important for rental property owners, remember that you may be losing $20 to $40 each day your property sits vacant — and that's money you never get back again! So if you have a property that looks great with a four-color flier, spend the extra $20 and generate those important rental leads today!

In the following sections, I explain how to create and distribute fliers for the maximum positive impact on your rental property.

Making high-tech fliers

With the wide availability of word processing programs, making great-looking rental fliers that contain all the pertinent info, plus a photo and a map, is very easy. Although the widely used word processing programs have everything you need to make basic fliers, I highly recommend you invest in basic desktop publishing software. Several great desktop publishing programs are available, but two of the easiest to use are *Microsoft Publisher* and *PrintMaster*. These programs have templates that simplify the process and provide you with the graphics and additional features to make your flier look sharp.

Another invaluable tool for all rental property owners is a digital camera, which helps you prepare advertising that works! A high-quality photo can easily separate your flier from the others. Check out Figure 7-2 for a great example of a flier that effectively uses photos to draw attention to a property.

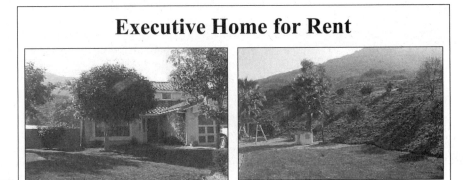

Figure 7-2: Fliers with good photos are a great way to attract attention to your property.

> # Executive Home for Rent
>
> The top-rated Horizon school district and plenty of room! 4-bedroom, 3-bath executive home with over 2,250 square feet of living space and a 3-car garage. Master bedroom suite has over 500 square feet and large walk-in closet. Other bedrooms are oversized with large closets. Plus, a large home office with shelves. Large fenced backyard is perfect for children and pets. Pets are welcome! Separate fenced pool and spa. Lush, mature landscaping, air conditioning, full-size washer and dryer included. Fireplace in family room, formal dining room with bay window, upgraded appliances. Side-by-side refrigerator, double oven, range top, dishwasher, disposal, trash compactor, shutters, intercom, and CD stereo system throughout home, built-in bookcases and lots of storage. Available on 7/1. 423 Sycamore. $1,995 per month. First month's rent plus $2,000 security deposit will move you in!
>
> Call 555-1212 today and mention this flyer for a free credit check.

Some people think a handwritten flier actually has greater appeal and implies that the owner is a nonprofessional who has a rental unit at a below-market rental rate. This reasoning may be true, but I believe having a sharp, easy-to-read, typeset flier with a high-quality photo and detailed map provides superior results.

Although your goal is to rent your property quickly, the reality is that you'll be marketing your rental unit over a couple of weeks. This guideline is particularly true if you're able to start your marketing during the current tenant's notice period. One of the problems with fliers (just like political placards) is that it's difficult to know which ones are current and which ones are stale. I recommend putting a date on your fliers and keeping them fresh. You should also consider having a series of fliers with a different look, each promoting a different open house. Include the monthly rent on your fliers so prospects can immediately determine whether your property is in their price range.

Distributing fliers

The key to success when it comes to fliers is distribution. Either pass out your fliers personally or consider hiring a reliable individual to distribute them door-to-door in the area where your rental unit is located. You can also have the fliers distributed to locations that current and prospective renters are likely to visit.

Make sure you never place your fliers into an official U.S. mailbox, because doing so is illegal. If you're considering direct mail distribution, contact a firm that specializes in direct mail services.

Although it's often suggested that renters look for a new rental in the last two weeks of the month, I've noticed that in most areas you can always find renters on the market throughout the entire month. Begin distributing your fliers as soon as possible. Each week, distribute the latest version with the current info and dates so that they're fresh.

You can target fliers to a specific geographic area, which can be very effective in reaching good rental prospects. You can distribute fliers to local employers who often have housing referral offices or employee bulletin boards, or you can post them in the housing referral offices at local military installations and universities. Be sure to get permission before posting your fliers or else they'll quickly disappear, and you'll have created enemies instead of allies who can help you fill your vacancies! Fliers, like all forms of advertising, are only as good as their distribution, so be sure to distribute them in the high-traffic areas where renters are most likely to see them.

Focusing on rental publications

Most major metropolitan areas have one or more rental publications that offer display advertising of rental properties. Following are two widely circulated rental pubs (both of which also have a presence on the web):

- *For Rent* offers biweekly, full-color rental advertising for most major cities with 100+ publications covering more than 190 markets. It offers ¼-, ½-, and full-page ads, which are generally listed by geographic area. *For Rent* has a handy index that allows prospective tenants to search for certain features. This pub promotes the fact that its biweekly format allows owners and property managers to change ad content more often. *For Rent* also offers a Spanish-language publication called *Apartamentos Para Rentar* in many areas of the country.

✔ *Apartment Guide* is available monthly, with editions for the major metropolitan areas in all 50 states. Its page format is smaller than *For Rent,* and it says that its size is an advantage because it's easier for rental prospects to carry and use. *Apartment Guide* offers full-color ½- and full-page ads, and it categorizes the ads in sections that relate to certain geographic segments of a metro area.

Rental publications are primarily designed for the larger rental housing communities and are a cornerstone of these communities' marketing programs. Most rental publications offer smaller display ads designed for medium-size rental properties. However, unless your property has several vacancies at the same time, using a rental publication may not be cost-effective.

Strategic distribution equals success in all advertising. Rental publications demonstrate this truth clearly as they battle for positioning on the shelves of major grocery stores and convenience store chains. They race to get the best locations for their curbside racks and make sure that all the major employers and military bases have a good supply of their latest issues. In most major metropolitan areas, rental publications are a dominant source of rental traffic.

If you're thinking about advertising in a rental publication, take the time to determine which one has the best distribution in your area for your target market. For example, you may have determined that the local hospital and medical services facilities just a few blocks from your property are potentially a great source for rental prospects. If you find that only one rental publication is distributed on-site to employees, start evaluating it to see whether it can offer you advertising that meets your needs and is within your budget.

Creating chat: Community bulletin boards

Community bulletin boards can be very effective advertising avenues in certain small areas or college towns. Often the local laundromats, pharmacies, hospitals, community centers, or grocery stores have bulletin boards where you can post information at no cost. You may find that you're limited to a 3-x-5-inch card, but you can tailor your posting to the people who'll be most interested in and attracted to your property. Post several identical cards so that interested prospects can simply take a card with them. This tactic also allows you to use the back side for more information, including a detailed map and directions to your property.

If your property has unique features, like a garage or large backyard, you may have some additional promotional opportunities. Carefully evaluate your property and determine its unique aspects and the specific target market most interested in these specific elements. For example, a property with a large yard appeals to renters with pets, so a listing on the bulletin boards found at the local pet store, veterinary clinic, or groomer may reach that specific target market. Likewise, a property with a garage appeals to patrons of an auto supply or hardware store.

A disadvantage to this advertising technique is that you may promote your possibly vacant rental unit to some people who may be more interested in having a party or stealing your appliances than renting the unit. One way to minimize this problem is to post on community bulletin boards while the unit is still occupied and clearly state that the property will be available at a future date. You should also consider indicating that the current tenant shouldn't be disturbed.

Going where the jobs are: Local employers

The local employers in your area are a great source for rental prospects. Employees of these companies likely have stable jobs and are looking for long-term rentals. Many companies have employee assistance or housing referral offices that work with their employees to help them find reasonably priced housing. Most rental properties located in metropolitan areas are located near at least one major employer. As a sharp rental property owner, you may have already determined that the employees of certain major firms are part of your target rental market.

Likewise, the major firms in your area have a vested interest in their employees being able to find good-quality and affordable rental housing in close proximity to their location. Progressive employers are always looking for inexpensive ways to assist their employees and improve morale. To capitalize on this desire, you can offer all employees of companies that participate in your corporate referral program an incentive to rent at your property, such as waiving the application fee, allowing the security deposit to be paid over the first 90 days, or even discounting the monthly rent.

Meandering through other tactics to try

If the other marketing tactics listed in this chapter don't appeal to you, you may find success through property brochures, direct mailings, leasing agencies, or broker referrals. Although most owners of small- to medium-size rental properties don't find these services advantageous, you may want to consider the following as part of your marketing plan:

- ✔ **Property brochure:** A property brochure isn't necessary for most small rental property owners. However, if you have a property with more than ten units, you should seriously consider developing a basic one. The benefit of a brochure is that the prospective tenant can take the information with her and easily share it with a coapplicant. I recommend a simple tri-fold brochure that can be printed on both sides of 8½-x-11-inch paper. With a basic word processing or desktop publishing program, you can easily create a customized brochure for your property. It should include a floor plan and an area map that highlights the key places for employment, shopping, schools, and transportation.

- ✔ **Direct mailings:** The key to success with direct mailing is to have a good flier or brochure combined with a mailing list that reaches your target market. If you've already developed your flier or brochure, using this same marketing piece in a direct mail advertising campaign is a natural next step. Of course, like all advertising, direct mail is only effective and cost-efficient if you can get your specific marketing piece into the hands of a prospective renter when he's looking for a place to rent. Use an outside direct mail firm for the most time- and cost-efficient handling of direct mail. Because postage is expensive and direct mail lists with individual names are often outdated, don't attempt to send personalized mailings; instead, send the mail to "Resident" at a specific address.

- ✔ **Leasing agencies:** *Leasing agencies,* or rental locator firms, often have working relationships with major corporations and relocation services and have excellent tenants looking for high-end rentals, usually in major metropolitan areas. Some offer their services for no charge to the renter and are compensated by the property manager when the prospect signs a rental contract. Other leasing agencies charge tenants for their service and are only compensated when they find a rental unit that meets the renter's needs.

Tenants relocating to an area typically don't have the time to search for a property and want the leasing agency to handle matters for them. They also aren't often candidates for purchasing a home because they're only staying for a specific assignment or because they want to rent in the area before making a purchase decision. You often encounter a trade-off with these renters: They're usually very well qualified, but they're not as likely to rent long term. But the reality is that not all tenants stay for a long period, anyway, and if you know that a certain tenant will only be with you for a set period (such as a one-year lease), you can adjust the rental rate to reflect this term.

✔ **Broker referrals:** Besides selling real estate, many real estate agents are also in the business of referring renters to property managers. Many of the calls real estate agents receive are from individuals relocating from other areas who contact an agent inquiring about a future home purchase. Although they may have long-range plans to purchase, they often rent while they become familiar with the area.

Real estate agents don't mind referring renters to an owner or property manager because they know that today's renter may likely be tomorrow's home purchaser. Real estate agents are also very interested in referral fees from owners or property managers. Although the referral fee may be a small amount of money compared to the potential commission the real estate agent can earn on a sales transaction, agents are willing to be patient and accept a small reward in the short run, knowing that the big money will be earned down the road.

Check the laws in your state because some states prohibit the payment of commissions to anyone other than real estate licensees.

The agent will likely stay in touch with your renter periodically, encouraging the renter to buy rather than continue renting. And aggressive real estate agents have been known to try to earn a referral fee from another landlord when the renter's lease expires with you. I suggest you discuss this concern with your real estate agent in advance to avoid any misunderstandings, especially if you're likely to be a future source of more rental referral fees.

Chapter 8

Handling Prospects When They Come A'Calling

In This Chapter

▶ Making a good first impression

▶ Using your phone as your primary business tool

▶ Handling rental inquiries over the phone

▶ Getting your prospects to visit your property

*I*n virtually all instances, the landlord-tenant relationship begins with the initial rental inquiry. This inquiry can be a traditional phone call or an electronic communication, such as an e-mail, a text message, or maybe even a "tweet." If you successfully master the proper handling and prequalifying of rental prospects and become skilled at selling them on your rental property, you'll find owning and managing rental property to be a profitable and pleasant experience.

Armed with the info in this chapter — and some practice — you can become adept at quickly screening prospects and convincing the qualified ones that you have the rental unit they want. In this chapter, I explain the importance of preparing for communication with prospects, using the phone and electronic media as effective marketing tools, and handling prospects all the way from the first contact to the rental showing.

Understanding Why First Impressions Are Important

Most everyone knows the old adage that you only get one chance to make a first impression. That's sage advice for most businesses, but it's especially true when people are looking to make such an important decision as which rental property will be their next home.

Successfully securing long-term tenancies with qualified tenants can be influenced by that first impression. Your rental property isn't the only one on the market, and your rental prospects have many options, so remember that you're competing for the best renters with everyone in your area who has a vacant rental property. You need to make a positive impression to stand out from your competition.

Do you ever go to a restaurant and feel like everything is so chaotic that you're never going to get the best service or meal? You probably leave and don't even give the restaurant a chance to surprise you with a good experience. This behavior is human nature, and the same concepts are true in rental housing. Prospective tenants are looking for the peace of mind and reassurance that they're making the right decision about something very important — where to live.

Being organized and professional from your very first contact through the entire rental process instills confidence in your prospective tenants that you have the ability to meet their housing needs. A professional attitude and presentation also let them know that if problems occur with the property, you're likely to address their concerns promptly.

The way you advertise or promote your property is part of making the first impression in rental housing, but the chief impression-making factor is the first time you have contact on the phone or in person with prospective tenants. One way to make a positive first impression is to be easy to reach and responsive to rental inquiries. In today's high-tech, easy-to-communicate world, people's expectations to be able to request and receive information have never been more demanding. Nothing turns off prospects faster than an inability to get in touch with you. Even the most diligent prospects only call, e-mail, or text once or twice before giving up and moving on to other properties. Of course, if you answer prospects' calls promptly on your cellphone but are distracted because you're at the grocery store or your child's soccer game, don't expect to secure a rental property showing.

If you're taking a call outside of what one might consider business hours, the prospect will understand. Simply say, "I'm so glad you called. I happen to be in line at the grocery store and will be tied up for just a few minutes. I want to give you my full attention, so can I call you back at the number that appears on my screen [repeat the number] in 10 minutes?" Then be sure to keep your promise.

I do think that an old-fashioned, two-way phone conversation is essential unless absolutely unrealistic (such as if your rental prospect is in the military and is contacting you from a time zone 12 hours from yours). So you may need to send that instant reply e-mail, text, or tweet and ask to set a mutually convenient time for a phone call in which you can provide and receive the important information that both parties need to determine whether your rental unit is worthy of further inquiry.

You also need to be prepared with all the information necessary to present your property in the best light to your prospects and to answer their questions. To remember each prospect, take good notes on tracking forms so you can recall which features the prospect liked most about your property, as well as any concerns he expressed.

Taking notes on conversations with rental prospects can be challenging if you're driving or engaged in another activity that makes note-taking impossible. Develop a system for recalling those important conversations as soon as possible. Personally, I've found that sending myself an e-mail or a text with the details of the conversation is helpful. Later on, I can take those e-mails or texts (or even notes written on scraps of paper or on my tablet or smartphone) and consolidate them into a single note or file.

People like to feel important and that they're really being listened to. Being able to recall prior conversations or correspondence can be a powerful tool in ultimately closing the sale and securing a rental contract.

The telephone's importance in property management

Some property management books recommend never placing your phone number in your rental ads. Instead, they suggest you market your property strictly by advertising and by holding open houses, where interested tenants can all view the property at the same time. Open houses allow prospects to prowl through the property, getting the information they want while you're preoccupied and have little contact with them. You usually can't meet and greet them individually, learn about their needs, and make them feel important in this venue.

In my experience, omitting your phone number from your ads eliminates a large number of qualified prospects who don't have the time for or interest in racing all over town to attend open houses at properties that may not even meet their needs. Your most qualified prospects are often people who value their time very highly. I can assure you that in today's high-tech world, your competition is making it much easier for the best rental prospects to narrow their choices to just a few properties, and you won't make it to those prospects' short list if you can't

answer their questions electronically or at least in a preliminary phone call. Consequently, the Internet and e-mail can help your prospects solidify their interests in your property, but that's where the usefulness of electronic communication ends. Ultimately, your prospects need the type of specific information they can only receive through a phone call.

You may think that you're able to conserve some of your *own* time by not accepting phone calls, but you'll have a different opinion after your first three-hour open house, where only a couple of unqualified prospects show up. Or, even worse, you may not get any prospects at all. Now *that* is a counterproductive afternoon!

Spend the necessary time talking with your prospects. Don't just take the quick and easy route offered by electronic communication. E-mail plays a prominent role in communications during a tenancy, but the phone is your primary business tool when dealing with prospective tenants.

After your prospects are willing to make a commitment and apply for your rental property, you need to have your rental application and rental contract, with all addenda, ready for their review. A disorganized rental property owner doesn't get a second chance. Being prepared allows you to focus your energies on evaluating each prospect to find the most qualified applicant who'll be your next long-term tenant.

Valuing Phone Conversations above All Other Communication Methods

Although the recent trend toward electronic communication (think e-mails and texts) has made keeping in contact with prospective tenants much easier, the phone is still your most important communications tool. The direct, instantaneous, two-way communication of a phone call is extremely valuable. (Just think of all the misunderstandings that can occur due to the limitations of e-mail and text messaging.)

Working vacation

I enjoy traveling and need to stay in touch with my property management office, so I always like to have the latest high-tech communication devices. Throughout the more than 30 years I've been in property management, I've seen a tremendous evolution in technology — from the large brick that was my first cellphone in the late '80s to the latest-generation Android tablet I now use. Today's devices combine 4G Internet access, e-mail, cellphone, camera, contact database, and calendar all in one — something unheard of in the early days of cellphones.

The ability to be contacted anytime, anywhere has its pros and cons, but I feel this communication technology allows me to travel more than in the past and still be available as necessary to properly manage my rental properties and interact with my tenants, vendors, and staff. Now I can travel to most parts of the globe and still receive e-mail messages and phone calls on my trusty tablet. Of course, this accessibility can lead to unpleasant surprises on your bill, such as receiving a non-emergency call from a tenant billed at $8 per minute while you're on a world cruise. Though the costs of these services are dropping quickly, they're still rather pricey in some areas of the world, so be sure to check with your communications provider about roaming charges before traveling to find out the most effective way to communicate from your destination.

An alternative to having your own tablet or smartphone when you travel internationally is making use of Internet cafés or the expanding number of locations offering wireless Internet access. With these sites, you can find inexpensive Internet connections virtually anywhere in the world and access web-based e-mail through a number of services (such as Google Gmail, Microsoft Hotmail, and Yahoo! Mail).

Trust me when I say that the advances in technology are extremely important for efficiency in owning and managing your rental property and for allowing you the opportunity to find some rest and relaxation. Isn't technology at work a wonderful thing?

The Internet and e-mail can be useful for your prospects by helping them solidify their interests in your property. But that's where the usefulness of electronic communication ends. Ultimately, your prospects need the type of specific information they can only receive through a phone call because they're likely to have many questions that can't be simply answered via e-mail or text. Likewise, you want to be able to ask them important questions to make sure they meet your rental criteria. Trust me; you'll benefit from hearing the hesitation or uncertainty in the voice of your prospective tenant when you ask her about her recent tenant history, her ability to pay rent, or whether she has any pets.

Spend the necessary time talking with your prospects. Don't just take the quick and easy route offered by electronic communication. E-mail plays a prominent role in communications during a tenancy, but the phone is your primary business tool when dealing with prospective tenants.

I recommend having a phone plan — cellphone, smartphone, or land line — that makes you available as much as possible. Look for features such as caller ID and voice mail.

In addition to your name, include on your voice mail system the following information about your rental:

- ✔ Your website address, if you have one (your website can provide prospects with so much more information than you can ever provide in a recorded message)

- ✔ Location, including directions

- ✔ Number of bedrooms and square footage

- ✔ Rental rate and security deposit requirements

- ✔ Qualifying information, such as minimum income and whether pets, excluding service animals, are accepted

- ✔ Property features and benefits

Preparing for Rental Inquiry Phone Calls

Whether or not you were ever a Boy Scout, you're probably familiar with the Boy Scout motto, "Be prepared." This motto applies to the management of rental properties in many ways, but one of the most important is being prepared when the phone rings. If you handle rental inquiry calls properly, you make your life much easier and also get the tenants you want. In the following sections, I discuss the importance of preparation and the steps necessary to make sure you're ready when the phone rings.

Even though prospects can find a lot of information about your property online, the rental inquiry phone call is a critical step that marks the beginning of the rental process. The purpose of this call is to get to the next step: showing the rental unit. Master the art of the rental inquiry phone call, and most of the time you can set appointments with only qualified rental prospects. And that's the name of the game in property management!

Having the basic tools ready

Advertising costs you a lot of time and money, so you don't want to waste time looking around for a pen, some paper, and your notes about your property when the phone starts ringing. You also don't want to take phone calls on your smartphone or cellphone if you're not in a position to devote the proper attention to the caller. Rental prospects can tell the difference between the prepared property owner and the one who doesn't seem to have a clue. They also form an impression of how you're likely to handle any problems they may encounter with the rental unit. Most sharp renters (and those are the ones you want) are looking for a professional, businesslike owner, so that's what you need to be.

The benefits of a professional phone technique are one of the main reasons I recommend having a separate business location for the management of your properties. This location doesn't have to be a separate office in a commercial setting; it can simply be the corner of your bedroom or an office at home. Consider having a separate phone line — or a separate cellphone or smartphone — as well. I know you can get a distinctive ring tone (and that is an improvement), but a separate phone line allows you to quickly distinguish between personal phone calls and rental business phone calls. It also helps you treat each kind of call accordingly.

You can find many great resources on the proper use of the phone in business, and the very first advice these resources typically offer is how to answer the phone and what to say. But when it comes to the management and leasing of rental properties, I believe that success with the phone begins with being prepared to use it *before* your first rental inquiry call. In the next few sections, I cover some basic tools to have on hand before your first call comes in.

Guest Card

A Guest Card, like the one shown in Figure 8-1, can assist you in gathering information from your rental prospect such as his name and phone number, how he heard about your rental unit, and his particular needs in terms of move-in date, size, and other requirements. This information can help determine whether your property meets his needs and wants.

To access a copy of the Guest Card that you can use, simply pop in the CD or click the link in the table of contents.

Guest Card

Name _____ Date of initial call _____ Time _____

Current address _____ City _____ Daytime Phone _____

Rental location (s) discussed _____ Cell Phone _____

How did you learn about our rental? _____ Email _____

When will you need to move in? _____ How many bedrooms do you need? _____

How many people will be living in the rental? _____ What size rental are you looking for? _____

What would you feel comfortable with as a monthly rent? _____

What do you do for a living? _____ Do you work? ___ Where? _____

Where are you living now? _____ How much parking space do you require? _____

What is wrong, if anything, with your current rental property? _____

Why are you looking to move at this time? _____

What types and sizes of pets do you have? _____

When can you drive by the rental property? _____ Mentioned Equal Opportunity Housing? ____

What other rental properties have you seen/plan to see? _____

Notes_____

_____

_____

Follow-up

Rental location(s) shown _____ Date shown _____ Quoted rent/deposit _____

What did prospect like best about the rental unit? _____

Objections, if any? _____

Most important features and amenities to prospect _____

Rental application completed? _____ Holding deposit? _____ Date to follow-up _____

Figure 8-1:
Guest Card.

You can also use the Guest Card whether you show your property to a prospective tenant or need to follow up on qualified prospects. Finally, you can use it to track the rental advertising source, which allows you to make sure you continue using only the advertising media that pay off.

One of the primary reasons to track your rental calls is so you can clearly see the results generated by your advertising. The number of phone calls isn't the most important factor in determining which advertising medium is the best for your property. The key factor is the number of *qualified* rental prospects they attract. Getting just a few calls from very qualified prospects is much better than getting a number of rental inquiries from unqualified prospects (which is just a waste of your valuable time and money).

Property Knowledge Sheet

One of the best ways to answer your rental prospect's questions is to prepare a Property Knowledge Sheet (see Figure 8-2) for each rental property location. This document contains all the basic information about the property, such as the size and type of the unit and the unit number if it's in a multi-unit property. Additionally, it should include the unit's age, type of construction, and other important details.

Pop in the CD or click the link in the table of contents to access a digital version of the Property Knowledge Sheet.

Property Knowledge Sheet

Property Information

Rental address _____ Unit # _____ City _____ Zip code _____
Office hours (if any) _____ Square footage of unit(s) _____
Unit mix—Studios _____ 1 Bedroom _____ 2 Bedroom/1 Bath _____ 2Bedroom/2 Bath _____ Other _____
Rent—Studios _____ 1 Bedroom _____ 2 Bedroom/1 Bath _____ 2Bedroom/2 Bath _____ Other _____
Application fee _____ Security deposit _____ Concessions _____
Age of rental _____ Type of construction _____ Parking _____
Recreational facilities _____ Laundry _____ Pets _____
Storage _____ Utilities (who pays?) _____ AC/Heat _____
Appliances _____ Floor coverings _____
Special features/comments _____
_____
_____

Community Information

School district _____ Grade school _____ Jr. high _____
High school _____ Jr. college _____ College _____
Trade school _____ Pre-school (s) _____
Childcare _____ Places of worship _____
Police station _____ Fire station _____ Ambulance _____
Electric _____ Natural gas _____ Telephone _____ Cable _____
Water _____ Sewer _____ Library _____ Post office _____
Hospital _____ Pharmacy _____ Vet _____
Other medical facilities _____
Nearby employment centers _____
Transportation _____
Groceries _____ Other shopping _____
Local services _____
Restaurants _____
Comments _____
_____

Rental Market Information

Rental competitors/rental rates/concessions _____
_____
_____
Our competitive advantages _____
_____
Our disadvantages _____
_____

Figure 8-2:
Property
Knowledge
Sheet.

Courtesy of Robert S. Griswold

A thorough Property Knowledge Sheet also contains important information about the neighborhood and general area. Just like the chamber of commerce or visitor's information bureau, you want to be able to answer questions about your locale. Rental prospects are very interested in knowing about employment centers, transportation, local schools, childcare, places of worship, shopping, and medical facilities. You can really make a positive impression on prospects if you can tell them where the nearest dry cleaner, child-care center, or Thai restaurant is located.

You want to have all this vital info from your Property Knowledge Sheet at your fingertips so that you can be ready to answer your prospect's questions, especially if you're competing with large, multifamily rental properties. The more you know about your property and the surrounding area, the more easily you can find some important reasons for your prospect to select your unit over the competition's. Knowing such details can make the difference between success and failure.

The time you spend answering all a prospect's questions can provide you with useful information. Be sure to take good notes about the source of your rental traffic and any important comments made by each prospect. Then you can improve your chances of securing a lease from this prospect and incorporate this feedback into your future advertising for that same property.

For example, maybe prospective renters indicate that they had trouble finding the property. This is a common problem and one that successful rental property owners know is a serious challenge. If your prospects can't find the property, they probably won't rent from you. ***Remember:*** You're competing with a lot of other rental property owners, and the best-qualified renters don't need to make extraordinary efforts to find a good-quality rental property.

Comparison Chart

You may find that you have a vacancy in a *soft rental market,* when the market has a lot of rental units available. Using a *Comparison Chart* can be very helpful in this kind of market, especially if your property has distinct advantages over others nearby. Keeping an updated Comparison Chart is really a marketing strategy commonly used by the owners and managers of large rental properties, but the concepts of it are helpful for the owners of small- to medium-size properties, too.

A Comparison Chart can

- ✔ **Provide useful information to prospective renters who may not be aware that they're comparing apples to oranges when looking at various rental properties:** Comparison Charts are particularly useful to rental property owners who may have a competitive advantage that's not readily apparent to uninformed prospects. For example, your rent may be slightly higher than the rent charged by your competition, but you may pay for the utilities, whereas tenants at your competition's apartments have to pay for their own utilities. This scenario is becoming a more likely example with the advent of many larger properties installing submetering for utilities, as discussed in Chapter 17.

- ✔ **Level the playing field and allow you to inform your prospective tenants of the actual costs of your rental housing (and the competition's housing):** Another potential advantage of your property may be that it has reserved parking, but the competition requires its tenants to scramble for parking spaces on the street. Or maybe your units have much more square footage than the competition. Many older properties are more aesthetically pleasing, with mature landscaping and beautiful shade trees. These are all factors that may not be readily apparent to prospective renters, and they can give you the upper hand over the competition.

Check out Figure 8-3 for an example of a Comparison Chart highlighting four properties. In looking at the chart, prospects can see that, although Sunshine Apartments has the lowest rent, when you add in the $75 monthly utilities, its tenants are paying $25 more per month than they'd pay at Maple Grove, and they don't get the reserved parking, on-site maintenance, lush landscaping, or free credit check. In this situation, Maple Grove Apartments is the obvious better deal for tenants, even though the monthly rent is higher. Madison Avenue Apartments and Camelot Townhomes, however, both level out at $700 per month when the utilities are taken into consideration. But Madison Avenue Apartments has better landscaping, and Camelot Townhomes has reserved parking. In this situation, tenants would need to decide which of these perks is more important. The key point: By providing an honest Comparison Chart, you save your prospective tenants legwork and highlight the advantages of your apartment over others.

If you're reading a hard-copy version of this book, the accompanying CD has a blank template you can use when making your own comparisons. If you're reading a digital version of this book, simply click the link in the table of contents to access a sample Comparison Chart.

Comparison Chart

Property	Rent	Owner Paid Water and Heating	Tenant Paid Water and Heating (with estimated costs)	Reserved Parking	Onsite Maintenance	Lush Landscaping	Free Credit Check
Sunshine Apartments	$600	No	Yes ($75/month)	No	No	No	No
Madison Avenue Apartments	$625	No	Yes ($75/month)	No	No	Yes	No
Maple Grove Apartments	$650	Yes	No	Yes	Yes	Yes	Yes
Camelot Townhomes	$700	Yes	No	Yes	No	No	No

Figure 8-3: Use a Comparison Chart to highlight your property's competitive advantages.

Courtesy of Robert S. Griswold

Answering the phone

As your key marketing tool, when your rental phone line rings, you need to stop what you're doing. Take a deep breath and even close your eyes briefly so you can be focused on the call. Be sure to answer the phone no later than the third ring; rental prospects generally have a list of calls to make, so they're rarely patient. If you don't answer in the first few rings, they'll begin dialing the next phone number on their list and probably won't take the time to call you again.

Because positive first impressions are always important, remember that the goal of your initial contact is to project a friendly, helpful, and professional image. These two pointers can help:

- **Have a smile on your face and speak clearly.** This is one phone technique that really does make a difference. Your positive attitude and enthusiasm can make an important first impression. Even if you're not in the best of spirits at the moment the phone rings, don't sound rushed or hurried. You don't want your prospects to feel that they're imposing upon you.

  If you sound disorganized and hesitant on the phone, the prospects will likely feel that you're incompetent and not the type of rental property owner whom they can trust and count on if they have a problem or need a repair. However, if you come across in your initial contact as polite, knowledgeable, organized, and confident, they'll respect your skills as a rental management professional. Prospects will see that you treat the rental of your property as a business, not a casual hobby.

- **Control your atmosphere to maintain a professional image.** If you run your rental management business from your home and a prospect calls and hears children screaming in the background or other distracting noises, you'll be making an unprofessional impression. Controlling your environment can be especially challenging with the advent of cellphones because you may not be in a location where it's safe (if you're driving) to take phone calls. In these situations, let the call go to voice mail and call the prospect back at your earliest convenience.

As with any business, you may find that a rental inquiry call comes in when you're right in the middle of another situation that can't wait. Or you may think that if you're not prepared, it may actually be better to let your voice mail system or answering machine take a message. I suggest you still answer the call right away and give your caller the choice to be placed on hold or tell her you can call her right back if she prefers. The majority of prospects aren't willing to leave a message, and you lose an opportunity to speak with them personally as a result. Asking the caller if she can call back in a few minutes is a risky strategy and one that I don't recommend because the odds of her calling back are remote. Remember that the majority of calls to small rental property owners require leaving a phone message, and you can really stand out by answering your calls personally.

If you're fortunate enough to have an exciting and chaotic home life, you need to make sure you can distinguish between rental inquiry calls and general household calls. For a nominal charge, many phone service providers offer a call waiting service that gives you two phone lines for one phone number. You can also have two separate lines or a service with distinctive ring tones so you can distinguish your personal calls from your rental business calls. If other members of your household pick up the phone during your conversation, you can easily get distracted, so let your family know how to tell the difference between regular calls and business calls.

Providing and obtaining the basic info

Rental inquiry calls are different from most of the calls you normally make in business. I often find that both parties are simultaneously trying to eliminate the other as a prospect and to get as much information as possible without giving out any information of their own. But this approach isn't the best because you're trying to make a phone presentation of your property. Instead, you need to have a give-and-take approach whereby you share the basic information that prospects need while making an initial assessment of their qualifications.

The beginning of many rental inquiry phone calls follows a standard pattern. Being aware of this pattern and knowing where your parts fit in can help you successfully make a professional and positive impression in the first few minutes. Here's how to handle the start of a basic rental inquiry call:

1. **Let the caller inquire about your rental unit and whether it's still available.**

   The caller also typically asks about the unit's size and the rental rate. Always answer his questions directly.

2. **Greet the caller by name to develop a rapport.**

   People generally like to be called by their names. If the caller hasn't already volunteered this information, you may want to mention your first name again and ask for his name. If he gives you his full name, be sure to ask his permission for you to call him by his first name. Sometimes a prospect provides his last name only. In this case, show respect by using an appropriate title when you call him by his surname.

3. **Ask the prospect for a return phone number.**

   If you have caller ID, verify that you have the best phone number to reach him. Don't assume that the number he called from is the best return number.

After you get past the initial formalities, begin prompting the caller for the information you both need. For example, you need to know when the prospect is looking to move in, how many people (and the number, type, and size of pets, if applicable) will be residing in the rental, and what he's comfortable with as a monthly rent.

An easy way to remember the basic questions you need to ask are to remember the six *w*'s — who, what, where, when, why, and how (yes, I realize that's technically five *w*'s and one *h,* but you get the point). Remember to use your notes and provide the prospect with immediate feedback so that he knows you're interested in his call and are really trying to determine whether your rental unit meets his needs.

Following are some examples of questions you can use to help determine your prospect's requirements:

- When will you need to move in?
- How many bedrooms do you need?
- How many people (including minors) will be living in the rental?
- What size rental are you looking for?
- What would you feel comfortable with as a monthly rent?
- How long do you intend to live at this property?
- What specific features or facilities are you looking for in your next home?
- How much parking space do you require?
- Where are you living now?
- What's wrong, if anything, with your current rental property?
- Why are you looking to move at this time?
- Where do you work (or attend school)?
- What do you do for a living?
- What's your gross monthly income?
- What types of pets do you have?
- When can you drive by the property?
- How can I reach you by phone?
- How did you learn about this property? Sign? Craigslist or other ad? Referral? Website? Flier?
- Are there any questions I haven't answered?

This basic initial give-and-take of questions and answers helps you and the prospect quickly determine whether the conversation is worth continuing. The prospect is looking for the opportunity to eliminate your property if you don't have what he needs at the time that he needs it. Likewise, if it appears that your property may be a good fit, you still need to explore whether the prospect is qualified and meets your screening requirements.

Be careful not to sound as if you're interrogating the prospect. Most of the questions in the earlier list don't give the caller much chance to talk — the prospect can answer them with one or two words. The conversation won't feel friendly if you just keep firing questions at the caller. Your goal is to let the prospect volunteer as much information as possible and to use the questions as prompts to keep a good two-way communication flowing. So don't feel as if you need to get all this information over the phone; you can fill in the blanks when you meet at the property.

Take notes on this Q & A so you can summarize each prospect's needs and wants during the initial phone conversation. Bring these notes to rental showings so that you know what aspects of your property are of greatest interest to each renter. Plus, people really appreciate the fact that you care enough to write down and remember what they're looking for instead of just trying to sell them what you have to offer.

Selling the prospect on your property

A key element to success in selling a rental prospect on your property is your ability to build rapport with the prospect on the phone. As you answer her initial questions, take the opportunity to highlight some of the desirable or unique aspects of your rental. For example, if the prospect asks about the number and size of the bedrooms, you can reply, "The house has four bedrooms, each with a separate closet. The master bedroom is very large at 15 feet by 12 feet. Will this accommodate your needs?" Or maybe you can say, "The backyard is completely fenced and is very large. Do you have any pets?"

Your goal is to turn the features of your property into benefits for the prospective tenant. To do so, you need to listen to what the prospect wants and then "sell" the specific feature of your property that fulfills that need. You do this by painting a picture of the property in her mind. For example, if your prospect asks about the recreational facilities and says she enjoys working out after a stressful day at work, you might mention that your property has a swimming pool and then ask whether she'd find a refreshing swim to be a good stress reliever after a long day.

You definitely want to tell your story about what a great rental property you have. Then, when you've grabbed the prospect's interest and determined that your unit meets her needs, you want to begin evaluating her qualifications in light of your requirements and needs. If you fail to hook the prospect, you never get to the next step. Of course, you want to be sure to prescreen the prospect during this initial phone call so that you invest your valuable time only with qualified prospects.

The goal of the rental inquiry call is to get the qualified prospect to see your property. You can't — and shouldn't — sign a rental contract on the phone!

Prequalifying the prospect over the phone

After you pass a prospective tenant's basic needs requirements, begin asking your own qualifying questions. You need to confirm when the prospect is looking to move, the size of the rental he requires, and his financial qualifications. Both you and the prospect need this basic information, and together you go through this ceremonial dance with the goal of advancing to the next stage — the showing of the rental unit.

But how do you know what to ask or what to listen for when prequalifying prospects? Read on for some guidance to help you find the best tenants for your rental property.

Holding a balanced conversation

Think of a rental inquiry call as a tennis match, with each side taking a turn presenting questions and gathering the answers needed to make a decision. Ultimately, both parties must agree that the unit meets the needs of the prospect and the prospect meets the owner's tenant screening criteria. This is the first step toward achieving your main objective of the call — getting a commitment from the prospect to make an appointment to see your rental unit in person.

Using open-ended questions and a pleasant manner, obtain basic information from the prospective tenant to determine whether he meets your rental requirements. Your goal with *open-ended questions* is to get your prospect to talk to you and give you the information you need. For example, "Why are you moving at this time?" is an open-ended question. *Closed questions* can be answered with a yes or no or one or two words. "What size apartment are you looking for?" is a closed question.

You want to achieve a balance between open-ended and closed questions. A good rule of thumb is not to ask more than three closed questions before inserting one that's open-ended. Doing so keeps the discussion from feeling like an interrogation.

You should also determine whether you're speaking with the actual decision-maker or whether this prospect is really gathering information for someone else. Although you always prefer to deal with the primary decision-maker from the initial contact on, you need to be skillful in prequalifying all the prospects without alienating your immediate contact because the immediate contact is likely to have considerable influence on the decision as well.

The answers to your basic questions determine whether you need to go on to the next step. For example, if currently you have only a studio apartment available, there may be no need to show this unit to a prospect who says that six applicants are planning to live in it. However, some fair housing advocates may claim you're discriminating on the basis of familial status or national origin if you don't show it.

Your goal during the rental inquiry call is to give the caller enough information about your property that he can determine whether he has enough genuine interest in it to make it worth his time to actually see it in person. Likewise, you want to obtain enough information about the prospect and his co-applicants to prequalify them for your rental property. Matchmaking is a two-way street.

Naturally, not every property is a match for every prospect. Your goal isn't to convince *all* the callers that they must see your property in person. Showing a unit to an uninterested or unqualified prospect is one of the most frustrating experiences in a rental management career. Showing property to qualified and interested prospects, however, is one of the most important factors in successful time management for rental property owners and managers.

Eyeing the qualities of desirable (and not-so-desirable) tenants

You can begin the process of prequalifying your rental prospect over the phone instead of waiting until you meet him when he tours the property or completes a rental application. By chatting with a prospective tenant during the first phone call, you're starting the all-important screening process right then and there.

Determining whether a prospect is qualified is easy if you know what to look for. Of course, you need to verify this information before making a commitment to rent your property, but if you can say yes to each of these statements, chances are you have a qualified prospect:

- ✔ You have a rental of the appropriate type and size available when the prospect needs it.
- ✔ The prospect meets your minimum qualifying standards for income, credit history, and employment history.
- ✔ The prospect has enough cash to pay the entire first month's rent and the full security deposit.
- ✔ At least one of the prospects is of legal age to sign the rental contract.
- ✔ The proposed number of occupants is appropriate for the particular rental unit.
- ✔ The prospect has an acceptable rental history and is vacating current living accommodations legally without any unpaid rent or other amounts owed.
- ✔ The prospect is willing to live within your property guidelines, such as no pets or no smoking allowed in the rental unit.

When trying to identify qualified prospects, you also want to watch out for less desirable prospects who don't meet your rental criteria. During the rental inquiry call, make sure you're not dealing with a *professional tenant,* someone who jumps from rental to rental frequently. Even during your first call, certain red flags may indicate you're dealing with someone who's trouble, such as a prospect who asks very few questions about the property and the area but is very interested in things like your move-in special or whether you can lower the rent or allow the security deposit to be paid over the first three months.

If a prospect seems interested in moving in too quickly, watch out. Although you may think that finding someone who wants to move in right away is great for cutting your rent loss, this eagerness may be an indication that the person has something to hide or is just looking for his next landlord victim. Maybe his current landlord just served him with eviction papers for nonpayment, and he needs to leave before he's physically removed. It can take up to two or three months for eviction actions to become a matter of public record, so your prospective tenant's credit report may turn up clean initially even if he's had recent problems. Be wary of subtle hints of trouble as early as the first phone call.

Handling phone objections

If you've done your homework, you're well prepared and know the answers to questions about the rental unit and the surrounding area. Being prepared for rental inquiries includes anticipating reasonable objections and providing honest answers to your prospect. Your goal isn't to convince the unqualified prospect who truly isn't a good match for your property to waste everyone's valuable time and come see the unit when it obviously won't work. Instead, your goal is to anticipate some of the more common objections and have info ready that allows you and the prospect to determine whether the mutual interest is high enough to warrant going to the next step — showing the unit.

I once managed a rental property with a centralized location that was also right under the flight path of a major airport. The ideal location near major employment and recreational centers made the property very desirable, but the proximity to the airport was quite obvious, and it was well-known that many properties in the area had significant problems with noise. Almost all the rental prospects who visited the property raised this concern, but even many of the callers brought up the noise because they were familiar with the area. What they didn't know was that when the property was built, the architects designed the rental units with special double-pane soundproof windows and extra insulation so that interior noise wasn't a problem. Knowing the perception of properties in the area, we mentioned the soundproofing features right upfront in our phone rental presentation.

Creating a sense of urgency

When you ask your prospect to come out and see your property, you may get a noncommittal response or an excuse that she can't make it no matter how many different appointment times you offer over the next week. Of course, the most popular excuse you can expect to hear is that she's just begun calling, and your rental ad is the first one she called on. This statement may be true, so you need to be polite and patient. But if you're truly her first call, then it's likely she called you first for a reason — your advertising made your rental sound like her best option. So patience can be a virtue, as long as you're not *too* patient.

Be honest, but don't hesitate to let the prospect know you've already received or will soon be receiving many more rental inquiry calls. Let her know that it's your intent to sign a rental contract with the most qualified rental prospect, but that you also process the rental applications in the order in which you receive them. So if you have two or more qualified applicants, you may lean toward the first qualified prospect who submitted an application. This knowledge creates a sense of urgency for the caller.

If you anticipate receiving interest in your property from multiple callers, set up one or two open houses so you can show the property to several interested prospects in just a couple of hours instead of making multiple trips. In tight rental markets, this method often creates a competitive or even auction-like environment, in which one prospect doesn't want to lose out to another. There's nothing like a little competition to instill a call to action in potential renters!

You may hear the complaint that your older, 20-unit rental property doesn't have individual washers and dryers in every unit, as offered in competitive properties in your area. Instead, your property features a centralized laundry room with new washers and dryers and a large folding table for tenants' convenience. Anticipating that some prospects are looking for individual washers and dryers and will raise an objection when you don't have this feature means you're prepared. You know that the competitors have smaller units with less storage because the washer/dryer takes up important closet and storage space. You also know that your competitor's tenants have to pay for water, and that the in-unit washers/dryers come with high utility charges and small capacities, whereas you pay for the water usage at your property, and your central laundry provides all the utilities and allows tenants to do several loads in the time it would take to do just one. These are important facts that you can politely mention to the prospect over the phone. When showing the rental unit to a prospect, you can provide her with the Comparison Chart covered earlier in this chapter.

Converting phone calls to rental showings

If your initial phone conversation goes well, the prospect will want to tour your rental property. You've already invested a lot of time and energy into the rental inquiry call, so this is the moment of truth when you find out whether your prospect is really interested in your rental. Maybe he's just gathering information for a future move or checking out similar rental properties to determine whether the rent increase he just received from his current landlord is justified.

You've answered a lot of questions, taken careful notes highlighting the prospect's needs and wants, and built up a rapport. You wouldn't have invested this much time in a prospect unless you felt that your rental meets his needs and that he's likely to pass your tenant screening criteria. So now isn't the time to become passive and tell him to call you back if he's interested. Nor is it the time to sheepishly suggest, "Stop by the open house this weekend, if you're in the neighborhood."

You need to be assertive and come right out and ask him to visit your property so you can personally show him your rental unit and be sure to set a specific appointment. If the prospect shows any signs of hesitating, you need to directly ask him if something's wrong. The prospect may then admit that he's just filed bankruptcy or that he plans to use your property for an iguana farm. Asking questions is one of your best tools; be sure to do it.

The prospect may indicate that he's interested in the property based on your conversation, but he wants to drive by it before actually making an appointment for a showing. This arrangement is fine and can be another useful tool in maximizing your efficiency as a rental property owner. Two scenarios can happen if the prospect wants to do a drive-by before scheduling a showing:

✔ He calls back and asks for an appointment or asks for the time of your next open house, and you can rest assured he'll show up.

✔ He drives by the property and finds that it's not suitable for him.

In both cases, allowing the prospect's drive-by is a positive step. In the former case, the prospect isn't presold on the area and curb appeal of your property alone; in the latter, the prospect doesn't waste your time scheduling a personal tour.

Many rental management advisors suggest you improve your efficiency by allowing prospective tenants to tour your property on their own. These advisors suggest giving prospects the combination to a lockbox at the property or allowing them to drop by and pick up a key. These advisors usually recommend that you ask for a $25 cash deposit or that you hold a prospect's driver's license as an incentive to return the key. I strongly advise against such a practice because you may find that a prospect has stripped the appliances or severely damaged the property while inside. Or worse, a prospect may decide your property is perfect and just move right in!

Many prospects make a showing appointment only to drive by the property a few minutes before the appointment and then skip the appointment if they don't like what they see. Another common scenario is when a prospect has already decided that your rental isn't going to be his next home, no matter how great the interior and how competitively you price the rental. But he feels guilty and doesn't want to skip out on you, so he shows up for the appointment and goes through the motions of looking at everything for close to an hour. Just imagine how many hours are wasted because your prospect takes the opportunity to gauge the neighborhood and curb appeal of the property before meeting for a scheduled showing but goes through the charade anyway. This is why giving the prospect your mobile phone number can increase your efficiency.

Planning Ahead for Open Houses and Walk-Throughs

One of the most time-consuming tasks of owning and managing rental property is filling vacancies. And the biggest time trap for most owners who don't have a system already in place is the rental showing. If you were to schedule a separate appointment with every interested rental prospect, you'd be making trips back and forth to the property constantly. Unless you live or work very close to your property, you can quickly find that you're spending hours showing the rental to one prospect after another. That's why having a strategy for showing your rental — whether you plan to have an open house or set up individual appointments — is the best way to go. The next few sections can help you formulate that strategy.

Holding an open house

Because your time is valuable and you have many qualified prospects interested in seeing your property, you may want to consider holding an *open house.* An open house allows you to efficiently show the property to several interested prospects within a couple of hours. A successful landlord doesn't make a dozen trips to show property to a dozen different prospects. Open houses are also beneficial because having multiple prospects viewing the property can create a sense of urgency and competition, which often generates multiple applicants for your property.

One of the other benefits of holding an open house is that many prospects feel more comfortable touring a property with other prospects around. These folks may be concerned about meeting someone they don't know in a vacant rental property. And you, too, should be very concerned about your own personal safety for the same reasons. Holding an open house can eliminate, or at least reduce, any safety concerns you — and your prospects — may have.

However, it's nice to be able to focus on one prospect at a time. So it may be beneficial to actually schedule appointments during the open house time frame but stagger them a bit so you can spend a little quality time getting to know each candidate.

Select a time for your open house that's convenient for you and most working people (preferably during daylight hours). For example, an open house on Saturday from 11 a.m. to 2 p.m. usually gives rental prospects a good opportunity to see your property at a convenient time for them. In the summer months, a weekday afternoon from 4 p.m. to 7 p.m. may be a good option. Combining a weekday afternoon open house with one on the weekend can also be very effective. That way, virtually all prospects can fit the showing into their busy schedules.

An open house promoted strictly in a newspaper ad isn't a good idea because you may end up with many unqualified renters walking through your property. But an open house where you invite all qualified prospects whom you've spoken with in response to your ad is a good way to efficiently lease your rental and create that sense of urgency and competition among prospective tenants.

Scheduling individual appointments

If you're in a depressed rental market or find that you need to fill a vacancy during the holidays, you may not be able to generate enough interest from prospects to schedule an open house for multiple renters. In this case, you need to be prepared to show your unit in the evenings and on weekends because that's often when prospects are available. Of course, you can still try to consolidate your appointments to a certain time frame, but don't push this scheduling too far. Asking prospects to conform to your calendar may turn them off.

If you have to schedule individual appointments to show your property, be sure you have the mobile phone numbers for your prospects. Almost everyone has a cellphone or smartphone these days, so call or text each person to verify the rental showing before making a special trip to the property. By calling, you're also reassuring the prospect that you'll be there and won't be delayed.

Crime is a concern in virtually all parts of the United States. Making an appointment to show a stranger your property can be an opportunity for someone criminally inclined. Be alert and take reasonable steps to protect yourself. If you ever have an uneasy feeling about a prospective tenant, decline the showing rather than risk personal injury. Limit your showings to daylight hours and bring someone with you, if at all possible. If you'd prefer, tell your prospect to meet you outside, right in front of the property or at another nearby public location, and require a picture ID before showing the unit. You can then use your cellphone or smartphone to call, text, or tweet a family member or friend and tell that person the name and driver's license number of your prospect. If you want, have someone call you on your mobile phone to check in throughout the showing. (*Note:* A text or tweet isn't enough in this case; you want the prospective tenant to hear the phone ring.) Of course, if you ever feel uncomfortable, be polite yet firm, end the rental tour, and leave immediately. Don't ever put yourself in a dangerous situation!

Providing directions to the property

When you have a commitment from a prospect to come to the property for an open house or showing, make sure you provide clear and easy-to-follow directions from anywhere in your area. Online and smartphone mapping programs are so prevalent and sophisticated that you can always ask prospects where they're coming from and find the exact directions to get them to your property. You can then verbally offer these step-by-step directions to your non-tech-savvy prospect.

Ask prospects whether they have a pen to write down the directions. It may seem silly, but by writing down the directions to your property, the prospect's commitment to keep the appointment is strengthened.

For your technically advanced prospects, you can simply forward the directions right to their tablet, smartphone, or mobile device. These prospects really just need your property address and they can provide their own personalized directions from their location to your property.

Because many of your prospects likely have Internet access, the need to provide directions to your property may not seem to be a priority. However, giving directions may not be quite as simple and unimportant as you think. Often the online directions prospective tenants have access to don't offer the most scenic or time-efficient path to your property. You always want to offer your own directions or at least suggest a route that approaches your property from a certain direction.

Carefully consider the best route for your prospects. Take into consideration the traffic conditions they'll face at the time of the open house or appointment. Think about which route presents the neighborhood in the best light. You want the route to be direct, but don't hesitate to have prospects come in from a different direction if doing so provides them with important information, such as the great shopping, schools, or other benefits of the area near your property.

Chapter 9

Strutting Your Stuff: Making Your Property Stick Out

In This Chapter

▶ Taking prospective tenants on a tour of your rental property

▶ Persuading prospects to rent with you

▶ Giving tenants the scoop on the environmental safety of your property

*T*o successfully rent your property, you need to show prospective renters why yours is better than all the others on the market. After you take the steps to prepare your property (see Chapter 5) and market it (check out Chapter 7), it's time to let prospective renters see what you have — and entice them to sign on the dotted line in the process.

In this chapter, I cover the proper way to show a rental unit, handle objections (which are really a sign of interest by your prospective tenants), and close the deal. I also make sure you're aware of important governmentally required disclosures that all rental property owners or managers must share with their tenants.

Showing Your Rental Unit

When your rental prospects arrive, you want to make a good first impression. Be sure to greet them with a smile and introduce yourself. Ask them whether they found your directions accurate and easy to use. Ask for their names and shake their hands. Refer to the notes you made on the telephone prospect card during your initial phone conversation to let them know you remember speaking with them (flip back to Chapter 8 for tips on how to conduct this conversation). This thoughtfulness gives prospective tenants a good feeling that you're not just going through the standard rental spiel.

Listen to any questions or concerns that may have come up since you spoke on the phone, and ask whether they have any other needs that they're looking for in a rental property that you haven't already discussed.

Don't let your prospects just wander through the rental unit by themselves. (Of course, this general rule is particularly true if you're showing an occupied rental unit.) Listen carefully to your prospects and anyone accompanying them as you informally guide the party through the unit. Pay close attention to the features your prospective tenants indicate are of particular interest or to any comments they make during the walk-through. But be careful not to come across as too pushy or overselling because this behavior turns off a lot of qualified prospects who dislike pressure-selling techniques. For more information on preparing your rental for walk-throughs, see Chapter 5.

No matter whether you're showing a vacant rental or an occupied rental, the next two sections focus on what you need to do to get your property rented.

Showing a vacant rental

If you're showing a vacant rental, act more like a tour consultant than a tour guide during the unit tour. Don't be too controlling; instead, let the prospects view the rental in the manner that suits them. Some prospects go right to a certain room, which gives you a clue about the importance they place on that aspect of the property. Of course, if the prospects hesitate or are reluctant to tour on their own, you can casually guide them through the rental property yourself.

There are as many different ways to show a rental unit as there are rental property owners. Remember the information provided by each prospect and customize the tour by beginning with the feature or room you feel has the most interest for him. Don't head straight to *your* favorite feature. When in doubt, start with the kitchen and then transition to the living areas and the bedrooms.

Keep the following pointers in mind when showing a vacant rental:

- ✓ **Encourage your rental prospects to see the entire rental property.** Don't overlook any garage or storage areas and the exterior grounds or yard, if applicable. You want to be sure prospective tenants have an opportunity to observe the conditions of all portions of the property and ask any questions. Besides being a good sales technique, doing so minimizes future claims that you discriminated against a prospect by selectively showing your property.

- ✓ **Listen and observe the body language and facial expressions of your prospects while they walk through the property.** When you begin showing the interior of your rental, avoid making obvious statements such as, "This is the living room," or, "Here's the bathroom!" That is insulting. They can see what the room is used for. Instead, ask them how they'll arrange their furniture or entertainment center. Try to incorporate any needs they've expressed into the tour of the unit. You don't need to oversell if your prospective tenants seem pleased, but you should feel free to point out the benefits of your property. (Take in prospects' reactions and comments; then chime in with something along the lines of, "It sounds like this neutral-colored carpet will go great with your living room furniture" or, "The view of the sunsets from the kitchen is so relaxing.")

✔ **Have a tape measure with you.** Vacant rental units look smaller than occupied ones, so a tape measure can assist your prospects in immediately determining that their bedroom set will fit in the master suite. Know the standard dimensions for both king- and queen-size beds and the typical sizes of nightstands and dressers. It helps if your prospective tenants can begin to imagine themselves living in the unit. If your prospects express concerns that their furniture won't fit in your rental, consider this strategy: Set up a partially or fully furnished model rental unit to demonstrate what furniture will fit inside. Although this tactic may not be feasible for most single-family homes or condos, it can work quite well for medium to larger apartment properties that regularly have vacant units or have a market for furnished rentals. Smaller rental properties can use a *vignette,* which is a rental unit decorated with towels, books, and knickknacks to give the unit personality. Sometimes you can even close the sale by offering to give new renters these small items.

If you're holding an open house, you may find yourself dealing with multiple prospects who all seem to have better timing than a synchronized swimming team. Do your best to courteously greet and speak with each prospect individually. At the very least, cover the basic information and get the first prospects started on the property tour before beginning to work with the next prospects. Be sure to communicate clearly that you'll answer all questions and treat all prospects openly and fairly to avoid any allegations of favoritism or discrimination. If at all possible, try to take one prospect on a tour at a time because you're less effective spreading your attention among several prospects.

Showing an occupied rental

If you're showing an occupied rental unit, be sure to consider the inherent advantages and disadvantages. On the plus side, your current tenant can be a real asset if she's friendly and cooperative and takes care of the property, because prospective tenants may want to ask her questions about her living experience. But not all tenants take the same level of care with your property or want to help you re-rent it when they're getting ready to move.

Always keep these tips in mind when showing an occupied rental unit:

✔ **Consider your current tenant's attitude.** If she is being evicted, isn't leaving on good terms, or has an antagonistic attitude for any reason, don't show the unit until the property is vacated. Your tenant's cooperation will be required, but you may be able to complete your rent-ready preparation work and any upgrades at this time as well. This strategy also works if your current tenant hasn't taken good care of your property's grounds

or landscaping or if her furnishings may be objectionable to some prospective tenants for any reason. Remember me mentioning that one of my
rules is "no surprises"? That applies strongly here. Never show an occupied unit that you haven't previewed first.

✔ **Know your local laws regarding showing occupied units.** In most
   states, if the tenant is at the end of her lease or has given a notice to
   vacate, the owner is specifically allowed to enter the property to show
   the unit to a prospective tenant. Of course, you must comply with state
   laws, which require you to give your current tenant advance written
   notice of entry prior to showing the unit. She may agree to waive the
   notice requirement, but make sure you have this agreement in writing.

✔ **Work with your tenant to coordinate scheduling.** Do your best to
   cooperate with the current tenant when scheduling mutually convenient
   times to show their rental unit. Be sure to respect her privacy and avoid
   excessive intrusions into her life. To ensure the cooperation of your
   tenant, you may even want to offer her a small bonus after she vacates,
   as a part of her security deposit disposition.

✔ **Try to get copies of recent utility bills from your current tenant.**
   Having current bills on hand is helpful if your prospective renters have
   any questions about utility costs. Prices for electricity, natural gas,
   water and sewer, and trash service are becoming significant items in the
   budgets of many renters. You don't want your new tenant to be financially unable to handle the typical monthly utility costs of your unit,
   because this difficulty may affect her ability to pay your rent. If your
   property has "green" or energy-efficient features or appliances, you may
   be able to use low utility costs as a marketing tool.

Although the current tenant may legally be required to allow you and your
prospects to enter the unit for a showing, she doesn't have to make any effort
to ensure the property is clean and neat. Nor is she required to help you in
your efforts to impress the prospect. Keep this fact in mind when deciding
whether you want to show your unit while it's still occupied. This is also the
reason why a financial incentive can result in a more cooperative tenant.

Taking the First Steps to Get the Renter Interested

Although some rental units may rent themselves, the reality is your success
as a property manager may be directly enhanced if you become skilled in
properly presenting the best features of your unit. You should use the meeting with your prospective tenant to evaluate whether the unit is a good fit for
the tenant.

This section walks you through the steps of prequalifying your tenant, handling objections, and closing the sale with a completed rental application. I also cover the advantages of priority waiting lists and holding deposits.

Prequalifying your prospect during the rental showing

While you're touring the rental, prequalify the prospective tenant by verifying the information he provided during your initial phone conversation. Refer to your notes and confirm his desired move-in date and ability to pay the rent, the number of occupants, the rental rate, and other important information. Also, make sure he's aware of your rental policies and any limitations on pets or other important issues.

You don't want to be abrupt or refuse to let him begin looking at the property until he answers numerous questions. However, verifying the basics upfront can save a lot of time if there's a misunderstanding or if the prospect's needs change. Your time (and theirs) is valuable, which is why you want to politely yet directly confirm as early as possible that there are no deal killers for either you or the prospective tenant.

If you don't take the time to review the information a prospect provided to you on the phone, as well as your rental terms and expectations, you may find the prospect glossed over certain problems or indicated your rental policies were just fine when they really weren't. Of course, this individual's strategy is to wait until you think you've successfully rented the unit and are just about to sign on the dotted line when he springs the truth on you. Maybe his dying aunt has suddenly asked him to care for her 100-pound Doberman, or his paycheck was delayed and he can only pay your security deposit in installments. You don't need these surprises, so confirm all the basics sooner rather than later!

Resolving your prospect's objections

Almost every rental prospect expresses some concerns or reservations about the property, the area, your rental rate, or other terms. No rental property exactly meets the needs of each prospective tenant, so don't be caught off guard when you inevitably run into objections.

Objections come in many forms. Some are a test to see whether you'll lower the rent or make some improvements to the property. Others are sincere issues that are generally more tangible and specific in nature.

If you've been listening carefully to the prospect and taking notes, then you can anticipate and handle some objections before she even brings them up.

In many instances, objections can actually present an opportunity to reassure your prospect that your property meets her needs.

If the prospect raises a question and you don't know the answer, make a note and promise to get back to her as soon as possible. Avoid the temptation to give an immediate answer that may not be right. Why? Because some prospects ask questions they already know the answers to just to test your sincerity. You can overcome most objections if you discuss them openly with the prospect and provide honest feedback. Giving the prospect a response and attempting to answer positively is important.

Convincing your prospect

After you qualify the prospect, you need to convince him that you have the best rental unit available. Renters want more than just a place to live. They want to feel they can communicate with you if a problem arises. They also appreciate when someone shows an interest in their needs and expectations about their potential new home. And by showing an interest, you're clearly setting yourself apart from other property managers. You don't want to be nosy or aggressive, but I believe prospects accept rental units that aren't exactly what they're looking for if they have positive feelings about the owners or managers.

I realized how important the property manager can be to renters when I transferred a popular manager from one property to another very early in my property management career. Ginny had been our on-site manager at a 300-unit rental property for nearly five years before we gave her a promotion to a 400-unit rental community a few miles away. I was shocked when more than 50 of Ginny's current residents decided to give notice and move with her to the larger property (despite the higher rents and less desirable location). Ginny had established a trusting relationship with these residents. She proved a determining factor in their rental decision. They were willing to pay more rent and suffer the substantial inconvenience of moving just to have Ginny as their on-site manager.

I've never seen a rental unit that can rent itself; *you* need to make the difference. No matter how closely your unit meets your prospects' needs and wants, they often hesitate and doubt their own judgment. You don't need to be pushy, but you should be prepared to actively convince prospective tenants that your property is right for them.

The best way to avoid problem tenants who pay late, damage your property, or disrupt the neighbors is not to rent to them in the first place. Screening your next tenant begins with the very first phone call. Tell the prospect you'll run his credit report and call his references. Don't waste your time convincing prospects who don't seem to fit your criteria for a high-quality, stable tenant.

Inviting your prospect to sign on

When you've convinced your prospect that your unit is the right one for her, it's time to close the sale. This is one area where many rental property owners and managers suddenly get cold feet. They do a great job handling the initial telephone inquiry, preparing and showing the property, and even resolving objections, but when it comes down to asking the prospect to commit, they become shy and freeze.

Today, many of your prospective tenants may first contact you via e-mail or text from their smartphones or tablets. Text and e-mail are wonderful communication technologies, but they're often used improperly as a substitute for a good old-fashioned phone call, in-person meeting, or showing of the rental unit. These days, even tenants relocating from another part of the world have the ability to make affordable phone calls. Always respond to a prospective tenant's e-mails promptly and professionally and answer any basic questions, but your goal should be to get the prospect in a two-way dialogue on the phone.

Your goal is to receive a rental commitment from the prospect by having her complete your rental application and pay any pre-move-in screening fee, her first month's rent, and a full security deposit on the spot. Of course, you still need to thoroughly screen the prospect and confirm she meets your rental criteria before asking her to sign a rental contract.

If, despite your best efforts, the prospect is still undecided, make sure she gives you a holding deposit. Remind her that you may make a deal with the very next prospect, and she'll be out of luck. Of course, if you have a lot of demand for your units, you should develop a priority waiting list, which is covered later in this chapter.

Having your prospect complete a rental application

You need to offer every interested prospect the opportunity to complete a written rental application for two important reasons:

✔ **You want to have all the information so you can begin the screening process and select the best tenant for your property by using objective criteria and your rental requirements.** The rental application is the key document you use to verify information and conduct your entire tenant screening procedure. I cover tenant screening in more detail in Chapter 10.

✔ **You want to avoid having prospects accuse you of discriminating against them by not permitting them to fill out the rental application.** Don't prejudge an applicant. The prospect may have already volunteered enough information about his financial situation and tenant history that you believe it would be a waste of time and effort for him to complete an application. Even in such a situation, always be sure to offer your application to every rental prospect of legal contracting age and keep even the rejected applications for four years.

Pop in the CD or click the link in the table of contents to access a sample Rental Application.

Have several rental applications and pens available at the property. Although you want to offer an application to every prospect, you don't want to just hand them out and let the prospects leave without making commitments.

Here are some important guidelines to remember when having prospects complete rental applications:

✔ **Every prospective tenant who is currently 18 or older should completely fill out a written application.** This rule applies whether the applicants are married, are related in some other way, or are unrelated roommates.

✔ **Before accepting the application, carefully review the entire form to make sure each prospect has clearly and legibly provided all requested information.** Pay particular attention to all names and addresses, employment information, Social Security or Individual Taxpayer Identification numbers, driver's license numbers, and emergency contacts. Ask for documentation about any discrepancies in the information provided on the application and through third-party credit reports or employment verifications. Also, ask about any gaps in employment. Any blanks should be marked with "N/A" if not applicable so that you can tell those items weren't inadvertently overlooked.

✔ **Each prospective tenant must sign the application authorizing you to perform your pre-move-in screening, verify the provided information, and run a credit report.** You can't legally obtain and review a consumer credit report without an applicant's permission.

✔ **All prospective tenants need to show you a current driver's license or other similar government-issued photo identification so you can confirm that they're providing you with their correct names and current addresses.** Identity theft is a growing concern; make sure you know exactly who you're renting to.

You may be asked by the prospect — or you may decide on your own — to go over the rental application with him and assist him in providing the information. If you do so, be very careful to ask only questions that are part of the application. Avoid asking questions that may directly or indirectly discriminate. Don't ask the applicant about his birthplace, religion, marital status, children, or a physical or mental condition. You *can* ask him whether he has ever been convicted of a crime and whether he's at least 18 years old.

Holding your prospect's deposit

Some rental prospects are willing to make firm commitments, but they either won't or can't give you the full security deposit and first month's rent. Maybe they just don't have the funds at the time, or maybe they want to reserve your rental while looking for a better property. In these situations, you may want to ask for a holding deposit to allow you to take the unit off the market for a limited time while you obtain a credit report or verify other information on the rental application.

Don't allow the prospect to reserve your property with a small holding deposit for more than a couple of days. Two days gives you more than enough time to screen the prospect; any additional time the unit is off the market often translates into rent you never see. After you approve the prospect, try to have her sign the rental contract. If the prospect still insists she needs additional time, have her agree to pay the daily rental rate or refund her holding deposit and continue your search for more interested prospects.

By taking the rental unit off the market, you forgo the ability to rent it to someone else. If the prospective tenant fails to rent your property for any reason, you've potentially lost revenue while the unit has been vacant and reserved. On the other hand, rental prospects don't want to pay rent while you're running them through your tenant screening process. The solution is to use a written Holding Deposit Agreement and Receipt, which outlines the understanding between you and the prospective tenant.

To access a sample Holding Deposit Agreement and Receipt, pop in the CD or click the link in the table of contents.

If you use a holding deposit, you must have a written agreement or you're likely to encounter a misunderstanding or even legal action. State laws regarding holding deposits vary, yet they're almost uniformly vague and can easily lead to disputes. My advice is to never retain funds from a holding deposit that exceed the total of the daily rental rate for the days you actually had the unit off the market. If you're perceived to have collected more money than the rental value for the "lost days," then your former prospective tenant will have a fairly persuasive argument should the matter ever be heard in court.

Developing priority waiting lists

If you have several qualified rental prospects interested in your rental unit, you'll only be able to rent to one of them. This is an excellent position to be in, but it may indicate that your rent levels are lower than the market will allow, and you can consider raising your asking rents. Use the tenant selection criteria covered in Chapter 10 to select the most-qualified prospect.

 If you have other qualified prospects, you may have other units at the same property, or in close proximity, that would interest them. If those other units aren't available right at the moment, you may be able to offer your prospects a spot on your *priority waiting list,* which is just a way for you to keep track of qualified tenants for whom you simply don't yet have available rentals instead of turning them away. Being in this situation is a dream come true for many rental property owners or managers.

If potential tenants express a desire to rent your property at a future date and you know other rentals are available in the area, the prospects may be interested because your rents are lower than market value. (Otherwise, they'd simply find another comparable rental somewhere else instead of waiting.) If you have a long waiting list, make sure it's because your property is desirable — not because you're charging too little in rent.

Some prospective tenants are simply looking for a great rental property several months in advance. Although you can't hold your property vacant and off the market until these folks are ready to rent, you can lock them in for one of your units that may be coming available at the time they're prepared to move. This situation is especially typical for prospects relocating from out of town and making a trip to look for a rental a few weeks or months before they officially move. You may be able to pre-rent your units even before they become vacant (and that's a great position for any property manager to be in).

 When you create a priority waiting list, don't just write the prospects' names on a piece of paper. This approach gives you no commitment, and the chances of those prospects returning to rent from you are slim. Prospective tenants' levels of commitment increase if you prequalify them, take partially refundable deposits, and give them written confirmations that they're on your priority waiting list. Note that the partially refundable deposit here is different from a holding deposit because you don't actually have a currently vacant unit, and thus you aren't losing any rent with a unit sitting vacant. You may even want to offer to lock in a rental rate if they rent from you within a certain number of months.

Inform your prospects that they're on the waiting list. Also, if you own multiple units, be sure to let your prospects know you can't guarantee that a certain property or unit will be available when they're ready to move in because you can't control when your current tenants will vacate. Give prospective tenants the right to cancel and let them know that the portion of their deposits not used for the tenant screening process is fully refundable at any time.

As with all rental policies, you need to apply your priority waiting list policy uniformly to all prospects for fair housing reasons. If you've already prequalified your waiting list prospects, then a policy of first come, first served makes a lot of sense. So if you have a priority waiting list, be sure to let all prospective tenants know about it and don't restrict anyone from being added to the list. Otherwise, you can be accused of discrimination.

Handling Mandatory Disclosures and Environmental Issues

One of the major challenges to being a successful rental property owner is keeping abreast of the constantly evolving health and safety requirements in your state that affect rental properties. In addition to providing your tenants with a clean and habitable property, you need to take precautions to ensure the rental is a safe and healthy environment.

Although failing to meet required state and federal disclosures leads to definite legal implications and substantial liability, most rental property owners genuinely don't want to see their tenants get sick or injured. In the following sections, I cover some of the most common issues facing rental property owners today.

New federal, state, and local legislation is constantly under consideration, and rental property owners must stay current with all requirements or face serious consequences. Visit the CD or click the link in the table of contents for links to state landlord-tenant laws to find out about any state disclosure requirements.

Lead-based paint

As a rental property owner, you need to be aware of the dangers of lead and the federally required disclosures regarding it. Most states now have lead hazard reduction laws in place, some of which require testing and careful maintenance, in addition to the federal disclosure requirements.

Although lead-based paint isn't a hazard when in good condition, it can be a serious problem (particularly for young children) when it cracks, peels, or turns to chalk because of age. Lead has been banned from paint since 1978, but even to this day, older housing units may contain paint manufactured before that time. You can't tell whether paint contains lead just by looking at it; a special lead test is the only way to verify its presence.

Lead-based paint isn't easy to remove. If your property has lead-based paint, hire a licensed contractor to address concerns about lead. Unfortunately, removing lead can be quite expensive. Often the best solution is to manage the lead in place rather than completely remove it because the removal processes of sanding and scraping can release large amounts of lead dust.

If you have any concerns about lead hazards, review the extensive resources available from the Environmental Protection Agency (EPA) and the National Lead Information Center (NLIC) by visiting www.epa.gov/lead or by calling 800-424-LEAD (800-424-5323).

Most rental property owners use a Lead-Based Paint Disclosure form (see Figure 9-1) to ensure they've complied with the Residential Lead-Based Paint Hazard Reduction Act of 1992 (see the nearby sidebar for more info). Access this form on the CD or via the link in the table of contents, print it online at www.epa.gov/lead/pubs/lesr_eng.pdf, or contact the NLIC at 800-424-5323 for a copy.

The Residential Lead-Based Paint Hazard Reduction Act (42 U.S. Code § 4852d) also requires you to provide tenants with an information pamphlet from the EPA titled "Protect Your Family from Lead in Your Home." You can get this pamphlet online at www.epa.gov/lead/pubs/leadpdfe.pdf in both English and Spanish. The pamphlet is also available in other languages (namely Arabic, Russian, Somali, and Vietnamese) at www.epa.gov/lead/pubs/leadprot.htm. You can receive clarification on the law from the NLIC by calling 800-424-5323. A few states (including California and Massachusetts) have their own pamphlets on lead-based paint hazards that the EPA has authorized for distribution in lieu of the EPA pamphlet.

Whichever pamphlet you provide your tenants, be sure you comply with the federal law and keep a copy of the disclosure form signed and dated by the tenants. You must keep this written record of compliance with the disclosure requirements on hand and readily available for review for a minimum of three years in case of an investigation or audit. Remember that you need to make the required disclosure only once, even if a tenant renews an existing lease.

Rental property owners or managers who fail to follow the federal regulations for lead-based paint can face significant fines. To enforce these regulations, the federal Housing and Urban Development (HUD) agency and the EPA are working together to investigate complaints from prospective tenants and/or current tenants who believe they may have been exposed to lead-based paint. If a tenant doesn't receive the required EPA or approved state information pamphlet or the disclosure statement, the owner or property manager may be subject to one or more of the following penalties:

- ✔ A notice of noncompliance

- ✔ A civil monetary penalty of up to $11,000 per violation for willful and continuing noncompliance

- ✔ An order to pay the injured tenant up to three times his or her actual damages

- ✔ A criminal fine of up to $11,000 per violation

WARNING!

Recently, the EPA and HUD began aggressively enforcing these regulations and levied significant and well-publicized fines against rental property owners and managers who haven't complied with the law. Government testers have been known to pose as prospective tenants, and federal agents have scoured leasing and maintenance records looking for evidence that property owners or managers knew or should have known about the existence of lead-based paint hazards on their property. This is *not* an area where you want to tempt fate. Make sure you comply with this law and keep the required documentation on file in an easily retrievable location for at least three years.

Disclosure of Information on Lead-Based Paint and/or Lead-Based Paint Hazards

Lead Warning Statement

Housing built before 1978 may contain lead-based paint. Lead from paint, paint chips, and dust can pose health hazards if not managed properly. Lead exposure is especially harmful to young children and pregnant women. Before renting pre-1978 housing, lessors must disclose the presence of known lead-based paint and/or lead-based paint hazards in the dwelling. Lessees must also receive a federally approved pamphlet on lead poisoning prevention.

Lessor's Disclosure

(a) Presence of lead-based paint and/or lead-based paint hazards (check (i) or (ii) below):

    (i) _____ Known lead-based paint and/or lead-based paint hazards are present in the housing (explain).

    _____

    _____

    (ii) _____ Lessor has no knowledge of lead-based paint and/or lead-based paint hazards in the housing.

(b) Records and reports available to the lessor (check (i) or (ii) below):

    (i) _____ Lessor has provided the lessee with all available records and reports pertaining to lead-based paint and/or lead-based paint hazards in the housing (list documents below).

    _____

    _____

    (ii) _____ Lessor has no reports or records pertaining to lead-based paint and/or lead-based paint hazards in the housing.

Lessee's Acknowledgment (initial)

(c) _____ Lessee has received copies of all information listed above.

(d) _____ Lessee has received the pamphlet *Protect Your Family from Lead in Your Home.*

Agent's Acknowledgment (initial)

(e) _____ Agent has informed the lessor of the lessor's obligations under 42 U.S.C. 4852(d) and is aware of his/her responsibility to ensure compliance.

Certification of Accuracy

The following parties have reviewed the information above and certify, to the best of their knowledge, that the information they have provided is true and accurate.

Lessor	Date	Lessor	Date
Lessee	Date	Lessee	Date
Agent	Date	Agent	Date

Figure 9-1:
As a property owner, you're required by law to give a lead-based paint disclosure form like this one to any tenants or prospects if your property was built before January 1, 1978.

Courtesy of U.S. Environmental Protection Agency

Painting a clearer picture of lead-based paints

The federal Residential Lead-Based Paint Hazard Reduction Act of 1992 covers all dwellings built before 1978 and requires rental housing owners or their property managers to notify tenants that the property may have lead-based paint. Testing for lead-based paint or removal isn't currently required under federal law. However, you must disclose any known presence of lead-based paint or hazards and provide all tenants with copies of any available records or reports pertaining to the presence of lead-based paint and/or hazards.

In addition to all housing constructed after January 1, 1978, some limited rental property exemptions from federal lead-based paint disclosure regulations do exist. Exempt properties include the following:

- Housing for the elderly or persons with disabilities (unless any child under 6 is living there or is expected to live there)

- Short-term rentals of 100 days or fewer

- The rental of an individual bedroom or similar room in a residential home

- Certain university housing, such as dormitory housing or rentals in sorority or fraternity houses

- Zero bedroom units, such as studios, lofts, or efficiencies

- Housing that has been inspected and certified as lead-free by a state-accredited lead inspector (meaning the complete absence of lead-based paint, not just encapsulated)

Be sure to contact the EPA or your state health and environmental agency for specific information. If you're advised that your property is exempt, be sure to receive written verification before ceasing to follow the federal requirements.

In pre-1978 properties, lead-based paint is usually found on the following surfaces:

- Doors, door jambs and frames, railings, and banisters

- Exterior painted surfaces

- Interior trim

- Porches and fences

- Windows, windowsills, and horizontal painted surfaces

In 2011, the EPA began enforcing the Renovation, Repair and Painting Rule (RRP Rule). It requires contractors who conduct renovation work in residential buildings built before 1978 to be a "lead-safe certified firm" and follow specific work practices to prevent lead dust contamination. The program aims to reduce the amount of lead dust created during renovation, repair, and painting of rental units and common areas and affects renovation contractors, maintenance workers in the rental housing industry, and painters and employees of other specialty trades. These workers must attend EPA-approved courses taught by a government-approved trainer.

Some of the requirements outlined in the RRP Rule include distributing information to building occupants to notify them of the work being conducted, obtaining written certification from the adult occupant that the information has been received, posting signs defining the work area, isolating the work area by closing windows and doors, and covering ducts or other openings that can't be sealed with plastic sheeting. The specific lead dust reduction practices also include covering the floor with plastic or similar material, negatively pressurizing the work space, storing daily waste under containment that prevents the release of dust, disposing of the waste in a sealed bag approved by the EPA, and placing all waste in a lined container and disposing of it at an EPA-approved site. You can find further information concerning lead-safe work practices at www.epa.gov/lead/pubs/renovation.htm.

> *Note:* The RRP Rule typically doesn't apply to minor maintenance or repair activities (such as patching holes) where less than 6 square feet of lead-based paint is disturbed in a room or where less than 20 square feet of lead-based paint is disturbed on the exterior, but this doesn't include window replacement, demolition, or prohibited practices.

Asbestos

Asbestos has received a lot of media coverage over the last 25 years. You may remember the federal government's concerns about asbestos in schools and the major efforts to remove asbestos-containing materials from those facilities.

Asbestos is a mineral fiber that historically was added to a variety of products to strengthen them and provide heat insulation and fire resistance. In most products, asbestos is blended with a binding material so that, as long as it remains intact, fibers aren't released into the air, and no health risk occurs. Asbestos fibers are microscopic and can be positively identified only with a special type of microscope. Products containing asbestos aren't usually labeled.

Asbestos was commonly used until 1981. Now, it's estimated that more than 3,000 products still in use today contain asbestos. These products, which can be found in many rental properties, include acoustic ceilings, vinyl flooring and tile backings, flooring *mastic* (a type of adhesive), building insulation, wall and ceiling panels, carpet padding, roofing materials, pipe and duct insulation, patching and spackling compounds, and furnaces.

Do *not* assume that a property built or remodeled after 1981 doesn't contain asbestos products.

The concern in most rental properties is that asbestos-containing materials may be disturbed, causing them to release microscopic fibers, which can be inhaled into the lungs. For example, many older apartments have popcorn or acoustic ceilings containing asbestos, which can be disturbed by installing a ceiling light or fan. The asbestos fibers don't self-destruct but remain in the air for a long time, increasing the risk of disease. Some asbestos materials are *friable,* meaning they crumble into small particles or fibers. Asbestos-containing materials can also crumble easily if mishandled. Even if the material was originally intact, asbestos can be released into the air if the material is sawed, scraped, sanded into a powder, or subjected to some mechanical processes.

A common cause of the release of asbestos is inappropriate or unsafe handling of asbestos-containing materials during remodeling or renovation of the property. If you plan to do any renovations that may disturb asbestos or plan to demolish your building, federal law requires a comprehensive survey before the work begins. Any asbestos found during the survey must then be handled appropriately. To be valid, the survey must be conducted by trained asbestos personnel.

Check with your local and state officials for any disclosure requirements they may require. Some jurisdictions insist asbestos materials be disclosed to tenants, along with a warning not to disturb them.

According to the American Lung Association, if you have asbestos-containing substances in your rental property, do the following:

- ✔ **If the substance is in good condition and the asbestos won't be disturbed, leave it alone.** Be sure to warn the tenants not to disturb these materials and have them notify you immediately if these materials are damaged in any way.

- ✔ **If the material is damaged and can release fibers in the air, have it repaired or removed.** Always seek the advice of a professional environmental firm to evaluate and recommend the best course of action concerning asbestos.

    - • Repair usually involves either sealing or covering asbestos material. Sealing is also commonly referred to as *encapsulation* and involves coating materials so that the asbestos can't be released. Encapsulation is only effective for undamaged asbestos-containing material. If materials are soft, crumbly, or otherwise damaged, sealing isn't appropriate, and the substances should be removed by a qualified professional.

    - • Removing asbestos-containing materials is an expensive and hazardous process to be completed only by trained personnel using special tools and techniques, and should be a last resort. You should hire a licensed contractor who specializes in removing asbestos-containing materials because improper removal can increase the health risks to the workers, yourself, and your future tenants.

    Unauthorized removal of asbestos can be illegal. Punishment can include hundreds of thousands of dollars in fines or prison.

Asbestos is a very dangerous material if disturbed or in poor condition. Don't attempt to test for asbestos on your own. Hire a professional environmental testing firm because the act of breaking open potentially asbestos-containing material to obtain test samples may release asbestos into the air and create a very dangerous situation.

The lowdown on asbestos

The federal Occupational Safety and Health Administration (OSHA) has developed regulations that apply to any building constructed prior to 1981. These buildings are presumed to have asbestos unless the owner tests the property and verifies that asbestos or asbestos-containing materials aren't present.

Exposure to asbestos can lead to an increased risk of lung cancer; *mesothelioma,* a cancer of the lining of the chest and the abdominal cavity; and *asbestosis,* a condition in which the lungs become scarred with fibrous tissue.

No known safe exposure level to asbestos exists. However, when the asbestos is intact and can't become airborne, exposure to it isn't a problem. Smokers who inhale exposed asbestos fibers have a greater risk of developing lung cancer than nonsmokers. Although most people who get asbestosis have usually been exposed to high levels of asbestos for a long time, even a short but significant exposure can cause harm. The symptoms of asbestos-related diseases don't usually appear until about 20 to 30 years after the first exposure to asbestos.

Radon

Radon, a radioactive gas, is a known cancer-causing agent that the EPA cites as the second leading cause of lung cancer in the United States and that claims 20,000 lives annually. Found in soil and rock in all parts of the country, radon is formed as a byproduct of the natural decay of the radioactive materials radium and uranium. Radon gas is invisible; it has no odor or taste. Its presence in the interior of buildings has been found to cause lung cancer. However, most radon found in buildings poses no direct threat to human life because the range of concentration is generally below the minimum safe level.

Although currently no federal requirements exist regarding disclosure or even testing for radon gas, it's a potentially serious health issue and one that's receiving more attention. Be aware of radon levels in your rental units and check with local authorities for more information about the prevalence of radon and appropriate precautions you should take to avoid radon exposure. (Florida and New Jersey have been particularly aggressive in addressing the radon problem.) Be sure to check with your local authorities for any specific disclosure requirements and always test if you discover that radon levels are high in your area.

Although radon may be found in all types of homes and buildings throughout the United States, it's more likely to occur in the lower levels of tightly-sealed, energy-efficient buildings, where insulation limits the flow of air from the inside to the outside and ventilation is poor.

Testing for radon

The only way to know whether your property has radon at unhealthy levels is to conduct short-term and/or long-term radon testing. Fortunately, radon tests are inexpensive and easy to use. The quickest way to test for radon is with a short-term test, which remains in your home anywhere from 2 to 90 days, depending on the device. Long-term tests remain in your home for more than 90 days. Because radon levels tend to vary from day to day and season to season, a long-term test is more likely to tell you your home's year-round average radon level than a short-term test.

You have two choices when testing for radon:

- **Do it yourself.** Do-it-yourself radon test kits are available in hardware stores, and some laboratories provide kits through mail order. Make sure you get one that meets EPA standards or your state's requirements — the test kit usually says so on the package. The price of a simple, short-term test kit starts at about $10 (or about $20 for a long-term kit) and includes the cost of having a laboratory analyze the test. Discounted test kits are available from the National Safety Council by calling 800-767-7236.

- **Hire a professional.** For information on the detection and removal of radon, you can call the EPA National Radon Hotline at 800-767-7236 or visit the EPA website at www.epa.gov/radon. This website has contacts for state agencies that regulate radon, plus information on finding a qualified radon reduction provider.

If your tests reveal radon in one particular unit of an apartment building, have all the other units tested immediately and notify all other tenants in the building of the problem promptly. Remember that even if your radon test shows low radon levels in one unit, other parts of the building may have high levels.

Repairing a radon problem

Fixing a radon problem usually involves repairs to the building. Therefore, you as the building owner, not your tenant, are responsible for having this work done. If your property has high radon levels, you can take steps to see that the problem is fixed by installing equipment, such as fans, blowers, and ducts, to reduce radon gas levels. The EPA advises that radon reduction costs between $800 and $2,500 for a single-family home, with an average cost of $1,200. For a larger rental property, the costs depend on the size and other characteristics of the building.

Radon reduction work generally requires a trained professional. To find out which radon reduction system is right for a building and how much those repairs will cost, consult a professional radon contractor. The EPA and many states have programs set up to train or certify radon professionals. Look online for your state radon office, which can provide a list of individuals who've completed state or federal programs. It can also provide a list of EPA-approved radon *mitigators,* or reduction specialists, in your state.

Sexual offenders

All 50 states have a version of *Megan's Law,* legislation that requires certain convicted sexual offenders to register with local law enforcement, which maintains a database on the whereabouts of registered sex offenders and often makes this information available to the public.

Megan's Law is named after 7-year-old Megan Nicole Kanka of Hamilton Township, New Jersey, who was raped and murdered in the summer of 1994 by a convicted child molester who was living in her neighborhood without her parents' knowledge. Less than 60 days after Megan's abduction, New Jersey passed Megan's Law, which required making information about the presence of convicted sex offenders in local neighborhoods available to the public.

In 1996, a federal version of this crime prevention law was passed, requiring the Federal Bureau of Investigation (FBI) to keep a national database of all persons convicted of sexual offenses against minors and violent sexual offenses against anyone. Prison officials are required to inform convicted sex offenders of their legal obligation to register with state law enforcement authorities. The state agencies are required to give local law enforcement and the FBI the registered addresses for each convicted sex offender. Local law enforcement authorities are then permitted to release the collected information as necessary to protect the public, but active community notification isn't mandatory.

Unfortunately, states aren't very consistent in their efforts to maintain this database and make it available. The federal law allows each state to decide how to use and distribute the database information. The three options are

- ✔ **Widespread notification with easy access:** This option allows notification to the public, including methods such as posting the names and addresses on the Internet or on a CD-ROM.

- ✔ **Selective notification with limited access:** This alternative allows notification only to those groups most at risk, such as schools and day-care centers.

- ✔ **Restricted notification with narrow access:** This option allows access only for a particular name or address.

Although registration is mandatory, often the addresses provided aren't verified or the convicted sex offender may move and fail to reregister at his new address. Also, the accuracy of this database can vary widely based on the age of the information.

Some states require property owners or managers to provide a disclosure statement to each tenant advising her of the availability of the Megan's Law database. Whether you're required by state law to give your tenant a Megan's Law disclosure, if you're ever asked by a prospective renter about Megan's Law, be sure to refer her to local law enforcement authorities and make a written and dated note of the conversation for your files. For specific information on the requirements of Megan's Law in your state, call your local law enforcement agency, contact the Parents for Megan's Law (PFML) hotline at 888-ASK-PFML (888-275-7365), or check www. parentsformeganslaw.org.

Chapter 10

Eenie, Meenie, Miney, Mo: Selecting Your Tenants

. . . .

In This Chapter

▶ Recognizing the value of proper tenant screening and written criteria for your process

▶ Confirming your applicants' information

▶ Informing applicants of the outcome

▶ Knowing the laws surrounding fair housing

. . . .

*W*hen you own rental property, one of your most important tasks is screening and selecting tenants. Because the process of screening tenants is time-consuming, you need to have a system in place for doing it efficiently.

Basically, for tenant selection and screening, you develop and use objective, written tenant selection criteria; consistently screen all applicants against these minimum criteria; and select the first qualified tenant based on your review.

Even after you've been managing rental properties for many years, you still won't be able to just look at a rental application and know whether the applicant is qualified. But with a system, tenant screening really isn't that difficult; it just requires assertiveness, diligence, and patience. You have to check the prospect's references, credit history, income sources or assets, stability of income, and rental history. And you can't cut corners. Selecting a bad tenant is much worse than having a vacant rental unit. So choose your tenants wisely and profit in the long run.

Another critical part of choosing your tenants is making sure you handle the selection process without bias, abiding by all fair housing regulations. This concept can be a murky issue, but it's an important one you need to pay attention to, no matter what your situation, so that you're not slapped with a discrimination lawsuit. The guidance I provide in this chapter helps you navigate these unfamiliar waters with ease.

Understanding the Importance of Screening

If you're like many rental property owners, you may be thinking, "Screening? Isn't that just a waste of time? After all, I trust my gut instinct when I meet people. I know which ones are good and which ones are trouble." Although verifying all the information on your prospective tenant's rental application does take time, it's time well spent. Relying on your instincts is inaccurate, arbitrary, and illegal.

To increase your chances of finding a stable, long-term tenant and avoiding charges of discrimination, your tenant selection criteria and screening process must be clear, systematic, and objective. Put this process in writing to ensure you apply it consistently and fairly to *all* applicants.

Establishing solid tenant selection criteria and performing a thorough tenant screening process doesn't guarantee a good tenant, but it does significantly improve your odds of finding one.

Setting up a systematic screening process is particularly critical if you own only a single rental or a small, multi-unit rental property. *Professional tenants* (people who go from property to property damaging the units and/or not paying rent) are experienced and shrewd. They know that the large, professionally managed rental properties have detailed and thorough screening procedures that attempt to verify every single item on their rental applications. If certain items don't check out, the professional property manager doesn't just trust her feelings on the prospective tenant. Professional tenants know that small rental property owners are easier targets because the novice owner is more likely to bend or ignore the rules than the professional.

Sometimes the mere mention of the tenant screening process is enough to make the prospect fidget and shift into the classic "I'm just looking" mode. Don't rush a prospect or allow one to hurry you through the tenant screening and selection process. Hold your needs in check. If the property is sitting empty with a mortgage payment due and you haven't had any takers, you feel anxious when a prospect surfaces. You may be inclined to accept any applicant, but don't do it. Take a breath and remember that you developed the minimum screening criteria, and now you must follow them. The wrong decision can be financially devastating, particularly if you have just a couple of rental units with monthly debt payments.

Establishing Tenant Selection Criteria

Tenant selection criteria are written standards that you use to evaluate each prospect's qualifications as a tenant. Determine your exact minimum qualifications and adhere to them. Of course, your written criteria can't be discriminatory or violate any federal, state, or local fair housing laws. (I explain how to avoid housing discrimination complaints later in this chapter.)

These criteria help you treat all applicants fairly to avoid claims of discrimination. Written guidelines are also useful as an objective evaluation technique to minimize the chance that you may be swayed by a charming prospect or a convincing explanation and find yourself lowering your standards and allowing a not-so-desirable tenant to occupy your valuable rental property.

The following sections break down the importance of tenant selection criteria and how you can develop your own.

Why having criteria is important

Giving all prospective tenants an overview of your rental screening procedure and requirements upfront lets them know exactly what you're looking for in a qualified rental applicant. Because these criteria are the minimum standards you accept, prospects know why their application may be rejected.

Developing your own tenant selection criteria has several benefits:

- ✔ **Rental applicants know you're aware of and comply with all fair housing laws.** You want to make sure your tenants know that you'll evaluate them objectively and fairly and that you promote equal opportunities in housing.

- ✔ **Rental applicants understand that rental activity and the preparation for it are dynamic processes.** Certain units may or may not be available even within the same day for legitimate business reasons. Outlining this policy and maintaining good records can minimize accusations of discrimination.

- ✔ **Rental applicants are aware that you abide by the reasonable occupancy limits suggested by most federal and state standards, while being conscious of the unit's limitations.** With the high cost of housing in many areas, some tenants want a smaller rental unit; you need to make sure that your property can handle the intended number of occupants while complying with standards.

- ✔ **Rental applicants know what to expect from your process of evaluating applications.** They know that you thoroughly verify the information on all applications, that the process takes one or two days, and that you charge an application fee to cover your costs for the screening process.

- ✔ **Rental applicants realize that you evaluate everyone applying for your unit consistently and fairly.** They can review your requirements and evaluate their own qualifications to see whether applying is even worth their time and, if you require, the payment of an application fee.

More than 90 percent of your applicants are going to be good tenants who pay their rent on time, take good care of their homes, and treat you and their neighbors with respect. You just need to carefully guard against those few bad apples, so don't hesitate to deny prospects who don't meet your standards.

How to create your criteria

To establish your tenant selection criteria, review what you're looking for in a tenant. Your notion of the ideal tenant may differ from someone else's, but here are five important traits to look for:

- ✔ Someone who'll be financially responsible and always pay his rent on time
- ✔ Someone who'll respect and treat the property as if it were his own
- ✔ Someone who'll be a good neighbor and not cause problems
- ✔ Someone who'll be stable and likely to renew his lease
- ✔ Someone who'll leave the premises in a condition the same as or better than he found it

To get the best results in selecting your tenants and ensure your rental prospects understand your tenant selection criteria, develop a *Statement of Rental Policy,* which is a formal, written statement explaining your screening criteria. Be prepared to defend the reasons for each requirement.

Pop in the CD or click the link in the table of contents to access a sample Statement of Rental Policy. Your policy standards may be more or less stringent, depending on your rental market and experience. But no matter what, you need to be sure your standards comply with all state and local laws. I strongly advise having a local attorney who specializes in landlord-tenant law review your Statement of Rental Policy in advance.

Give your Statement of Rental Policy to every applicant over the age of 18 (as well as emancipated minors) along with the rental application. If you have a multi-unit property with an office, clearly post the policy where all applicants can see it. If you don't have an office, insert the policy in an acrylic or similar holder and place it in clear view on the rental unit's kitchen counter or another area where all prospects can see it as they walk through.

You aren't required to provide your rental prospects with copies of your tenant selection criteria, but doing so is a good practice. Although you must offer all prospects rental applications and process each one you receive, you can benefit when prospects make their own decisions not to apply for your rental based on the criteria you've set up. The key is to follow these criteria without exception and have the information available if you're challenged.

Some rental property owners feel more comfortable discussing the tenant selection criteria right from the first rental inquiry call (which I cover in Chapter 8), whereas others wait and distribute copies only to those individuals who actually apply. You need to decide which policy works best for you and then apply it consistently.

Always be very thorough when you perform tenant screening and use the same process with all applicants. That includes your policy of discussing your standards with some tenants on the phone but with others only when they meet you to view the property. You run the risk of being charged with illegal discrimination if you vary your screening process and/or deviate from your written standards for certain applicants. Many legally acceptable reasons to deny a rental application exist, but be sure that your requirements are clearly understood and are followed consistently just to be safe.

The fact that you carefully prescreen all prospects is a positive factor not only for you but also for your rental applicants, your current tenants, and your neighbors. In fact, you have a responsibility to your current tenants to weed out the unqualified prospects with a track record of disrupting the neighbors everywhere they go. Good rental prospects appreciate the fact that their neighbors had to meet your high standards, too.

Doing the right thing is the first step in avoiding litigation, but documenting every step of the way is necessary so you have written evidence to help defend yourself if litigation can't be avoided.

Verifying Rental Applications

Bad tenants don't walk around with the word *deadbeat* printed on their foreheads. The tenant screening process requires you to be a detective, and all good detectives verify each fact and take thorough notes. You want to ensure that the prospect meets your minimum standards as outlined in your Statement of Rental Policy (see the preceding section). The following sections explain what info from the rental application you need to confirm before allowing a tenant to move in.

I recommend that you use a Rental Application Verification Form, like the one available on the CD or via the link in the table of contents, to collect and review the necessary information that allows you to properly evaluate your applicant's qualifications.

Keep copies of all rental applications, the corresponding Rental Application Verification Forms, credit reports, and all other documentation for both accepted *and* rejected applicants for at least four years. That way if anyone ever claims you discriminated against her, your best defense will be your own records, which clearly indicate that you had legal rental criteria and applied them consistently.

Confirming identity

The first step you should take in verifying a rental application is to personally meet each prospective adult tenant if you can. Require each prospect to show you a current, government-issued photo ID so you can confirm that each applicant is providing you with the correct name and current address. (*Note:* Government-issued photo IDs can include reliable identification from other countries.) Advise your applicant that if you approve his application, you'll need a photocopy of his ID to keep in his tenant file. Initial the rental application to record that you did indeed verify this information.

Inquire about any discrepancies between the application and the ID. Even if the explanation seems reasonable, be sure to write down the new information. Maybe an old address appears on the photo ID, which you can check out further through a credit reporting agency.

Having a photocopy of the ID for each adult tenant can be very important if a dispute concerning the tenant's identity arises in the future. In these situations, you need to be able to clearly show that you positively identified the tenant upon move-in. You could face a possible issue regarding timing, however, because someone may argue that you denied an application based on his appearance on his ID, attached to his application. Thus, it's wise to make copies after you approve the application.

Applicants from outside the local area applying electronically is becoming increasingly common. In such cases, require that the application be notarized so you have more assurance that the applicant is who he says he is.

Going over occupancy guidelines

Take a look at the rental application information provided by the prospective tenant concerning the number of persons planning to occupy your property to ensure that the anticipated use is within your established occupancy guidelines.

One of a property manager's major concerns is excessive wear and tear of the rental unit. Clearly, the greater the number of occupants in a unit, the greater the possibility for wear and tear. Unfortunately, questions about occupancy have no simple answers. Landlords are interested in how restrictive their rules can be without causing discrimination against families. Larger households have a tendency to include children; therefore, fair housing agencies are interested in minimum occupancy standards set by landlords. For example, the federal Department of Housing and Urban Development (HUD) guidelines state that property managers can likely limit occupancy to two individuals per bedroom. However, you must follow state and local restrictions as well. In California, for example, the state's Department of Fair Employment and Housing has formulated the *2 + 1 minimum occupancy standard guideline,* which states that a property manager must allow at least two individuals per bedroom, plus an additional occupant for the unit. In other words, three individuals may occupy a one-bedroom unit, five individuals may occupy a two-bedroom unit, and so on. These guidelines aren't safe harbors, however, because the agency may expect a higher limit for unusually large units.

Contact your local or state housing agency for information on its occupancy regulations and remember that you must always apply the most generous occupancy standard.

In addition to occupancy standards, you also have to consider maximum occupancy limits. These restrictions are usually set by state and local health and safety boards or building codes based on the square footage or size of the unit and its number of bedrooms and bathrooms. The maximum occupancy permitted under these codes is often as high as seven persons in a one-bedroom unit, but try to keep the occupancy of your unit closer to the minimum than the maximum.

Unless you have a more generous state or local requirement, I recommend using the 2 + 1 minimum occupancy standard guideline. Although federal and most state and local occupancy standards allow a more restrictive policy, the burden of proof is on the property owner. If you feel you have a legitimate basis — meaning a supportable, nondiscriminatory business reason — for having a more restrictive occupancy standard, hire a consultant and have her make an independent evaluation and recommendation.

Pregnancy is often included in familial status protection. Don't deny a household based on the projected number of occupants when a child is born in the future. It's also wise to address in your policy the issue of a violation of occupancy standards by the addition of any minor. Otherwise, your standards will become meaningless. Consider having a rule that allows the occupants to stay until the end of their lease or a certain number of months, whichever is longer.

Investigating rental history

You need to confirm all applicants' rental history. To do so, contact their current landlord and go through the questions on the rental history portion of the Rental Application Verification Form. When you first contact the current landlord, listen carefully to his initial reaction and let him tell you about the applicant if he decides to do so.

Asking for references from two previous landlords on all applicants is a good practice. Some applicants may provide you with letters of reference or even copies of their credit reports. This behavior often occurs in many competitive rental markets, where only the prepared tenants have a chance to get a quality property. Although the more information you have, the better the decision you can usually make, carefully evaluate the authenticity of any documents your prospects provide. Accept these papers but always perform your complete tenant screening process to independently verify all information.

Current or prior landlords may not be entirely forthcoming with answers to many of your questions. Most likely, they're concerned that they'll have some liability if they provide any negative or subjective information. If the information you receive from the current landlord about your applicant is primarily negative, you may not need to check with any prior landlords. However, be wary that the current landlord may not be entirely honest; he may be upset with the tenant for leaving his property or he may not say anything bad about a problem tenant so that he can get the tenant out of his property and into yours.

When a current or prior landlord isn't overly cooperative, try to gain his confidence by providing him with some information about yourself and your rental property. If you're still unable to build rapport, try to get him to at least answer the most important questions objectively and preferably in writing. You can offer to send (by fax or e-mail) a list of short questions that he can choose to answer or not. Ask questions like these:

> ✔ Did the residents pay rent on time? If not, how many times were they late?
>
> ✔ Were there noise complaints?
>
> ✔ Does there appear to be excessive damage?

The old standby question of "Would you rent to them again?" is now considered subjective and therefore possibly discriminatory. You're better off not asking it.

Another useful screening tool is to request that each prospective tenant provide copies of his water and utility bills for the past year. Doing so verifies prior addresses and gives you an idea whether the applicant pays bills on time. (A rental prospect who can't pay utility bills in a timely manner is very likely to have trouble paying your rent.) You may also want to inquire with local law enforcement to see whether its records show any complaints at a tenant's prior address.

Validating income sources

Although credit reporting agencies may provide information on your applicant's employment or other sources of income, they typically don't have all the information you need to properly evaluate this extremely important qualification criterion.

Independently verify the information and phone number the applicant puts on her application if you have any doubts about their authenticity. You may have reason for concern if an employer is a major corporation and the telephone isn't answered in a typical and customary business manner, for example. You also need to be careful that you confirm the sensitive questions about compensation and stability of employment only with an appropriate employer representative.

Occasionally, you may find that an employer doesn't verify any information over the phone. So be prepared to send letters requesting the pertinent info and include a self-addressed, stamped envelope, or see if the employer will send the info by fax or e-mail to speed up the process. If the employer will only respond by mail, be sure to tell your rental prospect that you may have a delay in providing her with the results of your tenant screening process.

Your applicant should provide you with proof of her employment or other sources of income. This proof may be in the form of recent pay stubs, bank account statements, and other proof of income or assets. No matter how strong the information is, verify it directly with the employer or the other source of income.

Always require written verification of all sources of income that an applicant uses to meet your income qualification requirements. If you can't verify the income, you don't have to include it in your calculations to determine whether the applicant meets your minimum income requirements. Keep the following points in mind as you verify income:

- ✔ **For an applicant who relies on sales, commission income, or bonuses, review at least six consecutive months of pay stubs.** Of course, the best policy is to require all applicants with any income other than salary to provide copies of their signed tax returns for the last two years. Although you must be careful to determine that it's an authentic document, I have yet to find a rental prospect who overstates annual income on a tax return.

- ✔ **Pay close attention to applicants who seem to be overqualified or anxious to be approved and take possession of your rental unit.** Remember the old saying, "If it sounds too good to be true, it probably is." This adage definitely applies in the world of rental property, so keep it in mind at all times.

- ✔ **Be particularly careful of applicants who seem to have plenty of cash to pay your security deposit and first month's rent but who don't have verifiable sources of income that seem consistent with their spending patterns.** The applicant may be involved in illegal activity, and you may need to evict him later at considerable expense and loss of income. Rental property owners can even lose their properties under certain circumstances if they fail to take action to eliminate the source of illegal activity on their property.

Several states and local jurisdictions have laws prohibiting a rental property owner from denying an applicant because he receives public assistance. California has gone further to include source of income as a state-protected class, which means you can't have a requirement that the applicant must be employed but simply that he has legal and verifiable income or financial resources to meet your stated requirements.

Traditionally, the source of income protection was to guard against discrimination of individuals who receive governmental assistance, but it's been expanded to include limitations on landlords who want to offer favorable terms to certain individuals based on their employment.

If you're in an area where source of income is a protected class, you may find you're violating fair housing laws if you have policies that favor employees of certain companies or if you favor specific types of employment — some property owners offer discounts to teachers, police, firefighters, and similar occupations. Also, you may find that some screening companies give extra "points" for length of employment. That practice would be a problem in a state that provides source of income protection.

Finally, be aware that some states include government subsidy payments as part of their source of income protection. In those states, all landlords are required to be open to renting to persons with government vouchers that pay for part of the rent.

If it looks too good to be true, it probably is!

I once managed a large rental property in a major city. I regularly visited the property and performed an inspection of both the physical aspects and the rental office procedures. One area of ongoing examination was the new rental application, which I reviewed to ensure that it was being properly completed by each prospect and that the tenant screening process was being applied uniformly.

During one of my visits, I reviewed an application for a one-bedroom apartment that was in the process of being screened. The on-site manager spoke very highly of this young person who had just graduated from high school, was looking for his first apartment, and listed an income of $750 per week. The manager then told me how, with more than $3,000 per month in income, this applicant was financially qualified.

Having been in rental management for many years, I was curious about the weekly income, so I took a look at the application and noticed that the individual listed the local sports facility as his employer. Sure enough, upon subsequent inquiry of the employer and then the prospect, it became apparent that the applicant did indeed earn $750 per week. The problem was that he earned this amount only during the six months of the professional baseball season and only in the two weeks per month that the local team played games in town. This situation is a reminder of the importance of thoroughly inquiring into and verifying all claimed income or assets.

Reviewing credit history

You can and should check out an applicant's credit history by obtaining a *credit report.* This document shows all current and previous credit cards and loans, with rating information on the timeliness of payments when due, plus all public record entries such as bankruptcy and judgment. Through a credit report, you can figure out whether an applicant has been late or delinquent in paying her rent or other living expenses.

What to look for in a credit history

Following is a list of what to consider when reviewing a credit history:

- ✔ **A pattern of financial responsibility:** You want your prospective tenant to have a history of prudent or conservative spending. Avoid applicants who seem to be using excessive credit and living beyond their means. If they move into your property and experience even a temporary loss of income due to illness or a job situation, you may be the one with an unexpected income loss as a result!

- ✔ **An accurate address:** You want to be able to verify prior living situations, so carefully compare the addresses contained on the credit report to the information provided on the rental application. Under the federal Fair Credit Reporting Act (FCRA), if you're notified by your consumer credit report provider of an address discrepancy, ask the rental prospect for an explanation. Maybe she was temporarily staying with a family member or simply forgot about one of her residences. As the prospective landlord, you need to have reasonable procedures to investigate and form a reasonable belief of the applicant's identity. Of course, be sure to contact prior landlords and ask all the questions on the Rental Application Verification Form just to make sure the applicant didn't neglect to tell you about that residence for a reason.

- ✔ **A false Social Security number:** You want to make sure you're reviewing the credit report of your actual applicant. People with poor credit or tenant histories have been known to steal the identity of others, particularly their own children, by using someone else's Social Security number. One way to prevent this problem is to make sure your credit reporting service provides a Social Security number search. (Check out the nearby sidebar for more info.)

You must keep information obtained in credit reports strictly confidential and can't give it to any third parties. With the growing problem of identity theft, you need to make sure you keep all tenant and prospect personal information in a secure file. In some states, the applicant is entitled to a copy of her credit report upon request, and federal law allows anyone denied credit on the basis of a credit report to obtain a free copy of the report.

Asking for a Social Security number or not?

Problem: Some rental property owners or managers require applicants to provide a Social Security number (SSN). However, such a policy may risk a fair housing complaint because only U.S. citizens or immigrants authorized to work in the United States can obtain an SSN. Many people (like those with student visas) simply don't qualify for one. Also, with the increased concern about identity theft and privacy rights, some of your rental prospects who *do* have an SSN may not feel comfortable providing it on your rental application.

Solution: An alternative to the standard SSN can be an Individual Taxpayer Identification Number (ITIN), which is issued upon request by the IRS to anyone earning income while living in the United States. Credit reporting bureaus can use the ITIN the same way they use the SSN to provide you with information on your applicant's credit history.

Problem: A person isn't required to have an SSN or ITIN, so failing to screen without one could have a discriminatory "effect" based on national origin. Therefore, you should consider having a method of screening based on all other factors besides SSN or ITIN.

Solution: Some screening companies indicate that such screening isn't possible, but it's really a matter of software. The ultimate result is that the applicant may not qualify — not because you didn't screen based on a lack of SSN or ITIN but rather because of a lack of available information when screening was done without them.

Problem: Another concern with the SSN is that some credit reporting bureaus provide rental owners and property managers with eviction information that may be inaccurate or misleading. The credit bureaus' databases often include information about every eviction filed against an applicant, regardless of whether the matter was ultimately resolved in the tenant's favor. Being confronted with an erroneous eviction filing can be very disconcerting for falsely accused rental applicants.

Solution: If your applicant has an eviction filing on her credit report, you need to inquire further and see whether it was filed in error, dismissed, or resolved in her favor. In the meantime, know that most credit reporting bureaus are making efforts to ensure their individual databases reflect actual court judgments and not just filings.

Where to get your applicant's credit history

A credit report contains valuable information that can assist you in determining whether your rental applicant meets your resident selection criteria. However, the federal Fair Credit Reporting Act (FCRA) has very complicated restrictions on the proper use of this sensitive information. To get a consumer credit history, you need to contact a tenant screening service in your area. You can find many companies that work specifically with the rental housing industry by going through your local NAA affiliate or your local IREM chapter.

The info you'll receive from the tenant screening service is based on the databases and records of the three dominant consumer reporting agencies:

✔ **Equifax:** www.equifax.com

✔ **Experian:** www.experian.com

✔ **TransUnion:** www.transunion.com

With the wide choice of tenant screening services available, you may have a hard time deciding exactly what you need. I recommend you use a service that offers the following:

✔ A retail or consumer credit report

✔ An eviction search or tenant history

✔ An automated cross-check of addresses

✔ A Social Security number or Individual Taxpayer Identification Number search

✔ An employment or income and prior landlord reference verification

✔ A criminal records search (not mandatory, but highly advisable if your tenant screening service can search records for the area within the United States where your prospect has previously resided)

Be advised that even if you use a tenant screening service to conduct all or part of the screening process, you're still responsible for any legal deficiencies. Make sure the company you hire follows the written criteria you've approved. (I explain how to establish tenant-selection criteria earlier in this chapter.)

The Internet is quickly changing the tenant screening procedures for many rental property owners. Consumer credit reports, tenant history, and criminal records search services are now available from your computer in a matter of seconds. This instant access often allows you to approve your applicant in minutes or hours, which can be a strong competitive advantage. Many tenant screening firms are entering this electronic market locally and nationally, and all offer impressive services designed to save you time and help you fill your vacancies faster. Using technology can improve the efficiency of your information collection for tenant screening and provide you with more details to make a better decision. However, don't rely strictly on computers and forget to personally contact past landlords, verify the applicant's income and employment, or consider your own dealings with the applicant. Rental property ownership and management is still, and always will be, a people business.

What charges are involved

The cost of a tenant screening credit report varies widely. On an individual basis, tenant screening can run between $30 and $50. When you start adding an investigative or criminal records search in multiple areas, this expense can go much higher. Establish the specific level of screening services you want and then be consistent to avoid discrimination claims.

If you join a tenant screening service, you can get discounts of 50 percent or more on each credit report. Some companies offer memberships with minimum monthly fees. But only owners of multiple rental properties who run at least one tenant screening per month really benefit from membership. If you run fewer than a dozen tenant screenings annually, you'll usually find it cheaper to just pay a higher fee per report.

If you own just a few rental units, you may find that joining your local NAA affiliate is a better deal than paying $30 to $50 per tenant screening. Not only do you have easy access to reasonably priced tenant screening services and consumer credit reports through your local NAA affiliate, but as a member you can take advantage of the NAA's education opportunities, publications, and forms.

Click the link in the table of contents or pop in the CD to find a complete list of NAA affiliates and information on the organization's educational programs and professional designations.

Charging an applicant for tenant screening or a consumer credit report if you don't actually run one is illegal. If you receive a large number of rental applications, review them in the order you receive them, one at a time. If the first applicant fails to qualify, begin processing the next application. Check your state laws to make sure you don't exceed any legal maximum charges and be sure to return any unused credit check fees to those individuals for whom you don't run the credit check. Try to keep your tenant screening fees as low as possible and set them based on the fees paid to a tenant screening company, the value of your time or salary expended, and any indirect expenses (such as phone calls) for checking rental history. Of course, always be aware of your state or local laws regarding tenant charges.

Checking criminal history

Rental property owners' liability is increasing all the time. One area of particular concern is criminal acts committed by tenants. In most states, rental property owners have no legal duty to ask about or investigate the criminal backgrounds of applicants or current tenants.

Since the events of September 11, 2001, federal, state, and local law enforcement have made great efforts to standardize reporting of criminal activity. However, in many areas of the country, only a county-level criminal records search is possible. Additionally, many states only indicate felony conviction records and don't list convictions for misdemeanors involving violence, sexual misconduct, or dishonesty.

What's in a name?

I've served as an expert witness in many interesting litigation matters concerning real estate. One of my more memorable assignments was to consult with the Legal Aid Society of Alameda County, based in Oakland, California. It had received complaints from several people who claimed they were being repeatedly denied rental housing even though they had excellent jobs and perfect credit.

After a brief investigation, it became obvious that the problem was a particular Bay Area tenant screening service that wasn't accurately identifying rental applicants. When an applicant with a fairly common name was run through its database, the company provided the property owner with negative information on evictions and poor credit patterns. Unfortunately, because its information wasn't carefully screened and verified, the data wasn't applicable to the actual applicant. Some very responsible and qualified applicants were turned down simply because they had the same name as an individual with a very poor credit report.

The lesson? Always verify an applicant's name, Social Security number or Individual Taxpayer Identification Number, and several former addresses to ensure you're using the correct information in your screening efforts. Compare the Social Security card (if available) with information showing the approximate date and general geographic location of its issuance. You know you have a problem if your applicant is over 40 and was born and raised along the East Coast, yet the credit reporting agency indicates that the Social Security card was originally issued in Arizona in the last few years.

When reviewing an applicant's criminal history, you need to consider convictions only and not simply arrests. Because the U.S. legal system is based on the idea that someone is innocent until proven guilty, you should deny only those applicants who have criminal convictions. However, it's not really that simple. The federal Fair Housing Amendments Act considers past drug addiction a disability, and prior drug-use felony convictions alone may not be sufficient grounds to deny an applicant. (Fortunately, current drug use or the sale, manufacturing, or distribution of illegal substances isn't protected under federal fair housing laws.) Some states also limit the ability to deny housing to registered sex offenders, while HUD doesn't. Properties subject to federal subsidized housing programs may have a defense against state discrimination claims based on the HUD program requirements for criminal screening. Always seek legal advice if you have any questions about the findings of a criminal records search.

With many tenants moving from area to area, performing a thorough criminal records search in every location the applicant may have lived can be cost-prohibitive. Many property owners request a criminal records search only if the applicant indicates that he's been convicted of (or pled guilty or no contest to) a felony or a misdemeanor involving violence, sexual misconduct, or dishonesty. Be diligent in looking for any indications that may provide a clue to possible criminal activity, such as gaps in rental history while the prospect was incarcerated.

Consistency is the key to all tenant screening activity, including your efforts to minimize the chances of renting to someone who may present a direct threat to the health or safety of others. You need to establish a policy of either inquiring about past criminal history or running a criminal records search on *all* rental applicants to ensure that you apply your screening process uniformly.

Talking with all personal references

Although you may expect that all of a prospect's personal references share only glowing comments about how lucky you'd be to have the applicant as your new tenant, investing the time to call all the prospect's references is important for several reasons. You may find someone who tells you that the applicant is her best friend but she never loans him money or lets him borrow her car. Plus, if you call the given references and find that the contacts are bogus, you can use this information as part of your overall screening of the applicant.

Consider having a clause in your rental criteria and application that states that the misrepresentation of screening information constitutes a basis for denial. You may even want to incorporate such a clause into your lease as a basis for eviction. Of course, the enforceability of such a statement depends on state eviction laws and the local judges who interpret them.

Dealing with guarantors

If your rental prospect doesn't meet the criteria outlined in your Statement of Rental Policy, you may consider approving her application if she provides a cosigner or *guarantor*. The guarantor needs to sign a Guarantee of Lease or Rental Agreement form; however, a guarantor must be financially qualified and screened or the guarantee is worthless.

Signing a separate Guarantee of Lease or Rental Agreement is better than asking the cosigner to simply sign the rental contract because doing so avoids any confusion about whether the cosigner lives in the unit if you need to regain physical possession with an eviction action.

You can access a sample Guarantee of Lease or Rental Agreement by clicking the link in the table of contents or popping in the CD.

Require your guarantor to complete a rental application, pay the application fee, and go through a verification of income screening. This process is similar to your procedure for the applicant except you don't need to verify rental or criminal history. Keep in mind that the guarantor won't actually be living at the unit and thus will have his own housing costs. So to ensure that the guarantor can meet all his own obligations and cover your tenant's rent in case of a default, you need to account for the guarantor's cost of housing before comparing it to your income requirements.

For example, if the proposed guarantor has a gross monthly income of $4,000 with a $1,000 mortgage payment, he has an adjusted gross income of $3,000. Assuming you have an income standard that requires the tenant to earn three times the monthly rent (and assuming the guarantor meets all your other screening criteria), this person can be the guarantor for your prospect as long as the rent doesn't exceed $1,000 per month. Or you could just establish a higher standard for guarantors, such as four or five times the rent or whatever you think provides you with reasonable security for payment.

An application approval could be conditioned upon the payment of an increased amount of security deposit instead of, or in addition to, a guarantor. Be sure to check applicable deposit laws to be sure that the amount doesn't exceed the maximum allowed.

Although a guarantor can be very important and can give you extra resources in the event of a rent default by your tenant, out-of-state guarantors aren't as valuable as in-state ones. The challenge you face is that, in many states, you're required to file a claim against the guarantor in the county in which the guarantor resides. This will likely require you to obtain an attorney who can file the lawsuit and appear in court in that court's jurisdiction. Enforcing the rental contract guarantee against an out-of-state party can be very difficult or even financially unfeasible.

Making your final decision

Selecting your tenant is one of the most important decisions you make as a rental property owner because choosing your tenant has a significant positive or negative impact on your success. Ideally, you've already established written tenant screening criteria and a system for evaluating the qualifications of your rental applicants; if you haven't, flip back to the previous sections in this chapter.

Although you need to carefully follow fair housing guidelines, never compromise your tenant screening criteria or allow yourself to be intimidated into accepting an unqualified applicant. HUD and state fair housing agencies have consistently ruled that rejecting an applicant who doesn't meet your objective tenant screening criteria isn't discrimination, even if the applicant belongs to a legally protected class.

Some fair housing advocates recommend that you have a policy of considering the applications in the order you receive them and accepting the first prospective tenant who meets your rental criteria. I feel that as long as you're consistent in your tenant selection methods that you should select the tenant who's best qualified. However, you need to be prepared for other qualified applicants who may feel they weren't treated properly. Clearly document your business reasons for selecting a certain applicant. Legitimate business reasons can include higher income, more assets, much better references, superior credit report, and a willingness to sign a longer-term lease.

If you use the first-qualified-applicant method, be sure to note on the application the date and time it was both submitted and approved, and indicate that from that point, the rental unit is no longer available. This information can be helpful if qualified applicants from protected classes claim you discriminated by accepting an application submitted after theirs or allege that you refused to show available units by claiming they were rented.

Some tenant screening services offer *risk scoring* of your applicant based on scoring models that they claim are designed to objectively predict an applicant's likelihood of fulfilling lease obligations. If you use one of these services, make sure you can meet the disclosure requirements of the federal Fair Credit Reporting Act (FCRA). Only use a tenant screening service that's willing to provide your denied applicants with a written, detailed notice of denial to rent that meets all FCRA requirements. If a credit score is used in setting material terms of credit or in taking adverse action, the FCRA requires you or your tenant screening service to disclose the tenant's credit score, the range of possible credit scores under the model used, the provider and the date of the credit score, and the factors that adversely affect the credit score ranked in their order of importance.

Notifying the Applicant of Your Decision

Rental property owners are legally allowed to choose among rental applicants as long as their decisions comply with all fair housing laws and are based on legitimate business criteria (see the preceding section to get an idea of what counts as a legitimate business reason). Regardless of whether you accept or reject an applicant, be sure to notify him promptly after you make your decision.

If you approve the applicant, contact him and arrange for a meeting and a walk-through of the unit prior to the move-in date. Don't notify the other qualified applicants that you've rented the property until the new tenant has signed all legal documents and you've collected all funds due upon move-in.

One of the most difficult tasks you face as a rental property owner is informing an applicant that you've denied his application. You obviously want to avoid an argument over the rejection, but even more important, you want to avoid a fair housing complaint based on the applicant's misunderstanding about the reasons for the denial.

If you deny an applicant, notify him in writing. If you notify the denied applicant by phone only, you may have difficulty giving all the required details and disclosures. A written notice of denial to rent avoids a situation in which the applicant may unintentionally (or sometimes intentionally) form the opinion that you're denying his application in a discriminatory manner and file a complaint with (HUD) or a state or local fair housing agency.

Using a Notice of Denial to Rent form to tell the applicant in writing of your decision is an excellent idea. This form helps you document the various and valid legal reasons for your rejection of the applicant. This simple checklist also allows you to provide the applicant with the information required by the FCRA. If you reject an applicant based on his credit report, the FCRA requires you to notify the applicant of his rights. You should provide the denied applicant with a letter containing the mandatory disclosures so that you have proof you complied with the law. (You must also provide this information even if you've approved the applicant but require him to pay a higher security deposit, only offer him a month-to-month rental agreement, or require a cosigner — see "Dealing with guarantors" earlier in this chapter for more on cosigners.)

If you're reading a hard-copy version of this book, you can find a sample Notice of Denial to Rent form on the accompanying CD. If you're reading a digital version, simply click the link in the table of contents to access the sample form.

Whether you use the Notice of Denial to Rent form or prefer to craft a rejection letter, make sure the document you send includes the following:

✔ The names, addresses, and phone numbers of all credit reporting agencies that provided you with information.

✔ A notice that the credit reporting agency only provides information about credit history, takes no part in the decision process, and can't give reasons for the rejection.

✔ A notice that the applicant has the right to obtain a free copy of the credit report from the credit agency if he requests it within 60 days of your rejection.

✔ A notice informing the applicant that he has the right to dispute the accuracy of the information on the report. He can also demand a reinvestigation or provide the credit reporting agency with a statement describing his position.

✔ A notice that if information was received from a person or company other than a credit reporting agency, the applicant has the right to make a written request within 60 days of receiving this notice for a disclosure of the nature of this information.

Keep a copy of all rejection letters for at least four years.

Avoiding Housing Discrimination Complaints

If you're in the rental housing business for long, you'll hear about a shocking settlement or award against a rental property owner for violating a fair housing law. Many of these awards or settlements can exceed $100,000 (and some have exceeded $1 million).

You may even have read about the facts of certain fair housing cases and thought to yourself that the defendants deserved to lose and that a discrimination case will never happen to you. That's probably true if you're an educated owner and you know and abide by all federal, state, and local fair housing laws. The problem arises when property owners are unaware that their policies or practices are considered to be discriminatory. For example, you may think that you're just being a courteous and caring landlord by showing only rental applicants with children your available units located on the ground floor. But not giving applicants without children the same treatment you give others can be a form of discrimination, even if that wasn't your intent.

Federal and state laws prohibit discrimination against certain protected classes in rental housing. These laws affect your tenant screening and selection process, and I cover the issues surrounding these laws in the following sections.

The ins and outs of fair housing

Discrimination is a major issue for rental property owners, and it has serious legal consequences for the uninformed. If you don't know the law, you may be guilty of various forms of discrimination and not even realize it until you've been charged.

The U.S. legal system acknowledges two types of fair housing discrimination:

  ✔ **Treating members of protected classes differently from the way you treat others who aren't members of that protected class:** For example, say you have two applicants with similar financial histories, tenant histories, and other screening criteria, but you charge one applicant who's a member of a certain protected class a larger security deposit. You may be subject to a fair housing discrimination inquiry or complaint on the basis of different treatment.

✔ **Treating all prospects equally, but having a disparate impact because of an individual's minority status:** If your occupancy standard policy is too restrictive, you may be accused of familial status discrimination based on *disparate impact,* which is when a policy is the same for all applicants but has a much different effect on certain applicants and essentially creates an additional barrier to rental housing for families. Although you've set an occupancy standard policy that's applied equally to all tenants, your policy may be deemed to discourage applicants with children. This scenario is an example of possible disparate impact.

The federal Fair Housing Act prohibits discrimination on the basis of race, color, religion, national origin, sex, familial status, and physical or mental handicap. Several states and many major cities have laws to protect individuals affected by other issues that aren't specifically protected under federal fair housing laws. Examples include age, occupation, educational status, medical status, sexual orientation, source of income, victims of sexual abuse, and physical body size.

Although several states still have laws prohibiting unmarried couples from living together, many prohibit any distinction based on marital status. The majority of states have very broad fair housing laws forbidding all arbitrary discrimination on the basis of an individual's personal characteristics or traits. Such laws can prohibit the use of someone's appearance as a basis for housing decisions. For instance, if someone has tattoos or piercings or wears clothing that could be construed to be typical of a gang member, you can't safely use that information as a reason for denial of the person's application. Always be sure to fully understand the fair housing requirements and limitations that apply to your rental property.

When renting your property, keep some of these specific pointers in mind:

✔ **Be careful not to inadvertently favor one sex as renters.** For example, some rental property owners may have the perception that male tenants aren't as clean or quiet as female tenants. Conversely, some owners with rental properties in rough areas may believe that male tenants are less susceptible to being victims of crime. As a result, these owners may attempt to restrict female tenants to upper-level rental units. Don't allow any stereotypes or assumptions to enter into your tenant selection criteria. Tenants should be allowed to choose any unit for which they are qualified.

✔ **Consider adding fair housing posters in another language if you have a rental unit in an area where a significant portion of the local population doesn't speak English.** HUD offers free fair housing posters in many different languages so that you can easily find one that's most applicable to your locale.

I include several of these fair housing posters on the CD. (If you're reading a digital version of this book, you can download the posters via the link in the table of contents.)

✔ **Pay attention to age-related issues.** Although the Fair Housing Act doesn't specifically state that age is a protected category, many states and localities have laws that directly address the issue of age. Whether someone is old or young, the age isn't the real focus; the applicant's ability to qualify under your rental criteria is. Typically, you can deny rental applicants younger than 18 but seeking to be treated as an adult, unless they're currently or were previously legally married, an active-duty member of the military, or emancipated by court order. In these cases, you must treat them just like any other adult rental applicant.

Following are three main exemptions to the *federal* fair housing laws:

✔ An owner-occupied rental property with four or fewer units.

✔ Single-family housing rented without the use of discriminatory advertising or without using an agent to facilitate or handle the leasing.

✔ Housing reserved exclusively for seniors that's intended for and solely occupied by persons 62 or older (which includes spouses and adult children but excludes caregivers and on-site employees). Also, HUD-certified seniors' properties where 80 percent or more of the households are occupied by at least one person who's 55. In both cases, the exemption is only against claims of age discrimination.

Many states, and even local governments, have passed their own legislation that may apply to your property and affect the aforementioned exemptions. Don't count on an exemption, and be sure to abide by all fair housing laws that may be applicable to your property, even if you think you're exempt. Abiding by all fair housing laws eliminates any potential complaints and is also simply the right thing to do.

Steering and chilling

Steering means to guide, or attempt to guide, a rental applicant toward living where you think she should live based on race, color, religion, national origin, sex, familial status, physical or mental handicap, or another protected class. Steering is an illegal act that deprives persons of their right to choose to rent where they want. HUD has clearly indicated that not showing or renting certain units to minorities is one form of steering. Another form according to HUD is the "assigning of any person to a particular section or floor of a building" based on any of the protected classes listed previously.

Rental property owners often have only good intentions when they suggest that a rental prospect with children see only rental units near the playground. However, you may not substitute your personal preferences but must offer the prospective tenant all the available units and let her decide completely on her own. Your failure to offer such an applicant an opportunity to see *all* available rental units is steering — and a violation of fair housing laws.

Steering can be subtle or direct. Some examples of steering include

✔ Limiting families or persons with disabilities to ground floor units

✔ Offering families or minorities only units near the playground or by the laundry room or elevator because noise makes these units less desirable

✔ Relegating families to certain buildings or sections of a building, or having separate family and adult buildings

A similar concept is known as *chilling,* which is making comments or establishing rules designed to discourage certain applicants from renting. Some examples of chilling include

✔ Pointing out property hazards to applicants with children that you don't point out to all applicants

✔ Showing only undesirable units in the hope that the applicant doesn't rent

✔ Questioning disabled or elderly applicants about their disabilities or whether they can care for themselves or should live alone

✔ Telling certain applicants something negative about the property that isn't true

Be very careful not to make any suggestions or comments that can be misinterpreted as steering or chilling. Give all applicants the same information on the area, the property, and the full range of units available so that they can decide for themselves which units they want to see.

Children

Federal and state legislation has virtually eliminated adult-only housing except for certain HUD-certified seniors' properties. I always recommend that rental property owners openly accept renters with children. Families tend to be more stable, and they're looking for a safe, crime-free, and drug-free environment in which to raise their children. Along with responsible pet owners, who also have difficulty finding suitable rental properties, families with children can be excellent, long-term renters. And typically the longer your tenants stay, the better your cash flow.

Some owners are concerned about renting to families with children because the property has hazards that may be dangerous for children. For example, the property may not have any safe areas for children to play. Although you may truly have only the children's best interests in mind, the parents have the right to decide whether the property is safe for their children. Of course, you do need to take steps to make your property as safe as possible by posting speed limit signs in your driveway or including restrictions on recreational use of driveways and parking areas.

Be careful not to discourage applicants with policies and guidelines for the conduct of children unless these rules are *safety-related*. For example, don't institute a policy against children riding bicycles on the property. Instead, you can have a policy that says *no one* is allowed to ride bicycles on the property. (This way, the policy doesn't discriminate against children; it's uniformly applied to all.) Avoid using any words that are obviously directed at children, such as *minors, toys, tricycles, diapers, playing,* and the like. Use terms like "all residents and guests," "personal property," "waterproof garments for controlling incontinence," and "recreational use." Make sure all your policies are age-neutral except for certain health and safety issues. For example, some states have specific laws requiring rental owners to have policies that, in order to use swimming pools or spas, children under 14 must be accompanied by an adult.

Charging applicants with children higher rents or higher security deposits than applicants without children is illegal, as is offering different rental terms, such as shorter leases, fewer unit amenities, or different payment options. The property's facilities must also be fully available for all tenants, regardless of age, unless a clear safety issue is involved.

Reasonable accommodations

The federal Fair Housing Act requires property owners to make reasonable accommodations for tenants with physical or mental handicaps (called *disabilities* in many state laws; the terms are interchangeable) so that they're able to enjoy the property on an equal basis with tenants who don't have disabilities. The cost of these accommodations usually involves a reasonable expenditure by the landlord, or the tenant may offer to make the accommodations at his expense or by contributing a portion of the overall cost if the expense is considerable. Requests for reasonable accommodations are valid if made verbally, but you should ask the tenant to make the request in writing. If that's not feasible, you can put the request in writing and have the tenant verify the information and sign or initial it.

The fair housing regulations state:

> "It shall be unlawful for any person to refuse to make reasonable accommodations in rules, policies, practices, or services, when such accommodations may be necessary to afford a handicapped person equal opportunity to use and enjoy a dwelling unit, including public and common areas."

You're required to make reasonable adjustments to your rules, procedures, or services upon request. You must refrain from assuming someone has a disability or inquiring if someone does. You must consider each request for a reasonable accommodation seriously.

Examples of reasonable accommodations that you may be required to offer include

- ✔ Providing a parking space that's wider and closer to the rental unit of a tenant with mobility impairments

- ✔ Arranging to read all management communications to a tenant with poor vision

- ✔ Allowing a tenant who receives income from a government agency to pay on a biweekly rather than monthly basis or allowing a change in the usual rent due date

Reasonable modifications

Federal law requires rental property owners to allow a tenant with disabilities the right to modify his living space at his own expense (except in project-based, HUD-subsidized housing, in which the landlord may be obligated to pay for reasonable modifications; see Chapter 21 for more on HUD-subsidized housing). The modifications can only be to the extent necessary to allow the resident an equal opportunity to use and enjoy the premises. If the modifications will make the unit unacceptable to the next tenant, the landlord may require that the current tenant agree to return the rental unit to its original condition upon vacating the property. The owner can also require the tenant to pay the funds necessary to perform the needed restoration into an interest-bearing escrow account.

Reasonable modifications that tenants may request to make at their expense include

- ✔ Ramps at the rental unit entry

- ✔ Lower light switches and the removal of doors or widening of doorways to allow for wheelchair access

- ✔ Grab bars or call buttons in bathrooms

- ✔ Lower kitchen cabinets and the removal of base cabinet doors

- ✔ Service animals allowed in the pool area, even though you don't permit other animals there (although arguably not *in* the pool because of health issues that make the accommodation unreasonable under the circumstances)

- ✔ Roll-in showers

The modifications must be reasonable. You can require the tenant to obtain your prior approval and ensure that the modification will be made in a workmanlike manner, including any necessary government approvals or permits. You can also require the tenant to provide verification that he fits the definition of a disabled person and that a disability-related need exists for the modification if the disability and the need aren't apparent. But you can't ask about the nature or extent of the specific disability that necessitates these changes.

Companion or service animals

If you have a no-pets policy, keep in mind that fair housing law requires rental property owners to make "necessary and reasonable accommodation." One specific common accommodation is not having any limitations or not discouraging occupancy by tenants who need a *support animal.* Companion or service animals that assist tenants with daily life activities aren't pets; they're exempt animals and must be allowed in all rental properties, regardless of any no-pet policies. Fair housing laws also prohibit you from requiring an animal or pet deposit or increasing the tenant's security deposit because she has a support animal. Further, you can't make any rules limiting the types or breeds of animals (for example, allowing German shepherds only) or an unreasonable size restriction. You can, however, establish reasonable rules of conduct for the animals and should note that the tenant is still responsible for any damages done by the animal.

Some tenants seek the accommodation of a companion animal based on their need for comfort or companionship, and federal law requires property owners and managers to grant the request if the tenant's claim is true and reasonable. The best method of determining reasonability is to obtain verification pursuant to the HUD and the U.S. Department of Justice (DOJ) guidelines from 2004. They provide that written verification can be submitted by a reliable third party, a peer support group, a nonmedical service agency, or the tenant's healthcare provider. The last verification method allowed is self-verification. This category usually applies to situations in which a tenant provides a landlord with copies of paperwork from the government, indicating that the tenant receives payments because she's disabled.

To avoid claims of discrimination or favoritism, set a consistent policy of requesting official verification before allowing any companion animals. Of course, like all potential housing discrimination issues, failing to consider a tenant request can lead to serious legal consequences.

Determining what's reasonable in the eyes of fair housing officials is always murky, so look at each request individually to make a proper decision. For example, most households only request one animal, but you may face situations in which more than one animal may be reasonable. If you're uncertain as to whether a particular request is reasonable, seek direction from local fair housing agencies or legal counsel whenever possible. Ask these representatives to provide you with their written opinion or send you a letter outlining their verbal directive; be sure to keep copies of this documentation in your rental files.

Americans with Disabilities Act

The Americans with Disabilities Act (ADA) has limited requirements for many rental property owners because it applies only to the public areas and not the private or common areas of residential properties. Under the ADA, all areas of a property to which the public is invited must be accessible by individuals with disabilities. For example, a rental property with an on-site office (and other public amenities, like rental unit models) must be accessible to persons with disabilities.

Note that common area amenities may become subject to the ADA by virtue of the landlord inviting the public to use them. Examples include a clubhouse used as a polling place, a pool used for YMCA swimming lessons, and so on. Thus, it is advisable to determine which amenities will be limited to use by tenants and guests and which (if any) will be open to the public.

The removal of existing physical barriers at the rental property owner's expense is required whenever it's "readily achievable and technically feasible." The ADA also establishes parking requirements if the residential property provides public parking, such as prospective resident spaces.

Often you'll be able to simply restripe your parking areas to provide the required parking, but be careful because many local municipalities have specific parking requirements for multi-unit rental properties. Before you make any changes, make sure your new parking layout meets the minimum parking requirements for your property zoning. Check with your local building and code enforcement office for details.

The ADA applies to all residential properties, even those built prior to the passage of the law. Owners of residential properties occupied prior to March 13, 1991, are required to remove barriers to accessibility, but they aren't required to make changes that may cause undue hardship. Owners of properties occupied after March 13, 1991, must comply with the ADA and the federal Fair Housing Act, too. Professional complainants seek out ADA violations in both residential and commercial rental properties, so know what you're responsible for accommodating.

If you have a rental property with public areas, you may want to consider using the services of a qualified contractor, architect, or engineer with specific ADA knowledge to conduct a physical assessment and evaluation of your property and make compliance recommendations. Also consult your rental housing legal advisor if you have any questions about ADA compliance. For more information on ADA requirements for residential rental property owners, visit the federal DOJ ADA website at www.ada.gov.

If your prospective tenant has a physical or mental disability that substantially limits one or more major life activities or if he has a record of having such a disability, you must allow him to make reasonable modifications to your property, including common areas, if necessary for him to use the rental housing. Conditions qualifying as *physical* or *mental disabilities* are evolving, but this term can include mobility, hearing, and visual impairments; chronic mental illness; chronic alcoholism; AIDS or AIDS-related illness; or mental retardation. Many state and local laws are expanding the definition of their protected categories, so be sure to check with legal counsel if you ever have any questions regarding the rights of your tenants under federal or state fair housing laws.

Sexual harassment

In the world of property management, *sexual harassment* occurs when you refuse to rent to a person who rejects your sexual advances or when you make life difficult for or harass a tenant who resists your unwanted advances. Most rental property owners understand the concern and find such behavior unconscionable. Yet this problem often arises when owners hire someone to assist them with the leasing, rent collection, or maintenance requirements at their properties. If the vendor or contractor commits sexual harassment, the owner is accountable because the offender is the employee or agent of the owner.

Make sure you have a clear written policy against sexual harassment, provide an open-minded procedure for investigating complaints, and conduct thorough and unbiased investigations that lead to quick corrective action if necessary.

Part III

The Brass Tacks of Managing Rentals

The 5th Wave

By Rich Tennant

"I'm well aware that I ask a lot from my rental applicants, Mr. Harvey. However, sarcasm is rarely required."

In this part . . .

Managing rental property involves a lot more than just managing the property itself. Working with tenants — from orienting a tenant to your rules prior to move-in to having the paperwork in order when a tenant moves out — is what you spend a huge chunk of your time doing. So the chapters in this part take you through that relationship step by step. I show you how to help tenants at move-in and move-out, increase the rent without losing your tenants, and retain the good tenants and deal with the bad ones. Chances are you can find the answer to any question you have about your tenants in this part.

Chapter 11

Moving In the Tenants

- -

- -

*A*fter selecting your new tenants, you still have to complete one very important step to ensure you establish a good landlord-tenant relationship: moving them into their new home. To guarantee that the tenants' move-in process goes smoothly, you need to hold a tenant orientation and rental property inspection meeting, which allows you to present the rental property and your ownership and management skills in the best possible light. You also need to make sure your new tenants understand and agree to the policies and rules you've established for the property.

In this chapter, I outline the important steps to start your landlord-tenant relationship off on the right foot, including scheduling the move-in date and the tenant orientation meeting, conducting the preoccupancy inspection and documenting the unit's conditions, providing important policies to tenants in a written format, and using creative ideas to welcome your tenants on move-in day.

Moving is very stressful for most people, and if your new tenant has a bad move-in experience, this feeling can last for months or even stay on her mind throughout the tenancy. The timing of the orientation is critical. On move-in day, there's a great deal of activity, and your tenant's mind is preoccupied. Her furniture is waiting to be unloaded, helpful friends and relatives are anxious to begin their tasks, and the new tenant has difficulty focusing on the details of her lease and the rules of occupancy. Try to schedule the brief orientation meeting at a less hectic time — usually before move-in day. Although you can't guarantee your new tenant a simple and painless move, you can take steps to ensure you're organized and ready to handle any complaints or concerns about her new home.

Establishing the Move-In Date

When you inform your prospective tenant that you've approved his rental application, you need to determine a mutually agreeable move-in date. You may have discussed this date during your initial telephone conversation or when you showed the property, but be sure to raise the issue again to guarantee you're in agreement.

After new tenants are approved, some suddenly stall on setting the move-in date. They may stall because they're still obligated under a lease or 30-day notice at another rental property and don't want to double pay. Unless you're willing to suffer rent loss that you can never recover, insist that the tenant begin paying rent to you on the originally scheduled move-in date. The time for your new tenant to negotiate the move-in date was *before* you approved him.

Tenants often request to move the weekend before the start of their lease date in order to provide adequate time to complete the move and secure willing and available help. Owners often allow early occupancy if the unit is ready and even forgo the day or two of rent as a kindly move-in gesture. This can start your new tenant off with a positive feeling, but I'd caution you to ask your new tenant to provide proof that both utilities and insurance coverage are in place as of the date of physical occupancy.

In some situations, your rental unit may not be available on your mutually agreed move-in date. Perhaps the prior tenants didn't vacate when they said they would, perhaps the unit was in much worse condition than you anticipated, or perhaps you just weren't able to complete the required prep work in time. If the unit won't be available as promised, communicate with your new tenant immediately. Often, a new tenant can adjust his move-in date as long as you give him reasonable notice. If he can't adjust the date, try to work out another arrangement.

Sometimes new tenants ask whether they can move just a few items into the rental unit before your preoccupancy conference. Don't allow it! You create a landlord-tenant relationship simply by letting the tenants have access to the unit without you present or by allowing them to store even a few items in the unit. If you have to cancel the rental for any reason, you then need to go through a formal legal eviction that can take several weeks.

Meeting with a Tenant Prior to Move-In

After you and your tenant decide on a move-in date — but *before* the tenant actually moves in and takes possession of the unit — you need to meet to deal with some of the technicalities, like walking through the property, signing paperwork, and handing over the keys. The following sections walk you through each step of the move-in process.

Set up a meeting with the tenant on the move-in day or a few days before. At this meeting, you review your property policies and rules, review and sign all the paperwork, collect the move-in funds, conduct a thorough property inspection, and complete an inspection checklist.

Although the rental property should be in rent-ready condition before you show it to rental prospects, it can get dirty or dusty quickly if there's any delay between showing the property and moving in the new tenants. So before meeting with your tenant prior to move-in, make one last visit to the unit and go through your rent-ready inspection checklist again just to make sure you don't encounter surprises when move-in day arrives. (See the section "The inspection checklist" later in the chapter for more info.)

Covering the rules with your new tenant

When you meet with your new tenant, start by giving her a copy of your house rules, which may look something like those in Figure 11-1. (Pop in the CD or click the link in the table of contents to access the same information in print-ready form.) Give her a chance to read over the rules and ask questions, and provide clarification as necessary. Then ask for her signature, which indicates she has received and understands the rules and agrees to abide by them.

The term *rules and regulations* tends to sound rather imposing to most tenants. Some rental housing owners and managers use the term *policies and guidelines,* but I feel that you need to make it very clear that these are legally enforceable rules, not optional guidelines. Your house rules are separate from your rental contract, which is drafted by an attorney using lots of formal and hard-to-understand terminology. The rules you draft should be more informal and conversational in tone than your rental contract. Be sure to use clear language that's neither harsh nor demeaning. Because your house rules are a part of your lease, you should have your lawyer give them a quick read. Casual tone and language can put a softer spin on the document but may make the rules more susceptible to misinterpretation and more difficult to enforce, and could even lead to a fair housing discrimination complaint.

Many owners and managers of single-family or small rental properties don't worry about detailed rules and regulations because they think the rental contract covers it all. But setting up some basic rules that you can easily change through written notice to the tenants is a good idea. This tactic shows that you and your tenants are on the same page and gives you flexibility in managing your property.

Policies and Rules

We are proud of this property and we hope that your living experience here will be pleasant and comfortable. The support and cooperation of you, as our tenant, is necessary for us to maintain our high standards.

This is your personal copy of our Policies and Rules. Please read it carefully as it is an integral part of your rental agreement. When you sign your rental agreement, you agree to abide by the policies and rules for this rental property, and they are considered legally binding provisions of your rental agreement. If you have any questions, please contact us and we will be glad to help.

This document is an addendum and is part of the Lease or Rental Agreement, dated _____, by and between _____, Owner, and _____Tenant, for the premises located at: _____.

New policies and rules or amendments to this document may be adopted by Owner upon giving 30 days written notice to tenant.

Guests: Tenant is responsible for their own proper conduct and that of all guests, including the responsibility for understanding and observing all policies and rules.

Noise: Although the Premises are well constructed, they are not completely soundproof and reasonable consideration for neighbors is important. Either inside or outside of the Premises, no tenant or their guest shall use, or allow to be used, any sound-emitting device at a sound level that may annoy, disturb, or otherwise interfere with the rights, comforts, or conveniences of other tenants or neighbors. Particular care must be taken between the hours of 9:00 p.m. and 9:00 a.m.

Parking: No vehicle belonging to a Tenant shall be parked in such a manner as to impede passage in the street or to prevent access to the property. Tenant shall only use assigned and designated parking spaces. Tenant shall ensure that all posted handicap, fire zones, or other no-parking areas remain clear of vehicles at all times. Vehicles parked in unauthorized areas or in another tenant's designated parking space may be towed away at the vehicle owner's expense. Vehicles may not be backed in, and repairs and maintenance of any sort are not allowed on the premises. All vehicles must be currently registered and in operative condition. No trucks, commercial vehicles, recreational vehicles, motorcycles, bicycles, boats, or trailers are allowed anywhere on the Premises without advance written approval of the Owner. All vehicles must be parked properly between the lines of the parking space. Tenant shall ensure that their guests abide by all of these parking policies and rules.

Patios/Balconies and Entry Areas: Patios/balconies and entry areas are restricted to patio-type furniture and are to be kept clean and orderly. No barbecues or similar cooking devices may be used on the Premises without advance written approval. No items may be hung from the Premises at anytime, and all entryways and walkways must be kept free from items that could be a hazard. Owner reserves the right to require that items that detract from the appearance of the Premises be removed immediately upon request. No unauthorized storage is allowed at any time.

Wall Hangings: Pictures may be hung on a thin nail. Mirrors, wall units, hanging wall or light fixtures, etc. need special attention and professional installation. Please contact the Owner for approval in advance as damage to the Premises will be the responsibility of the Tenant.

Trash: Tenant is responsible for keeping the inside and outside of the Premises clean, sanitary, and free from objectionable odors at all times. Tenant shall ensure that all trash, papers, cigarette butts, and similar items are sealed in trash bags and placed in appropriate receptacles. No trash or other materials shall be allowed to accumulate so as to cause a hazard or be in violation of any health, fire, or safety ordinance or regulation.

Figure 11-1:
A sample first page of policies and rules (also known as house rules).

Courtesy of Robert S. Griswold

When you establish your house rules and have your new tenant review them, keep these points in mind to reduce the chances of future headaches:

✔ **Frame your house rules in a positive light.** Review the rules with several of your friends and colleagues to find better ways to say the same thing. Be clear, direct, and firm, yet not condescending. And watch out for the *no index,* which happens when many of your rules are too blunt and negative, such as "No glass in the pool area," "No storage on your balcony," and "No riding bikes on the grounds." Although each of these rules is reasonable and important for the safe and efficient operation of your property, you can say the same thing in a more positive way. For example, instead of saying, "No riding bikes on the grounds," you can say, "Please walk your bikes in the common area." Or instead of saying, "No glass in the pool area," you can say, "We gladly allow beverages by the pool in unbreakable plastic containers." Phrasing the rules in a positive tone and minimizing the no index makes the rules — and you — seem friendlier to your tenant.

✔ **Verify that your house rules are reasonable and enforceable.** They must not discriminate against anyone in a protected class. The term *protected class* refers to the federal antidiscrimination laws that protect classes of people because of race, color, gender, national origin, religion, and familial status.

✔ **Make sure your house rules avoid any reference to children, unless the reference is related to certain health and safety issues.** For example, you can have a rule that states, "Persons under 14 must be accompanied by an adult while using the spa," because legitimate safety concerns exist regarding unattended children in spas. But a rule that says, "Children aren't allowed to leave bicycles in the common area" is inappropriate because it singles out children and implies that adults can leave bikes in the common area if they want. A better way to handle this issue is to use wording that isn't age-specific, such as, "No one is allowed to leave bicycles in the common area." With this verbiage, the rule applies to everyone and doesn't discriminate based on age.

✔ **Regularly review and modify your house rules based on situations you encounter.** But remember that you're not running a prison camp, and you don't want to alienate a tenant by harassing her with rules or controlling her day-to-day life. Just because one tenant demonstrates poor judgment doesn't necessarily mean it's time to create a new rule.

Every time you revise your house rules, put the date on the document so that your tenants know which rules are the most current. Remind your tenants that these rules supersede any prior versions and have them sign the document to indicate that they've received the revised house rules and will comply.

And then there was light

With the high cost of utilities, you need to be certain you and your tenants are on the same page regarding who is financially responsible for the rental unit's utility charges. Tenants usually aren't real eager to begin paying for utilities, so be sure your procedures clearly state that your new tenant must immediately contact the utility companies and put the utilities that are her responsibility in her name. Most rental property owners have the utilities revert to their name when the unit becomes vacant for unit turnover and rental showings. So if your new tenant doesn't change the utility billing information, you may end up paying for some of her utility bills.

One way to make sure your new tenant handles this matter promptly is to confirm that she's dealt with the utilities prior to giving her the mailbox key.

An even better way to avoid paying for the tenant's utilities is to provide contact information for all utilities at the tenant orientation meeting and then require your new tenant to contact the utility companies and establish the bills in her name while in your presence. You may also be able to handle the utility issues online, including verification that the tenant has taken responsibility as of the move-in date.

In many states, rental property owners are required to disclose whether tenants are financially responsible for any utility services outside of their rental unit. For example, exterior common area lighting may be connected to a rental unit, or a common area natural gas grill may be connected to a tenant's gas meter. In some states, landlords must give tenants an appropriate rent credit for the common area utilities they help pay. Check the laws in your area and be sure to disclose this kind of information if you're so required.

Reviewing and signing documents

Tenants and property owners alike are usually aware of all the legal paperwork involved in renting a home. And although sifting through all that legalese isn't fun for anyone, doing so is important. Property owners and tenants each have specific legal rights and responsibilities that are outlined in these documents, and being aware of what you're agreeing to — and being sure your tenants know what they're agreeing to — is crucial.

In the next several sections, I outline the documents you need to go over with your new tenants and have them sign.

Rental contract

Be sure your tenant understands that when he signs your lease or month-to-month rental agreement, he's entering into a business contract that has significant rights and responsibilities for both parties. Before your tenant signs

the rental contract (or any rental contract addenda), carefully and methodi-
cally review each clause.

Certain clauses in the rental contract are so important that you should have
the tenant initial them to indicate that he's read these points and understands
his rights and responsibilities in relation to them. For example, the tenant
should initial the clause concerning the need for him to obtain his own renter's
insurance policy to protect his property and cover him for liability claims (see
Chapter 19 for tips on educating your tenants about renter's insurance).

Never give a tenant the keys to the property before he's signed your required
legal documents. Even if the tenant fails to sign the rental contract, an oral
landlord-tenant relationship is established when you give him the keys to the
unit, and when you rely on oral agreements, you and the tenant are likely to
disagree on the terms. Regaining possession of your rental unit can be a long
and expensive process, so be sure that every adult occupant signs all documents prior to handing over the keys.

Speaking of keys, have your new tenant initial that he's received X number
of keys for the property and acknowledge that you had the locks rekeyed or
changed since the last tenant vacated. It is also advisable to fully explain the
charges that your tenant will incur for a lock-out or loss of the keys, entry
cards, or gate or garage door opener. Your tenant may think you or someone
you pay is available 24/7 to open the door for him, when the reality is that
these can be expensive problems to solve and items to replace. Explaining the
consequences in advance should keep the tenant cautious and avoid these
challenging situations.

Environmental disclosure forms

If you haven't already done so, be sure to give your new tenant copies of the
required legal and environmental disclosure forms, plus the Environmental
Protection Agency pamphlet for lead-based paint hazards, which is also
required under federal law for most properties built before 1978. (Turn to
Chapter 9 for more info on disclosure of these hazards.)

Mold addendum

Mold is a common term for a variety of fungus types found virtually everywhere
in the environment — both indoors and outdoors. Blaming elevated mold levels
for alleged health problems caused by exposure to certain mold spores, which
are often called *toxic mold,* is a fairly recent phenomenon. Such claims are very
controversial, and currently, no federal regulations exist regarding permissible
exposure limits or building tolerance standards for mold.

Mold can occur anywhere as long as it can find sufficient humidity or moisture and a food source, such as drywall or other common building materials.

You can prevent mold, but doing so requires cooperation between you and your tenants.

Because the tenant has day-to-day control over the rental unit, you can't possibly know about mold problems as soon as they develop or know about all the conditions in the unit that can lead to mold. Emphasize to your tenants the importance of avoiding conditions that increase the chances of mold growth and instruct them to immediately notify you of any suspected problems such as unexplained moisture or leaks.

To minimize the possibility of mold concerns at your property, give your tenant a Mold Notification Addendum (see Figure 11-2) to educate him on how he can help prevent mold growth through proper daily lifestyle and housekeeping measures. This addendum indicates that you've inspected the condition of the property and deemed it free of damp or wet building materials upon tenant move-in. It also verifies that no known issues of water intrusion, visible mold, or mildew exist. Be sure your tenant carefully reviews the addendum and signs his acknowledgment, and then give him a copy of the signed form for his records.

To access a sample Mold Notification Addendum from the California Apartment Association, simply pop in the CD or click the link in the table of contents.

Smoke detector agreement

Inform your new tenant of the importance of smoke detectors. You may even want to create a Smoke Detector Agreement, an example of which you can find on the CD (if you're reading this book in digital form, click the link in the table of contents). This document helps you be certain that your tenant fully understands the importance of this vital safety equipment and realizes that he must make sure the smoke detectors remain in place, operate properly, and have electrical or battery power. Check your state and local fire and building codes to ensure you're in compliance with the type, number, and location of detectors required by law in each rental unit.

Many tragic accidents have occurred in rental properties where fires broke out after tenants had removed or disabled the smoke detectors because they were annoyed with false alarms triggered by smoking or cooking. Some tenants fail to regularly test the smoke alarms or replace the batteries as needed. It is not legally required, realistic, or desirable from the tenant's perspective to have you enter the rental unit for routine testing of the smoke detector. All tenants need to understand that you can only address conditions brought to your attention, so they must be actively involved in ongoing inspections of the rental unit to ensure their own safety.

MOLD NOTIFICATION ADDENDUM

Page _____
of Agreement

This document is an Addendum and is part of the Rental/Lease Agreement dated _____ between
(Date)

_____(Owner/Agent) and _____(Resident)
(Name of Owner/Agent)   (List all Residents as listed on the Rental/Lease Agreement)

for the Premises located at _____, Unit # (if applicable) _____
(Street Address)

_____. CA _____.
(City)   (Zip)

It is our goal to maintain the highest quality living environment for our Residents. The Owner/Agent has inspected the unit prior to lease and knows of no damp or wet building materials and knows of no mold or mildew contamination. Resident is hereby notified that mold, however, can grow if the premises are not properly maintained or ventilated. If moisture is allowed to accumulate in the unit, it can cause mildew and mold to grow. It is important that Residents regularly allow air to circulate in the apartment. It is also important that Residents keep the interior of the unit clean and that they promptly notify the Owner/Agent of any leaks, moisture problems, and/or mold growth.

Resident agrees to maintain the premises in a manner that prevents occurrence of an infestation of mold or mildew in the premises. Resident agrees to uphold this responsibility in part by complying with the following list of responsibilities:

1. Resident agrees to keep the unit free of dirt and debris that can harbor mold.
2. Resident agrees to immediately report to the Owner/Agent any water intrusion, such as plumbing leaks, drips or "sweating" pipes.
3. Resident agrees to notify the Owner/Agent of overflows from bathroom, kitchen, or unit laundry facilities, especially in cases where the overflow may have permeated walls or cabinets.
4. Resident agrees to report to the Owner/Agent any significant mold growth on surfaces inside the premises.
5. Resident agrees to allow the Owner/Agent to enter the unit to inspect and make necessary repairs.
6. Resident agrees to use bathroom fans while showering or bathing and to report to the Owner/Agent any non-working fan.
7. Resident agrees to use exhaust fans whenever cooking, dishwashing, or cleaning.
8. Resident agrees to use all reasonable care to close all windows and other openings in the premises to prevent outdoor water from penetrating into the interior unit.
9. Resident agrees to clean and dry any visible moisture on windows, walls, and other surfaces, including personal property, as soon as reasonably possible. (Note: Mold can grow on damp surfaces within 24 to 48 hours.)
10. Resident agrees to notify the Owner/Agent of any problems with the air conditioning or heating systems that are discovered by the Resident.
11. Resident agrees to indemnify and hold harmless the Owner/Agent from any actions, claims, losses, damages, and expenses, including, but not limited to, attorneys' fees that the Owner/Agent may sustain or incur as a result of the negligence of the Resident or any guest or other person living in, occupying, or using the premises.

The undersigned Resident(s) acknowledge(s) having read and understood the foregoing.

_____   _____   _____   _____
Date   Resident   Date   Resident

_____   _____   _____   _____
Date   Resident   Date   ·   Resident

_____   _____
Date   Owner/Agent

Figure 11-2:
A Mold
Notification
Addendum.

Courtesy of the California Apartment Association

The importance of smoke detectors

I once managed a great 70-unit apartment building that looked like it was pulled straight from a Gene Autry movie set. It had a very Western motif, with wood everywhere — covered wooden walkways, completely enclosed wooden carports, and wood decks. This property was a termite's dream! But it was also a significant fire risk. And that's exactly what one crazed friend of an evicted tenant must have thought when, in the middle of the night, he doused one of the apartments with gasoline and lit a match.

The intense fire spread quickly. Luckily, the on-site manager was walking back to the property from a movie and saw the fire soon after it started. He immediately alerted all the tenants in the adjoining units before calling the fire department. It's a good thing he did because it turns out that one tenant had taken her smoke detector down because of false alarms from cooking, and another tenant had taken the batteries out of his smoke detector just a few days before, when his portable radio needed batteries!

This event will always be a vivid reminder to me that smoke detectors can save lives, but the only way they can do so is if they're properly maintained.

Animal agreement

Marketing your rental property to tenants with pets can be very profitable because you usually have lower turnover and higher rents. If your new tenant has pets, you need to have her complete and sign an Animal Agreement. This document outlines your house rules regarding your tenant's animals. (Pop in the CD or click the link in the table of contents to access a sample Animal Agreement.)

A good animal policy clearly stipulates exactly which animals are acceptable at your rental property. It may just be semantics, but you don't want to get to court and have your tenants argue that the large iguana that damaged your rental unit isn't subject to your rules because it's not their "pet." I recommend broadening your rules from merely "pets" to "animals in general."

After the initial move-in, tenants may be tempted to take advantage of your policy and bring in additional animals or pets. For example, your tenant may decide that the small poodle you agreed to is lonely and needs the company of a Great Dane in your studio rental unit! Tenants often have heartwarming stories about how they've added new animals to the mix, but you need to retain control over the numbers, types, and sizes of the animals on your property. One way to do so is to meet and photograph the animal so there's no doubt as to what you've approved. Also, remember that small puppies can grow into large dogs, so make sure your policies anticipate the animal at its *adult* size. Also, note that smaller isn't always better. Some small breeds are noisier than their larger counterparts. Pets tend to be as responsible as the tenants who care for them, control them, and pick up after them.

> ## Pythons and piglets and goats, oh my!
>
> In managing rental properties over the years, I've seen just about every type of pet you can imagine. I once took over management of a small rental property where the owner allowed the tenants to have pets. I wasn't too concerned until it became obvious that the prior management company didn't have any limitations. I soon found out that we had everything from the usual dogs and cats to a large Burmese python and a potbellied pig. One tenant even had two goats on his patio. Strictly define exactly which animals are acceptable on your property or you may be in for a big surprise.

Keep current photos of all animals living on your property in the individual files of their owners. This practice may seem ridiculous, but no matter how large your security deposit is or how strict your rules are, animals have the potential to cause significant damage. Determining the source of the problem can be difficult if you can't accurately identify the guilty animal and its owner. Having a photo can also help if the original animal passes and the "replacement animal" doesn't meet your limitations.

Collecting the money from your tenant

During your pre-move-in meeting (and before the tenant has the keys to the place), be sure to collect the first month's rent and the security deposit. Payment may be in the form of a cashier's check or a money order but not a personal check (after all, you have no way of knowing whether it'll clear). Be sure to give your tenant a receipt for payment, and also let him know whether your rent collection policy allows him to pay his future rent payments with a personal check.

Although cash is legal tender, have a firm policy *against* accepting cash unless doing so is absolutely necessary. Regularly collecting cash for your rents can make you a target for crime. Tenants often move in on the weekends and in the evenings, so you don't want to have cash on you or at your home until you can get to the bank. Of course, if someone assists you in your rent collections, he's also at risk (not to mention the fact that cash is harder to keep track of, and your assistant may be tempted to skim off some of it for his own needs).

Prior to handing over the keys to your new tenant and allowing him to take possession, you need to insist on having the cash in hand through *good funds* (as opposed to *insufficient funds,* where a person writes a check and doesn't have the money to cover it in his account). Most owners guarantee the receipt of good funds by requiring cash, a bank cashier's check, or a money order. But many rental property owners aren't aware that both cashier's checks and money orders can be stopped. Financial institutions and convenience stores allow the purchaser to stop payment because these financial instruments can be lost or stolen. However, bank cashier's checks and money orders are superior to personal checks because they do represent good funds and won't be returned to you because of a lack of money to cover them.

If, despite my strong advice, your tenant persuades you to accept a personal check, then at least don't give him access to the property until you've called and verified with his bank that the check will be honored. Your best bet is to take the check to the tenant's bank and cash it or at least have it certified. If the bank certifies the check, it's guaranteeing that the tenant has sufficient funds available, and the bank will actually put a hold on the funds. Of course, cashing the check is the only sure way to collect your funds because a devious tenant can always stop payment on even a certified personal check.

Check scanners are now available from some financial institutions for a fee (or for free to their larger customers). These devices can process personal checks by scanning the micro-encoding on the bottom of the check and essentially making a bank deposit remotely. You can cut down on the processing time of a check and know immediately whether it's good simply by using one of these scanners.

You can't judge a book by its cover

I once had a resident manager who'd been in the rental management business for many years. She'd rented to hundreds of tenants and was consistently one of my best managers, with very high occupancy and rarely any uncollected rent. She used to tell me how, over the years, she followed all fair housing laws but began to feel as though she could "read" a person and had even developed a sort of sixth sense to anticipate which prospective tenants weren't likely to pass our thorough screening process.

One Saturday afternoon, a very well-dressed man in his 30s came in to see an apartment. He drove a fancy car and wore several pieces of expensive jewelry. He looked at a couple of apartments and then said he'd take the larger unit at the back of the property because he preferred privacy. He said that he'd just arrived in town and had been staying at a nice hotel in the area, but he was anxious to get settled and wanted to know if he could move in the next day. The man was quite charming and very smooth. In fact, he was so charming that this seasoned resident manager didn't wait for the results of the tenant screening process. Instead, she accepted a personal check for all his move-in funds, even though this tactic was clearly against company policy. Unfortunately, his personal check bounced, and it took more than two months to evict this "gentleman" from the rental unit. When we finally got possession of the unit, we found that this individual was quite a salesman — he'd installed more than a dozen phone lines in his apartment for his telemarketing operations.

Inspecting the property with your tenant

The number one source of landlord-tenant disputes is the disposition of the tenant's security deposit. You can avoid many of these potential problems with proper procedures before the tenant takes possession of the rental unit. But to do so, you need to walk through the property with your tenant before move-in and go over the following matters.

To avoid disputes over security deposits, record the rental unit's condition before the tenant moves in using photos and/or video. In addition to your inspection checklist (see the next section), you'll have some visual evidence to help refresh the tenant's memory or to show the court if the matter ends up there. If you use a video camera, be sure to get the tenant on video stating the date and time, if she's cooperative. If your tenant isn't present, bring a copy of that day's newspaper and include it in your recording. With photography, be sure to include a caption or descriptions with all photos and provide a running, detailed narrative with the recording.

The inspection checklist

Your inspection checklist is just as important as your rental contract. By using an inspection checklist at both move-in and move-out time, you can take care of many problems. The purpose of the inspection isn't to find all the items you or your maintenance person forgot to check; you should've already looked carefully through the unit to ensure it meets your high standards. The purpose of the move-in inspection is to clearly demonstrate to the tenant's satisfaction that the unit is in good condition except for any noted items and to establish the base-line condition should any damage be noted when the tenant vacates.

When properly completed and signed, an inspection checklist documents the property's condition upon acceptance by and move-in of the tenant and serves as a baseline for the entire tenancy. If the tenant withholds rent or tries to break the lease by claiming the unit needs substantial repairs, you can prove the unit's condition upon move-in by referring to the checklist. And when the tenant moves out, you're able to clearly note the items that were damaged or weren't left clean so that you can charge the maximum allowed under your state or local laws before returning the remainder of the security deposit.

Make sure you do the following when having a new tenant sign this form:

- ✔ **Physically walk through the rental unit with your new tenant and guide her through the inspection form.** Let the tenant tell you the conditions she observes and make sure your wording of the noted conditions and comments accurately describes everything in detail.

If doing this walk-through with your tenant isn't possible, then you should complete the move-in/move-out inspection checklist on your own and ask that all adult occupants review and sign the form as soon as possible upon move-in. Inform the tenant that you'll be glad to deliver her mailbox key after you have the approved form in hand. I never seem to get anything but bills and junk mail myself, but I've learned that the mailbox key is a very useful tool in motivating a tenant to promptly review and approve the inspection checklist.

✔ **Print legibly and be as specific as possible when noting the condition of each item.** Indicate each item's condition — new, excellent, very good, dirty, scratched, broken, and so on — but also include details, such as writing "the built-in timer doesn't work" rather than just saying that the oven is "broken." That way your tenant understands that the oven does in fact work and knows she won't be held responsible for this specific item upon move-out. If you only comment on dirty or damaged items, a court may conclude that you didn't inspect or forgot to record the condition of an item that you're now claiming was damaged by the tenant. You may think everyone knows and agrees that all items without any notation are in okay condition, but the tenant will likely tell the court that the item was at least somewhat dirty or damaged and that you shouldn't be able to collect for it.

Whenever possible, have the tenant actually fill out the checklist legibly in her own handwriting. If a dispute arises later that finds its way into small claims court, the credibility of the form will be stronger if the tenant was the one who completed it.

Of course, remember that your tenant may discover that an item doesn't work after move-in. So you need to be a bit flexible. For example, the oven may have tested in working order, but when initially used by the tenant, it doesn't heat properly. The shower head may have tested well for temperature and pressure, but both are found to fluctuate when put to normal use. But these are items that you'll quickly address, and the rental unit should be in good working condition in all ways except those few noted wear-and-tear issues that you and the tenant agree can be left, such as a small stain on the carpet or a slight indentation in the kitchen countertop.

When used properly, a move-in/move-out inspection checklist not only proves the existence of damage in the rental unit but also pinpoints when the damage occurred. Don't fall for one of the oldest tenant ploys in the book. Tenants often try to avoid walking the rental unit with you upon move-in because they want to avoid charges for damage that occurs during their actual move-in. Save yourself some trouble and require your tenant to walk through the rental premises and agree that all items are in clean and undamaged condition *before* she starts moving in her boxes and furnishings.

Always note the conditions of the carpets and floor coverings because this is one of the most common areas of dispute with tenants upon move-out. Although you shouldn't charge tenants for ordinary wear and tear, they should pay for the damage if they destroy the carpet. Indicate the carpet's age and whether it's been professionally cleaned as part of your rental turnover process. When a tenant leaves after only six months and has destroyed the carpet, you can guarantee she'll remember the carpet as old, dirty, and threadbare. The tenant's selective memory won't recall that the carpet was actually brand-new, or at least in very good condition, and professionally cleaned upon her move-in!

If you discover any problems during your inspection walk-through, note them on the inspection form and take steps to have them corrected, unless the corrections aren't economically feasible. For example, you may have a hairline crack along the edge of the bathroom countertop. If you determine refinishing or replacing the countertop is too costly, just note the condition on the inspection form so that your tenant isn't erroneously charged upon move-out.

✔ **Be sure your inspection checklist reflects any repairs or improvements made after the initial walk-through inspection.** For example, if you and your tenant note on the form that the bathroom door doesn't lock properly, you should then have that item repaired, necessitating an update to the inspection form that your tenant must initial.

✔ **Be particularly careful to note any and all mildew, mold, pest, or rodent problems.** Doing so is important because these are health issues that you must address immediately before the tenant takes possession. There's been a trend toward tenant claims of an uninhabitable rental property or a unit that violates health and safety regulations. These claims often result in requests for rent reduction or even litigation. To prove you turned over the rental property in good condition, note on your inspection checklist that no indication of any of these issues exists. If problems persist after move-in despite your best efforts, consult with the appropriate licensed professional to evaluate the sources of the conditions, the necessary responses, and remedial actions, and advise the tenant of any potential health risk.

✔ **Be sure to give your tenant a copy of the completed and signed checklist for her records.** That way the tenant can review her own copy when she moves out if there are charges.

I like to use the California Apartment Association's Move-In/Move-Out Itemized Statement at my properties. To access this document, pop in the CD if you have a hard-copy version of this book or click the link in the table of contents if you're reading a digital version. The first column of the checklist is where you note the unit's condition before the tenant moves in. The last two columns are for use when the tenant moves out and you inspect the unit with her again. Often, you don't immediately know the estimated cost of repair or replacement, so you can complete that portion of the checklist later and include a copy of it when you send your tenant her security deposit disposition form. (Chapter 15 has the scoop on how to figure out how much of the security deposit to return to a departing tenant.)

The nitty-gritty details

When your tenant moves in, you don't want to assume he knows everything about the property. Take a few extra minutes during your walk-through with the tenant to do the following:

- ✔ **Provide your tenant with the appliance manuals or at least copies of the basic operating instructions.** These manuals get lost over the years, but many manufacturers have manuals online that you can download.

- ✔ **If you have natural gas appliances or gas heat, instruct your tenant to contact the local utility company if he has any questions or concerns.** This step is particularly important if he detects the sulfur smell commonly associated with a gas leak or has any concerns or questions about proper operation of the appliances. The tenant should also contact the utility company or your maintenance person if he needs to relight a pilot light.

- ✔ **Tell your tenant where the utilities are and how to shut them off.** Utilities may need to be shut off because of severe weather, a water leak, an electrical short, or fire on the property. If you have a serious storm or earthquake, your tenant needs to be able to immediately turn off the natural gas supply as well. Provide your tenant with an inexpensive special wrench, available from the natural gas utility company. Attach it to the gas meter with a simple cable so that your tenant or maintenance person can have it handy in case of an emergency.

Giving your tenant an informational letter

The key to success in managing rental properties is to develop an efficient system that reduces the time you spend managing your rentals. A good way to minimize your phone calls from tenants is to provide them with either a tenant handbook or a Tenant Information Letter (like the one in Figure 11-3) that outlines all your policies and procedures that are too detailed to include in your rental contract. You can also attach details on the proper operation and care of appliances, plus other important info your tenant needs to know about the rental unit.

Tenant Information Letter

Tenant Name(s) _____
Rental Unit Address _____

Dear _____,

We are very pleased that you have selected our property to be your home. We hope that you enjoy living here and would like to share some additional information that will explain what you can expect from us and what we will be asking from you:

1. Owner/Manager:

2. Rent Collection:

3. Notice to End Tenancy:

4. Security Deposits:

5. New or Departing Roommates:

6. Maintenance and Repair Requests:

7. Lockout Procedure/Lost keys:

8. Renters Insurance:

9. Guest Occupancy Policy:

10. Annual Safety Inspection:

11. Utility shut-off locations:

12. Trash collection or recycling programs:

13. Parking:

Please let us know if you have any questions.

Sincerely,

_____   _____
              Owner/Manager   Date

I have read and received a copy of this Tenant Information Letter.

_____   _____
              Tenant   Date

_____   _____
              Tenant   Date

Figure 11-3:
Tenant
Information
Letter.

Courtesy of Robert S. Griswold

Customize your tenant handbook or information letter to present the house rules you've implemented for each rental property (see Chapter 4 for guidance on setting house rules). Although this information should be customized for each property, here are some of the basic items to include:

✔ Property manager name and contact number

✔ Procedures to follow in case of an emergency

✔ Rent collection information, including when rent is due, how and where payment is to be made, and how late fees and other charges are calculated and handled

✔ Requirements for ending the tenancy, including the notice requirement

✔ Procedures for the return of the security deposit

✔ Handling of new or departing roommates

✔ Proper procedure for requesting maintenance and repairs

✔ Reminder to check and test smoke and carbon monoxide detectors

✔ Reminder to immediately contact owner/manager if water intrusion/leaks or any sign of mold/mildew is present

✔ Lockout procedure and charges for lost keys

✔ Renter's insurance requirements

✔ Guest occupancy policy

✔ Annual interior unit inspection walk-through policy, if any

✔ Utility shut-off locations, including a separate diagram for the individual unit and information on how to shut off the utilities

✔ Essential appliance information, such as what not to place in a garbage disposal and how to keep refrigerator coils clean

✔ Trash collection and recycling program information

✔ Parking policies

✔ Property rules and policies

✔ Community association or homeowners' association rules and policies

Many tenants misplace this information when they need it most during the tenancy, so many professional rental owners and property managers are using the Internet to improve the efficiency of managing their properties. You can put the majority of this information online in an electronic tenant handbook that you can update as necessary.

Remember that having this information online may be efficient and handy, but it's not in lieu of giving your tenant actual physical copies of all items upon move-in. You should also give your tenants in writing any changes to the tenant handbook, and, as required by law, provide in writing any changes in legal terms or rules and policies.

Distributing the keys to your tenant

Distributing the keys is a very serious issue that has significant liability for rental property owners and managers. A problem in key control can allow access to a tenant's rental unit, potentially leading to theft or crimes involving serious bodily injury. Keys require careful handling and should be stored only in a locked metal key cabinet or safe.

As the property owner, you're obligated to take reasonable measures to ensure the well-being of your tenants. Tenants must have the ability to control unauthorized entry into their rental. This means that, as the owner, you need to ensure that doors, windows, and locks are in working order and up to the local industry standard. Include an entry lock set and a sturdy deadbolt with at least a $\frac{13}{16}$-inch throw on all exterior entry doors. Provide peepholes on the main or primary exterior entry door as well.

Some states have laws specifically requiring rental property owners to provide window locks. Whether legally required or not, I recommend you provide locks for all windows that can be opened. Install window locks on upper-level windows as a safety device and as a way of minimizing the chance that young, unsupervised children may fall from an open window.

For the convenience of your tenants, have a single key that works all entry locks for their particular unit and also operates common area or laundry room locks.

One of the least desirable aspects of managing rental property is handling tenant lockout calls. Tenants rarely seem to get locked out of their rental units during normal daylight hours, so you need to inform your new tenants about your lockout and lost key policies and charges. Set up a policy that acknowledges the difference between a lockout during reasonable business hours and nonworking hours. For example, you can charge the tenant $20 for a lockout Monday through Friday from 9 a.m. to 6 p.m. and $40 for a lockout at all other times.

Changing the locks between tenants is extremely important. Prior tenants may have retained copies of the keys and may return to steal or commit some other crime. You can purchase and install an entirely new lock or have your maintenance person or a locksmith rekey the existing lock. If you have several rental units, substitute the existing lock set with a spare lock set. Keep several extra lock sets in inventory so you can rotate locks between units upon turnover. Have your new tenant sign a statement indicating she's aware that the locks have been changed or rekeyed since the prior tenant vacated. Then give her a copy of the locksmith receipt for her records.

The importance of changing locks between tenants

As the host of a live weekly radio show on real estate for more than 14 years, I was often amazed at some of the stories I heard from callers. I'll never forget the call I received from a tenant in a small multi-unit rental property who was shocked to find out that another tenant had a key to his unit. Apparently, one of the tenants had loaned his key to a family member who got confused and inadvertently entered my caller's rental unit. When the caller confronted the property owner, the owner wasn't very concerned and didn't understand the tenant's concern. He stated that he always used the same locks so that he didn't have to carry around extra keys if he needed access to a rental unit in case of an emergency. Lesson: Make sure all your locks are uniquely keyed!

The rental housing industry relies on locks, and until recently, technology hasn't really changed. But following the lead of the hospitality and lodging industries, rental property owners are beginning to see many more options that offer better security and key control for rental housing. The cost of many of these systems is coming down, but it still remains too high for the average rental property owner with just a few rental units. But this advancement is an important trend that will be beneficial for owners, property managers, and tenants down the road.

If you have a master key system for your rental properties, be extremely careful with it. Don't keep any extra copies or loan the master key to anyone whom you don't trust implicitly. Although locksmiths are required by law to have written authorization prior to duplicating a key marked "Do not duplicate," remember that an individual who wants a copy of your key to commit a crime isn't likely concerned about breaking the law by illegally copying the key.

Setting Up the Tenant File

You need to be able to immediately access important written records, and one way of doing that is to have an organized filing system to ensure you don't waste time searching aimlessly for a lost or misplaced document. The best way to accomplish this goal is to set up a new tenant folder for each tenant at the time of her move-in that includes the following:

- ✔ Tenant contact and information form
- ✔ Rental application

- ✔ Rental application verification form
- ✔ Credit report
- ✔ Other reference information, including criminal background report, if any
- ✔ Holding deposit agreement and receipt, if applicable
- ✔ Signed rental contract
- ✔ Lead-based paint disclosure form
- ✔ Smoke detector agreement
- ✔ Any other addenda to the lease or rental agreement
- ✔ A move-in/move-out inspection checklist
- ✔ Photos or DVDs of the unit, taken at move-in

Set up a file folder for each of your rental properties with individual files for each tenant. Turn to this file throughout the tenancy, adding to it all new documents such as rent increases, notices of entry, maintenance requests, and correspondence. Keep tenant files for four years after the tenant vacates. And remember that your tenant's file contains personal information such as Social Security numbers, credit reports, and bank account numbers. With the concerns about identity theft, you want to always protect these files as if the information were your own and store the files in a locked container.

Preparing a Welcome Package for Your New Tenant

Tenant satisfaction and retention are critical to success in rental management. One way to make a positive first impression is to provide your new tenant with a welcome package when he moves in. Welcome packages can be very elaborate or just a few inexpensive but thoughtful items.

Give your new tenant a simple welcome package with a few useful items, such as a couple of bottles of spring water in the refrigerator, a bar of soap and a roll of paper towels in the kitchen, a few change of address forms, a pad of scratch paper and a pen by the phone, and a roll of toilet paper in the bathroom. A discount coupon or a gift certificate for a free pizza is another great way to impress your new tenant.

Another simple idea that really impresses new tenants is offering one or two hours of free maintenance assistance when they first move in. Every new tenant needs to hang a few pictures, install a paper towel holder, or do some other minor maintenance work to make your rental unit feel like home, so why not offer a helping hand?

All your efforts to make a great first impression by offering some free maintenance can backfire if the tenant doesn't clearly understand the limitations of your offer or if the maintenance person is rude or doesn't do quality work. Provide your new tenant with a list of suggested items for your maintenance person and be sure to have your tenant sign a simple disclaimer form waiving his right to sue you or make a claim if your maintenance person damages his favorite picture while hanging it on the wall.

Chapter 12

Collecting and Increasing Rent

*I*f location is the most important element in real estate investing, then collecting rent in full and on time is the most important element in managing your rental investment. But how can you make sure your tenants pay their rent on time every month? The reality is that most tenants don't have significant cash resources, and many live from paycheck to paycheck. So if a tenant's paycheck is delayed, her car breaks down, or she has an unexpected major expense, then her ability to pay the rent in full and on time is in jeopardy. And because the tenant's funds are so tightly budgeted, when she falls even one month behind on rent, catching up again is even more difficult. Fortunately, you can take steps to increase the likelihood that you'll get all your rent money, all the time.

You can begin laying the foundation for successful rent collection before you rent your property. The best preventive measures include targeting your advertising to responsible tenants and establishing a thorough and careful tenant screening and selection process. (I tell you all about the tenant selection process in Chapter 10.)

Collecting the rent is a key part of property management, as is keeping your rent competitive with the market. Raising the rent to reflect trends in your area is also a necessary part of managing rental properties. Many property owners hesitate to raise the rent for existing tenants, but trust me when I say that you can do so effectively, without risking the loss of your tenants.

In this chapter, I fill you in on what you can do to guarantee that you're getting paid on time and that you're charging a competitive rent.

Creating a Written Rent Collection Policy

The keys to rent collection success are establishing policies and procedures and firmly enforcing rent collection. Setting up a rent collection policy, putting it in writing in your lease or rental agreement, and repeating it to your tenants in the tenant handbook or information letter is the best way to ensure their understanding. No single rent collection policy works for *all* property owners, but every policy should cover when rent is due, where it's paid, and how it's paid. I offer considerations for each of these key issues in the following sections.

Be sure to point out that each tenant is jointly and severally responsible for the full payment of rent. *Jointly and severally* is a legal term that means each of your tenants is responsible for paying the rent. So regardless of any agreement between co-occupants or roommates, every tenant can be legally required to pay the entire rent, not just his share. Use this phrase on the lease immediately after the insertion of the tenants' names and note the meaning when you sign the lease agreement with the tenants.

Review your rent collection procedures with each adult occupant of your rental unit before accepting his rental application so that no one misunderstands how important you consider the prompt payment of rent. Then make rent collection a featured topic of your pre-move-in orientation meeting with tenants, when they review and sign the rental contract.

When rent is due

I recommend that you require your tenants to pay the full monthly rent in advance, on or before the first day of each month. This method is the most common, and many state laws require it unless the rental contract specifies otherwise.

That said, you and your tenant can determine that the rent is due on any mutually agreeable date during the month. This approach may make sense if your tenant receives income or financial assistance payments on certain dates. For example, you may have a tenant who receives a check on the 10th of each month, so you set the rent due date for the 15th of each month.

Some owners make the rent payable on the date the tenant first moved in. For example, if the tenant moves in on the 25th of the month, then his rent is due on the 25th of each future month. This practice is legal and may be acceptable if you have only a few tenants and are willing to keep track of each due date, but making all your rents due on the first of the month makes life simpler and avoids confusion.

If your rent due date falls on a weekend or a legal holiday, most states allow the tenant to pay by the next business day. This policy may not be mandatory in your state, but adopting it is a good idea.

Although rent is traditionally paid in full at one time, you may agree to let your tenant divide up the rent and pay twice a month, every week, or in some other time frame. Try to avoid accepting more frequent payments, because your goal is efficiency, and handling the rent collection process as few times as possible is definitely more efficient.

Be careful to document that any differences in rental collection terms are based on legitimate business decisions or else your actions may be seen as favoring one tenant over another. Of course, you may have a tenant who formally requests an accommodation in payment terms under fair housing laws. In this case, seek advice from local landlord-tenant legal counsel.

In addition to fair housing concerns, think about the ramifications of accepting rent based on the tenant's scheduled receipt of income rather than your usual rent due date. By accommodating the tenant, you're tacitly acknowledging that he needs that payment to afford the rent. But one of the fundamental tenets in rental housing management is to avoid tenants who can't afford the rent. If your tenant needs that income to pay your rent that month, you have no safety net if the tenant's check is lost in the mail, his car breaks down, or he's temporarily laid off from his job.

To avoid surprises and delinquent rent, you don't want your tenants' finances to be so tight that they need this month's income to pay this month's rent. Check out Chapter 10 for tips on selecting tenants with enough financial resources to pay this month's rent with cash on hand.

Prorating rent

Life would be simpler if all your tenants moved in and out on the first day of the month, but they don't. If your tenant's occupancy begins in the middle of the month, and your rent collection policy states that all rents are due on the first of each month, then you need to prorate the tenant's rent at move-in. Following are two basic ways to prorate the rent at the beginning of your new tenant's occupancy:

> ✔ **If your tenant moves in toward the end of a month, collect a full month's rent (for the next month), plus the rent due for the prorated portion of the current month.** For example, if your tenant takes occupancy on June 25, then upon move-in, collect six days' rent for the period of June 25 to June 30, plus a full month's rent for July. A new tenant is usually glad to oblige if just a few days are prorated.

✔ **If your tenant moves in early in a month, collect a full month's rent prior to move-in and then collect the balance due for the prorated rent on the first day of the next month.** For example, if your tenant moves in on May 10, then before he takes occupancy, collect a full month's rent that covers the period of May 10 through June 9. Then on June 1, collect the balance due for June 10 through June 30 (21 days' worth). By July 1, the tenant is on track to pay his full rent on the first day of each month.

Don't let your new tenant move in without making at least a full month's rent payment. Though the tenant may want you to accept just the prorated rent for that month, you don't want to turn over your rental unit for a small payment of only several days' rent.

Unless otherwise agreed, you normally uniformly apportion rent from day to day using a 30-day month. Divide your monthly rental rate by 30 to determine the daily rate and multiply your answer by the number of days in the partial rental period. (*Note:* This formula applies to February as well.)

Providing a grace period

Many rent collection policies allow for a *grace period* that provides tenants with a few extra days to pay their rent in full before incurring late charges. Most tenants incorrectly believe that if they pay rent within the grace period, their payment is legally on time. However, the rent is due on or before the due date. If paid later, it's considered delinquent from a legal perspective, regardless of the grace period's terms.

Make sure your rental contract and the tenant information letter are very clear about the fact that the rent is due on or before the due date and that it's technically late if paid during the grace period.

Grace periods are optional in most states and can be any number of days in length. However, a few states (including Connecticut, Delaware, Maine, Oregon, and Rhode Island) have mandatory grace periods or restrictions on serving a *notice to pay rent or quit* (a legal notice demanding rent payment), so be sure to check your local and state laws. Unless restricted by law, I recommend you set up your grace period to expire on the third of the month and allow an extra day or two if the third falls on a weekend or holiday.

In most states, you don't have to wait until the grace period expires to begin your collection efforts with tenants who show a pattern of being late. You can even serve legal notices demanding the rent payment. Your rental contract should contain a specific provision that you have the right to refuse payment after the expiration of your legal demand notice so you aren't obligated to accept an offer of rent from the tenant and can move forward with eviction, if necessary.

Where rent is paid

You can collect your rent in several ways, but unless otherwise agreed, many states require that you collect the rent on the premises. Although stopping by the unit allows you the opportunity to see your property, it isn't time-efficient unless you live on or very close to your property, especially if you have to make multiple trips. The benefits of in-person collection also depend on your tenants' expectations. Tenants in low-rent properties often expect you to come by and collect the rent in person, whereas renters in middle- to higher-rent properties tend to think you're too nosy if you personally come by for the rent.

If you'd rather not collect the rent in person, you can have your tenants pay in one of the following ways. Just make sure you agree on this information when each tenant signs the rental contract.

✔ **Tenants can mail the rent to you.** For most rental property owners and tenants, the most popular way to remit the rent payment is to have the tenants mail it. Because collecting rent by mail is only effective if your tenants pay on time, I strongly suggest you make doing so extremely simple for your tenants by providing them with stamped, preaddressed envelopes. Giving tenants several envelopes at once is efficient as long as they don't lose them or use them to pay other bills.

If you and your tenants agree that the rent will be mailed, you may run into a major question: Is the rent considered paid when it's postmarked or when you receive it? Check your local laws and have a clear, written agreement in your rent collection policy. Absent any legal requirements, I recommend you consider the rent paid when the payment is postmarked. By mailing the payment on time, tenants are acting in good faith, and you don't want to unfairly penalize them if the mail is delayed.

✔ **Tenants can bring the rent to your home or office.** Although this method may be very convenient for you, many tenants object to having to personally deliver their monthly rent. For this reason, my experience is that asking tenants to deliver the rent to you isn't the most reliable method to assure getting it on time. Instead, this request places an additional burden on your tenant when your goal is to simplify the rent collection process for everyone involved.

The issue of where rent is paid is moot if your tenants are willing to make their payments electronically. Check out the later "Digitizing the day-to-day: Electronic payments" section for details on this method of paying rent.

How rent is paid

Your rental contract should clearly indicate how tenants should pay rent: by personal check, cashier's check, money order, cash, or electronic payment. Regardless of the method, give your tenants a receipt for all money received.

Digitizing the day-to-day: Electronic payments

Technology is making the rent collection process much more efficient and timely. Rental owners and property managers can now benefit from their financial institution's ability to process hundreds of rent payments in a matter of minutes. Due to improvements in software automation and *security encryption,* which prevent the theft of confidential information, electronic payments are actually more secure than the conventional check payment method.

Several companies now offer technology for the electronic transfer of funds to allow tenants to pay their rent. The computer software enables you to download the details on all payments processed each month. You're automatically notified if a tenant doesn't have sufficient funds to cover the transfer so you can enforce your regular rent collection policies. Check with your local IREM chapter or NAA affiliate for more info on these companies.

Most tenants are quite comfortable paying electronically rather than writing out and mailing a check each month. With electronic payments, a tenant simply fills out a form one time, and the preauthorized amount is deducted on a designated day (usually between the first and fifth of each month) from his bank account and deposited directly into your account.

If you want to set up your tenants to pay electronically, refer to the Tenant Automated Clearing House (ACH) Debit Authorization Form on the CD. (If you're reading a digital version of this book, click the link in the table of contents to access the ACH form.) Consult with your financial institution for the necessary banking information to ensure payments are properly credited to your rental property account.

Putting pen to paper: Checks

For many rental property owners, accepting checks (personal, cashier's, or money order) is routine. Most tenants have a personal checking account, and paying by check is easy for them. Check processing has also improved greatly with new federal regulations for the banking industry that allow checks to be scanned and converted to an electronic funds transfer. Check with your financial institution to see whether you can use this technology to simplify your rent collection, provide immediate access to the funds, and eliminate several trips to the bank.

Some property owners request postdated checks in advance from their tenants with the idea that they'll already have the rent payment in hand, and the tenants just need to make the funds available to cover the check. I strongly advise against accepting postdated checks. Often these checks aren't good, and many state laws consider a postdated check a promissory note. You may be unable to file an eviction action for nonpayment of rent while the note is pending.

Payment by check is conditional. If the check isn't honored for any reason, it's as if the tenant never paid, and late charges and returned check charges should apply. Check scanning can give you immediate notice that funds aren't available, allowing you to contact the tenant and promptly begin collection efforts.

Never accept second-party checks, such as payroll or government checks. Instead, institute a policy that all rent payments made after the grace period must be in the form of a cashier's check or money order.

Busting out the big bucks: Cash

Although some tenants may want to pay rent with cash, avoid accepting it whenever possible. Turning down cash is always difficult, and your tenants may remind you that cash is legal tender. However, according to the U.S. Department of the Treasury, you have the legal right to refuse cash because accepting cash

- **Can make you a target for robbery:** Even if you use a safe, your risk is increased.

- **Can add the risk of employee theft, if you have employees:** Plus, you're potentially putting your employees in danger.

- **Attracts tenants who may be involved in illegal businesses that deal primarily in cash:** Although many employees in legitimate businesses derive income, at least partially, from cash tips (wait staff and beauticians, for example), so do drug dealers. Criminal tenants don't want to have their activities tracked and prefer properties where cash payments are allowed. Don't make your rental property more attractive to the criminally inclined.

Clearly state in your rental contract that you don't accept cash under any circumstances. Reinforce this policy early in the relationship and don't accept even small amounts of cash for rental application fees or late charges. However, if a tenant is facing eviction and offers full payment in cash, you may want to accept the funds at a place where you feel safe (your home or office) because you may find that the eviction court isn't inclined to allow you to terminate the tenancy if you refuse the proposed cash payment for the entire amount due.

Managing multiple rent payments

When you have multiple tenants in one of your units, you'll probably receive several payments for portions of the total rent due. And you may not receive all the payments at the same time or for the proper amount. When you call the tenants, some of them may say that they paid their share and that you need to track down one of the other tenants.

How your tenants choose to divide the rent between them isn't your problem, and accommodating your tenants by accepting multiple payments can cause administrative nightmares. It can also lead roommates to erroneously believe that they're not responsible for the entire rent. You're better off having a firm

policy of requiring one payment source (either check, money order, or electronic payment) for the entire month's rent. This practice offers more than just administrative convenience. Legally, each roommate in your rental property is *jointly and severally* liable for all rental contract obligations, meaning that if one skips out, the others owe you the entire amount.

Encourage your tenants to let the delinquent roommate know that, although they've all paid a portion of the rent, they're on the hook until the balance is paid. After all, your tenants are in a better position to track down their elusive roommate than you are.

Good accounting practices suggest that you clearly document all your income and expenses. The IRS may consider auditing your rental housing if it learns of frequent cash transactions at your property.

Dealing with Rent Collection Problems

Tenants don't always pay rent on time and in full, which is why you need to have policies in place for the most common problems you'll encounter in rent collection. These rules should outline the specific penalties for late payments, bounced checks, insufficient funds, and failure to pay in full. I cover some of these key issues in the following sections.

Apply your rent collection policies — including charges for late payments, dishonored payments, and partial payments — consistently with all tenants. If you don't, you can be accused of discrimination by simply allowing some tenants to pay late or by accepting multiple payments from some roommates and not from others.

Collecting late rent

One of the most difficult challenges for a rental property owner is dealing with a tenant whose rent is late. You don't want to overreact and begin serving threatening legal rent-demand notices because doing so creates tension and hostility if the tenant has a legitimate reason for the delay. Then again, late rent can be a very serious issue.

Communication is the key to keeping your response in line with the magnitude of the problem. Remain calm and businesslike, and focus on determining why the rent is late before taking any action. If you're having trouble collecting rent on time, consider these options:

- ✔ **E-mail or mail your tenants monthly payment reminders or invoices.** Although electronic payments are the best approach, some owners find that a rent coupon book (just like a mortgage payment coupon book) can be helpful in improving their rental collections.

- ✔ **Call slow rent payers routinely.** Landlords and property managers seeking payment of delinquent rent aren't subject to the regulations set by the Fair Debt Collection Practices Act, so you can call tenants at home *and* at their places of business. (Although you may not want to bother your tenants at work, don't feel bad calling there as long as you're respectful and professional. You do have a right to know when to expect your rent.) When you call, remind these slow payers that the rent is due on or before the first of the month. You can also remind them that you expect your rent to be a top priority among their various financial obligations.

  If you're forced to make reminder calls every month, consider the extra time you're spending on these tenants because your time is too valuable to baby-sit them. If they consistently fail to pay the full rent on or before the due date, don't renew the contract; make sure to give a written notice to terminate the tenancy.

- ✔ **Go to the rental unit and speak directly with tenants.** Don't be shy, or else paying the rent will quickly become a low priority for your tenants. But remember to document your visit with a written notice to the tenant. You may need to show it to a judge at some point in the collection process.

The most effective way to collect rents and determine whether you should exercise a little patience is to contact your tenants directly. Simply mailing a rent reminder or hanging a late notice on the front door can be effective with tenants who just need a reminder, but these tactics typically don't get the job done with tenants who are financially strapped and likely to respond only to direct personal contact.

When contacting tenants, your goal isn't to harass them but to remind them about rent payments or to be solution-oriented and work out an agreement to get your rent. Whatever agreement you reach, make sure that it's in writing and that the tenants sign it.

If you're having trouble locating a tenant, check with her neighbors or call the emergency contact listed on her rental application. Check to see whether the utility company has been told to cancel the utilities; maybe the tenant has skipped town without notifying you.

Your rent collection policy is the most critical element in your rental agreement. As the landlord, you need timely payment of rents. After all, you likely use these funds for your mortgage, taxes, and insurance payments or other expenses. The most common mistake I see landlords and managers make is breaking their own rent collection rules. They allow rents to be paid late, accept excuses, fail to send timely collection or legal notices, and find themselves housing tenants who are weeks — even months — behind in rent payments. So you *must* be firm in your rent collections.

Charging late fees

More than a dozen states have laws addressing restrictions on late charges, so be sure to check with your local NAA affiliate before establishing a late fee policy, and read your state statutes for late fee guidelines and restrictions. Generally speaking, though, implementing and enforcing a late charge policy makes sense, as long as it's reasonable and relates to your actual out-of-pocket costs or expenses incurred by the late payment.

Don't allow tenants to form the impression that your late charge policy approves of late rent payments as long as you collect the late charges. Your late charge should be high enough to discourage habitual lateness but not so high as to be unreasonable. Send written warnings to tenants who regularly pay late (even if they pay the late charges), clearly indicating that their late payments are unacceptable and are a legal violation of the terms.

You can assess late charges in one of several ways:

✔ **Flat fee:** The most common late charge is a *flat fee,* which can be any set amount, due immediately after the grace period. Typical flat fees range from $30 to $100 and are usually set at 4 to 6 percent of the monthly rental rate. One problem is that many tenants are only one or two days late, making the flat late charge unreasonable. Property owners in this situation often end up waiving the flat fee, especially if it's at the higher end of the range. If the matter ever goes to court, the tenant usually challenges the fee, and the court may throw it out.

✔ **Percentage late fee:** A *percentage late fee* is calculated as a percentage of the rent payment and ranges from 4 to 8 percent of the monthly rental rate. The customary late fee percentage for late rent payments is either 5 or 6 percent, but be aware that some states have legal limits on late charges expressed as a percentage of the rent.

✔ **Daily late fee:** If you use a *daily late fee,* you set a daily late charge with a reasonable cap or maximum fee. I've found that a late charge of $5 per day, with a maximum of $50, works very well. A tenant who is only one day late pays a nominal $5 late fee. A tenant who is eight days late pays a heftier $40. The purpose of the cap (which you can also express as a percentage of the rent, such as a maximum of 5 percent) is to keep the late charge reasonable. By the time you get to the cap (at ten days late), you'll have already sent the proper legal rent-demand notices.

The flat fee and the percentage late fee methods both fail to provide an incentive for the tenant to pay rent promptly. After the late charge has been incurred, the tenant often finds other financial obligations more important than your rent. Assessing a daily fee, on the other hand, offers the incentive some tenants need to get their rent in sooner rather than later.

Waiving the late charge excuses late payment of rent and can send the wrong message to your tenants. If you routinely accept late payments and waive the late charges, you can't suddenly change your attitude and begin eviction proceedings the next time a tenant pays late. Instead, you need to provide a written notice that you're once again actively enforcing the strict rent collection terms of your rental contract. You also need to be consistent in applying your late charge policy to all tenants equally — or risk facing claims of discrimination. This also causes issues in court. Judges often rule that if you break your own rules, they're no longer rules that can be enforced against your tenants. As difficult as it is to be firm at times, you must show consistency.

If you receive a late payment by mail, always keep the envelope with the postmark in case the tenant wants to dispute the late charge.

Except where restricted by law, you need to evaluate your own increase in costs as a result of late rent payments to determine what a reasonable late charge should be for your property. Put this amount in writing and be prepared to explain your policy if challenged in court. Additional costs may include phone calls and in-person meetings with the tenant, the preparation and sending of warning letters and required legal rent-demand notices, time and costs spent preparing delinquency lists, and additional accounting and bank deposits when you receive the funds.

Early-payment rent discounts: Yes or no?

Some landlords have tried to get around late charge problems by using early-payment rent discounts to entice their tenants to pay rent on time. These landlords set the rent in the rental contract slightly higher than the market rent and then offer tenants a reduced rent if it's paid in full and on time. For example, if a landlord wants $900 in rent and a $75 late charge, she sets the contracted rent at $975 with a $75 discount if the tenant pays on or before the third of the month.

Although this tactic may be creative, the U.S. legal system has consistently determined that the actual rent is the discounted amount. The courts view giving a large discount for an on-time payment the same as charging an excessive late fee.

Don't play the early-payment rent discount game. If you're challenged, your case will be thrown out of court. At least two large class-action lawsuits on this specific practice have been ruled in favor of the tenants, and the landlords were levied with major legal costs and severe financial penalties. This practice is a scam, and the courts have seen right through it. If you want more rent money, raise your rent amount. If you want tenants who pay on time, carefully screen your prospects. Establish a reasonable and fair late charge policy and apply it uniformly to all tenants.

Handling returned rent payments

Dishonored rent checks or electronic payments can cause major problems for your rent collection efforts, so you need to charge tenants a fee when you're unable to collect good funds per your rent collection policy.

Often, when you contact your tenant, she'll have some excuse for the returned item and tell you that her payment is now good. Check with your bank about its policy for handling dishonored electronic payments. For old-fashioned paper checks, I recommend you go to the tenant's bank and cash the check immediately instead of depositing it again. Or you can get the check *certified,* which means the bank reserves the funds for payment when you deposit it in your bank. ***Note:*** Unless you receive good funds before the end of your grace period, your tenant is also responsible for late charges.

Demand your tenant immediately replace a returned check with a cashier's check or money order. After a tenant's check is returned a second time, regardless of her excuse, require the tenant to make all future payments electronically or with a cashier's check or money order (both of which are guaranteed to have sufficient funds). ***Note:*** Tenants can still cancel their electronic payments or request a stop payment on a cashier's check or money order, so be sure to process the transaction right away.

Like late charges (covered in the preceding section), dishonored electronic payment and returned check charges should be reasonable. Try setting the fee at $25 to $35 per returned item, or slightly higher than the amount your bank charges you.

Dealing with partial rent payments

Occasionally, you'll encounter a tenant who isn't able to pay the full rent on time. She may offer to pay a portion of the rent with a promise to catch up as the month proceeds. Your written rent collection policy shouldn't allow partial payments of rent, and deviating from this standard generally isn't a good idea.

In some instances, however, allowing for partial rent payments may make sense. If your tenant has an excellent rental payment history and you can verify that this partial payment is a one-time situation, then you're probably safe in accepting a partial rent payment. Of course, you need to be careful and watch for the tenant who's delaying the inevitable and stalling you from pursuing your legal options.

If you do accept a partial payment, prepare the proper legal notice for nonpayment of rent or draw up a written notice outlining the terms of your one-time acceptance of the partial rent payment, including late charges. Then present the tenant with the legal rent-demand notice or written agreement when she gives you the partial payment. This way, you can be sure she understands your terms.

In most areas, the acceptance of a partial payment voids any prior legal notices for nonpayment of rent. If your tenant is causing trouble besides the delinquent rent (read: breaching any other terms of the lease), don't accept any partial payments or you'll have to begin your eviction proceedings from scratch. In most states, after you begin the legal process for an eviction, you may demand full rent plus all late fees and other penalties, including legal and court costs. Should you accept any partial payment before the court hearing, the legal notice is voided, and in some cases you must refile the eviction action.

Always apply rental payments to the oldest outstanding past-due rent amount, even if the tenant tries to indicate the payment is for a different time period.

Rewarding timely payments

Because timely rent collection can make or break your career as a rental property owner, you may want to offer your tenants incentives to pay on time. If you have several rental units, one good way to motivate your tenants to pay the rent is to offer a monthly prize drawing for everyone who pays rent in full by your due date. Of course, you need to carefully outline your rules in writing and make sure you don't violate any local or state laws.

The drawing should be simple and easy for your tenants to understand. Limit eligibility to tenants who are current with their rent, and automatically enter tenants when you receive their full rent on or before the due date. Inform tenants of the time and place for the drawing and try to hold it in a common area at one of your properties. You can also give a second entry to tenants who pay early, but be sure your rules disqualify a winner whose rent payment is later returned for any reason.

The prize can be a gift certificate to a local store or restaurant. (Often, the merchant is willing to discount or donate the prize if it gets some good publicity from your drawing.) You may even want to offer a discount off the next month's rent. Either way, consider sending out a written announcement congratulating your monthly drawing winner.

Serving legal notices

If you're having trouble collecting rent from one of your tenants, you may need to pursue legal action. In most states, you don't need to wait until the end of the grace period to serve a legal rent-demand notice, but you should serve it personally whenever possible. But be aware that some states forbid the service of legal documents by the plaintiff (in this case, the plaintiff being you, in a legal action against your tenants). So check your state statutes because you may need to have the tenant served by another employee or a contracted process server. Contact your local NAA affiliate for the process-serving requirements in your area.

Legal notices for nonpayment of rent and similar breaches of the rental contract vary widely from state to state. The generic forms available from office supply stores may be ineffective or even invalid in your region. Contact your local NAA affiliate or the National Association of Realtors member board in your area for current and legally correct forms.

Raising the Rent without Sending Your Tenants Running

Increasing the rent is one of the most difficult challenges rental property owners face. You may be wondering how to raise the rent, worrying that tenants will leave or questioning how rent control ordinances may affect your efforts. I help clear up these murky waters in the following sections.

Figuring out how to raise the rent

The best way to establish your rent increase is to regularly review the local rental market to determine the current market rental rate for *comparable properties* — ones that are of similar size and condition and that have the same features and amenities. Turn to Chapter 6 for more information on evaluating the competitive rental market and setting rents.

Unless you're in a rent-controlled area, you have no limit on the amount or frequency with which you can increase the rent of a month-to-month or periodic tenant — with proper legal notice. If your tenant is on a lease, you need to hold off on raising rent until that lease expires. You can raise the rent as much and as often as your good business judgment and the competitive rental market allows. But don't be too aggressive or you'll lose your best tenants. Trying to get that last $25 per month can cost you a vacancy with significant turnover costs, plus the lost rent that's likely much more than $25 per month! I also recommend that you don't raise rents in small amounts too frequently, which tenants view as a nuisance. Even in a rental market with rising rents, you want to limit your rent increases to no more than once or twice per year and ensure that the amounts are justified and reasonable in the eyes of your tenants.

Many wise rental property owners intentionally keep their rents slightly lower than the maximum amount the competitive market will allow as part of a policy to retain the best tenants.

Be careful when raising the rent so that you're not accused of retaliatory rent increases. An increase immediately after a tenant complains to the local health department or building code enforcement agency, or an increase for one tenant that's much higher than what other tenants received, is likely to lead to problems. As always, your best defense is to have a sensible rent increase policy, keep good records, and be consistently fair and equitable with all your tenants.

Keeping your tenants (relatively) happy

Whether you raise the rent for the first time in several years or raise it on a semiregular basis, most tenants naturally have a negative reaction to a rent increase. So you need to do your homework and make sure that your increases are reasonable and justified. When the rental market is tight, adjust your rent by small amounts with greater frequency rather than large amounts less often. Most tenants don't leave over a small rent increase.

Before increasing your rent, be sure to determine what improvements you're going to make in your property's common area or, better yet, in the tenant's unit. I suggest setting a budget equivalent to three to six months of the rent increase and making an immediate upgrade to the tenant's unit. Often, just painting and cleaning or replacing the carpet helps your tenant accept the rent increase. Tenants also appreciate new plumbing or light fixtures.

Although you're legally required to give only a 30-day notice in many cases, I recommend a minimum rental-increase notice of 45 days. If the rent increase is significant (10 percent or more), a 60-day written notice is advisable. Some owners fear that giving their tenants notice also gives them plenty of time to find another rental. However, if you set your increased rent properly and treat your tenants fairly, you want your tenants to have the opportunity to compare the new rental rate to the market conditions.

If possible, inform each tenant personally of the pending rent increase and be sure to follow up by legally serving a formal written notice of the increase and keeping a copy in each tenant's file. The letter doesn't have to be a literary work, but you may consider attaching any market information obtained from your market survey (see more about market surveys in Chapter 6) so your tenants can see you've made an informed decision.

Realizing how rent control may affect you

If you don't live in California, Maryland, New Jersey, New York, or the District of Columbia, then you don't have to worry about rent control limiting your rental rates. But if you live in one of these regions, know that many of the larger cities and certain surrounding communities have rent-control laws that regulate many aspects of the landlord-tenant relationship.

Although the local rent-control ordinances differ by area, they all feature regulations that landlords must know and that may be broader than simply limiting the setting or adjusting of rental rates. These ordinances also invoke specific requirements that must be met prior to increasing the rent.

If you own rental property in a rent-controlled city, you typically must register your property with the local rent-control agency. Always have a current copy of the rent-control ordinance on hand and be sure you have a good understanding of all the regulations or procedures you must follow. The services of a landlord-tenant legal expert are extremely important for all rental property owners, but especially so in jurisdictions with any form of rent control.

Chapter 13

Keeping the Good Tenants
(And Your Sanity)

. . . .

In This Chapter

▶ Retaining your tenants by recognizing and fulfilling their wants and needs

▶ Reducing turnover by enticing tenants to renew their leases

. . . .

An occupied rental unit is the key to your success as a property manager. Yet this basic fact is something many rental property owners quickly forget. Advertising your vacancy, having a well-polished presentation, knowing all the latest sales closing techniques, implementing a thorough tenant screening program, and moving in your prized tenants with efficiency are all key parts of your job. But the day your tenant moves in is the day your most important job begins: keeping your good tenants satisfied and happy.

You want your best tenants to stay and pay. If you offer a quality rental experience at a reasonable price, you'll have lower turnover than other rental properties. You can achieve this goal by treating tenants with the same personal attention and courtesy you demonstrated when you first spoke to them on the phone or gave them a tour of the property.

Knowing what your customers want is the key to success in any business, and as a rental property owner, your tenants are your customers. In this chapter, I tell you what most tenants are looking for in a rental experience so you can make sure you're meeting those needs. I also give you some tips on getting your tenants to not only enjoy their experiences at your property but also want to renew their leases.

Knowing What Tenants Want

If you're trying to raise your level of tenant satisfaction (and that should always be your goal), you need to determine what your tenants want and how to deliver that to them. The following sections reveal what your tenants are basically looking for.

Out of sight shouldn't be out of mind

In my early years as a regional property manager, my wife and I lived on-site at one of the properties I oversaw for a large firm. We lived across the shared stairwell landing from Beatrice, one of the kindest and quietest neighbors you could ever have. Beatrice was a widow who kept to herself and only ventured out a handful of times per week for church and bridge club. She always paid her rent early and never complained. So what's the problem?

Well, Beatrice not only didn't want to bother any of the neighbors but also didn't want to be a burden on anyone and even failed to ask for routine maintenance. So when she eventually vacated her apartment, our on-site management staff were quite surprised when they did their pre-move-out walk-through with her: Only one stove burner worked, and one of the two toilets hadn't worked in years. It took a crew of three handymen a full week to turn over her apartment. When the property's on-site manager asked Beatrice how she could live with so many problems in her apartment and reminded her that two full-time maintenance pros lived on-site, Beatrice's only comment was that she could see how busy everyone was, and she didn't want to bother anyone, as she was sure that her problems were manageable. Besides, because she lived alone, she only needed one burner and one toilet!

Checking in on tenants periodically — even the quiet ones — can be worth a fortune in time and money if you can discover issues early, before they become expensive problems at move-out.

Timely and effective communication

Most tenants are concerned about a variety of fairly obvious issues. Good tenants don't like noisy neighbors, unkempt common areas, broken or unserviceable items in their units, or unsubstantiated rent increases. Fortunately, you can solve most of these problems if you exercise good communication and follow sound management practices.

Nobody likes to be ignored, particularly people who have a problem and are seeking a solution. Tenants expect you to care. If you fail to return their calls, are slow to make repairs, or fail to answer their questions honestly, they'll feel that you're not keeping up your end of the bargain. If you seem uncaring or nonchalant about tenants' concerns, they'll get the message that you don't value their business. The perception of apathy is often created by the unwillingness or failure to communicate. If you give your tenants the impression that you care about them only when their rent is late, you're headed straight down that apathy path.

Keep your tenants informed. No one likes surprises, and tenants are no different. If the pest control company cancels its service call, let your tenants know right away. If the walk-through with your new lender is rescheduled, call or e-mail your tenants instead of arriving unexpectedly with a weak apology. Common courtesy goes a long way.

Quick responses to maintenance requests

One way to set your rental management apart from your competition is to handle tenant maintenance requests quickly and professionally. Providing prompt resolution to your tenants' problems keeps them happy.

If a new tenant notes any problems after moving in, don't view these complaints as negatives. Instead, think of them as opportunities to let your tenant know you care. By quickly and professionally addressing the problems, you actually improve your tenant relations. Successful rental owners don't have to be perfect; they just need to admit a problem exists, communicate openly and candidly, and take the steps to resolve the issue.

A common complaint about rental owners is that they're unwilling to maintain, and especially upgrade, their units for current tenants. In my experience, this complaint is valid. Refusing to repaint, recarpet, or upgrade the appliances for a great tenant makes no sense. After all, if you don't do it for the great tenant you already have and that tenant gets frustrated with your lack of effort and moves out, you have to do the work anyway to be competitive in the rental market and attract a new, unproven tenant.

Unfortunately, in my experience, most owners and property managers will do almost anything for a new tenant, including making upgrades to the rental unit, while making the good, long-term tenants get by with the old carpet and appliances. Put yourself in the place of your long-term tenant. How would this make you feel?

Rental property owners often also overlook punctuality when it comes to making repairs. Undoubtedly, you're a very busy person, so you can easily lose sight of the fact that your tenants are busy, too. If you tell your tenants that you'll call or meet them at a certain time, do so — or, at the very least, call or text to let them know you're running late. Require your property manager, maintenance personnel, and contractors to treat your tenants with the same level of respect.

Treating your tenants as important customers can be the best decision you ever make. When working with a tenant concern, ask yourself how you'd want to be treated. Treating your tenants in this manner makes your tenant relations much more pleasant, dramatically decreases your tenant turnover, and improves your net income — a win-win situation for all!

Consistent respect for their privacy

The vast majority of tenants hate rental owners who fail to respect their privacy. In most states, the property manager or owner can enter the premises only with advance written notice or a tenant's permission, except in an emergency situation that's a threat to the property or a life-safety issue. Examples include pressurized water floods, fire or natural gas leaks, or any other imminent threat to life or limb. In such situations, always leave a note indicating that you had to enter the rental unit; include the date and time, as well as the reason.

The minimum required written notice of entry is 24 hours in most states. A few states require two days' notice, and many don't have any specific law at all. In these cases, 24 hours is generally considered reasonable notice. (Pop in the CD or click the link in the table of contents to access additional information about state laws regarding required notification for entering a tenant's rental unit.)

Legally, you may have to notify the tenant in writing only a few days in advance of when you want to enter the unit, but that isn't enough notice to maintain a positive and mutually respectful relationship with your tenants. Even though you own the property, the last thing you want your tenants to feel is that their home isn't really theirs. If you don't respect your tenants' privacy in their own home, they'll be less likely to show respect for you or your property during or at the end of their tenancy.

Your request for entry should only involve normal business hours. A few state laws offer specific day and time parameters, but many don't. Without the guidelines, some rental owners feel that as long as they give proper legal notice, they can enter the rental whenever they want. However, I recommend limiting your entry to Monday through Saturday from 9 a.m. to 6 p.m., unless the tenant requests or voluntarily agrees to a different time.

Equal enforcement of house rules

A frequent source of tenant complaints is the property owner's failure to enforce reasonable *house rules,* the policies and regulations you set for your property (check out Chapter 11 for info on establishing house rules). In fact, good tenants actually want and appreciate fair and reasonable policies and rules. They know that they'll be quiet and respectful of their neighbors, and they want to know that their neighbors must reciprocate. Establishing house rules for your properties and enforcing them fairly are all part of the job of managing rental property.

Too often I've seen owners who shy away from conflict. They just hope that problems will solve themselves. To be a good owner and property manager, you must be comfortable with rule enforcement. In most instances, addressing problems quickly lessens their severity.

Fair rental rates and increases

Rent increases are always unpopular, and if you don't handle them properly, they can easily lead to increased tension, tenant dissatisfaction, and a vacancy. No one likes to pay more, but, of course, the good stuff in life isn't cheap. Most tenants don't mind paying a fair and competitive rent, as long as they're convinced they're receiving good value for their money.

Although they may initially be upset with the increase, your tenants may be thinking to themselves that you can now finally address their peeling paint and missing window screens. Better yet, you might ask your tenants if such issues exist before imposing the rent increase. If your rental property has these issues and you increase the rent, address those problems right away to keep your tenants satisfied.

Increasing your price isn't a sin — after all, you're running a business. But common sense and prudence dictate that you explain to your tenants the reasons for the rent increase and what benefits are in it for them.

Recognizing the Ins and Outs of Renewing Leases

Tenants who renew their leases — thus locking in solid, long-term commitments — are a sign that you're doing a good job in your initial tenant screening and selection process and that you're keeping your tenants satisfied and meeting their needs. Lease renewals are one of your most productive activities as a rental property manager. Of course, despite your best efforts, not all tenants are good candidates for lease renewal, but renewing a lease with a current tenant clearly has a benefit over a lease with a new tenant. After all, you have a track record with your current tenant; you know her rent payment history and whether she treats the property and her neighbors with respect. You can never be 100 percent sure of that kind of information when you start from scratch with someone new.

Plus, your tenant knows what to expect from you as a property owner. She knows your standards for maintaining the property, your interest in and response to her requests, your house rules (and whether you enforce them fairly), and the courtesy and respect you have for her privacy. Your tenant has a certain comfort level with you, and as long as you're willing to be competitive with your rental rate, it's in her best interests to stay.

The info in the following sections helps you keep the good tenants around.

Reducing your turnover

One of the most effective ways to be successful in the rental housing business is to retain those tenants who are your best customers. Reducing turnover not only keeps the rental income flowing but also lowers your expenses. The tenant retention process really starts the moment the tenant moves in, and one fundamental step in that process is simply keeping track of when your leases expire.

Although renewing leases can reduce turnover and provide many benefits, renewing a lease in a strong rental market may not be in your best interest because a lease prevents you from raising the rent or changing any terms. Plus, with a lease in place, evicting a problem tenant is much more difficult. A tenant who wants a lease renewal may seem like a blessing, but you need to be certain that he treats your property properly and that the rental rate is competitive before signing a new long-term lease extension.

Understanding the costs of turnover

When a tenant moves out, you incur extensive turnover costs for maintenance, painting, and cleaning, and you lose rent for every day the unit sits vacant. The greatest wear and tear to your units occurs during the moving process. So if you can minimize the number of times you change tenants, your property will hold up better over time and won't incur as much cumulative damage that makes it look tired, even with routine repairs. For example, you can patch holes in drywall from furniture nicks, but the result's never quite like new unless you have an exceptional contractor.

In addition to maintenance and repair expenses, tenant turnover adds to your advertising costs and requires your time and effort to show the rental unit and screen each applicant. And after all that, you still may not have a tenant who'll treat your property and the neighbors respectfully and be prompt with rent payments.

Following is a look at what the typical costs are for a turnover of a $1,500 per month rental home that takes six weeks to re-rent, plus marketing and rental unit preparation charges.

Costs	Dollar Amount
Lost rent	$2,250
Advertising and signage	$400
Maintenance and repair parts	$175
Maintenance labor	$450
Painting	$475
Cleaning	$250
Total turnover cost	$4,000

Notice that the total cost is more than 2½ months' rent and doesn't include new floor or window coverings or any appliance replacement!

You may be able to legally deduct some of these costs from your tenant's deposit if he only lived in the property a short time, but this analysis doesn't include your time if you self-manage or the turnover fees from your property management company to cover its out-of-pocket expenses. Only you can put a value on your time, but the typical property management company charges from 50 percent to 100 percent of the monthly rent as a leasing fee.

Convincing tenants to re-sign

To avoid turnover, you need to get your tenant to re-sign his lease. Unless the lease contains an automatic renewal clause, it expires on the date specified. If you want your tenant to stay, don't be afraid to ask him to sign another lease that's effective when the current one expires. Contact your tenant at least 45 to 60 days prior to his lease expiration.

Keep the following in mind as you work to retain your good tenants and reduce turnover:

- **Plan your lease renewals so you don't have vacancies during those times of year when rental traffic is slow.** Many rental owners blindly seek the 12-month lease renewal as if that's the only option. When you're reviewing your upcoming lease expirations for tenants whom you want to renew, why not try something different? Structure the new lease expiration dates in your favor. Avoid times when other leases are expiring and select expiration dates that occur in more favorable seasons, when rental activity is strong in your local market. For example, most rental markets are traditionally slow from mid-November until mid-January, so if you have a lease that's up in the second week of November, offer your tenant a 16- or 18-month lease. The new lease then expires in the spring.

- **Provide exemplary customer service at all times.** I find that the customer service practices of certain retailers keep me coming back again and again. You can have that same customer service attitude. Anticipate your customers' needs and work to reinforce their positive image of your property and your ability to quickly respond to and competently address legitimate concerns that they raise.

✔ **Contact your strong tenants before their leases expire and discuss their satisfaction.** Doing so gives you a pretty good idea of which tenants are strong candidates for lease renewal. Remember, these quality tenants have the most leverage because they're so desirable. So if you want to impress a quality tenant with your proactive customer service, I suggest contacting him by phone two to three months before the current lease expires. Briefly review the service requests he has made to date to confirm whether he's satisfied with your response. Always ask whether you can do anything else for him. After he recovers from the shock that you're calling and you have a genuine interest in his needs, he'll tell you whether any problems exist so you can address them now rather than later. Most tenants are quite conservative in their requests.

Low turnover is financially rewarding, but you should resist the temptation to renew the lease of a tenant who doesn't pay rent on time or who creates other problems. If you're uncertain but cautiously optimistic that your tenant will pull through some temporary issues and be the great long-term tenant you want, don't offer a lease. Keep the tenant on month-to-month instead until he can demonstrate enough stability to warrant a new lease.

Listen and consider your tenants' requests

Throughout the 30 years that I've been a rental housing owner and manager, I've found many industry quirks that simply don't make any sense. One baffling mistake is the knee-jerk denial of a tenant request to make needed upgrades during the tenancy. One of the most common requests from tenants is to replace the carpeting. The standard rental owner's reaction is that he changes carpeting only on tenant turnover. Why institute a blanket policy that upgrades can only be made between tenants when the goal is to keep the same tenants for many years? I recommend first evaluating whether the request is reasonable and whether the tenant created the poor condition of the current carpeting.

Clearly, you don't want to replace the carpet for a tenant whose pet just ruined it; that's a rational reason to deny the request unless the tenant wants to pay for some or all of the cost. But if your inspection reveals a true need to replace the carpet, then you need to make the proper business decision. If the current tenant vacates and you have to replace the carpet to attract a new tenant, why not replace the carpet for your current good tenant? So often, rental owners and property managers summarily deny upgrade or improvement requests from tenants without proper consideration. Rethink this standard practice and give your good tenants a reason to stay. And while you're at it, why not also offer assistance removing and returning the tenants' furniture?

Offering incentives for tenants to stay

One of the main differences between rental property owners who enjoy their rental housing experience and former owners who tell horror stories is the ability to find and retain good, long-term tenants. If you can master the skill of attracting, screening, and holding on to your best tenants, you'll find that being a rental property owner or manager may even be enjoyable. Offering incentives to your tenants is an easy way to get them to stick around.

One successful technique I've used to keep properties in the positive cash flow mode and to keep those good tenants happy is a Resident Appreciation Day. Call your tenants in advance and bring them some breakfast treats or juice and gourmet coffee to start their day.

You can show your appreciation in hundreds of inexpensive yet meaningful ways, and the incentives you offer are limited only by your imagination and your budget. Following are some ideas to help get those brain juices flowing:

- ✔ Coupons for free DVD rentals, pizza, or other items
- ✔ Gift certificates to a popular local restaurant, the local mall, or a general merchandise store
- ✔ Movie theater passes
- ✔ Professional carpet cleaning or another type of pro cleaning service
- ✔ Two hours with your maintenance person for use at the renewing tenant's discretion (which can even involve moving furniture, hanging wall decorations, or anything else to make your rental unit the tenant's home)

Most good tenants like to have a landlord who demonstrates a sincere concern for them and is willing to invest the time and funds necessary to make sure they always have well-maintained property. So why not make a few upgrades to the unit a couple months before the tenant's lease expires as a reminder that you care about the tenant's satisfaction?

When you offer incentives to entice your tenants to stay, develop several choices for them that reflect the current and expected market conditions. If the rental market is weak, you need to be more generous than if you're in a tight rental market. Offer your tenants renewal incentives that improve your unit for future tenants (think mirrored closet doors, built-in water filter systems, security screen doors, ceiling fans, intrusion alarms, new kitchen countertops, new plumbing or lighting fixtures, or built-in microwave/stove hood units). Or another approach is simply to ask, "What would it take for you to remain with us for another lease term?"

An excellent way to improve your property and allow your tenant to personalize her home is to give her a list of comparably priced service items or unit upgrades and let her choose which upgrade she wants. You can have your contractor paint a few accent walls (in a tenant-selected color from a palette you control) or install quality wall coverings. Or you can give your tenant a few options to choose from for new, upgraded window coverings. This way, you send the message that you value her input and strive to reward her business.

In a competitive rental market with increasing rents, most tenants who intend to stay are glad to renew their current leases or even sign new leases at higher but still reasonable rents. Perform a rental market survey before setting the rent for any extended-term lease renewals so you know your rental rate is fair to both you and the tenants.

Renewal incentives are great if they make sense, but some creative, well-meaning ideas with frightening and unintended consequences are out there. For example, I once saw an incentive for "one free late rent payment" if a tenant renewed the lease. Is that really something you want to encourage? Another head-scratcher is to return the tenant's entire security deposit upon lease renewal if she has a history of prompt rent payment. My advice is never, never, never (did I mention never?) give back the security deposit until your tenant vacates the property! I can tell you hundreds of stories about the problems of not having a security deposit to keep tenants honest and responsible. That small amount of money is your best insurance against damage to the rental unit. After all, even the best tenants are careless when they know you aren't holding any security deposit.

Following up with tenants after move-out

Sometimes good tenants leave, and that's out of your control. Just make sure you maintain a professional relationship with them, because you never know when they may refer you to a co-worker, friend, or family member.

One of the most common reasons a tenant leaves or doesn't renew a lease is the intent to purchase a home. Although homeownership is a very worthy goal, you may want to advise your tenant about other options. For example, if you want to entice her to stay, you may offer a lease option (see Chapter 21 for more info) or a long-term lease at a fixed amount that provides rent stability. A number of calculators are available on the Internet to help people determine whether they're better off renting or buying, given their overall financial situation. Let tenants know their options without discouraging them from buying if that's really best for them.

Make sure departing tenants complete tenant exit surveys. This survey may not help you retain your moving tenants, but asking some basic questions about the reason for their move gives you valuable, candid feedback on what they liked and disliked so you can make appropriate changes for the future. And when you seek their feedback, why not ask them if they'd please refer other good tenants (like themselves) in the future?

Chapter 14

Dealing with Problem Tenants

- -

In This Chapter

▶ Knowing how to handle typical tenant problems

▶ Considering options other than eviction

▶ Navigating your way through the eviction process

▶ Being prepared for situations beyond the norm

- -

*A*lthough the proper tenant screening and selection techniques greatly improve your success in picking good tenants, they aren't a guarantee. At some point in your rental property management tenure, you're sure to come across a problem tenant or two. Some tenants avoid paying rent, disturb the neighbors, damage property, or keep a growing collection of inoperative cars on the front lawn, and you need to take steps immediately to remove these tenants and replace them. But other tenants — like the one who pays his rent a few days late every month or the one who sneaks in an animal even though pets aren't allowed — are more subtle in the problems they present, and their behavior may not warrant eviction. This chapter gives you tips for handling some common tenant problems and suggests valuable alternatives to eviction. It also prepares you for some scenarios you may encounter so you know right away how to deal with them.

Recognizing and Responding to Common Tenant Problems

The level of response you take toward a problem tenant depends on how severe the problem is and how frequently it occurs. Some issues — including nonpayment of rent, additional occupants not on the rental contract, noise, and unsupervised children — are breaches of the rental contract and clearly call for serving a legal notice.

Documentation is critical whenever you have a problem with a tenant. Even minor problems are worth documenting because, over time, they may add up or increase in severity. If you need to evict a tenant, you must have written documentation of as many elements of the entire situation as possible because you'll likely have the burden of proof if you end up in court.

The next few sections highlight several of the more common problems you may experience with your tenants and how to handle them.

Late or nonpayment of rent

One of the toughest issues you'll encounter is how to deal with a tenant who consistently pays her rent late or, even worse, doesn't pay her rent at all. In other respects, the tenant may not create any problems, but she just can't seem to comply with the contract's payment requirements. You may have to serve a Notice of Nonpayment of Rent to get the tenant to pay — and even then, she may not include the late charge with her payment. In my experience, this nagging problem doesn't go away unless you put a stop to it.

When you're faced with a tenant who just can't seem to get her rent payment in on time, you have many factors to consider (such as whether the tenant is creating any other problems for you or other residents), but the strength of the rental market is usually the most important issue. If it's a renter's market and you know that finding another tenant will be difficult, you may be willing to be more flexible.

Specific legal notices are available in most states (from your local NAA affiliate) to deal with the issue of nonpayment of rent, but you should document other violations of the rental contract in writing using a Lease or Rental Agreement Violation Letter, which you can access by popping in the CD or clicking the link in the table of contents.

Don't ignore the problem of a tenant who consistently pays late. You're not doing your tenants any favors by allowing them to fall behind on their rent, which is probably their largest monthly financial commitment. Clearly inform her in writing that she has breached the rental contract, and be sure to do so each and every time she pays late. If you fail to enforce timely rent payment obligations or your late charges, the tenant can later argue that you've waived your rights to insist on compliance with the contract's rent payment provisions or to collect future late charges. Inform the tenant in writing that chronic late payments are grounds for eviction, even if you're not necessarily willing to go that route just yet. (Chapter 12 describes how to handle late payments and late charges.)

Additional occupants

Tenants frequently abuse the guest policy by having additional occupants in their rental units for extended periods. But you may have trouble determining the difference between a temporary guest and a new live-in occupant. Be sure that you have specific guest policies as part of your rental agreement or house rules. If you suspect your tenant has added another occupant, talk to him to find out what's going on. Point out your guest policy, but be sure to get his story before jumping to conclusions. This practice is sound not only because it's considerate but also because you need to avoid claims of discrimination, particularly if the additional occupant is a child.

In the case of children (where custody is an issue), I suggest you add them to the lease or rental agreement because they really aren't guests but family members. Because legally they're minors, they don't need to complete a rental application or go through your prospective tenant screening process, as adults would. If the addition of the child causes the household to exceed your occupancy, have a written policy for handling the situation differently from the addition of an adult (see Chapter 10 for suggested policies).

If your tenant doesn't comply with your guest policy, immediately send him a Lease or Rental Agreement Violation Letter indicating that the additional occupant must be formally added to the rental contract as a tenant or must leave as of the notice's expiration. (**Remember:** All new adult occupants must complete a rental application, go through the tenant screening process, and sign the rental contract if approved.) If the tenant fails to cooperate, you may need to take legal action.

Pop in the CD or click the link in the table of contents for a Lease or Rental Agreement Violation Letter, which you can modify for your needs.

A common guest policy in the rental housing industry is to allow guests to stay in the unit for up to 14 consecutive days. But savvy tenants just ask their guests to leave for a day or two and then return. Although tough to enforce, I suggest modifying your guest policy to limit visits to a total of no more than 14 days in any 6-month time frame. You should uniformly enforce this policy to the best of your ability to avoid allegations of discrimination.

Proving occupancy can be difficult. The receipt of mail or the presence of a vehicle on the property for excessive periods of time is often solid proof. Local law enforcement and your mail carrier can be of great assistance here.

You must be careful when determining whether an additional occupant is a rental contract or guest policy violation if the individual may qualify under fair housing law as a *caregiver,* which is a disability accommodation. Typically, a caregiver isn't on the rental contract, isn't responsible for rent payment, and often can be a family member. You can screen him for behavior issues but not for credit because a caregiver isn't responsible for rent. Don't have caregivers sign the lease; instead, have them enter into a caregiver agreement that indicates that they're living on-site only for the purpose of performing assistance services and that they agree to follow the house rules, except that they're exempt from senior housing age restrictions. Seek the advice of legal counsel if you have any questions.

Inappropriate noise level

Unreasonable or excessive noise is likely the most common complaint that landlords and property managers receive from tenants, and it's easy to downplay the seriousness of the issue — especially if you live across town! But unreasonable or excessive noise is a nuisance by law in most areas. You don't want a few noise complaints to spiral into a tenant taking official action against you or refusing to pay her rent because of her "loss of quiet enjoyment" of the property. Many jurisdictions have noise ordinances, and some allow action such as fines or violation notices to be taken against you as well as your tenant. Tenants may also find that their local small claims court is willing to give them a healthy rent credit for their loss of sleep!

You usually hear about a noisy tenant from one of the tenant's neighbors. The neighbor may or may not have already made her concerns known directly to the noisy tenant. If she has and the noise continues unabated (or she isn't willing to take any action), then, as a first step, you should contact the tenant, explain that there's been an anonymous complaint, and inform the tenant that you expect him to live quietly with his neighbors. Confirming the substance of your conversation in a follow-up letter to the noisy tenant is wise.

If the unacceptable noise continues, tell the complaining tenants that they can always contact law enforcement and file an official complaint as soon as the noise level becomes a problem. Then they should let you know that they've done so.

Have a policy that requires all tenant complaints regarding neighbors — especially noise — to be in writing. Neighbors usually don't want to go to court to testify; they just want you to quickly solve the problem and allow them to keep their anonymity. But if the noisy tenant disputes the charges, the courts are usually reluctant to accept your unsubstantiated testimony. A report from law enforcement and a written complaint made simultaneously by a neighbor carry a lot of weight. If tenants don't send you a written complaint, write them and state that you're still waiting for them to document the problem, that you can't do much without their cooperation, and that you'll recount what you understand they told you and correct any mistakes in a responsive letter. If tenants fail to provide a written complaint, this confirmation letter at least has some value. Although it would be hearsay and inadmissible to prove that the noise occurred, it may be admitted in court to show that management received complaints.

Unsupervised children

Under federal law, with the exception of the limited number of HUD-certified senior housing properties, you must accept children at your rental property. Unfortunately, one of the toughest dilemmas you'll face is dealing with a tenant's unsupervised child on the grounds of your property. If you don't do anything and the child gets hurt, you may be sued for failing to take reasonable action. But if you don't handle the matter properly, the tenant may claim that you're discriminating against families with children. In this case, you need to be able to prove that you acted reasonably and consistently.

If you become aware of an unsupervised child at your property who is in a potentially dangerous situation, immediately contact the parent or caretaker or, if the situation is serious, escort the child home to her parent(s). Take the child home again if the problem happens a second time but also send a letter to your tenants warning them of the seriousness of the matter. If the written notice isn't effective, you can always call the police or social services while advising your tenants, in writing, that an eviction may be warranted. Diplomacy is essential here, as nothing can hit a nerve as quickly as someone accusing a child of misbehaving.

You can't require general supervision of children, but you can address any health and safety issues or lease violations for disturbance of others. If your tenants fail to properly supervise their children and the children damage your property, don't just talk to the children about the problem. Immediately contact the tenants and officially advise them of the health and safety issues or lease violations, stressing the fact that they're responsible for the actions of all household members and guests and that disturbances or property damage by tenants of any age is unacceptable. Communicate in writing or provide a letter confirming your conversation. This kind of action is usually sufficient, but if the damage is severe or continues, notify the tenants in writing, bill them for the damage, and warn them that any continued problems will result in eviction.

Exploring Alternatives to Eviction

Evictions are both expensive and emotionally draining. They can also be costly in terms of lost rent, legal fees, property damage, and turnover expenses. And they can earn a negative reputation for your rental property with good tenants in the area. Always consider the costs of any decision you make — in dollars, in reputation, and in tenant relationships. Be sure to evaluate each situation carefully and only turn to eviction as a last resort.

When you're looking for an alternative to evicting a problem tenant, such as the solutions presented in the following sections, don't underestimate the importance of communicating with your tenant. Be sure to document any conversations you have or agreements you reach in writing, and make sure both you and the tenant sign and get a copy of the paperwork.

If the most likely outcome of an issue with a tenant is an expensive and time-consuming eviction, do your best to minimize or cut your losses. A court judgment against a tenant without any assets doesn't help your cash flow, but a nonpaying or bad tenant is much worse than no tenant at all. Your primary goal should be to regain possession of the rental unit and find a new tenant as quickly as possible.

Negotiating a voluntary move-out

Although you may feel strongly that your tenant should keep up his end of the rental contract, you may come out ahead by avoiding legal action and not having to worry about him anymore. You may be able to negotiate a voluntary move-out with your tenant, in which you forgive the unpaid rent if he agrees to leave by a mutually agreed upon date. Another approach is to agree to refund the tenant's full security deposit immediately after he vacates the property (as long as no significant damage has been done to it).

If you agree on a voluntary move-out, don't count on a verbal agreement. Make sure you get it in writing.

Using mediation or arbitration services

If you aren't able to reach an agreement with your tenant about a voluntary move-out, consider taking your dispute to a neutral third-party mediation or arbitration service.

- ✔ *Mediation* is an informal opportunity for both parties to resolve their disputes with the assistance of a local mediation group at little or no cost. It typically involves only the parties to the dispute (you and your tenant).

- ✔ Often confused with mediation, *arbitration* is legally binding and enforceable and can be a relatively quick and inexpensive alternative to litigation. It often involves attorneys, witnesses, and experts in addition to you and your tenant.

Many organizations offer both mediation and arbitration services, so if mediation doesn't resolve the issue, you can always try arbitration. Check with your local legal bar association for referrals.

Taking your tenant to court

Rather than eviction, you may want to consider taking your tenant to small claims or municipal court. Rental property owners in many states can turn to small claims or municipal courts to resolve the issue of the rental unit's possession in an eviction. Courts with limited jurisdiction are often used to resolve landlord-tenant matters restricted to monetary demands. The jurisdictional limits for these courts range from $2,000 to $15,000, but the majority are $5,000 or less. Consult with your local court for its limits.

The popularity of court TV shows means almost everyone is generally familiar with the roles of the participants in, and the procedures of, small claims courts. Although this knowledge can make the participants more comfortable with the format, note that most small claims or municipal court proceedings aren't as entertaining in real life as what you see on TV because there matters are handled quickly and efficiently and edited down to just a few minutes. If you plan to head to court with your tenant, don't be afraid to be overly prepared. Consider using labeled "exhibits" for all your documentation in a chronological order that supports your claim. Be sure to bring copies for the court and your tenant.

Giving 'Em the Boot: Evicting a Tenant

Some tenants just don't pay their rent; others violate the rules or are involved in criminal activities. In these situations, after you've explored your other options, you may have no other reasonable alternative but an eviction. The eviction process, which I give you an overview of in the following sections, can be intimidating and costly, but keep in mind that allowing the tenant to stay only prolongs the problem.

The eviction process varies greatly from state to state, and many attorneys who specialize in representing rental property owners offer guidebooks that outline the specific legal steps for an eviction action in your area. Your local IREM chapter or NAA affiliate can provide attorney references; you can access contact information for both groups by heading to the CD or clicking the link in the table of contents.

Serving legal notices

To evict a tenant, you need to follow the applicable law as well as the contract. For a fixed-term lease, some states don't require service of a notice of nonrenewal. If the contract requires the resident to give you notice in order to leave at the end of the lease term, most courts interpret that duty to be reciprocal, and you have to give the resident notice to obtain the legal right to file an eviction upon lease expiration. Of course, even if a notice isn't legally required, it's wise to inform the resident in writing that the lease won't be renewed in a reasonable time before it expires.

If the tenant stays beyond the lease's expiration and you accept rent, a month-to-month tenancy is created on the same terms as the lease. In a month-to-month tenancy, you have to terminate the tenancy by giving an appropriate, legal Notice of Termination. You can generally terminate month-to-month tenancies with written, 30-day notices, although some states and some subsidized programs require a longer period.

Although the terminology varies from state to state, three other basic types of legal notices are required, depending on the circumstances:

✔ **Pay Rent or Quit notices:** These notices are given to tenants who haven't paid rent and require tenants to pay the rent or move out. Tenants are typically allowed from 3 to 10 days to pay in full, depending on the law in your state, but some jurisdictions allow up to 30 days. Be careful not to include late fees or other non-rent charges in your Pay Rent or Quit notice because many courts will determine that the notice is overstated, and you may lose your case.

✔ **Cure or Quit (or Perform Covenant or Quit) notices:** This paperwork is given to tenants who've violated one of the terms or conditions of the rental contract. It gives tenants a limited number of days (determined by state law) to cure the violation or vacate the premises; if they fail to do so, they're subject to an eviction action. The most common violations are to remove an unauthorized pet or occupant or to pay a fee other than rent, such as late charges, returned check fees, or a utility.

✔ **Notice to Quit or Unconditional Quit notices:** These documents are the most severe types of notices and require tenants to vacate the premises without the opportunity to cure any deficiency. Most states discourage the use of these notices unless tenants are conducting illegal activity, have repeatedly violated a significant term or condition of the rental contract, or have severely damaged the premises.

Filing a formal eviction action

If your tenant doesn't cure the violation or leave the property after receiving the appropriate legal notice, she isn't automatically evicted. Instead, you must begin a formal eviction process by following these steps:

1. **You file the required forms with your local court and arrange to have the tenant properly served with a summons and complaint.**

   The complaint is usually a preprinted form, and you can only seek unpaid rent and actual damages. Many times, daily rental damages continue to accrue during the pendency of the action, and they can be added to the judgment granted at the end of the court process.

   Serving a legal notice isn't simply a matter of mailing the notice or slipping it under the tenant's door. You must have an authorized person attempt to physically deliver the legal notice to the tenant face to face. If the notice can't be delivered directly to the tenant, there are usually procedures for substitute service or posting and mailing pursuant to a court order. Every state has specific rules and procedures as to what exactly constitutes *proper legal service,* including who can serve notices, the method of delivery, the specific parties who can be legally served, and the amount of time the tenant has to respond to the legal notice. Check with your attorney for the requirements in your area.

2. **By law, a trial date is set, and your tenant has a certain number of days to file an answer to your summons and complaint.**

Tenants usually either deny the allegations you've made in your eviction action or claim that they have an *affirmative defense* (a legal justification for their actions). The tenant may deny your allegations, for example, if she has a canceled check showing that the rent was paid and your records are in error.

Frequently, tenants know that they've materially breached their rental contracts and voluntarily leave the premises. Or sometimes tenants settle with you out of court.

If your tenant settles informally, you must officially dismiss your court eviction action because doing so is the proper way to treat your tenant and it also preserves your reputation with the court. After all, courts have limited resources and don't respond well to parties who resolve their matter and fail to file a timely dismissal. Also, failing to dismiss an eviction action can result in a negative credit standing for your tenant.

3. **If your tenant doesn't file an answer in a timely manner, the eviction action proceeds to court without the tenant.**

   This scenario is known as an *uncontested eviction.* The court requires you to prove your case, but the tenant isn't there to respond to or deny your charges. Typically, you can easily prevail in this situation, as long as you have good documentation.

4. **If your tenant files an answer and appears at court, each party receives the opportunity to present its evidence before the court makes a ruling.**

   This scenario is known as a *contested eviction.* In the alternative, the parties can enter into a formal written settlement right before trial. Then the judge signs the settlement and it becomes a court order. If a settlement isn't reached, the parties proceed to present evidence in the courtroom. If you're prepared and professionally present the facts in a well-supported case, you can generally win. However, the courts can be very harsh if you've acted illegally or in a retaliatory or discriminatory manner toward the tenant.

   You may also have to show that you've properly and promptly responded to any complaints by your tenant during her tenancy, especially those that involve allegations of health and safety violations or uninhabitable conditions at your property.

A tenant may be able to argue that she's entitled to additional time to work out a payment plan for the unpaid rent or that she has a hardship that requires the court's leniency. Although not legally required in most states, courts have been known to allow a tenant an extension because of inclement weather, an appeal of the ruling, or the improvement of the tenant's health or other personal situation.

Some jurisdictions show extra leniency during the fall and winter holidays, so you may want to be more diligent to get your matter to court quickly if the holidays are approaching.

5. **If you win the eviction lawsuit, you must present the judgment to local law enforcement.**

   The local law enforcement gives the tenant one final notice before going to the rental unit and physically removing the tenant and her possessions. Arrange to have someone meet the law enforcement officers at the property at the designated time, and have the locks changed after you receive legal possession of the unit.

Following the do's and don'ts of the eviction process

Although the eviction process is rather straightforward in most areas, you still want to ensure you don't do anything to jeopardize the proceedings. I can't guarantee that the process will run smoothly, but if you keep the following do's and don'ts in mind, you can alleviate many headaches:

- ✔ **Do use an attorney.** The filing and serving of eviction actions are governed by very precise and detailed rules. The smallest mistake can result in delays or even the loss of your case on technicalities, regardless of the fact that the tenant hasn't paid rent or has otherwise violated the rental contract.

- ✔ **Don't fail to properly respond to maintenance requests.** Even if you're in the middle of an eviction process with a tenant, you're *always* responsible for properly maintaining the premises. If someone gets hurt because of your failure to keep the property in good condition, you can be sued.

  Tenants and their attorneys are very sensitive to maintenance issues. Any failure to respond to a tenant's request for maintenance can be used as a defense in the eviction action.

- ✔ **Don't get too emotionally involved in an eviction process and make an irrational decision that can be construed as a self-help eviction.** A *self-help* or *constructive eviction* is a situation in which the owner takes illegal actions to effectively force the tenant to vacate the premises. Veteran rental property owners love to tell stories about the good old days when they could just change the locks or shut off the electricity or water to encourage a tenant to immediately vacate the premises. But in today's reality, no states tolerate these aggressive tactics, regardless of how bad the tenant may be. In many states, even reducing or eliminating free services such as cable TV can create a serious problem; the court can consider this move an illegal self-help measure, and the tenant can sue for significant penalties.

Collecting judgments

When you win in court and your tenant owes you for unpaid rent, damages, or legal fees, you've received a *money judgment* against the tenant. But the judgment isn't worth much unless you're able to collect. If you know that the tenant has a job or other unencumbered assets, in most states you can obtain a court order to garnish his salary or have local law enforcement seize his assets and sell them, with the net proceeds of the sale going to you.

The majority of problem tenants aren't easy to locate, so your best bet may be to hire a licensed collection agency to attempt to locate the tenant and collect your judgment. These agencies are usually paid on a contingency basis and receive a portion of the collected amount, typically ranging from one-third to one-half of the amount. Sometimes they add any out-of-pocket or hard costs of collection to the amount they retain. Although you may want to make your own efforts to enforce the judgment, remember that collection agency success rates and fees are often tied to the age of the bad debt. So the sooner you submit the judgment for collection, the easier it is for the agency to collect, lowering the fee you have to pay.

Your success in collecting judgments often depends on how hard you worked throughout the tenancy. The rental application typically contains valuable information for a collection agency, including the tenant's Social Security Number (SSN) or Individual Taxpayer Identification Number (ITIN), prior addresses, current and prior employment information, banking and credit card accounts, vehicle information, and emergency telephone numbers. If you require a tenant to complete this application, you verify its accuracy, and you keep the info updated, you have a great place to start hunting him down for collections.

Handling Unusual Tenant Situations

After a few years as a rental property owner, you may begin to think you've seen it all, but new and interesting twists always arise to keep rental management challenging. Knowing how to handle these unusual — yet surprisingly common — situations, some of which I cover in the following sections, can make life much easier.

Bankruptcies

One last-ditch effort some tenants make when they're in financial trouble is to file bankruptcy. There are several types of bankruptcies under the federal bankruptcy laws but only two that you'll likely encounter. The most common is Chapter 7, where debts are completely eliminated after paying a percentage of the amount owed to all identified creditors. But you'll also encounter Chapter 13, in which the debtor ultimately repays all debts in full, but the court approves a reorganization plan that allows the debtor to pay over an extended time frame.

Traditionally, many rental owners suffer severe financial blows when tenants file bankruptcy during the eviction process because doing so institutes an *automatic stay,* which immediately stops any lawsuit involving an eviction action. The rental owner must then petition the federal bankruptcy court for permission to proceed with the eviction by requesting a motion for Relief from Automatic Stay, which can delay the eviction process for several days to a few weeks.

The Bankruptcy Abuse Prevention and Consumer Protection Act of 2005, however, gives rental property owners some relief. Under this act, you can proceed with your eviction if you already have a judgment for possession when the tenant files for bankruptcy. The law also provides that the court can lift the stay in ten days if you can show that the tenant is using illegal controlled substances or is endangering the property.

Severe legal penalties exist for rental owners who violate an automatic stay, so as soon as you become aware of your tenant filing bankruptcy, immediately stop any collection or eviction efforts and contact a landlord-tenant legal expert. Your legal counsel knows what steps to take in each situation and can file pleadings with the federal bankruptcy court requesting a motion for Relief from Automatic Stay in order to proceed with the eviction, if necessary. *Note:* Even if you routinely handle your own legal work, have an attorney handle all tenant bankruptcy matters because bankruptcies are complicated, and you need good legal advice.

Illegal holdovers

Rental owners have a rough time when a tenant fails to vacate the property as mutually agreed upon in the rental contract. Unless you accept rent, tenants who continue to live at your property are referred to as *holdover tenants.* Many states require you to give holdover tenants a legal notice to vacate immediately; other states allow you to proceed directly with an eviction action.

A common trick used by savvy tenants (or ones advised by tenants rights attorneys or eviction delay firms) is to submit the rent and hope that it's cashed so any outstanding notice is voided or a new month-to-month rental agreement is created at the lease's expiration. If you have several rental units with tenants who mail or drop off the rent, you may be handling quite a few checks at once. To avoid this common mistake, you need to be extra careful that you don't inadvertently deposit the tenant's rent check. Make a copy of the check and return the original with a letter indicating that you'll be forced to proceed with eviction if the tenant fails to move out.

If you accept rent, you agree to a continuation of the tenant's rental, generally on at least a month-to-month basis, unless state law indicates differently.

Broken rental contracts

Although you may occasionally be faced with a tenant who refuses to leave as agreed, you'll surely encounter a tenant who leaves before the expiration of her rental contract and doesn't want to pay the balance of her financial obligation to you. In practically all states, you don't have the right to demand that the tenant pay the rent due each month for the balance of the rental contract.

So what can you do? First, confirm that the tenant has indeed given up her right of possession. Then take reasonable steps to mitigate or limit the ongoing rent and other charges to the departed tenant by preparing the unit for re-renting. In most states, you must make a reasonable effort to promptly re-rent the property, including the use of advertising or other standard rental marketing methods. If you don't make an effort, the tenant may be released from any further legal obligation to pay the balance of rent owed under the rental contract.

Handle the marketing of this rental unit just like any other unit. You don't need to lower the rent, lower your tenant selection standards, or give this rental priority over any other available unit. Of course, you can't be vindictive and attempt to make yourself rich either.

Tenants frequently dispute whether your efforts were reasonable in mitigating their financial obligations. If challenged in court, you need to show that you maintained detailed records clearly indicating the actions you took to re-rent the property, including dated copies of all documents. The tenant generally has the burden of proof, but courts are often sympathetic to tenants who may have hardships, so be prepared.

Tenants sometimes have legitimate reasons for breaking their rental contracts, and in these situations, they don't have any further obligations to you. These legitimate reasons are all subject to state and local laws, but they can include the following:

- ✔ Harassment of the tenant by the property owner
- ✔ An uninhabitable rental unit
- ✔ Violation of a significant rental contract condition

Some state or federal laws allow the tenant to leave under certain specified circumstances, such as job transfers, military transfers, or health reasons. Make sure you know the laws applicable in your area.

Pop in the CD or click the link in the table of contents to access state-by-state information on a landlord's duty to re-rent the rental unit.

Assignments or subleases

A tenant may approach you and request the right to assign or sublease his interest in the rental unit.

- ✔ If you allow an *assignment,* the new tenant takes over all aspects of the original tenant's rental contract, and you can take legal action directly against the new tenant.

- ✔ *Subleases* are a relationship solely between your tenant and the new tenant. You can't directly sue the new tenant for unpaid rent or damage to the property; all you can do is go after the original tenant.

Tenants usually only request the right to assign or sublease when they must suddenly relocate for personal or professional reasons. Typically, rental contracts prohibit subleases because you want to have a direct relationship with the occupant. Assignments are superior to subleases because you do have the opportunity to screen and approve the new tenant's application. Note that a complete prohibition against assignment or subletting is likely to affect your ability to pursue a tenant for breach of lease. Most judges expect that you won't refuse any reasonable offers to allow tenants to comply with their obligations through a third party.

Subleases needlessly complicate the landlord-tenant relationship and prevent you from directly taking legal action against the occupant of your premises. If the proposed occupant meets all your rental criteria, propose terminating the current rental contract and entering into a new one with him.

Departing roommates

On occasion, you may receive a notice that a tenant or roommate will be leaving the property in the middle of a lease. The departing tenant usually requests a partial refund of the security deposit, even though not all the individuals on the rental contract are vacating the premises. You should retain the entire security deposit until all contracted occupants have vacated the property (see Chapter 15 for more on dealing with security deposit disputes).

If one tenant chooses to vacate early, then the tenants need to resolve any security deposit issues themselves. For example, if a new roommate is moving in, that individual can inspect the premises and pay the departing tenant an agreed amount for her share of the security deposit. Or the remaining tenant can reach some other fair and equitable agreement with the departing tenant.

If the rental contract is going to change, require the departing tenant to complete a Deposit Assignment and Release Agreement (available on the accompanying CD or by clicking the link in the table of contents). This document releases you from liability.

Domestic problems

Couples (or any combination of two or more individuals) who rent the premises together and have domestic disputes provide a tough challenge for rental property owners. As with disputes between neighbors or roommates, you need to avoid getting involved. You lack the authority to side with one party or the other, so stay neutral, encourage the couple to resolve their problems themselves, and continue treating all parties fairly and equally.

Unfortunately, some disagreements between tenants involve domestic violence, and you may receive a request from one occupant to change the locks or remove one of the co-tenants from the lease. Don't agree to any such changes, regardless of the strength of the tenant's argument, without first seeking legal advice and requiring a copy of a restraining order or other appropriate court order from the requesting tenant. In some circumstances you may be able to avoid an argument about changing the locks because the other party may be willing to voluntarily leave or allow the changing of the locks. But to cover yourself, even if the other party is cooperative or isn't disputing the matter, insist on a verifiable letter or agreement documenting the other party's consent. Be careful not to discriminate against the victim of domestic violence by evicting her, especially if the perpetrator is no longer in the rental unit and doesn't return to the property.

Some state laws allow victims of domestic violence to give notice and breach their lease without penalty upon presentation of either a court order or a police report.

The Violence Against Women Act of 2005 prohibits public housing agencies and rental properties that accept Housing Choice Vouchers from denying an applicant because she's been a victim of domestic violence or stalking. Nearly 30 states have passed legislation protecting women in similar situations, so check with local legal counsel if you run into one.

Tenant deaths

If you have reason to suspect the death of a tenant who lives alone, try calling the tenant or banging loudly on his door. Check with any known family or the neighbors, and call the tenant's place of employment and the emergency contact number from the rental application. If you still aren't sure, exercise your right to inspect the rental unit in an emergency or contact the police or fire department.

When officials have confirmed the death and removed the body, you must immediately take reasonable steps to safeguard the deceased tenant's property, including denying access to the unit except for obtaining limited personal effects for a funeral. Secure the unit and allow access only to legally authorized persons or law enforcement. If you have any doubts about the authority or actions of the tenant's relatives or friends, contact your attorney for further advice.

At this time, you may also find yourself in the middle of a dispute as to who has access to the unit. Although you should be sympathetic to your tenant's grieving relatives, make sure you don't grant rental unit access to an unauthorized person or you may be held liable if Aunt Margo's prized goldfish-shaped cookie cutter turns up missing. When faced with this unusual situation, it's best to have your tenant-landlord legal expert assist you in determining who's authorized to access the rental and potentially remove property. Your goal is to get the unit back without any furnishings or personal property so you can re-rent it, but don't be in such a hurry that you fail to take the proper steps and find yourself accused of unintentional aiding in the theft of the deceased tenant's property.

Chapter 15

Moving Out the Tenants

· ·

In This Chapter

▶ Providing your tenant with the necessary paperwork to make move-out a breeze

▶ Assessing the rental unit at move-out

▶ Dealing with security deposit disputes

▶ Knowing what to do when a tenant abandons your property

· ·

*A*lthough hanging on to your great tenants forever would be nice, the reality is that all tenants leave at some point. Your goal is to make the experience as straightforward and painless as possible by maintaining clear communication and procedures. Don't just assume that your tenants are familiar with proper move-out procedures. Instead, have a proactive plan that involves your tenants in the process of preparing the rental unit for the next tenant. Communication and reasonable and mutually agreed upon expectations are the key here.

It may sound pessimistic, but start preparing for your tenants' eventual move-out when they first move in. The Tenant Information Letter (covered in more detail in Chapter 11) provides tenants with the legal requirements of move-out, as well as your expectations for giving proper notice. You can use the Move-In/Move-Out Itemized Statement (also explained in Chapter 11), which you complete upon move-in to establish the unit's baseline condition, to evaluate the unit's condition on move-out and calculate the appropriate charges, if any.

This chapter covers the importance of having a written notice (the Move-Out Information Letter) and proper procedures in place for returning the security deposit. It also helps you distinguish between damage and ordinary wear and tear and offers guidance on handling special move-out situations.

Requiring Written Notice of Your Tenants' Move-Out Plans

When giving notice that they plan to move, most tenants call or mention it when they see you, even though your rental contract most likely contains clauses that require written notice. Some tenants may put their notices in writing by sending you simple one- or two-sentence letters or e-mails but leave out critical information or important details. Although any type of written notice from a tenant is usually legal, a proper notice provides much more information.

To be sure you're complying with the law in all regards, require your tenants to use a Tenant's Notice of Intent to Vacate Rental Unit. This form contains important information, including the tenant's approval of your entering the unit upon reasonable notice to show it to workers, contractors, and prospective tenants. Be sure to include all agreed-upon terms, including the following:

- ✔ How the notice of entry must be given
- ✔ How much time must elapse before entry is allowed
- ✔ The number of hours you may access the unit
- ✔ Whether you can access the unit in the tenant's absence

Pop in the CD or click the link in the table of contents to access a version of the Tenant Notice of Intent to Vacate Rental Unit that you can print, fill out, and supply to your tenants.

When you receive verbal or written notice, honor the date of the notice, providing it complies with the notice requirement in your lease. But also insist that the tenant complete this form; doing so is simply good policy. If you don't have this info in writing, many misunderstandings can arise. You may not remember the move-out date and be caught off guard scheduling a new move-in only to find that the tenant won't be out until the following week. The most common reason tenants want to give only a verbal notice is so they can change the move-out date unilaterally as their plans change and blame it on your memory. Surprises aren't good business!

Time is truly of the essence when it comes to an occupant's move-out. Several states have deadlines for the accounting or return of the security deposit of only 14 or 15 days, and virtually *all* states require the security deposit accounting to be completed within 30 days. To make matters even more complicated for small-time landlords, some states have variable security deposit deadlines that range from 14 days to 30 days based on different parameters such as the type of rental agreement or whether you were provided a forwarding address. Be forewarned that some states levy penalties against landlords of up to three times the amount of the security deposit if the deadlines for accounting or return are not met. Check with your local tenant-landlord legal experts or NAA affiliate for the rules in your state.

Often rental property owners and managers receive less than the legally required notice or no notice at all. So how do you determine the tenant's financial responsibility in such cases? Say the required notice is 30 days, and the tenant gives you a written notice on the 10th of the month that she plans to vacate at the end of the current month. The tenant must vacate as agreed, but she's responsible for the full rent through the required 30-day notice period. In such instances, you may have a legal obligation to re-rent the property to mitigate the financial responsibility of the tenant; however, in situations where only a few days remain in the required notice period, most courts don't expect you to re-rent the unit.

Providing Your Tenant with a Move-Out Information Letter

Many tenants are afraid you're going to cheat them on their security deposit refund. After all, security deposit disputes are the number one issue in many small claims courts. Just as the Tenant Information Letter (covered in Chapter 11) helps get the landlord-tenant relationship off to a good start, the Move-Out Information Letter can help end the relationship on a positive note.

The Move-Out Information Letter (see Figure 15-1) thanks your tenants for making your rental unit their home and provides them with the procedures for preparing the unit for the final move-out inspection. It also informs them of your policies and method of returning their security deposit after any legal deductions.

You can access a printable version of the Move-Out Information Letter by clicking the link in the table of contents or checking out the CD.

Provide your tenant with a Move-Out Information Letter as soon as he gives his written notice to vacate. Although state law and your rental contract may contain information on the security deposit refund process, most tenants appreciate receiving this information so they know what to expect without having to search for their rental contract while trying to pack.

The Move-Out Information Letter reminds tenants that they can't apply their security deposit to the last month's rent and that it's only to be used as a contingency against any damages to the unit or for other lawful charges. If no portion of a tenant's deposit is called "last month's rent," you aren't legally obliged to apply it in this way. Unless your rental contract uses this wording, don't allow your tenants to try to apply their deposit toward their final month's rent or you may not have enough money on hand to cover any legally allowed charges. The only time that you apply the security deposit funds to rent is if unpaid rent is one of the "damages" you suffer, as the landlord, after the tenant has vacated.

Move-Out Information Letter

Tenant Name(s) _____

Rental Unit Address _____

Dear _____,

We are pleased that you selected our property for your home and hope that you enjoyed living here. Although we are disappointed to lose you as a tenant, we wish you good luck in the future. We want your move-out to go smoothly and end our relationship on a positive note.

Moving time is always chaotic and you have many things on your mind, including getting the maximum amount of your security deposit back. Contrary to some rental property owners, we want to be able to return your security deposit promptly and in full. Your security deposit is $_____. Note that your security deposit shall not be applied to your last month's rent as the deposit is to ensure the fulfillment of lease conditions and is to be used only as a contingency against any damages to the rental unit.

This move-out letter describes how we expect your rental unit to be left and what our procedures are for returning your security deposit. Basically, we expect you to leave your rental unit in the same condition it was when you moved in, except for ordinary wear and tear that occurred during your tenancy. To refresh your memory, a copy of your signed Move-in/Move-out Inspection Checklist is attached reflecting the condition of the rental unit at the beginning of your tenancy. We will be using this same detailed checklist when we inspect your rental unit upon move-out and will deduct the cost of any necessary cleaning and the costs of repairs, not considered ordinary wear and tear, from your security deposit.

To maximize your chances of a full and prompt refund, we suggest that you go through the Move-In/Move-Out Inspection Checklist line by line and make sure that all items are clean and free from damage, except for ordinary wear and tear. All closets, cabinets, shelves, drawers, countertops, storage, refrigerator, and exterior areas should be completely free of items. Feel free to check off completed items on this copy of the Move-In/Move-Out Inspection Checklist, as we will use the original for your final inspection.

Some of our tenants prefer to let professionals complete these items. You can contact your own professional or, upon request, we will be glad to refer you to our service providers so that you can focus on other issues of your move. You will work directly with the service provider on costs and payment terms, knowing that you are working with someone who can prepare the unit for the walkthrough inspection. Call us if you would like contact information or for any questions as to the type of cleaning we expect.

Please be sure to remove all personal possessions, including furniture, clothes, household items, food, plants, cleaning supplies, and any bags of garbage or loose items that belong to you. Of course, please do not remove any appliances, fixtures, or other items installed or attached to your rental unit unless you have our prior written approval.

Please contact the appropriate companies and schedule the disconnection or transfer of your phone, cable, and utility services in your name. Also, cancel any newspaper subscriptions and provide the U.S. Postal Service with a change of address form.

Please contact us when all the conditions have been satisfied to arrange an inspection of your rental unit during daylight hours. To avoid being assessed a key replacement charge, please return all keys at the time you vacate.

You have listed _____ as the move-out date in your notice. Please be reminded that you will be assessed holdover rent of $_____ per day for each partial or full day after the above move-out date that you remain in the rental unit or have possession of the keys. If you need to extend your tenancy for any reason, you must contact us immediately. Please be prepared to provide your forwarding address where we may mail your security deposit.

It is our policy to return all security deposits either in person or at an address you provide within _____ after you move out **and** return all keys. If any deductions are made for past due rent or other unpaid charges, for damages beyond ordinary wear and tear, or for failure to properly clean, an itemized explanation will be included with the security deposit accounting.

If you have any questions, please contact us at _____.

Thank you again for making our property your home. We have enjoyed serving you, and we hope that you will recommend our rental properties to your friends, family, and colleagues. Please let us know if we can provide you with a recommendation letter. Good luck!

Sincerely,

_____

Owner/Manager

Figure 15-1:
This letter can help end the landlord-tenant relationship on a positive note.

Courtesy of Robert S. Griswold

If the vacating tenant is a good one, ask whether you can provide him with a letter of recommendation. A positive reference can be very helpful to tenants, whether they're moving to a new rental property or buying a home. This kind of offer is welcome and courteous and is one that most tenants have never received from prior landlords. The bonus for you? If you offer to provide a letter of recommendation, tenants often work extra hard to make sure the rental unit is clean and undamaged to thank you for your positive comments.

Walking Through the Unit at Move-Out

After your tenant vacates your rental property, inspect it as soon as possible, preferably during daylight hours. Doing so allows you to determine what work you need to do to ready the property for a new tenant and to assess any charges that you need to deduct from the former tenant's security deposit.

A good way to motivate tenants to comply with your move-out procedures is to remind them that they'll receive the full sum of their deposit (plus interest if required by statute) if they leave the rental unit in clean condition, with no damage beyond ordinary wear and tear. (I clarify what ordinary wear and tear is in the later related section.)

To ensure the walk-through runs smoothly, you need to understand the process and how to handle the security deposit if you uncover damages. The following sections can help.

Getting the 411 on the walk-through

Many new landlords have been asked to perform the move-out inspection with some or all of the tenant's possessions still in the rental property, only to discover that creative tenants can hide damage very easily. So try to schedule the move-out inspection with your vacating tenant just *after* she removes all her furnishings and personal items, turns in all her keys, and either disconnects the utilities or converts them to your name as the property owner. In my experience, most damage actually occurs during the move-in and move-out, so another plus for doing the inspection at this time is that you can make sure the tenant doesn't do additional damage after the inspection while she's removing her possessions.

Unfortunately, you can't always arrange to do the inspection with your tenant after she has actually moved out. In this case, conduct the move-out inspection as soon as possible and preferably with a witness present (or at least a digital still or video camera). If you wait too long to inspect the unit and then discover damage, the tenant may claim that someone else must have caused the damage, and you may face an uphill battle in court.

I strongly recommend performing the final move-out inspection with the vacating tenant present. Doing so resolves many of the issues that can later become contentious enough to end in small claims court. If you live in a state that allows the tenant to be present when you're determining the proper security deposit deductions, consider doing that as well.

For California rental property owners

If you own rental property in California, you need to comply with special rules and procedures for vacating tenants. California landlords must provide their tenants with written notice stating that they're entitled to request and be present for an initial pre-move inspection. A vacating tenant can decline, but if he accepts, then the rental property owner or manager needs to provide him with feedback on what cleaning and repairs, if any, need to be addressed to receive his maximum security deposit back.

Tenants have been known to show up for the walk-through but deny that they know anything about the damaged items you find. Refer to your Move-In/Move-Out Itemized Statement (see Chapter 11) in these situations. If the checklist clearly indicates that the item was in good condition when the tenants moved in, their claim doesn't stand much of a chance. However, if the move-in remarks are blank or vague, you may have some problems justifying a deduction. *Remember:* As the rental housing professional, the courts hold you to a higher standard of record-keeping and usually interpret your vague documents in the tenants' favor.

Paying the security deposit — or not

Security deposit disputes are the number one problem in landlord-tenant relationships. Although the proper use of the Move-In/Move-Out Itemized Statement (see Chapter 11) eliminates many of these disputes, the definition of *ordinary wear and tear* is one of life's greatest mysteries (see the next section for help figuring it out).

Many owners see a tenant's security deposit as a source of additional income that's theirs for the taking. However, as a business practice, returning the deposit in full is actually much better for the owner. You can minimize arguments with former tenants and avoid small claims court by making only fair and reasonable deductions and providing the security deposit accounting and any refund within legally required time limits.

Refer to the CD or click the link in the table of contents for information regarding each state's time limitations for providing former tenants with an accounting or return of the balance of their security deposit.

Although state laws vary, typically the only lawful deductions from a tenant's security deposit are for cleaning, damages beyond ordinary wear and tear, keys, and unpaid rent. Therefore, the actual out-of-pocket costs to renovate the unit for the next tenant are greater than the legally allowed deductions because you must pay for all damage that falls within the scope of ordinary wear and tear. Be careful not to charge excessive deductions to try covering these expenses or you may fight a losing battle in small claims court.

Encourage tenants to earn the full return of their security deposit. Some states allow for a nonrefundable security or cleaning deposit, and in those states, you can even offer the tenant the opportunity to receive some or all of the nonrefundable deposit. This situation can be a win-win — the tenant can use the money, and you can quickly clean and sanitize the unit to begin showing it to prospective new tenants. Typically, you can't charge the outgoing tenant for lost rent incurred while maintenance and cleaning are being done. So if you can quickly prepare the unit and get it back on the market, you're well ahead of the game.

Tenants often request the chance to do some more cleaning or make repairs if you indicate that you're going to take deductions from their deposit. If you feel that they're capable of the work and can do it quickly, you may want to give them a second chance at cleaning or simple repairs (as is legally required in California). However, be wary of tenant repairs that can cost you more to correct later or that create liability issues. With the majority of repairs, you're better off refusing tenants' requests to fix them themselves.

Defining ordinary wear and tear

Legally, you're entitled to charge your tenant for damages beyond ordinary wear and tear. But virtually all disputes over security deposits revolve around this elusive definition. It's your job to be able to tell the difference between ordinary wear and tear and more serious damage that you can legally deduct from your tenant's security deposit.

The standard definition of *ordinary wear and tear* in most states is deterioration or damage to the property expected to occur from normal usage. The problem then is what's considered to be *normal usage.* Judicial decisions vary from state to state and court to court. If you ask 100 small claims court judges or commissioners, you'll likely receive nearly 100 different interpretations of this definition.

Generally, the longer your tenant has occupied the rental unit, the greater the expectation that the conditions that have deteriorated during the tenancy will be considered *ordinary wear and tear.* The bottom line? No hard and fast rules exist regarding what constitutes ordinary wear and tear and what the tenant can legally be charged. Table 15-1 gives you some ideas for comparison to help you determine what is ordinary wear and tear and what goes beyond ordinary into damage you can charge for.

Table 15-1	Ordinary Wear and Tear versus Damage
Ordinary Wear and Tear (Landlord's Responsibility)	**Damage beyond Ordinary Wear and Tear (Tenant's Responsibility)**
Smudges on walls, near light switches	Crayon marks on walls or ceilings
Minor marks on walls or doors	Large marks on or holes in walls or doors
A few small tack or nail holes	Numerous nail holes that require patching and/or painting
Faded, peeling, or cracked paint	Completely dirty or scuffed painted walls
Carpet worn thin from normal use	Carpet stained by bleach or dye
Carpet with moderate dirt or spots	Carpet that has been ripped or has urine stains from pets
Carpet or curtains faded by the sun	Carpet or curtains with cigarette burns
Moderately dirty miniblinds	Bent or missing miniblinds
Doors sticking from humidity	Broken hinges or doorframes

Using a Security Deposit Itemization Form

After you've inspected the rental unit and determined the proper charges, you need to prepare the Security Deposit Itemization Form. Complete this form and give the vacating tenant a check for any balance due within your state's maximum time guidelines. Most states allow rental property owners 14 to 30 days to complete the accounting, but several states have no specific legal deadline. Either way, make sure you don't wait until the last minute because the consequences in most states are severe, including forfeiting your rights to any deductions and punitive damages.

Pop in the CD or click the link in the table of contents to access a template for a Security Deposit Itemization form.

Send the security deposit accounting and refund, if any, as soon as you're sure of the final charges. Tenants need this money, and the longer they wait, the more impatient and upset they become — and the more likely they are to challenge your charges. Of course, you need to make sure your maintenance personnel have been through the entire unit carefully and found all tenant damage beyond ordinary wear and tear. (In theory, you can always seek reimbursement for items discovered after you refund the deposit, but your chances of collecting in this case are slim.)

Some tenants want to personally pick up the deposit as soon as possible, whereas others don't even tell you where they can be reached. Generally, you should mail the Security Deposit Itemization Form to the address provided by your tenant on the Tenant's Notice of Intent to Vacate Rental Unit. If you don't have your vacating tenant's forwarding address, send the form to his last known address, which may be your own rental unit. Perhaps he's forwarding his mail to a new address; if not, the check will be returned to you.

If your Security Deposit Itemization Form and refund check are returned undeliverable, be sure to save the returned envelope in case the former tenant claims you never sent the legally required accounting. Many states have very severe penalties for improper deductions or failure to provide the security deposit accounting in a timely manner. Check with your state laws to determine the proper disposition of the tenant's uncashed deposit refund check.

Be sure you're able to prove that you've met the legal requirements in terms of returning the deposit in a timely manner. Otherwise, the small claims courts may rule against you, because as a major player in the rental housing business, you're held to a higher standard of record-keeping.

You can send the deposit accounting and check via certified mail (as required by some states) to prove the date you sent it. However, it's much more cost-effective to go to the post office and ask for a *certificate of mailing,* which records the date you sent the check (and doesn't require the recipient's signature for delivery).

Tenants, particularly roommates or married couples in the midst of a separation or divorce, may fight among themselves over the security deposit. Legally, the deposit belongs equally to all tenants who signed the rental contract, unless otherwise agreed in writing. If you arbitrarily split the check between the tenants, you can find yourself liable to the other party.

In multi-tenant situations where you have a court order or a written agreement or instructions signed by all the tenants, always handle the deposit as directed. If you don't have a court order or a written agreement or instructions, follow these steps for paying out the security deposit:

1. **Make your deposit refund check payable jointly to all the adult tenants.**

2. **Prepare a mailing that includes the refund check for one of the tenants with a copy of the check to the others.**

   Leave it up to the tenants to handle the check's endorsement.

3. **Mail copies of your Security Deposit Itemization Form to each of the tenants at his respective forwarding address.**

Deducting from the security deposit

If you make deductions from the security deposit, be sure your paperwork is accurate and detailed. Because property damage deductions are only for damages beyond ordinary wear and tear, you need to be sure that your description of the item explains why the damage exceeds that.

For example, if you merely indicate "Pet damage — $100" on the Security Deposit Itemization Form, you may be challenged. However, if you provide details like "Steam cleaned carpeting in living room to remove extensive pet urine stains — $100" and include your actual receipt, you greatly improve your chances of winning if the matter gets to court or. (In fact, maybe you won't even be challenged in the first place.)

Every rental property owner can recall claims from former tenants protesting deposit deductions because they "left the property cleaner" than it was when they moved in. Fortunately, the advent of digital photography is a real advantage, and I strongly encourage you to liberally use this technology to fully document your deposit deductions.

Bust out that digital camera or video recorder and follow these guidelines when listing charges on your Security Deposit Itemization Form:

1. **Indicate the specific item that's been damaged.**

   List all damaged flooring, window coverings, fixtures, appliances, and pieces of furniture separately.

2. **Note the specific location of the damaged item.**

   Document the room and which wall, ceiling, or corner of the room the damaged item is located in. Use compass directions, if possible.

3. **Comment on the type and extent of the damage.**

   Be sure to describe the damage in detail by using appropriate adjectives, such as *filthy, substantial, excessive, minor, scratched, stained, soiled, ripped, cracked, broken, inoperative, missing, burned,* or *chipped.*

4. **Note the type and extent of repair done.**

   Describe the repair using words such as *spackle, patch, paint, steam clean, deodorize,* or *refinish.* Indicate if an item is so damaged that it has to be replaced and, if so, why. Indicating the item's age is helpful, especially if it was new when the tenant first occupied the rental unit, and its life span was supposed to exceed the length of the tenancy.

5. **Document the cost of the repair or replacement.**

   List exactly how much you spent or plan to spend based on a third-party estimate. Include copies of receipts whenever possible.

You may not know the actual charges for certain items until after the work is completed and you receive the contractor's final invoice. Plus, owners often don't discover some damages until the rental unit preparation work is underway. So during the walk-through, note that the item is damaged on the checklist and advise the tenant that you reserve the right to deduct the actual repair costs. When you know the actual charges, you can update the checklist and include a copy with your security deposit itemization.

If you won't know the final charges and deductions from the tenant's deposit before your state's deadline for the accounting and/or return of the deposit balance, make sure you send the tenant a written itemized accounting of the charges you *do* know and indicate that you're waiting for additional information. Also, include an estimated time that you expect to have the final charges and then send the final accounting and any remaining funds as soon as possible.

Don't withhold the entire deposit if you know the undetermined items are likely to be much less than the balance of the deposit. In those instances, conservatively estimate the potential remaining charges and refund the balance of funds, along with your explanation letter, by the deadline. Most judges consider this move a good faith effort and won't penalize you if the matter ultimately ends up in court.

Some rental property owners give all vacating tenants a *pricing chart* with a list of costs that will be charged for different services or damaged items. These owners believe pricing charts minimize disputes because the charges are predetermined and are given to the tenants in advance. They argue that the tenants will see how expensive repairs are and will take care of some of the work on their own. This method has some logic, but it also poses potential problems because prices frequently change and most courts insist on actual charges, not estimates. Also, many items can't possibly have preset prices for repair because different contractors may charge different amounts. Rest assured that a tenant won't pay up if your actual charge turns out to be much higher than the preset charge indicated on your pricing chart. But if the tenant challenges your deductions, and your actual invoice shows you paid less than what you charged the tenant, you'd better have your checkbook ready.

Dealing with Special Situations

Although you may have worked very hard to make sure everything goes smoothly during your tenant's move-out, a few special situations inevitably arise. And the more you know as a rental property owner about how to handle these situations, which I describe in the following sections, the less likely they are to become significant problems.

Forking out the dough: When damage and unpaid rent exceed the security deposit

As a rental property owner, you're probably going to encounter a time when a tenant's security deposit isn't sufficient to cover the unpaid rent and the damage caused by the tenant. Unless legally prohibited, allocate the deposit to first cover the damage and then cover the unpaid rent because it makes sense to apply the deposit to items that are more difficult to prove in court.

Say you're holding a $500 security deposit from a tenant when she vacates, owing $350 in delinquent rent. When you inspect her unit, however, you find $400 in damage beyond ordinary wear and tear. The total of the rent owed and the damages done is $750, but the deposit is only $500. What should you do? First, apply the $500 deposit to cover the full $400 in damage and allocate the remaining $100 toward the unpaid rent. You can then pursue the $250 delinquent rent balance with your rent collection ledgers and records as evidence to clearly prove this amount is owed.

Be sure to always record the actual costs for damages, even if you don't intend to pursue the tenant for the balance owed. This way, you can prove your expenses in court if you ever need to.

In most states, even if your lawful deductions exceed the departing tenant's security deposit charges, you must provide the tenant with a full accounting of the damages. You must do so even if you file a small claims lawsuit for the balance due. So be sure to always follow the required procedures for the accounting of the deposit.

Having your facts straight: When disputes arise about the security deposit

No matter how fair and reasonable you are with your security deposit deductions, sooner or later you're bound to have a former tenant challenge them. Even if your deductions were proper and you're sure you're right, going to court over this matter may cost you more than the deduction amount in legal fees. Often, the actual disagreement is over a relatively small amount of money.

For example, you may have deducted $100 for painting touch up, but your former tenant may believe that the charge should be $50. So you're arguing over a mere $50 difference. Explore possible negotiations to resolve the matter before going to court. If you're sure that your charges were fair, always maintain that in your discussions with your former tenant, even if you want to see whether a settlement is a possibility.

If you charge your tenants for damage to the rental unit either during their tenancy or afterward by deducting from the deposit, you need evidence to back up your claim in case a tenant disputes the damage. Digital photos or videotape of the damage can be effective tools to resolve disputes with tenants or prove your position in court. In fact, many courts now have video monitors that you can use to show the judge or jury your evidence. Just be sure you have possession of the unit or have given proper legal notice before entering it to videotape.

Reclaiming what's yours: When the rental is abandoned

Occasionally, tenants abandon your rental unit without notice. This discovery can be good news if you're taking legal action against the tenant because you're sure to save lost rent days and may be able to reduce your legal costs.

Each state has its own definition of abandonment, so make sure you comply with all state legal requirements before trying to determine that the rental unit is abandoned. The best way to know for sure is to contact the tenant and have him give you a statement in writing relinquishing his rights to possession of the unit.

Have a policy in place stating that your tenants must inform you if they plan to be absent from the unit for more than one or two weeks. This policy can be helpful in determining whether a property is abandoned or the tenant is just on a long vacation.

Consider giving the tenant a legal notice in order to enter the unit if you suspect that the tenant has abandoned your property. You can serve this notice by mailing a copy to your tenant at the unit address and/or by posting the notice on the front door as required by your state law. After you're inside the unit, look for additional evidence, including removed furniture, clothing, and toiletries; stale, spoiled, or missing food; and absent pets. You can also send your tenant a note or letter. If it's returned undeliverable or forwarded to a new address, that can be an indication your tenant has abandoned the unit.

If you already have an eviction action underway, your legal counsel may suggest that you continue the legal process until you receive possession. This way you can minimize your potential liability in the event that the tenant shows up later and claims the right to the rental unit. Or if no eviction action is in progress, be sure to serve the required legal notice of belief of abandonment. When you've met your state requirements, you can take possession of the unit and begin your turnover work to put it back on the rental market.

Dealing with abandoned personal property

One of a rental property owner's worst nightmares is discovering that a tenant has suddenly abandoned the rental unit and left all her furnishings and household items behind. More common, however, is finding that a tenant has moved out and returned the keys but left behind a few items of personal property. Often these items are junk that even your favorite charity will refuse to accept. But many landlords tell tales of the tenant who remembers (three months after she moved out) that she left her great aunt's diamond ring in her antique dresser.

When you first discover that your tenant appears to have left behind personal property, immediately try to locate the tenant and ask her to reclaim her property. Serve the appropriate legal notices as required by your state. (Note that state laws vary widely in terms of the standards for establishing that a tenant's personal property has been abandoned and your obligation in handling that property.)

If you're unable to locate the tenant or the tenant refuses to claim the items, you need to have an impartial witness assist you in preparing a written and photographic inventory of the abandoned items. If possible, carefully move the abandoned items into a secure storage area until you can proceed with the sale or disposal of the possessions per state law. If the personal property is extensive, hiring a third-party firm that specializes in such situations to prepare appraisals and conduct the sale or disposition is a good idea. Keep copies of all appraisals and photos for your records.

Several states allow the owner an automatic lien on the personal property to be used toward unpaid rent or storage costs. So after the expiration of legal notices, you can attempt to sell the items and generate funds to offset your associated expenses incurred, with any balance applied toward unpaid rent. Any excess funds beyond those items belong to the tenant.

In some states, selling or disposing of a tenant's abandoned property requires advance court approval. In others, you're bound to place abandoned property in bonded storage with removal supervised by an officer of the law. Be extremely careful to follow the specific legal requirements for your area before you sell, give away, or keep any of the tenant's abandoned personal property because the penalties for breaking the law can be very stiff.

Part IV

Techniques and Tools for Managing the Property

The 5th Wave

By Rich Tennant

"Don't worry, Mrs. Morse. As soon as the plumber's done patching the roof I'll have him call the electrician to finish wallpapering the dining room."

In this part . . .

A huge aspect of rental property management involves people other than your tenants — everyone from employees you hire to contractors you work with. And just as owning your own home involves a lot of maintenance work, the same holds true for owning rental property. Plus, as a landlord, you have to be aware of the safety and security of your property and your tenants. In this part, I cover all these issues so that whether you're managing a painting contractor or you want to be sure you provide your tenants with all the required legal disclosures, you have the information you need.

Chapter 16

Working with Employees and Contractors

In This Chapter

▶ Finding, hiring, and supervising employees

▶ Assembling a quality team of contractors and vendors

As your rental property business grows, you'll find that you're limited in how much work you can handle yourself, and you may begin to consider hiring employees. But before you jump into being an employer, you need to fully understand the responsibilities, financial consequences, and increased liability associated with having employees. You also need to determine how much an employee costs you versus how much that employee is worth to you based on the time-consuming aspects of rental management that the employee can take off your plate.

Extensive legal requirements and responsibilities also come with being an employer. So you may find that using independent, self-employed, insured contractors or hiring companies that can handle your maintenance and service needs is easier and less risky. In fact, you may actually end up better off financially by paying the higher cost of an independent contractor or service company than by employing your own on-site manager or maintenance person.

This chapter touches on the benefits and burdens of hiring employees to assist you in the management of your rental properties and tells you the proper way to locate, hire, and supervise contractors. Property management is a time-consuming job, but you can lessen the burden a bit by hiring people.

Surveying the Ins and Outs of Bringing Employees Onboard

If you own only a few rental units, you probably don't need any employees because you can handle all your duties by yourself or with the help of contractors. However, when you begin acquiring a large number of rental properties — either many small properties in scattered sites within the same general area or one or two larger apartment buildings — you probably need to hire at least one employee.

For most rental owners, that first hire is an on-site manager. On-site managers offer several advantages. They can handle many of the day-to-day problems; make sure the property is tidy and properly maintained, with good curb appeal; notify you or your maintenance person if an emergency occurs; assist in marketing vacant rental units; and resolve a budding conflict between tenants. However, on-site managers come with some disadvantages, too, namely the added expense, the liability inherent in having an employee, and the difficulty finding and retaining good, qualified help. But don't let these challenges stand in your way if a manager is an asset in your particular situation.

If you do decide to hire employees, check out the following sections for advice on managing them.

Establishing job duties, work schedule, and compensation

Before you begin looking for a new employee, you need to determine what that employee's job duties, work schedule, and compensation are going to be, and you need to put those details in writing.

Most rental property owners don't create written job descriptions for their on-site managers and maintenance personnel, but this is a mistake you don't want to make. If you rely solely on verbal agreements, disputes are sure to occur — and they're usually resolved in the employee's favor.

Some landlords have an unrealistic expectation of the time it takes to complete tasks satisfactorily. If you've ever done the work yourself, you have a very good idea of the time it takes. But if you're acquiring a larger building with older infrastructure and many more tenants, you may find yourself frustrated because the part-time employee you hired doesn't keep the building up to your standards in the 10 hours per week you agreed to pay him.

Many local NAA affiliates offer great on-site manager employment agreements written specifically to comply with federal and state employment laws. I recommend you use these NAA forms (available online for many states) to formally record your mutual agreement regarding duties, authority limits, compensation, hours, and rental unit credit, if applicable. (Be sure to check state laws concerning limits on the rental credit.) Also, take particular care to ensure that the employee has set hours and compensation that at least meet the federal or state minimum wage. Require any overtime to be approved in advance, unless there's an emergency. However, your policy should require that your employee immediately contact you after the matter is under control or, if the emergency is after hours, promptly the next business day.

Have your employees fill out a time sheet every day and be sure to pay overtime or allow compensating time off within the same pay period or within the limits of your state law.

WARNING!

Failing to clearly define a contract, carefully document hours worked, and strictly enforce limits on extra hours can lead to exorbitant claims for back pay and overtime from a disgruntled employee in the future, plus accrued payroll taxes and penalties.

CHECK IT OUT

Pop in the CD or click the link in the table of contents to access a sample time sheet, as well as several generic job descriptions from IREM that you can customize to your needs. And a friendly reminder: Be sure to have an attorney review all forms, especially legal documents.

Screening employees

Because your employees will have close contact with your tenants, make sure you screen all candidates before hiring them. Why screen? Because you can no longer rely on a résumé, an interview, and a list of references when making hiring decisions. And due to the minimal day-to-day supervision in many positions, the rental housing industry and building maintenance trades have historically been relatively easy areas for individuals with poor work history, alcohol or substance abuse problems, and serious criminal convictions to find employment. But many managers and maintenance personnel are in a position of trust; they often assist in the collection of rent and of cash from coin-operated laundry equipment, have regular tenant contact, and have ready access to building equipment and supplies and the rental units. Therefore, the liability for a rental owner who fails to properly screen employees or contractors is very high. If you choose to conduct your own background checks on employees, pay particular attention to work and residence history. Consider criminal background checks mandatory for any employee who will have access to money or unit keys.

When state law mandates having employees

In some areas of the country, laws actually require rental property owners to have an on-site manager if a single location has a certain minimum number of rental units. For example, rental properties with 8 or more units in New York City and properties with 16 or more units in California require an on-site manager or responsible party.

The employment screening process is much more difficult than tenant screening because of the numerous state and federal laws protecting prospective employees. These laws make it difficult for the small rental owner to meet all the legal requirements of hiring. If you own just a few properties, you may want to consider using outside employment firms for locating and screening potential employees.

Be sure to check with an employment law specialist before initiating a pre-employment screening policy to ensure your application procedures meet all legal requirements and to help you avoid federal law pitfalls. For example, a job applicant's credit history can be important if the employee will be handling money. Yet the federal Fair Credit Reporting Act (FCRA) covers employee background checks, and several mandatory disclosures are required. Also, the Americans with Disabilities Act (ADA) severely restricts an employer's ability to seek information about an applicant's medical history. The employee can volunteer information, but you can't ask questions concerning physical limitations, prior workers' compensation claims, lost time due to illness or injury, or prior drug and alcohol addictions. Be very careful; employers who violate the FCRA or ADA regulations can suffer significant penalties.

The following sections take you through the process of pre-screening employees before hiring them and explain the convenience of working with an employment-screening firm.

Walking through the process

Focus your pre-employment screening on education, job history, and personal references, plus a criminal background search and a drug/alcohol screening.

Have each prospective employee complete an employment application that lists his education, experience, and references, and have him specifically authorize your right to investigate the provided information. If you're hiring an employee who'll live on-site, require that he complete a separate rental application and rental contract, and be sure to include any other adult occupants, just as you would if this were a non-employee rental.

Next, prescreen your prospective employee on the phone. Describe the job requirements, hours, and compensation. Then discuss the applicant's current employment status; review his qualifications, skills, and experience; and reconfirm his interest in the position with the proposed work schedule and compensation. If there seems to be mutual interest, schedule an in-person interview and a tour of the rental property.

The evaluation and selection of your on-site manager is one of your most critical tasks, and you should make every effort to be diligent and objective. As my good friend, the late rental industry educator Dorothy Gourley, has advised owners for many years, your on-site manager needs to be fair, firm, and friendly — not always an easy combination to find in one person. The ideal candidate combines honesty and integrity, perseverance, and good communication or people skills. He also has a good employment history, the ability to work with you, and a professional, stable demeanor that complements your tenant profile. Prior experience isn't necessary if you're willing to train or provide educational opportunities from IREM or the local NAA affiliate.

Hiring an employment-screening firm

The ever-changing and more restrictive employment-screening regulations are creating a strong demand for employment-screening firms. I recommend using these firms, particularly those that specialize in the rental housing industry, whenever possible, especially if you own a smaller rental property.

WARNING!

Be wary of employment-screening firms that claim to be able to conduct a single national criminal database search. Not all states offer statewide searches, and the data is often inaccurate or dated in those states that do. Also, the statewide data typically only includes felony records, not serious misdemeanors, so the most thorough information must still be gathered on a county-by-county basis. Though the ability to conduct comprehensive employment screening is improving, the reality is that federal, state, and county law enforcement bureaus have outdated systems and don't always share information with one another.

I recommend specifying that you want your employment-screening firm of choice to conduct a criminal background check in every county where your prospective employee lived, attended school, and worked. This type of check costs more upfront, but it's a good investment that pays dividends and offers peace of mind in the long run.

Knowing your responsibilities

Being an employer has serious legal obligations and requirements. Besides being responsible for wages, employment taxes, and reporting, you're also accountable for properly supervising your on-site manager (or any employee) and can be held liable for her actions. So make sure your manager always abides by all fair housing laws, acts within the scope of her job description and level of authority, and has basic knowledge of the law.

The right on-site manager can make all the difference in the world. Be very competitive with your compensation and use recognition rewards and financial incentives that acknowledge positive results, such as low turnover, minimal lost rent due to vacancy and bad debt, and efficient expense control. A competitive compensation package is a wise investment that allows you to hire and retain the best on-site manager.

Employees are typically paid based on a salary or hourly wages. The exact amount varies based on their responsibilities and work schedules, but you still need to meet the minimum wage requirements in your area. You can often contact other rental property owners or your local NAA affiliate to obtain information on the wages and benefits you need to offer to stay competitive.

You're also responsible for your employee's tax withholdings, Social Security contributions, federal and/or state unemployment insurance, and workers' compensation insurance. Never agree to pay an employee in cash or in any manner that doesn't cover all the proper deductions for payroll burden, because you can be held responsible for paying all these sums (even the employee's share) if you're audited. Federal and state agencies look for abuse by businesses in the rental housing industry, where cash compensation is prevalent, so be sure to always comply.

To get all your paperwork in order, you need an Employer Identification Number (EIN), and I suggest you get a copy of IRS Publication 15, "(Circular E), Employer's Tax Guide." Both are available from the IRS by calling (800) 829-4933 or visiting www.irs.gov.

Although some states may not require you to carry workers' compensation coverage (insurance that pays employees and covers their medical expenses if they're injured or become ill as a result of their jobs) unless you have a minimum number of employees, I advise carrying it even if you don't have *any* employees. Although any contractor you hire to perform work on your property should have her own workers' compensation policy to cover all her employees, if someone gets hurt and the contractor has limited or even no coverage, you can bet that her injured employee will come after you for compensation. Don't take chances; you can often add this insurance to your standard policy for a nominal cost. Work with an attorney to make sure you're in full compliance with your state's workers' compensation laws.

Many rental owners prefer to have payroll handled by an accountant or a firm that specializes in this service. But you can also use an employee leasing company as the *employer of record,* an organization that's responsible for payroll, withholding taxes, workers' compensation, benefits, deductions, regulations, and reporting. You can pay the firm with a single check and let it deal with the paperwork. Check with your local IREM chapter or NAA affiliate for referrals.

Working with your manager

You have to walk a fine line between being an involved and caring rental owner and an overbearing micromanager who inhibits your on-site manager from properly running the property. Good managers treat the property as if it's their own and often make a major effort to keep it in excellent condition to maximize your net income. Of course, many incompetent managers out there only do what they're literally forced to do. Stay out of the way of the good manager and terminate the bad or uncaring one. Better yet, learn how to find, hire, and retain the good manager, and avoid hiring one who doesn't care.

Posting all the legalities

Federal law requires all employers — yes, even if you have just one employee — to display posters explaining employees' legal rights. This signage "must be posted in a prominent and conspicuous place in every establishment of the employer where it can readily be observed by employees and applicants for employment." Federal informational posters include the following topics:

✔ The Employee Polygraph Protection Act (EPPA)

✔ The Fair Labor Standards Act (FLSA)

✔ Job Safety and Health: It's the Law (OSHA)

✔ The Uniformed Services Employment and Reemployment Rights Act (USERRA)

The following federal posters should be visible based on certain conditions:

✔ Equal Employment Opportunity Commission (EEOC): Post this signage if you have 15 or more employees.

✔ Family and Medical Leave Act (FMLA): Post this signage if you have more than 50 employees in a 75-mile radius.

Some of the mandatory posters are available at no charge online at www.dol.gov/elaws/posters.html. Be sure to check whether your state has additional requirements or posters that supersede the federal law.

Your on-site manager must have the tenants' respect to collect rents, deal with problems, and respond to maintenance service requests. Back up the manager whenever possible. However, your manager must earn respect from you and the tenants. Backing up a manager when he's wrong can create a much larger problem.

When dealing with tenant complaints about your on-site manager, remain neutral and calmly investigate the facts before getting back to the tenant with a formal response. Never ignore a tenant's concerns, but always be sure to balance the need to investigate the complaint with well-reasoned trust of your employee.

Staying on the alert for danger signs

As I mention throughout this chapter, having employees increases your liability, particularly when it comes to violence and sexual harassment. Keep your eyes and ears open so you don't miss the following danger signs:

✔ Although it doesn't happen often, be careful if you ever have any indication that your employees display abusive tendencies, make threats, or show any signs of violent or disruptive behavior. You aren't always liable if one of your employees threatens or harms someone, but workplace violence is a concern throughout the country, and rental housing employees are often in positions of authority, with access to personal information and rental units. Watch for any signs of threats, illegal possession of drugs, or the illegal possession and/or use of weapons. If you become aware of any of these signs or if you find out about prior attacks or convictions for violent crimes, immediately contact your employment law specialist for advice on the proper response, which may include a written warning or the employee's immediate termination.

✔ Sexual harassment claims by tenants against managers, other employees, or contractors (or even other tenants) are a growing concern for rental property owners. You need to have a clear, firm, written, zero-tolerance policy against sexual harassment, and you must promptly and fairly investigate any complaints. Cases of employee or contractor misconduct have been a problem for years. However, recent litigation against owners is making this matter even scarier in cases where one tenant accuses another tenant of sexual harassment and alleges that the owner or manager either condoned such actions or failed to take proper steps to address the concerns. This territory is dangerous, so don't jump to conclusions; balancing the need for a prompt and accurate investigation against the rights of the accused individuals can be difficult. Immediately contact your attorney for advice when you're told about any sexual harassment allegations.

Firing an employee

In virtually all situations, you have the right to terminate an employee at any time, as long as you don't do so for an illegal reason. You can fire an employee who hasn't performed his job (including for committing acts of discrimination or retaliation against a tenant or prospective tenant). But an illegal reason would be if you tried to fire an employee who is a member of a protected class without good reason. As with any employment situation, always document any concerns about job performance in writing and discuss them with the employee as soon as possible.

If you need to fire an employee, be prepared to show that the termination was for cause and was carefully documented. Reasons for terminating an employee include

✔ Dishonesty

✔ Failure to follow the written job description

✔ Participation in illegal or criminal activity

✔ Poor job performance

✔ Theft

Although the logistics of terminating your employees probably aren't on your mind when you hire them, you need to have clear, written documentation about the process of parting company, particularly with on-site employees. Rental property owners often have legitimate concerns that a terminated on-site manager or other on-site employee may cause problems. Because they typically receive a rent discount, these ex-employees may take their time relocating unless you have a clear policy upfront.

TIP

Keep a written agreement clearly indicating that the rental unit is a condition of and incident to employment. Any rights to occupy the unit cease upon an employee's termination. Although some people advise giving on-site employees only 24 hours' notice to vacate, I believe that one week is reasonable to find a new place and make the move, particularly because these folks are now unemployed. You can always be flexible, but have a holdover rent clause in place that calls for rent at the rate of 125 percent of the current market rent as an incentive for former on-site staff to relocate quickly. Although the utilities and telephone service should be in the employee's name, if these items are included in his compensation for any reason, be sure to require him to put them in his name immediately.

Independent contractor versus employee status

As a rental property owner, you may routinely receive assistance from workers who perform jobs such as cleaning, painting, and landscaping. These workers are classified as either independent contractors or employees. You're responsible for the employment taxes of your employees, but independent contractors pay their own employment taxes. The advantage of classifying these workers as independent contractors is obvious. However, the IRS is investigating businesses that traditionally use independent contractors to be sure they're not classifying employees as independent contractors incorrectly.

The IRS has established detailed, comprehensive requirements to qualify as an independent contractor. For example, workers must provide their own tools and equipment, pay their own business and transportation expenses, hire and pay any assistants, offer services to the public at large, perform their services in such a manner that they have control over the process and the outcome, and be in a position to potentially incur a loss as a result of their work.

Most on-site managers, and possibly other maintenance workers, can't meet these stringent requirements. They usually are paid a salary or an hourly wage, work under the guidance and control of the rental owner or property management firm, and follow set hours and specific job responsibilities.

Check with your attorney or accountant, but my advice is not to even try to structure your relationship with your on-site manager as anything other than an employer-employee relationship. If the IRS or a state agency later determines that your independent contractor was really your employee, you'll be liable for back taxes, penalties, and interest. To make matters worse, you also must retroactively pay the employee's share of these employment taxes. See IRS Publication 15-A, Employer's Supplemental Tax Guide, for more information.

Building Your Contractor and Vendor Dream Team

Every rental property owner depends on contractors and vendors to assist with the proper management of the rental units. The real challenge for many owners is finding the right people or companies for the job and ensuring that they're paying a competitive price for quality services or materials. Not to worry, though. The following sections can assist you in assembling your team.

Whoever you hire, be sure to issue an IRS Form 1099, Statement of Miscellaneous Income, at the end of each calendar year to each independent contractor or vendor who isn't incorporated and was paid more than $600.

Recognizing what to look for

Having a list of competent and reliable contractors, vendors, and suppliers who price their services and materials fairly is crucial to successfully maintaining your sanity as a rental property owner. You can count on these high-quality individuals and firms for any need that arises at one of your rental properties. Unfortunately, finding them can be a real challenge, and you may be wondering where to turn. Locating and screening vendors is a constant process because the best contractors are often so busy that they can't handle all the work, leaving you to find another contractor.

You typically pay a major portion of your overall expenses to contractors and service providers, so spending these dollars wisely is important. You must ensure that the contractors are honest, dependable, and competent. To locate the better contractors, check with other property owners or the product service council of your local NAA affiliate or IREM chapter. (You can also use online services such as Angie's List and Yelp, but these sources haven't been in business long enough to have developed a niche in the rental housing industry and are more for homeowner projects.) Look for a contractor or vendor with a proven track record, all required insurance, a local business license and/or state contractor's license (if required), and a minimum of three to five years of experience. Also, be sure to obtain several references and call them before signing on the dotted line.

After you find a contractor, start her on a relatively simple job and supervise her carefully so that you can see the quality of her work firsthand and avoid any billing surprises. If you own one or only a few rental units, you have too much at stake and can't afford any problems or delays.

Giving a contractor unlimited, unsupervised access to a rental unit can be dangerous because you usually have very little, if any, personal background information on the contractor or her employees. Likewise, don't ever hire day laborers who congregate in front of your local home improvement or building supplier — the savings are illusory and the risks are tremendous.

In addition to good work, dependable response, and competitive pricing, when you hire contractors, you must insist that they provide a copy of their certificates of insurance, including current and adequate workers' compensation and liability insurance coverage. Contact your state contractors licensing board to ensure that your vendor's license is current and that she has any required bonds. This information is often available online at each state's official website. Even if you find a listing, be careful to make sure that the person or company is the exact same one as the license holder. (Many rogue unlicensed contractors use fake or stolen license numbers — often entities with similar names that can fool people who aren't extremely careful in performing their due diligence.)

Avoiding common pitfalls

I've found that the classic statement "You get what you pay for" is painfully true when it comes to working with contractors and vendors. Many rental property owners are so concerned about keeping their expenses down that they get into trouble by selecting contractors based strictly on pricing. Pricing is important, and the profit margins in rental housing require diligent conservation of financial resources, but you don't want to skimp on hiring contractors and vendors.

To avoid any potential problems down the road, watch out for the following:

- **Bids that are much lower than others:** The bid may be fine, but be sure you're not asking for trouble by hiring an unlicensed, uninsured contractor who doesn't pay or properly insure his workers. Avoid a painful lesson and just trust me that the cost to have another contractor clean up an unqualified vendor's mess isn't worthwhile.

- **Contractors who don't have full-time employees:** Some firms hire day laborers who don't have the required job skills. If something goes wrong, you can count on being on the wrong end of a claim or lawsuit.

- **Contractors who don't supervise their employees:** Make sure your contractors properly supervise their employees and require them to remove all debris from your property upon completion of the project. And hold them accountable if they do any damage.

- **Products and services that either barely meet the minimum or far exceed what you need:** You want to find the right balance between going with products or services that meet the bare minimum but also hold up under typical rental conditions. Overspending with customized or indulgent upgrades is wasteful and doesn't justify the added expense.

One example is window coverings. I've seen some property owners use inferior window coverings that don't even fit the window properly and don't last through one average-length tenancy with normal use. On the other hand, I've seen units with custom wood shutters or luxurious drapes that clearly were a waste of money for a rental. For most rental properties, a good balance is a quality vertical or miniblind product, although for some rental properties, good-quality drapery can be appropriate.

✔ **Quotes that aren't competitive or bidders who don't use identical specifications:** Have the firm with the best reputation and qualifications set the bid's scope, specifications, and proposed time schedule. Then you can let the other competitors bid using the same information, with the pricing deleted.

Not sure how to craft a Request for Proposal (RFP)? Pop in the CD or click the link in the table of contents to access a sample RFP I created for a major landscaping project. You can modify this document for any type of project at your rental property to ensure that you receive competitive quotes and that all the bidders quote on the same specs.

✔ **Service contracts with odd terms:** Some contractors or vendors propose multiyear contracts or ones with an automatic renewal clause. This is known as an *evergreen clause.* The contractor hopes that, after the contract is in place, you'll forget the renewal date, and the contract will automatically renew for successive periods, including rate increases, which are usually allowed per the terms. I strongly recommend avoiding any service contract that you can't cancel with or without cause upon a written 30-day notice. Even if you must pay a penalty to prematurely terminate the contract, you always want this option. Avoid service contracts with odd terms by having your attorney review all contracts before you sign them.

Also, although vendors initially say otherwise, all terms of the service contract should be negotiable. Unless this contractor has a monopoly in your area, seriously consider another if the one you're talking with refuses to negotiate.

✔ **Unclear billing and/or payment expectations:** Payments should be made in *arrears,* or after the work is done, and should be due generally in 30 days; more prompt payments should coincide with the completion and your approval of the work. If you're contracting out a very large project, you may want to authorize progress payments, but always withhold at least a 10 percent retainer for your final walk-through upon completion. Even if you're a small landlord, contractors will give best customer service to those that pay promptly.

✔ **Vendors who demand payment before the work is done:** Never pay for services in advance, unless the work requires some special order or customized product. Even then, pay only a small deposit. Unethical contractors have been known to demand large payments upfront and then suddenly file bankruptcy or leave town. Don't be a victim. Check with your state contractors licensing board for any dollar limits on advance payments required by contractors.

Hiring your tenant as a contractor — or not

Although hiring your tenant to perform work on your property can be very tempting, in most cases, you shouldn't. Your tenant isn't likely to possess the skills, qualifications, and tools or equipment to properly complete most repair work. You may also find that the job just doesn't seem to get done in a timely manner or that the tenant has unexpected cost overruns that can all be corrected with a rent credit. Another downside is that you'll likely be responsible if your tenant gets injured or causes an injury to someone else, so make sure that he has workers' compensation insurance or at least a decent health insurance policy.

If you do hire your tenant for any work that he's qualified to perform, handle it totally separately from the lease or rental agreement and pay him with a check only upon the satisfactory completion of the job.

Chapter 17

Maintaining the Property

In This Chapter

▶ Setting up a maintenance plan for your rental property

▶ Knowing what types of maintenance problems you're likely to face

▶ Responding professionally to your tenants' maintenance requests

*M*aintenance — the work required to keep something in proper condition or upkeep — is just part of the territory when you own rental property. Regular maintenance not only helps you keep your property but also is a standard legal requirement. As a rental property owner, you're legally required to properly maintain and repair your property to meet all building, housing, health and safety, and habitability codes. In legalese, this is called the *implied warranty of habitability*. In plain English, it means that, from the day the tenant moves in until the day the tenant moves out, you must keep the rental property in a safe and habitable condition. (The term *rental property* in this case includes the exterior yard or grounds of single-family homes and the exclusive-use common areas of multifamily rentals in addition to the property's interior.)

In this chapter, I explain why a good maintenance plan is essential for all rental properties. I also cover the most common types of maintenance and detail some sound procedures for handling property maintenance and saving money.

If you hire and oversee a contractor or maintenance person instead of doing the work yourself, find out enough about basic maintenance so you can make sure that whomever you hire is doing a good job.

Recognizing the Importance of a Maintenance Plan

One of the most common reasons why dissatisfied tenants leave a rental property is the rental owner's failure to respond to their basic requests for maintenance. But you can use this disappointment to your advantage when you show your well-maintained rental unit by informing your prospective tenants about your system for promptly addressing maintenance issues. If you have a solid maintenance plan in place, you'll consistently command higher rents and have much lower turnover thanks to satisfied tenants staying longer.

In 2003, a friend of mine conducted a survey of more than 8,000 residential tenants. More than 34 percent of the respondents said that prompt maintenance was the most important quality they looked for in a rental property. That was twice as many who cared about dishwashers, washers and dryers, or new carpet. When you demonstrate pride in your property by maintaining it, your tenants will partner with you to do the same.

A good maintenance plan includes regularly scheduled exterior property visual inspections. The frequency of these inspections varies depending on the location, type, age, and condition of your property, but you should perform them at least semiannually and again upon tenant turnover.

A customized property inspection checklist for each property is a good management tool. Pop in the CD or click the link in the table of contents to access a sample Apartment Exterior Inspection Report from IREM for inspecting the exterior of a small apartment building.

When you follow a maintenance plan, you can control your expenses and keep them to a minimum because you greatly reduce the need for emergency or extraordinary repairs (which always cost more). Things break and need to be replaced. For example, light bulbs burn out. Planning ahead by purchasing the right replacement bulbs in bulk at a good price and having them in stock ensures that you don't have to waste time running to the hardware store (and possibly pay full retail price) to buy one bulb. Your time is valuable, and you don't get the best pricing when you buy items individually. In your plan you should have the names of contractors and suppliers on hand so you can have the proper repair done the first time instead of having to fix a botched job. (You've probably seen the sign in the service repair shop that says "Repairs: $50 per hour. Repairs (after you tried to fix it yourself): $100 per hour.")

Because long-term, satisfied tenants are the key to financial success, you need to properly maintain the premises in order to avoid operating losses and potential legal problems. An ill-maintained property leads to higher tenant turnover and tenants of progressively lower caliber who are willing to accept the property's poor condition. A tenant can also use the property's shoddy shape as a reason to call the local housing inspector, withhold rent, vacate in the middle of a lease, defend an eviction, or even sue under state laws or special slumlord or habitability statutes found in most urban areas. Unhappy tenants talk, and bad news travels fast and far, especially with social media and many online rating sites. You can quickly develop a horrible reputation that will be difficult to overcome if you don't make tenant satisfaction and good maintenance a priority.

Although not required, consider taking a proactive approach to maintenance. You can include a clause in your rental contract allowing you access to the unit's interior to conduct an annual property inspection walk-through. Most tenants cooperate fully, but a few states prohibit you from entering just to inspect the unit without the tenant's advance permission. In these cases, or as an additional tool to improve your tenant relations, you can send your tenant a nonintrusive note and maintenance checklist that allows a quick response. Implementing this policy can protect you from claims of poor maintenance, allows for repairs when problems are small, and keeps your good tenants satisfied. However, this policy doesn't absolve the tenant from his ongoing responsibility to notify you immediately in writing of any concerns or needed repairs so you can respond promptly.

Your tenant has a responsibility to maintain the premises in a clean and sanitary manner and to properly use the premises in a usual and customary fashion. Always hold the tenant financially accountable for any damage caused to the property by his negligence or misuse.

Being Prepared for Maintenance Issues

Rental properties require several different types of maintenance, and you're sure to run into all of them at one time or another. Although every type of maintenance is critical, you need to respond to and handle each one in a unique way. The following sections address how to prepare yourself for the plethora of maintenance issues you'll encounter as a rental property owner.

My first employer in property management taught me the saying, "To own is to maintain." It's something worth keeping in mind when you find yourself having to do maintenance work on your rental property.

Emergency maintenance

Part of being a rental property owner is being prepared for emergency maintenance requests at all hours of the day (or night!). When you receive a maintenance call from a tenant, first you need to determine whether the request really is an emergency. *Emergency maintenance* is work that you must do immediately to prevent further property damage or to minimize the chance of endangering people. The most common maintenance emergencies typically involve plumbing, electrical, or access control/security problems.

In a maintenance emergency, immediately advise the tenant of what steps to take to limit any further damage. For example, if a pressurized pipe is leaking, tell the tenant to shut off the water supply at the angle stop nearest the source or, better yet, at the water meter; this simple step can prevent further water damage. Instruct tenants not to use appliances or electrical systems that are malfunctioning until they've been inspected or repaired.

 If a fire, flood, or gas leak emergency ever occurs at your property, or if a natural disaster hits the area, immediately shutting off the utilities may be imperative. Prepare charts and simple diagrams for each property indicating where to find all utility shut-off locations and the tools necessary to operate them — as well as instructions on which situations warrant shutting the utilities off. Always include the emergency phone numbers for the utility companies so your tenants can immediately contact them. (**Remember:** Tenants should only attempt to shut off the utilities on their own if the utility company or your own handyman or contractor isn't available and the situation warrants immediate action.)

 In many parts of the country, you may need to remind tenants that freezing outdoor temperatures can lead to water damage in unheated rental units. Tenants may want to turn off the heat when they go to work or when they're on vacation as a way to save money. But turning off the heat completely, leaving a window open in sub-zero temperatures, or setting the thermostat below 40 degrees can lead to freezing and bursting pipes, which can cause flood damage to floors, walls, and ceilings. I suggest you make heating the rental unit to a minimum of 50 degrees a requirement in your rental contract and send out a newsletter or reminder letter when the seasonal weather begins.

Preventive maintenance

A sound preventive maintenance program can reduce the number of maintenance emergencies at your property and enhance your cash flow. *Preventive maintenance* is regularly scheduled inspections and maintenance that extend the operating life of a property's building systems. Although preventive maintenance requires your tenant's cooperation, it often includes annual maintenance surveys or inspections of the unit's interior.

One great example of preventive maintenance is regularly lubricating the motors and replacing the filters in heating and air conditioning systems. When performed annually on a service contract, this preventive maintenance is very inexpensive, and the lubricated motors and clean filters lessen the strain on the equipment so that it lasts longer and operates with greater energy efficiency. Another example is periodically replacing the ball cock assemblies in toilet tanks. Especially if you pay the water bill, you want to make this inexpensive replacement at least annually. It can minimize the chance of running toilets, which are the most common source of significant wasteful increases of interior water usage in a home or apartment.

Preventive maintenance can often address problems when the conditions are still minor, thus saving significantly over future emergency repairs or replacement. It also reduces the cost of maintenance labor because maintenance personnel can work more efficiently by having all the necessary tools, parts, and supplies on hand. According to a study by IREM, 80 percent of the cost of most maintenance repairs covers labor and only 20 percent covers the actual parts and supplies. So, if you're replacing one exterior light bulb at the entry to your rental property and doing so requires a ladder and special tools to open the fixture, why not replace both bulbs while you're there? And be sure to also clean the fixture, too.

For even more savings, schedule preventive maintenance work during a contractor's slow season so you can obtain favorable pricing. For example, schedule your roof inspection and any waterproofing repairs during the dry season.

A temporary shut-off of utilities (particularly water) is often necessary in emergencies or while performing preventive maintenance and repairs at your property. Advising your tenants in advance, in writing, can minimize their inconvenience — and any requests for rent credits. The courts generally allow reasonable utility shut-offs as long as you're diligent in making the necessary repairs in a timely manner. (*Note:* You should have a clear understanding with your service contractors that they need to work efficiently and to the extent possible have all utility services back to full working condition at the end of each workday.)

Corrective maintenance

Although planning and performing preventive maintenance work is usually cheaper than fixing or replacing items, the reality is that if something breaks, you must fix or replace it in a timely manner, which is what *corrective maintenance* covers. Consequently, the most common tenant maintenance requests are for corrective maintenance. If you respond promptly and professionally, you'll earn a reputation as a good rental property owner.

Even with the best preventive maintenance in place, corrective maintenance is a normal part of any maintenance program. Anything in a rental unit can, and eventually will, break or need attention with normal usage, including toilets and sinks that clog, roofs or windows that leak, doors that stick, and appliances that malfunction. Most tenants realize that stuff happens, and the key to tenant satisfaction often depends on whether you have a system for efficiently accepting and responding to tenant maintenance requests. The reputations of great companies are often based on how they respond when things require attention. See this as an opportunity to build loyalty with your customers — your tenants.

Although smartphones, cellphones, or answering services or machines are still the best ways to communicate urgent maintenance requests, e-mail is the most popular with both owners and tenants for many nonemergency maintenance situations. E-mail (or a text) works well for owners, who often prefer not being interrupted by a phone call at a potentially inconvenient time. It also works well for tenants, who appreciate being able to send the request at any time of the day or night instead of having to wait until normal business hours to reach you. Upon receiving the e-mail or text, you can reply with a confirmation or ask for more details. You can even forward this communication directly to the maintenance contractor who'll be handling the service request. Either way, be sure to get the tenant's permission (preferably written) to enter the unit to fix the problem, and keep the tenant informed as to what will be done to remedy the situation.

Custodial maintenance

Custodial maintenance is the regular, day-to-day upkeep of the property and the most frequently occurring type of maintenance. The curb appeal and physical appearance of your property and grounds depend on regular patrolling and cleaning. In single-family rentals, the tenant typically handles this duty, and you should include the specific responsibilities in your rental contract. In larger rental properties, an on-site manager, maintenance worker, or groundskeeper should be responsible for daily inspection and cleaning.

Keep a list of routine maintenance items, including washing windows; hosing down parking areas, driveways, and walkways; and doing other tasks that keep the property's interior and exterior clean and presentable. Don't forget to keep the mailbox area and trash/recycling bin areas clean and free of litter as well.

The number one complaint of tenants, and the bane of all rental owners, is deferred maintenance. Not really a type of maintenance at all, *deferred maintenance* is the result of obvious needed repairs that landlords don't properly address in a timely manner. Common examples are peeling paint, rusting metal, broken screen doors, frayed carpet, cracked tile, overgrown landscaping, and minor roof leaks in the garage. Although every property has some deferred maintenance, your goal is to keep it to a minimum.

Cosmetic maintenance

Properties with great visual appeal are easier to manage and generate higher returns on your investment. So if you're willing to spend money to improve the unit's appearance both inside and out, you'll reap the rewards of *cosmetic maintenance*. Examples of this type of maintenance include replacing old countertops, installing new light fixtures, repainting, and installing new window coverings.

One of the most common complaints tenants make is that their landlord refuses to paint the property's interior every few years. Except for local rent control ordinances or the mitigation of lead-based paint, no federal or state laws require you to repaint the unit after any certain period for strictly cosmetic reasons. Of course, repainting the unit to keep your tenant satisfied if she's willing to pay more rent may be a good idea. This can also be a great lease renewal tool for a long-term tenant, but you need to be sure you're willing to cover the added costs of moving, protecting, and replacing the tenant's furniture and possessions.

Handling Rental Property Maintenance

Even though you may be assertive in properly maintaining your rental property through regular inspections and diligent interior maintenance upon tenant turnover, you'll always need to make repairs. To help you deal with this fact of property management life, the next few sections cover the important pointers you need to remember.

Responding to tenant maintenance requests

In many industries, the companies with the best reputations and customer loyalty are those that efficiently address complaints with a positive attitude. The rental property business is no different.

Your first knowledge of a maintenance problem or needed repair will likely be when your tenant contacts you. Typically, a service request comes to you via phone, e-mail, or text. Although you need to be respectful of your tenant's time, you also need to ask questions to gather a detailed description of the necessary maintenance and the precise location of the problem. This information allows you to make an educated decision as to the problem's urgency and who is the proper person to handle the work. It also gives you the chance to confirm that the proper tools, equipment, and parts are available at the first service call, if possible.

Make sure your tenants know they can't contact your maintenance person or contractor directly. A tenant may think he's doing you a favor by contacting the maintenance person directly and not hassling you with his problem, or he may remember another problem when the maintenance person is in his unit working on something else. Either way, require all service requests to be routed through management because you need to have a written record of all work requested and completed. Then, whenever a tenant contacts you with a maintenance problem, you can properly record all information in writing on a Maintenance Request Form (see Figure 17-1), regardless of how insignificant the problem is.

To access a sample Tenant Maintenance Request form you can use, simply pop in the CD or click the link in the table of contents.

Having proof that the tenant gave permission for maintenance personnel to enter the unit is essential. This proof can be visual (such as the tenant's signature or a copy of his request in e-mail or text form) or verbal (such as approval given over the phone). If the tenant makes the request only verbally, note the date and time and who gave permission to enter. If the tenant didn't specifically give permission for a maintenance person to enter the unit, serve a Notice of Intent to Enter Rental Unit, as legally required in your area.

Pop in the CD or click the link in the table of contents to access a sample Notice of Intent to Enter Rental Unit.

If you rely on an outside firm to handle your tenant maintenance requests, make sure all personnel who may be entering your tenant's unit are licensed and bonded. (Flip to Chapter 16 for tips on finding good contractors.) If your maintenance staff is on your payroll, this requirement is unnecessary.

Enter all tenant maintenance requests in a master log in chronological order. A good maintenance tracking system does much more than just record the service request and the fact that the tenant granted permission to enter. It can provide proof that the repairs were made, record the parts and materials used for the job, and serve as the basis of a billing record if the tenant caused the damage and needs to be charged for the service call. (See Chapter 20 for the scoop on computer software programs and manual maintenance tracking systems that simplify the paperwork.)

Always archive copies of Tenant Maintenance Request forms in the tenant's file and in a separate permanent maintenance file for each rental unit. If the tenant complains to authorities or makes allegations of a breach of habitability, Tenant Maintenance Request forms provide a repair history you can use to document that a tenant actually made a certain complaint and that you properly addressed it.

Maintenance Request Form

Maintenance Request Number _____

_____
Date

_____
Name

_____
Street Address   Unit number, if any

_____
City/State/Zip Code

_____   _____
Home Phone   Work or Alternate Phone

Service Requested (Describe very specifically):

_____
_____
_____
_____
_____
_____

Best time to perform service (Day and time): _____

Authorization: Owner/Agent/Service personnel are authorized to enter rental unit if Tenant is not present unless specific instructions have been given in advance to the contrary.

_____
Signature of Tenant

If verbal approval received, given by: _____. Received by: _____

Report of action taken
____ Completed, by _____ (Upon completion, describe problem/work done/materials used)
_____
_____

____ Unable to complete on _____, because _____
____ Outside professional assistance required, because _____
____ Will return to complete on _____

Charge cost to Tenant: _____ Yes   _____ No   If Yes, Reason _____
_____

Comments: _____
_____
_____

Received: _____   _____
             Date   Owner/Agent

Figure 17-1:
Tenant
Maintenance
Request
Form.

Courtesy of Robert S. Griswold

Your maintenance personnel and contractors are key in giving your tenants a positive or negative impression because they have direct contact with your tenants and are a reflection on you. Remind your maintenance pros that they're entering your tenants' homes and therefore must immediately identify themselves properly by using photo identification. They must always be appropriately dressed, well groomed, respectful, and courteous, and they should never smoke in a rental unit, unoccupied or not. They should also either remove or use protective coverings over their work shoes so they don't leave a trail across the tenant's clean floors. Your contractors must be businesslike and stick to the facts while keeping tenants informed about the status of the service request. They should also always completely clean up after themselves. And last but most certainly not least, they must always treat all tenants professionally and equally, or you can wind up facing fair housing discrimination claims.

Repair and deduct: Reimbursing tenants if repairs aren't made in a timely manner

In most states, if a tenant gives proper notice of a defect and you fail to properly address the issue and maintain the rental property in a safe and habitable condition after a reasonable period, the tenant has the right to have the defect repaired and then deduct some or all of the repair cost from a future month's rent.

If your state provides for the repair-and-deduct remedy, you need to fully understand the remedy's limitations and the rights and responsibilities of both you and your tenant. In most states, the tenant must follow a prescribed procedure to use the repair-and-deduct remedy, including providing proper notification to the rental owner and allowing her reasonable time to respond. Specific guidelines limit the types of defects covered, the number of times tenants can use this remedy, and the amount they can deduct (either as a set dollar amount or as a set percentage of the monthly rent).

Your goal should be to promptly respond to legitimate complaints about the property and to make sure that all maintenance work is done properly at a reasonable cost. When the tenant resorts to the repair-and-deduct remedy, you can face unpleasant consequences. The tenant may attempt to do the repair himself or hire a contractor who isn't skilled. Even worse, the tenant may hire a contractor who's very skilled but quite expensive and then send the bill to you.

If you have a tenant who pays less than the full amount of rent, claiming she had to have some repairs made without having given you any advance notice, then you need to contact her immediately. Depending on the legitimacy of the circumstances, you can agree to the reduced rent this time, but inform your tenant in writing that she must bring all future maintenance issues to your attention. If you don't, you may find your tenant discovering new and ever more creative reasons to repair-and-deduct as a way to lower her rent. (A real warning sign is when tenants attempt to charge you for their own labor.)

The bottom line? Always make repairs in a timely manner, and you won't have to face these problems to begin with.

Although responding to tenant maintenance requests can lead to excellent tenant relations, some tenants may have excessive demands. The best way to handle these tenants is to remain calm and courteous and to address *all* legitimate health and safety items or maintenance repairs that preserve your investment. It can be a fine line, but when tenant demands become unreasonable, trivial, and excessive, politely explain that providing extra service calls or cosmetic upgrades may necessitate an increase in rent to cover your additional expenses.

Keeping tenants from doing repairs

In most states, you can legally delegate some of your maintenance and repair tasks to your tenants, often in exchange for a rent reduction. However, you remain responsible for ensuring that the rental unit is habitable. Your tenants may be qualified and capable of handling many routine repairs, but you should really retain control of even the minor maintenance problems.

Initially, allowing your tenants to handle certain minor repairs seems to offer significant savings in cost and aggravation. However, most tenants lack the proper skills, training, special tools, or motivation to do the job properly. They may be willing to ignore or live with a problem that can be resolved inexpensively. But that little problem may soon become a major problem — and a major expense — leaving you with the responsibility of paying for it.

Although your tenant can probably handle many typical plumbing problems, be sure to instruct him to call immediately if the plumbing backup results in any amount of sewage overflow because this can be a significant health and safety risk. If plumbing clogs become common and they're not due to tenant misuse, they're likely the result of damaged pipes, roots in the waste line, or a blocked vent pipe. If this situation happens, immediately have a professional correct the problem at your expense.

Almost every rental property owner (especially if you have single-family rental homes) has a tenant propose to take care of the landscaping and the pool or spa. If your tenant is actually a professional landscaper or the owner of a pool service, then lucky you! If not, don't allow tenants to perform landscaping or pool/spa maintenance in exchange for lower rent. The landscaping at many properties can be worth tens of thousands of dollars — an investment that wilts to nothing if your tenant doesn't know how to properly care for it. Likewise, maintaining your pool or spa requires dealing with toxic chemicals that can lead to serious liability and costly repairs if they're not used by an experienced and qualified individual. This is also true for pest control beyond the household products available for the general public. Save yourself some hassle: Hire pros to service all aspects of your property and include their cost in your rent.

Tracking the life span of your appliances

Rental property owners often overlook the fact that they have a major investment in the appliances in their properties. Next to the physical structure itself, the appliances are some of the most expensive components of a rental property. So knowing the average life expectancy of each appliance and some easy steps you can take to properly maintain and often extend an appliance's usefulness makes a lot of sense.

The average life of an appliance varies dramatically based on the appliance's quality and the way the tenants treat it. So be sure to explain the proper use and care of all appliances to your tenants when they move in.

Here are the life expectancies for some commonly used appliances:

✔ **Dishwasher:** Dishwasher tubs are made of plastic or stainless steel, but you may still find a vintage porcelain-coated steel tub in an older property. The porcelain tubs rust out in 5 to 8 years if you have hard water, whereas the plastic tubs (the most common rental unit dishwashers) have a life expectancy of 10 to 12 years before they crack or fail. Unfortunately, this time frame is shortened if hard water mineral deposits damage and clog the pump, the impeller, or the float switch. Higher-end models now use stainless steel, but even on these, the most common problem is the need to replace rusted racks. Run a cycle with a lime or hard water deposit remover every few months for best performance. If you have a vacant unit, run the dishwasher every once in a while to prevent the motor and pump unit from freezing up or the seals and gaskets from drying out and becoming brittle.

✔ **Refrigerator:** This is one of the few appliances that runs almost continuously, but if properly serviced, a fridge can last 12 to 15 years. For longer life and maximum energy efficiency, brush or clean the condenser coils, usually located under the front bottom grill. You also want to make sure the defrost drain is clear and the drip pan is clean. Routinely clean and periodically check the fridge's gasket by closing the door on a dollar bill in several places. If the bill moves when you gently tug on it, replace the gasket. If you have an ice maker line, be sure to clean or replace the water filter every six months or as recommended. A crack or separation in this line can create a major flood and cause substantial damage.

✔ **Stove and oven:** These pieces have the longest life spans of any household appliance and can last 20 years or more because most of their parts are modular. Replacing the drip pans, thermostat, burners, controls, switches, light bulbs, and knobs is relatively easy. Check the gasket around the oven door periodically and make sure the exhaust fan is clean. Always use nonabrasive cleaners on all surfaces. Also, if the unit isn't built in, make sure that an anti-tip bracket has been properly installed.

✔ **Water heater:** This equipment can last 10 to 12 years with regular maintenance to maximize its energy efficiency and life span. Every three to six months, take a bucket and drain the water until it runs clear in order to remove mineral deposits and sediment that build up on the bottom and create a popping or crackling sound. Check the pressure relief valve, as well as all water lines and connections, and make sure the flue assembly is aligned and tightly sealed. For energy efficiency, buy a water heater with a thick, insulating shell and wrap a thermal blanket around it to keep heat trapped inside. Natural gas water heaters are generally much more cost-efficient than electric ones. Remember that with any natural gas appliance, carbon monoxide can be a significant health and safety risk (see Chapter 18), so be sure that only an experienced and competent handyman or contractor services the unit (you should always call the natural gas company to inspect the unit if you have any concerns). Though water should be adjusted or tempered by the tenant to avoid scalding injuries, be careful that the thermostat isn't set any higher than necessary to provide hot water throughout the property at a temperature not to exceed 120 degrees at the taps, as recommended by the International Plumbing Code.

All new appliances come with manufacturer warranties covering the cost of replacement or repairs if the appliances break down during the warranty period. Be sure to keep all appliance and equipment warranties, plus copies of all purchase receipts, in a readily accessible file for each property. Read the warranty before attempting a repair yourself or you may inadvertently void your rights to have the manufacturer replace or repair the appliance or equipment for free. (**Note:** After the basic warranty expires, many manufacturers offer extended service contracts for an annual fee, but these contracts generally aren't worthwhile if you have good quality appliances and a reliable service technician at your disposal.)

One of the main advantages of renting is that someone else is responsible for the property's maintenance and repair. Most tenants are relieved to know that you appreciate the opportunity to properly maintain the property and that they don't have to do a thing except alert you to problems when they arise.

Purchasing parts and supplies

As a rental property owner, you may have an uncanny interest in wandering through your favorite hardware store looking for obscure parts or flipping through a huge catalog for the latest sale on garbage disposals. Don't underestimate the importance of having reliable vendors with competitive pricing because the ongoing maintenance and repair of a rental property greatly exceed its original construction cost.

You can receive trade discounts from most rental housing industry vendors and suppliers just by setting up accounts in the name of your rental property or management business. These discounts usually apply to all purchases, but you can often find special volume or bulk discounts for commonly used items.

Shifting utility costs to tenants

Historically, utility providers installed one meter (a *master meter*) for an entire apartment complex, leaving the landlord responsible for all utility costs incurred at the property. In the last few decades, numerous states have mandated that gas and electric utilities directly meter individual apartment units. However, most water utilities allow the installation of a single master meter for an apartment building, regardless of the number of units. Because of this situation, an entire industry has evolved that's devoted to shifting utility costs from the landlord to the tenant. And guess what — the change is good for the environment, too, because it encourages energy conservation!

Landlords of multifamily rental properties may now choose to shift utility costs via submetering or allocation systems:

✔ *Submetering* involves the installation of individual utility meters, generally inside each residential unit, that record the unit's utility usage. Consumption in each unit is generally determined by a third-party utility billing company via a radio frequency system, which avoids any issues related to gaining entry into the unit or hiring meter readers. The readings are then used to calculate utility bills based on the local provider's rates. Be aware, though, that some companies only install in-line water meters on the hot water line and then estimate the total water usage, figuring that the cold water use is similar to the hot water use. Savvy tenants have been known to take advantage of this anomaly and then minimize their use of hot water by washing clothes in cold water. So, if you can only measure a single supply line, I suggest you submeter the cold water!

✔ *Allocation systems,* commonly known as *Resident Utility Billing Systems* (RUBS), employ specific formulas to allocate utility costs to individual apartment units. Common RUBS formulas include the number of occupants per unit, the square footage of each unit, or a combination of both occupancy and square footage. Under an occupancy-based RUBS, a unit with four residents pays approximately twice as much for utilities as a unit with two occupants.

Is one method really better than the other? Well, some of the benefits of submetering systems include a higher rate of conservation than what RUBS encourages (national studies have claimed from 25 to nearly 40 percent) and increased revenues. Submetering also makes tenants far more likely to report maintenance issues such as leaks and running toilets. Additionally, state and local governments have historically been more accepting of submetering programs than RUBS.

On the other hand, RUBS can be implemented without having to purchase and install submeters because they rely on a formula and not equipment to calculate the bill. The conservation savings aren't typically as great with RUBS because tenants don't have direct control over their actual individual use, but overall savings do exist.

With either method, a professional third-party company calculates the monthly charges and sends a utility bill to each tenant. Then the company either collects the money for the landlord or directs the tenants to pay the manager with rent. In addition to providing a user-friendly billing program for you and your tenants, these third parties can assist you with lease language and help ensure your utility billing system is compliant with all necessary regulations.

Whether you choose to investigate submetering or RUBS now or down the road, note that several areas in the United States have either mandated submetering of water or have considered such legislation in the last several years. This trend is likely to continue with the emphasis on green technology and the desire to conserve both water and energy.

Don't fall into the trap of buying items in greater quantities than you can immediately use if the items don't have long shelf life, regardless of the great savings offered at the time. A common mistake property owners make is buying tons of the latest discontinued paint on sale, only to be stuck with bad paint when it comes time to touch up the unit upon tenant turnover. Use the same standard color on all rentals so you can always find the color, buy in bulk, and do touchups as needed.

Another growing trend is purchasing parts and supplies online. Websites offer a wide variety of items, from appliances and plumbing and electrical fixtures to tools and hardware parts. They make the purchasing process very easy and typically offer free delivery. If you own just a few rental units, however, you may find that the savings are nominal unless you purchase in high quantities.

Chapter 18

Keeping Safety and Security in Mind

In This Chapter

▶ Handling and preventing crime at and nearby your rental property

▶ Enacting safety measures to protect your tenants and your property

▶ Shielding against environmental hazards

As a rental property owner, you need to take an active role in implementing policies and security measures for the safety of your tenants and their guests. Even if your property is located next door to the local police station, you still need to implement proper building security measures. Crime can strike anywhere, even in good neighborhoods. And even if crime isn't a problem in your area, you may face potential safety challenges from Mother Nature. Take the lead in working with local experts to prepare for the most likely natural disasters that may occur in your locale, including severe storms, wildfires, floods, hurricanes, tornadoes, and earthquakes.

Whether you're trying to ward off criminals or you're looking for ways to keep your property and tenants protected from hazardous environmental issues, I give you the suggestions you need in this chapter.

Tackling Crime in and around Your Rental Property

Crime's a fact of life for everyone, rental property owners and tenants alike. Tenants need to act prudently, but part of your responsibility as a rental owner is to make your property as reasonably safe as possible for your tenants and to alert them to their responsibilities as well. In the next few sections, I give you some tips for keeping crime to a minimum in your area and responding to it if and when it occurs.

Turning to crime prevention programs

Although you can't directly control the amount of crime in your rental property neighborhood, you can be proactive. The best way to do so is to check with your local police department and neighborhood association to see what programs are available in your area. The following sections highlight two of the more common ones.

The Crime Free Multi-Housing Program

One of the best crime prevention programs for rental property owners is available through most local law enforcement departments. The Crime Free Multi-Housing Program (www.crime-free-association.org/multi-housing.htm) unites rental property owners, local law enforcement, and tenants in an effort to fight crime and raise the local standard of living. This program has certified trainers with the nonprofit International Crime Free Association teach owners and managers how to help keep illegal activity out of their rental properties. This training is comprehensive and covers applicant screening techniques, proper preparation of rental contracts, warning signs of drug activity, crisis resolution, and ongoing management responsibilities. Tenants receive instruction on how to identify criminal and suspicious behaviors, and they're strongly encouraged to take responsibility to prevent crime from occurring.

After the training is complete and you demonstrate that you're screening prospective tenants, evicting problem ones, and using a Crime and Drug-Free Housing Addendum, your property can be certified as a Crime Free Multi-Housing Community. After certification, you can display signs at the entrances to your rental property to alert any prospective tenants that your property doesn't tolerate any criminal or drug-related activity.

Figure 18-1 shows what a sample Crime and Drug-Free Housing Addendum looks like. To access a copy that you can print, pop in the CD or click the link in the table of contents.

A large number of local law enforcement departments actively support this program in conjunction with a traditional neighborhood watch program, because the combination trains tenants to recognize crimes or suspicious activity and to report any to police. Law enforcement works one-on-one with owners, managers, and tenants by sharing information regarding criminal activities that have occurred in the community. The program's goal is to help these rental communities become certified and improve the quality of life for all.

Crime and Drug-Free Housing Addendum

This document is an addendum and is part of the Lease or Rental Agreement, dated
_____,

by and between _____,"Owner/Agent",

and _____"Tenant",

for the premises located at: _____.

In consideration of the execution or renewal of a lease of the Premises identified in the Lease or Rental Agreement, Management and Lessee agree as follows:

1.   Lessee, any member of Lessee's household, or a guest or other person under the Lessee's control shall not engage in criminal activity, including drug-related criminal activity, on or near said Premises. "Drug-related criminal activity" means the illegal manufacture, sale, distribution, use, or possession with intent to manufacture, sell, distribute, or use a controlled substance (as defined in section 102 of the Controlled Substance Act (21 U.S.C. 802)).

2.   Lessee, any member of Lessee's household, or a guest or other person under Lessee's control shall not engage in any act intended to facilitate criminal activity, including drug-related criminal activity, on or near said Premises.

3.   Lessee or members of the household will not permit the Premises to be used for, or to facilitate criminal activity, including drug-related criminal activity, regardless of whether the individual engaging in such activity is a member of the household or a guest.

4.   Lessee or members of the household will not engage in the manufacture, sale, or distribution of illegal drugs at any location, whether on or near said Premises or otherwise.

5.   Lessee, any member of Lessee's household, or a guest or other person under Lessee's control, shall not engage in acts of violence, including, but not limited to, the discharge of firearms on or near said Premises.

6.   Violation of any of the above provisions shall be a material violation of the Lease or Rental Agreement and good cause for termination of tenancy. A single violation of any of the provisions of this addendum shall be deemed a serious violation and a material noncompliance with the Lease or Rental Agreement. It is understood and agreed that a single violation shall be good cause for termination of the Lease or Rental Agreement. Unless otherwise provided by law, proof of violation shall not require criminal conviction, but shall be by a preponderance of the evidence.

7.   In case of conflict between the provisions of this addendum and any other provisions of the Lease or Rental Agreement, the provisions of the addendum shall govern.

| _____ | _____ | _____ | _____ |
| Date | Owner/Agent | Date | Tenant |

| | | _____ | _____ |
| | | Date | Tenant |

Figure 18-1:
Crime and
Drug-Free
Housing
Addendum.

Courtesy of Robert S. Griswold

The National Crime Prevention Council

A great resource for information is the National Crime Prevention Council, which offers a free checklist with advice and suggestions to help you evaluate the current safety features of your rental units and common areas. This information, which can also be useful for your home or office, is available online at www.ncpc.org/resources/files/pdf/neighborhood-safety/aptchk.pdf.

Paying attention to tenant questions and complaints about safety-related issues

When a tenant directly inquires about safety or security at your property, always provide an honest answer and inform him of any recent confirmed serious or violent criminal incidents. Of course, rental owners aren't routinely advised or aware of crime in the area or even in their own rental property. You obviously can't disclose what you don't know, but you should refer prospective or current tenants to local law enforcement for more information.

Although describing your building's security devices can be an effective marketing technique, you must take care to avoid inadvertently increasing your liability. This problem arises when you represent or even imply that your property is safer and more secure than other properties. If you make these kinds of claims, your security had better live up to your statements. In reality, no rental property is immune from crime. Crime can, and does, happen virtually everywhere, despite the best efforts of law enforcement.

So why not just exclude the words *safe, secure, security,* or any variations thereof from your vocabulary? Don't use them in your advertising, phone conversations, or vacancy showings because if your tenant ever becomes a crime victim, he'll certainly claim that your ads or comments gave him the expectation of security. Be honest with people, but be sure they understand that neither you nor law enforcement officials can guarantee any level of safety for them, their family and guests, or their personal possessions or vehicles. When discussing any building features, speak generically without embellishment. For example, if you happen to have an alarm device in your rental unit, don't refer to it as a *security protection system* or imply that the tenant's safety is assured because of this or any other building feature.

Test any alarm and demonstrate the proper use of all security hardware and devices in the presence of your tenants. Then have them sign an acknowledgment. Remind your tenants in writing to test these devices because they can fail or malfunction, and to call immediately for repairs or replacement.

Some rental property owners put disclaimers in their rental contracts that say the owner isn't responsible if a tenant suffers damage or an injury, regardless of the cause. Because they have this disclaimer in place, owners get careless and slow in responding to tenant complaints about lighting or malfunctioning window locks. But what these owners don't realize is that these disclaimers are almost certainly unenforceable. Many states have laws that invalidate these broad clauses because the disclaimers attempt to shift the owner's duty to properly maintain the premises in order to avoid responsibility for a tenant's injuries or damage. However, informing tenants of the following within your rental contract language is a good idea:

✔ You don't promise security of any kind.

✔ The tenants acknowledge that you don't and can't guarantee the safety or security of them, their family, or their guests.

✔ You don't guarantee the effectiveness or operability of security devices.

✔ The tenant should have renter's insurance (see Chapter 19).

See your local legal counsel for assistance preparing the proper language and documentation.

Responding to crimes when they occur

If a serious or violent crime occurs at your property, give your tenants written notification as soon as possible, along with any warnings or safety tips provided by law enforcement. Some owners are concerned that telling tenants about crime at the property or in the immediate area will lead to increased vacancies. You may occasionally lose someone this way, but warning your tenants so they can be more conscious of safety and security issues is important and helps prevent other similar crimes from occurring.

No specific rules exist about what crimes you should report to your tenants. But you should notify them of any crime concerning physical attack or bodily injury and also of any attempted or actual rental unit break-ins, burglaries, or robberies. A random car break-in or minor isolated vandalism on the property usually doesn't rise to the level of notification unless the incident occurs repeatedly. You can use a letter or memo to inform tenants about criminal activity; owners of larger rental properties can use the community website, newsletter, or a tenant meeting as a forum for discussing the issue.

The dated, written notification should tell your tenants that a crime has occurred. Be sure to include any information, composite sketches, or safety tips provided by law enforcement. Don't use the victim's name or address unless that person has requested you do so or unless you have advance approval. Remind tenants to be careful regarding controlled access areas and their surroundings and to call law enforcement immediately if they suspect a crime. Also, remind tenants that security is their responsibility. And be extremely careful that you, your on-site manager, or any other employees avoid making statements that can be used against you in any future legal action.

You have personal information on your tenants, including where they live and work, what cars they drive, and all their personal identification and financial information. Consequently, you have a tremendous responsibility to keep this information confidential. Institute a policy of not providing any information to anyone unless the tenant specifically gives you advance written authorization to do so. Securely lock all your property and tenant files in unlabeled file drawers to prevent intruders from rifling through these documents to target vulnerable tenants, such as elderly people or single women. You may also want to consider eliminating publically visible tenant rosters or at least limiting the information to only last names on controlled-access directories. Check with your mail carrier about putting the tenants' names only on the insides of the mailboxes.

Taking Necessary Security Precautions

One of the best ways to keep crime from occurring at your rental property is to make security a top priority. Although you can't guarantee to your tenants that your property is safe (you can see what I mean earlier in this chapter), you should do what you can to increase the likelihood that they won't encounter problems. In the following sections, I cover some security issues worth considering, not only for your property's safety but also for your tenants' well-being.

Keys and access-control systems

Rental unit locks are useless as security devices when keys aren't effectively controlled. Some properties employ a master key system where one single key works on all locks. Although this method is convenient, I strongly advise against using it because one lost key can require you to rekey an entire property. Instead, use a duplicate system with different keys for each lock.

Keep all owner or manager keys in a locked metal key cabinet or key safe. Don't label them with the tenants' addresses or unit numbers; rather, code them so that if they become lost or stolen, they can't be used easily. If a tenant reports a lost or missing key, change or rekey the lock instead of just giving her a duplicate key, unless she's sure the key is irretrievably lost. Charge the tenant a reasonable fee to cover your costs of getting a new key made. *Remember:* If you have contractors or suppliers working on-site, always arrange to have someone provide needed access instead of giving them a key.

Although you must always change or rekey all entry locks upon tenant turnover, some tenants want to change, rekey, or install additional locks during their tenancy. Doing so is fine as long as they give you a duplicate key so that you can enter the unit to resolve emergencies and make agreed-upon repairs. If you find an added or changed lock, verbally explain your policy and request a copy of the key. If the tenant doesn't want to give you a copy of the new key, send a polite but firm letter informing her of your policy. Ultimately, you may need to consider eviction if you aren't able to obtain a copy of the key.

More sophisticated card key and other access-control systems are now available and are regularly used in the hospitality industry. When combined with full-perimeter fencing, these card systems can be effective in controlling access, as long as your tenants cooperate and don't let anyone follow them in. Originally these systems weren't cost-effective unless you owned a larger rental property, but in the last decade or so, these systems have seen very significant drops in cost and are feasible at many smaller properties.

I've personally installed smart card access-control systems with great success. *Smart cards* are the size of a credit card and contain a small microchip that provides a unique identification number that's almost impossible to forge. You can install smart card readers at all access control points on the property, such as vehicle and pedestrian gates, as well as common area facilities. Another great feature of smart cards is that, with the use of an ATM-type station, they can store monetary value and be used for laundry machines, tennis court lights, or any other amenity that you want to charge for or control.

Just make sure you always invalidate any lost or stolen card keys.

In addition to keys and/or access-control systems, use standard security devices like deadbolts (preferably with minimum 1-inch throws) and locking passage sets. All wood entry doors should be solid core and have wide-angle peepholes or door viewers. Window locks and safety pins for all sliding glass doors, or even simple wood doweling for window tracks, are also extremely cost-effective yet valuable security devices. Make sure your tenant initials on her move-in checklist that all these security devices are operative and that she knows to contact you immediately if any locks or security devices are inoperative. Repair any broken locks or security devices immediately upon notification.

Make sure that any security devices you install are easy to operate and difficult to disable. A determined criminal can break into any rental community, but you want to make yours a more difficult target. Also, avoid installing security devices that create an illusion of security because they can actually lower tenants' guard and make them more vulnerable to crimes. For example, don't install phony security cameras or monitors in an attempt to deter criminal activity. Courts have routinely held that if such security measures are installed, the owner is required to employ the appropriate staff to oversee them. Never forget that you're in the rental housing business, not the business of installing and monitoring security systems.

Lighting

Effective outdoor lighting has many benefits to dissuading crime. Proper lighting is an extremely cost-effective way to protect your property and your tenants. It can serve as a deterrent to vandalism while illuminating your building walkways and the common areas to help prevent injuries to tenants and guests. The right lighting plan can also beautify your building and improve your property's curb appeal. Just remember that lighting is only effective if it's operative, properly located, and has the right type of fixture and light bulb for the intended purpose.

When lighting your rental property, keep these tips in mind:

- **Install appropriate lighting and keep the fixtures clean.** Too much lighting can be an irritant to tenants whose bedroom is 20 feet from the 5,000 watt bulb that illuminates the parking area. Make sure the lighting is appropriate for the space. Also, lights attract insects, so regularly clean your fixtures to keep them bug-free.

- **Replace any exterior lighting on clock timers with photocells that automatically detect darkness.** This step keeps your property well lit and eliminates the need to constantly adjust timers because the daylight hours vary with the seasons. Plus, photocells turn on the exterior lights on dark, stormy days. You can easily inspect and test your lights during the day by blocking the photocell sensors with tape to simulate darkness.

- **Establish a regular schedule for inspecting the common area exterior lighting and immediately repair broken fixtures and replace any burned-out bulbs.** The best time for inspecting and testing your lights is at night, when you can see that all fixtures are working properly and providing sufficient illumination in the correct locations. Proper lighting in parking lots is very important because many tenants routinely use parking areas after dark. Be sure to ask your residents to notify you of any inoperative lighting, and log your lighting inspections, repairs, and bulb replacements in your maintenance records.

Security firms

Most small rental property owners don't need on-site security firms or random patrols of their property. However, if you own rental properties in areas where security firms are necessary, you can choose from two common types: standing guard or drive-through services. *Standing guard services* can be quite expensive, particularly if you use them full time. A *drive-through and property lock-up service* that makes a predetermined number of random checks of the premises each evening (either by vehicle or on foot) and includes the securing of common area facilities is a cheaper alternative.

If you need a security service, you may want to hire part-time guard services with a schedule that constantly shifts the guards' days and hours. This way, you're balancing the high cost of security guards with a limited but random schedule to keep the criminal element deterred and guessing. Another option is having standing guards on some shifts interspersed with drive-throughs.

If you decide to hire a security firm, carefully interview and screen the company, including speaking to the actual guards who'll be assigned to your property. Always reserve the right to request a different guard and make sure he understands your expectations and behavior guidelines, including a strict policy against socializing with tenants.

Check the firm's references by calling current and past clients and inquire about the status of all required state and local licenses or permits, including a business license, security protection firm permits, or guard cards. Require a current certificate of insurance with general liability coverage of at least $3 million, with both you (the owner) and your rental property manager (if you have one) named as additional insureds. Request to be notified at least 30 days in advance of any lapse in coverage and require proof of workers' compensation and employer's liability insurance, plus auto liability insurance and a fidelity bond.

Your agreement should be in writing, clearly indicate that the security firm is an independent contractor, and feature a short termination notice requirement, because service from security firms can deteriorate very quickly.

Avoid armed guards unless absolutely necessary for your area. If a security firm indicates that armed guards are required at your location, immediately contact local law enforcement for confirmation of that opinion. And think seriously about whether you even want to own this type of property.

Law enforcement officers in some areas are allowed to offer their off-duty services to patrol your property, and some are even allowed to take their law enforcement vehicles home at night. This off-duty presence can be a powerful deterrent to the criminally inclined; however, you need to be extremely careful in establishing any such arrangement. Even if you offer a rent discount, you should use your standard rental contract with an addendum that clearly indicates the officer is an independent contractor and outlines the general services provided and the exact financial terms. Make sure your insurance covers the use of off-duty law enforcement and consult with your legal counsel to draft the documents. See Chapter 16 for more info on working with independent contractors.

Crime prevention and property protection measures should be appropriate for the standard in your community. Excessive measures can have a negative impact on prospects and tenants. You want them to be active and alert to their surroundings and take prudent self-protection measures, but at some point, instead of making them feel more comfortable, they may begin to wonder why so much attention to these issues is necessary. Landlords and property managers are not (and aren't expected to be) experts in crime prevention. So if you have issues or law enforcement brings concerns to your attention, it's best to ask law enforcement or other appropriate professionals to assist you and then follow their advice.

Prioritizing Tenant Safety

Though you can't guarantee and be responsible for ensuring your tenants' safety, you need to make sure that the rental unit and premises are reasonably safe at the time your tenant moves in and throughout the tenancy when you have knowledge of problems. The following sections highlight products and tactics you can use to keep your rental unit safe for its residents.

With tempered glass

Tempered glass is a type of safety glass manufactured by a special process so that it crumbles into small, granular pieces instead of splintering into dangerous, jagged shards. It's four to five times stronger than nontempered glass. Nontempered glass is found in many rental properties, especially older ones, and you may not even know it. As long as your property's nontempered glass is in good condition, you're not required to replace it because it's grandfathered in under the building code that was in effect at the time the property was constructed. However, you should be aware of this safety issue.

Whenever you replace shower doors, sliding glass doors, glass entry doors, glass closet doors, or any window in the kitchen or bathroom, I strongly encourage you to make sure your glass supplier and/or installer provides you with tempered glass. This is often required by code, but even if it isn't, the cost isn't much more but the safety factor is significantly improved with tempered glass. You may want to make this a standard part of the scope of your improvements when you look to renovate or upgrade your rental unit.

Tempered glass is often labeled with a small decal in the corner but not always. If you're unsure, consult with a professional glass installer or general contractor who's knowledgeable about glass.

If you have furnished rental units, don't purchase or rent any furniture containing nontempered glass. Most major national furniture rental companies don't even offer products with nontempered glass, but some low-end suppliers still import products with nontempered glass, which can be very dangerous when used in a residential rental property.

With safe cords (or no cords) for window coverings

The Consumer Product Safety Commission (CPSC) has identified window coverings with cords as one of the top five hidden hazards in homes. An estimated 1 billion (yes, *billion*) mini blinds, vertical blinds, or shades are in use in the United States, and children ranging from 7 months to 10 years old have suffered strangulation deaths or injuries when the window covering cord became wrapped around their necks.

Despite these statistics, this home-safety hazard is still unknown to many people. The danger is that an infant, toddler, or child can get entangled in corded window covering products that have loops, inner cords, or even long draw cords that can get wrapped around the child's neck and cause an unreasonable strangulation hazard. Research has shown that the greatest danger is with corded window coverings with exposed or accessible cords that are 7¼ inches or longer.

These products come from the manufacturer with labels and hang tags that warn of the potential hazard, but these labels and tags are often quickly removed or become faded or overlooked with subsequent tenants. The CPSC has had a safety campaign for many years to alert parents of this hazard, but it remains relatively unknown, especially to parents of children 3 years old and younger, who are at greatest risk.

The window covering industry has implemented voluntary retrofit programs and made significant improvements in the design and manufacture of its products, but these corded window products are abundant, although cordless products have recently become available.

Tenants may request that corded window coverings be removed from the rental property, but you're not required to make this accommodation. However, you may want to reach a reasonable agreement about the added cost of this change with your tenant, and you should certainly allow tenants to install their own cordless window coverings at their expense upon request.

You can also find other methods of securing the cords so they're less accessible to young children. These are often included in the packaging with new window coverings and should be installed if they're available. Or, if you have older window coverings already installed, you can purchase cord cleats and spring tension devices that help secure the cords and reduce the risk.

For more information on window cord safety, including free retrofit kits for many corded window covering products, go to the Window Covering Safety Council website at www.windowcoverings.org.

With anti-tip brackets for free-standing ranges

Though not a well-known hazard, a *free-standing range* (an appliance with an oven and a top-mounted cooktop, sometimes erroneously called a stove) can tip over if the oven door is opened and used as a place to sit or step up. This is primarily a hazard to small children who are curious to see what's cooking on the stove; the unsecured range can tip over and crush or burn the child.

Since 1991, the manufacturers of gas and electric ranges have agreed to voluntary safety standards to supply anti-tip bracket hardware and installation instructions with new ranges. Despite the availability of these anti-tip brackets, they're not widely used. In 2011, the Consumer Product Safety Commission expressed concerns that these brackets require special installation procedures that homeowners and/or installers may disregard. Additional voluntary measures have been developed, including more markings on the ranges as well as further warnings in the user's guide and installation instructions.

With appropriate enclosures and signage for swimming pools, spas, and hot tubs

One of the most desirable amenities for a rental home or multi-unit apartment community is a swimming pool, spa, or hot tub. But swimming pools and spas can create many safety issues for landlords and property managers. Be sure to check your local building code requirements regarding enclosure fencing and self-closing gates that can minimize the risk of accessibility by children or others who shouldn't be unattended near or in a swimming pool, spa, or hot tub.

Local health departments and similar agencies also have strict guidelines about additional safety equipment that must be present, plus proper water maintenance and testing/reporting procedures that you need to follow with written documentation. You also need to post the required signage and provide rules and/or lease clauses that remind your tenants about the unique dangers associated with swimming pools, spas, and hot tubs. These dangers include the need for constant adult supervision and safe practices, such as no glass and no running or diving. Of course, the most secure fence won't protect a child (or anyone who can't swim) if the person is left unattended inside a pool or spa enclosure.

Virginia Graeme Baker Pool and Spa Safety Act

The 7-year old granddaughter of former Secretary of State James Baker III, Virginia Graeme Baker, tragically drowned in a swimming pool in 2002 when she was trapped underwater by the suction of a spa drain despite the efforts of two adults to rescue her.

The federal act named after her requires that, effective December 19, 2008, all swimming pool and spa drain covers available for purchase in the United States must meet specific performance standards that prevent this type of tragedy. Further, public swimming pools, wading pools, spas, and hot tubs must meet these requirements as well.

A multifamily apartment building would be considered a public facility, while a single-family rental home likely wouldn't, as private pools, spas, and hot tubs built before the effective date aren't required to comply with this federal law. Nonetheless, I strongly urge all landlords and property managers to immediately contact a professional pool/spa maintenance company and verify that all their swimming pools, wading pools, spas, and hot tubs fully comply. This company can also advise as to any state or local requirements about pools, including the regular safety checks of all systems and drains.

Besides fencing and adult supervision, many jurisdictions require additional safety measures, including pool/spa safety nets or covers, pool/spa water alarms, gate alarms, and door alarms for all doors from the rental units or common area facilities that have direct access to the swimming pool.

Addressing Environmental Issues

Although crime is usually the first safety concern that comes to rental property owners' minds, important tenant safety topics also include those I outline in the following sections.

Fire safety

Fire safety is a critical issue for rental owners. Every year, several thousand Americans die in fires, and more than 100,000 are injured. Fires can spread quickly and fully engulf an entire room, rental unit, or home in a matter of minutes. Fire also produces poisonous gases and smoke that are disorienting and deadly.

Work with your local fire department to develop an evacuation plan for your property, including written notification to authorities of any rental units occupied by tenants with children or tenants with physical or mental challenges who may require assistance in an emergency.

Fire inspections are conducted regularly in most areas; when your property is inspected, you receive written notification of any deficiencies. You must address these noted items immediately, and you must contact the appropriate officials in writing to acknowledge that you've corrected the items and to request a new inspection. Be sure to obtain written confirmation that all items have been satisfactorily corrected.

In some areas, rental owners are required by law to provide fire extinguishers and to properly inspect and service or recharge them upon tenant turnover. A multipurpose dry chemical fire extinguisher can be a valuable and effective tool to quickly extinguish a small fire. If not required by law, evaluate your potential liability in the event the fire extinguisher is defective, used improperly, or unsuitably maintained by your tenant. If she gets hurt because the fire extinguisher you provided wasn't working properly when she needed it, you can be held liable. Fortunately, local fire departments are often willing to offer your tenants instruction on the proper use of extinguishers. Your insurance carrier may also conduct inspections and provide lists of safety issues or suggestions.

Fires are always serious, but the most dangerous ones are those that start while the tenants are asleep. That's one of the reasons all states require rental owners to install smoke detectors in all rental units. I strongly recommend installing smoke detectors in all rental unit hallways/exit routes and near, or preferably just inside, all sleeping areas, in compliance with applicable local building or fire codes and the alarm manufacturer's specifications. If you don't know your local requirements, contact your local fire department or building inspection agency for the exact specifications.

Always inspect and test the smoke detector according to the manufacturer's instructions upon tenant turnover. If a fire hurts a tenant because the smoke detector wasn't working properly when she moved in, she can sue you for responsibility. So be sure to keep written records of your inspection and testing of the smoke detector and have your tenant initial her rental contract or Smoke Detector Agreement (check out Chapter 11 for more on this document) indicating that the smoke detector was tested in her presence and that she can perform her own tests.

Also, be sure to immediately address all tenant requests for smoke detector inspections and repairs. Note such a request in your maintenance log, along with the date that the smoke detector was repaired or replaced. If the tenant is present, have her sign to acknowledge that the smoke detector now works properly. Smoke detector complaints are always a top priority requiring immediate attention, so keep new smoke detectors on hand for this reason.

Many rental units have electric baseboard heaters, which can be an efficient and effective way to heat individual rooms rather than the entire unit. However, your tenants need to be careful to make sure that furniture, bedding, and window coverings are kept at least 6 inches away at all times. If they haven't been used for some time, it's important to check for loose items that could restrict airflow or cause a fire if they're near the heating element. Also, be sure that the unit is attached securely to the wall and that the heating element cover is properly in place and will prevent any accessibility because the burn injuries can be severe.

Carbon monoxide

Carbon monoxide (CO), a colorless, odorless, and poisonous gas produced when fuel burns incompletely, can build up in a rental unit in mere hours. If the leak occurs when the tenants are asleep, they can easily lose consciousness, suffer a serious injury, or die before noticing anything's wrong.

The following items can all emit carbon monoxide:

- ✔ Fireplaces
- ✔ Gas appliances
- ✔ Gas or kerosene space heaters
- ✔ Gas water heaters
- ✔ Natural gas and oil furnaces
- ✔ Wood-burning stoves

When these items are working properly, carbon monoxide is safely vented to the chimney or another venting system. If they aren't vented properly, then carbon monoxide can build up within a rental unit.

Carbon monoxide detectors are now readily available. These devices are either hard-wired (some with a battery backup) or battery operated and emit a loud sound when an unsafe level of CO is detected. Currently, more than 25 states require carbon monoxide detectors in certain residential buildings.

Pop in the CD or click the link in the table of contents to access the list of states requiring carbon monoxide detectors, but note that the trend is for more states to require them.

Naturally, carbon monoxide poisoning is a particular concern for rental owners with properties in cold weather areas of the country, where tenants rely on some of these items to heat their rental units. Carbon monoxide detectors are only legally required in certain areas; however, I strongly advise installing one if your unit has a fireplace or uses carbon monoxide–producing heating appliances. Even if you don't, when in the rental unit upon request, have your on-site manager and maintenance personnel look out for any tenant misuse of a portable gas or kerosene heater because these devices are a major cause of carbon monoxide poisoning and death. They're inexpensive and can be installed by plugging them into electrical outlets in reasonable proximity to the carbon monoxide–producing source and/or as required by your state or local jurisdiction.

You should check all heating systems for basic operation prior to tenant move-in, but during the tenancy, your tenant needs to be proactive to safeguard her own health and safety. If your tenant alerts you to a concern about the system during the tenancy, you may want to have a pro from your oil or natural gas supplier inspect all heating systems. If your supplier doesn't offer this service, you can hire a professional heating appliance repair company. If you have fireplaces, you need to hire a chimney cleaning company to periodically inspect your chimney, chimney connections, and insulation for cracks, blockages, or leaks. Have the recommended work done as soon as possible and quickly respond to any tenant complaints about possible carbon monoxide poisoning.

Electromagnetic fields

Electromagnetic fields (EMFs) are controversial environmental hazards with varying scientific opinions regarding their potential danger to humans. Electric power lines, wiring, and appliances all create some level of EMF. Although the forces these sources create are minimal when compared to the normal electrical activity found within the human body, scientists can't agree definitively as to whether EMF exposure increases a person's chance of developing certain types of cancer, particularly childhood leukemia.

This potential problem is well beyond your control, but you should be aware of this issue in case you receive a tenant complaint. Because you can't insist that the electric utility remove its power lines and transmitters, the only viable solution for a tenant with legitimate concerns about EMF is to move. Evaluate the legitimacy of your tenant's concerns to determine whether it's in your mutual best interest to release him from his lease.

Mother Nature's wrath

Every region in the United States experiences its own set of challenges from Mother Nature, so make sure that you and your tenants are prepared for whatever natural disaster may be possible at your property. Every state and many local jurisdictions have emergency preparedness offices that can provide information and tips to help you and your tenants take the appropriate steps now, before an emergency happens. You can find these offices' contact info in the front of your local telephone directory.

The Federal Emergency Management Agency (FEMA) has many great resources available online to identify and assess your risk for hazards that can potentially affect you. Its website (www.fema.gov) even has a Hazard Information and Awareness section that allows you to see exactly what natural disasters or hazards have occurred historically in your area.

In many parts of the country, snow and ice accumulation can create danger-ous conditions. Many states and local municipalities have laws requiring owners to remove snow and ice from walkways or driveways; others don't. Either way, in most states, you aren't responsible if a tenant slips and falls on natural accumulations of snow and ice.

Mold

Mold is the common term for a variety of types of fungi commonly found in the natural environment. Mold is everywhere, and its effect on health has become an increasing concern for rental property owners and managers.

According to the Environmental Protection Agency (EPA), mold has the potential to cause health problems for some persons who have asthma or are allergic to certain types of mold. For these individuals, contact with specific molds can cause allergic responses such as sneezing, runny nose, red eyes, and skin rash. But mold can also irritate the eyes, skin, nose, throat, and lungs of nonallergic folk. Symptoms other than these reactions aren't com-monly reported as a result of mold inhalation.

You should inspect your rental unit for mold carefully before the tenant moves in and minimize the possibility of mold by quickly identifying and remedying the source of any moisture. But note that mold can develop under normal living conditions, particularly in high-moisture rooms like kitchens and baths. Chapter 11 discusses the specific paperwork you need your tenants to sign concerning mold.

If, despite their best efforts, your tenants suspect any issues of elevated mois-ture or smell or see any mildew or mold, they should notify you immediately. You must take claims of visible mold seriously, possibly by arranging for a maintenance person or contractor to investigate. Follow the EPA guidelines regarding mold removal (available at `www.epa.gov/mold`) and consult with experts if the problem is severe and persistent. In such cases, use qualified professionals and carefully document all communication to minimize the pros-pect of being sued by your tenants.

If you want more information about mold and how to minimize or get rid of it, I suggest you check out the following resources:

✓ "Guidelines on Assessment and Remediation of Fungi in Indoor Environments": This document, published by New York City's Department of Health and Mental Hygiene, is widely considered to be the first comprehensive document to establish best practices for mold assessment and remediation. You can find it online at `www.nyc.gov/html/doh/html/epi/moldrpt1.shtml`.

✔ "A Brief Guide to Mold, Moisture, and Your Home": This publication, produced by the EPA, is an excellent resource for both rental property owners and tenants. It's available at no charge from the EPA at `www.epa.gov/mold/publications.html`.

Bedbugs

Get a complaint from your tenant that he has bedbugs, and you'll have not only a practical pest control and maintenance problem to resolve but also a potential public relations nightmare on your hands.

Bedbugs are parasitic creatures the size of a sharp pencil point that feed on blood every five to ten days, causing skin irritations and itchy bites. (Just reading this information may make you start scratching for no apparent reason!) And they aren't picky, either; they're willing to feed on humans and pets alike. They're also resilient. In studies, researchers have discovered that bedbugs are capable of surviving several months to a year without feeding.

Bedbugs exist throughout the world, prefer warm climates and darkness, and generally do their feeding runs at night. Because bedbugs live solely on blood, having them in your home isn't a sign of dirtiness. You're as likely to find them in immaculate homes and hotel rooms as in filthy ones.

Bedbugs may enter your rental unit undetected via your tenant's clothing, luggage, containers, used furniture (they especially like mattresses, box springs, and couches), pets, and other items — anything where their flat-tened bodies make it possible for them to hide, which covers a lot because they fit into tiny spaces, about the width of a credit card. If there's a crack that will hold a credit card, you've found a potential bedbug-dwelling unit!

Over time, they may scatter from the bed throughout the bedroom, moving into any crevice or protected location they can find. They may also spread to nearby rooms within the same rental unit, although whether they can travel between apartments on their own is still debatable. Some experts insist they can't; others think they can follow electrical or plumbing lines, as well as crawl right under the walls separating adjacent apartments.

Although they're not a known carrier of diseases, bedbugs are a great nui-sance after they've fed because they lay eggs (and lots of them), typically in the creases or seams of fabrics. You can pick up bedbug egg casings on your clothes or shoes simply by visiting a unit that's infested.

Presently, the bedbug population appears to be increasing exponentially, and there's currently no effective treatment for completely eradicating the pests. Well, you could welcome the bedbug's natural predators into your unit — namely cockroaches, ants, spiders, mites, and centipedes — but I doubt your tenants will appreciate that.

The EPA and mold: What you can do

EPA guidelines emphasize that the key to mold prevention is moisture control and that drying water-damaged areas within 24 to 48 hours is important. They advise that, although eliminating all mold and mold spores from an indoor environment is impractical, you can clean up mold with detergent and determine and eliminate the source of the moisture. If you don't remove the moisture source, your mold problem will reoccur.

Although the Internet is full of websites promoting air testing, the EPA indicates that testing for mold is generally unnecessary if visible mold growth is present. You should proceed with mold cleanup and remediation per the appropriate EPA guidelines or the advice of a qualified professional. The EPA does advise that surface sampling using analytical methods recommended by the American Industrial Hygiene Association (AIHA), the American Conference of Governmental Industrial Hygienists (ACGIH), or other professional organizations may be useful after mold removal to determine whether an area has been adequately cleaned.

The EPA provides a cleanup and mold prevention guide for various materials and classifies mold contamination in different categories based on the surface area of the affected space. The EPA recommends different responses for areas of 10 feet or less (approximately 3 feet by 3 feet), areas of 30 to 100 square feet, and areas greater than 100 contiguous square feet. Consult a professional for mold contamination greater than 100 contiguous square feet.

For more info about mold, check out the EPA's website at `www.epa.gov/mold/mold resources.html`. I especially recommend you click the Ten Things You Should Know about Mold section for valuable help.

The following sections explain how to identify a bedbug infestation within your property and how to remove these annoying creatures.

You may want to consider supplying a Bedbug Addendum with your lease or rental agreement. This document acknowledges that the unit has been inspected for bedbugs prior to the tenant taking up residence and acknowledges the tenant's responsibility in preventing, reporting, and treating infestations. You can access a sample Bedbug Addendum from the California Apartment Association by popping in the CD or clicking the link in the table of contents.

Identifying a bedbug infestation

Like most pest control challenges faced by landlords and property managers and their pest management professionals, the key is tenant education and cooperation. Although bedbugs are routinely misidentified, get professional assistance as early as possible to minimize the chance of an infestation spreading to more than a single rental unit. Because your tenant occupies your rental property, any efforts to control bedbugs always begins with a notice to the landlord or property manager.

To spot a bedbug infestation, look for the following:

- Small dark spots, about the size of a pencil point. These are bedbug droppings, and they may bleed through fabric like a marker bleeds through paper.

- Any blood on sheets or pillowcases — it's a result of their bites.

- A peculiar musty or offensive odor that the bedbugs excrete from their glands.

- Miniscule white eggs and eggshells (about 1 millimeter in size).

- The dead skins caused by bedbugs shedding as they grow larger.

- Live bedbugs. (See `www.epa.gov/bedbugs/#biology` for a good image of what bedbugs look like throughout their different stages of development.)

- Signs of crushed bedbugs — rusty-colored or reddish stains on bedding or mattresses.

Removing bedbugs from your property

If you encounter bedbugs at your property and want to get rid of them, be prepared for the process to take some time and require a fair amount of patience — as well as a sizable expense. The good news is that you don't have to rely solely on pesticides. Instead, you can turn to an integrated pest management program that combines chemical and nonchemical treatments (such as applying excessive heat over an extended period of time).

Keep the following in mind when dealing with a bedbug infestation:

- Thoroughly clean *everything* found within the infested area.

- Remove the bedbugs' habitat. (Also, consider cleaning up clutter because bedbugs like to hide there.)

- If you choose to use pesticides, take extra care to follow the label directions to the letter — or just hire a pest management professional.

- Schedule follow-up inspections of the area to ensure the bedbugs haven't returned.

Of course, if you're unfortunate enough to have bedbugs at your property, you're probably extra concerned about how to prevent future infestations. Educating tenants about bedbugs is truly one of the best things you can do. For additional information, I encourage you to visit `www.epa.gov/bedbugs`.

Part V
Money, Money, Money!

The 5th Wave   By Rich Tennant

"Mr. Johnson, I think we've found the perfect rental investment property for you! By the way, how do you feel about ghosts, burial grounds, and curses?"

In this part . . .

Keeping track of your money is important no matter what business you're in, but it's especially important in property management. In this part, I make two not-so-fun issues you have to deal with as a rental property owner — insurance and taxes — easy to understand. I also give you some great tips for using computer software to assist you in keeping records and managing your finances.

Finally, after you have a little landlording experience under your belt, if you want to increase your cash flow (and who doesn't?), you may want to try your hand at some more unusual endeavors. Here, I present you with some options so you can figure out whether they're right for you and then use them to your advantage with few worries.

Chapter 19

Two Necessities of Property Management: Insurance and Taxes

As a rental property owner, two of the major financial responsibilities you must deal with are insurance and taxes. Knowing the rules before you get in the game is the best way to play, and in this chapter, I let you know just what to expect.

Cover Me, I'm Going in: Making Sure You Have the Insurance You Need

Some insurance companies want to sell you coverage against any possible danger or loss in the world. And a sharp insurance agent is a master at describing all sorts of horrible problems that can befall your property. If you want to make sure you're covered at a reasonable cost, you need to sift through the sales pitch and decide which type of coverage is right for you.

Your goal is to pay only for coverage for events and losses that are most likely to occur at your property. Buying hurricane insurance in Minnesota may not make a ton of sense, but purchasing the right insurance coverage is worth a lot.

You also need to be concerned about lawsuits and having the proper insurance coverage to defend yourself and protect your assets. Why? Because apartment complex owners and property managers tend to be sued quite frequently. Although that sounds intimidating, you'll likely be okay if you have sound ownership and management policies combined with insurance that's customized for your specific needs. The following sections help you determine what those needs are.

You'll always retain and need insurance, but don't assume that your insurance covers all potential losses. Your best defense against losses is to properly manage your rentals and assertively avoid, transfer, or control the inherent risks of owning and managing rental property. Seek the feedback and advice of your insurance agent or company, many of which will routinely inspect your property to help you identify and mitigate risks. Some companies even offer discounts if you implement some of their recommendations, and no or few claims over the years can lead to lower premiums.

Telling the difference among the types of insurance coverage you can get

The first step in getting the right insurance is understanding the different types of insurance available. The proper insurance coverage can protect you from losses caused by many perils, including fire, storms, burglary, and vandalism. Besides building coverage, a *comprehensive general liability* policy covers injuries or losses suffered by others as a result of defective conditions on the property. General liability insurance also covers the legal costs of defending personal injury lawsuits. Because legal defense costs are commonly much greater than the ultimate award of damages, if any, liability insurance is a valuable feature. Loss of rents or income insurance can also come in handy to keep up with the mortgage payments and other costs of ownership in the event of a loss that interrupts your income stream, such as a fire or natural disaster.

The coverage you can get as a rental property owner varies from company to company, so do the following when selecting one:

- ✔ **Interview and choose a qualified insurance broker or agent who understands your unique needs.** Have an in-depth discussion with several insurance agents about types and amounts of coverage, the costs, deductible amounts, and exclusions. Make a chart that allows you to compare several companies side by side.

- ✔ **Look at each company's ratings and its reputation for quickly and fairly handling and paying claims.** Although several rating firms exist, the most widely known is A. M. Best Company. It uses an *A* through *F* rating scale, just like in grade school. The top companies have an *A* or *A–* but preferably an *A+* or *A++* rating (as high as the scale goes).

> You can visit A. M. Best online at www.ambest.com and search for its Financial Strength Ratings on insurance companies you're considering. Remember to add a rating column to your comparison chart.

Insurance professionals are either independent brokers or exclusive agents who write policies for only one company. Talk with an insurance broker and a couple of company agents to ensure you're receiving the insurance coverage you need at the best value. Keep in mind that the lowest premium often isn't the best policy for your needs. Ask a lot of questions and insist on evidence that the company provides coverage with a *written binder,* a document issued by an agent to the insured prior to the formal issuance of the insurance policy. Always make sure that communications regarding insurance coverage and policies are in writing, and remember that your best proof of coverage (besides the actual policy) is a formal certificate of insurance that outlines who and what the policy covers.

Basic, broad form, and special form coverage

Three types of full-building insurance coverage exist:

- **Basic:** Most insurance companies offer *basic* building coverage packages that insure your property against loss from fire, lightning, explosion, windstorm or hail, smoke, aircraft or vehicles, riot or civil commotion, vandalism, sprinkler leakage, and even volcanic action. This coverage often doesn't include protection against claims alleging property damage or personal injury from mold or protection for certain contents, such as boilers, equipment, and machinery, unless specifically added as an endorsement. (Fair housing discrimination claims aren't typically covered either, but recently, coverage has become available.)

- **Broad form:** With *broad form* coverage, you get the entire basic package plus protection against losses due to glass breakage, falling objects, weight of snow or ice, water damage associated with plumbing, and collapse from certain specific causes.

- **Special form:** The broadest coverage available is *special form,* which covers your property against all losses, except those losses specifically excluded from the policy. This coverage offers the highest level of protection and is typically more expensive. However, many insurance companies offer competitive insurance packages specially designed to meet the needs of rental owners, so remember to shop around. Insurance agents often market their policies at favorable terms through NAA affiliates or to IREM members, so be sure to check these sources as well.

If you own multiple rental units, you may receive discounts (and better coverage!) if you have a single insurance policy that covers all locations. For example, if you currently own three properties, each with a $1 million policy, you can get a single policy with a $3 million limit at a more competitive cost. Doing so provides up to $3 million in coverage for each property. You can also benefit if you have an *aggregate deductible,* which is the portion of your loss that you essentially self-insure. The losses at any of your properties can be used toward meeting the aggregate deductible. Extremely competitive rates on group package policies are also sometimes available for the clients of professional property management firms.

Supplemental coverage

Flood, hurricane, and earthquake insurance are examples of coverage available for a separate cost. This coverage can be critical in the event of a natural disaster. However, these policies are often expensive and have extremely high deductibles, making them uneconomical for the average small rental property owner. Get quotes nonetheless and see whether supplemental coverage is something you think you can afford.

Seriously consider replacement cost coverage. An insurance company pays owners for losses in two ways: *actual cash value* pays the cost of replacing property after subtracting for physical depreciation; *replacement cost* pays the cost of replacing the property without subtracting for physical depreciation. The standard policies most insurance companies offer provide for actual cash value coverage only; you must specifically have an endorsement and pay extra for replacement cost coverage. In my experience, the extra cost is often well worth it.

If you decide to rent out your personal residence, immediately contact your insurance agent and have your homeowner's policy converted to a landlord's policy. A landlord's policy contains special coverage riders that aren't in the typical homeowner's policy. Because of the increased liability risk for rental properties, your insurance company may not even offer this coverage, whereas certain companies specialize in this business. Either way, make sure you possess proper landlord's coverage for your rental property or your claim may be denied. A single uncovered lawsuit can cost you dearly, whether or not you're ultimately found to be at fault, because the cost of litigation is so high. Plus, in some states, if you're found to be even 1 percent responsible for the plaintiff's claims, you could be required to pay all the plaintiff's legal fees, which could be greater than the actual awarded damages.

Umbrella coverage

Umbrella coverage, which is designed to supplement other policies, can be a very cost-effective way to dramatically increase your liability exposure. Your primary policy may have liability limits of $1 million, but an umbrella policy can provide an additional $1 or $2 million in vital coverage at a reasonable cost. Depending on the value of your property and assets, buying an umbrella liability policy with higher limits makes sense. The proper policy limits are always your decision as the owner, but seek and listen carefully to the advice of an experienced insurance agent.

I suggest you purchase your umbrella policy from the same company that handles your underlying liability insurance. Otherwise, you may find yourself dealing with conflicting strategies on how best to defend you in litigation.

Paying attention to coinsurance clauses

Some insurance companies have a *coinsurance clause,* which is the joint assumption of risk between the insurer and the insured and requires rental property owners to carry a minimum amount of coverage. If you carry less than the minimum amount, the company imposes a coinsurance penalty that comes out of your recovery. These penalties reduce the payment on the loss by the same percentage as the insurance shortfall.

If you carry only $1.6 million in coverage when you should have $2 million, you're only carrying 80 percent of the minimum required insured value. If the building suffers a loss, the insurance company will only pay 80 percent of that loss.

Other insurance coverage

A variety of other insurance options make sense for certain rental property owners. For example, a policy that includes *loss-of-rents coverage* provides income if your property is uninhabitable because of fire or another calamity and allows you to continue making your mortgage and other payments. The following nonstandard options are available:

- ✔ **Nonowned auto liability coverage:** If you plan to have any maintenance or management employees assisting you with your rental activities, consider buying this type of coverage. It protects you from liability for accidents and injuries caused by your employees while working and using their own vehicles.

- ✔ **Fidelity bond:** This type provides reimbursement if a dishonest employee steals your rents. An *endorsement for money and securities* can protect you from losses occasioned by the dishonest acts of nonemployees.

- ✔ **Building ordinance:** This type protects you in the event your rental property is partially or fully destroyed. It covers the costs of demolition and cleanup, plus the increased costs to rebuild if the property needs to meet new or stricter building code requirements, or the loss of value if the property can't be rebuilt to its prior condition.

Determining the right deductible

A *deductible* is the amount of money you must pay out-of-pocket before your insurance coverage kicks in. Deductibles can be expressed as a percentage (such as 10 percent) but usually can be purchased as a fixed dollar amount or cap that generally ranges from $250 to $500, or sometimes $1,000 for small rental properties. The larger the property, the higher the customary deductible, but also, the higher the deductible, the lower your insurance premium.

Evaluate the possibility of having a higher deductible and using your savings to purchase other important coverage. Contact your insurance agent for quotes on the premium reduction based on each level of deductible. To score a lower insurance premium, you must be willing and able to absorb the amount of a much higher deductible. And because you always want to minimize the number of claims, remember that you're unlikely to submit any claim for an amount that's just higher than your deductible. For example, if you decide you can increase your deductible from $500 to $2,500, you're realistically agreeing that you aren't going to submit any claim for less than $3,000 to $4,000, because making a claim for a small amount beyond the deductible doesn't make sense. Always contact your insurance agent to discuss any potential claims because not all claims negatively impact your future coverage or premium charges.

Letting your tenants know about renter's insurance

Renter's insurance is something your tenants obtain and pay for themselves; it covers losses to a tenant's personal property as a result of fire, theft, water damage, and so on. Tenants often think they don't need renter's insurance because they possess few valuables, but renter's insurance covers much more than just their personal possessions. It also provides protection against claims made by injured guests or visitors and offers supplemental living expenses if the rental unit becomes uninhabitable because of fire or smoke damage. And it protects the tenant in the event that he causes damage to another tenant's property.

Although the number of tenants with renter's insurance has increased significantly, the most recent Insurance Research Council study showed that 96 percent of homeowners have a homeowner's insurance policy, but only 43 percent of renters have a renter's insurance policy.

As a rental property owner, you benefit from renter's insurance because it covers any claims in the event that tenants start a fire or flood. Their premiums go up instead of yours. So to protect your property, be sure to place a clause in your rental contract that clearly states that every tenant must have renter's insurance. Depending on the policy limits, renter's policies typically cost from $150 to $300 per year, with deductible amounts of $250 or $500. As with car insurance, the insurance company only pays for losses over and above the deductible amount.

A *renter's insurance addendum* is a document that informs renters about insurance coverage so they can protect against loss. This document helps prevent misunderstandings about the owner's and tenant's insurance coverage and also allows you the option of requiring the tenant to obtain renter's insurance. To access a sample Renter's Insurance Addendum from the California Apartment Association, pop in the CD or click the link in the table of contents.

Renter's insurance is no laughing matter

The importance of renter's insurance was reinforced to me early in my management career when a bad fire occurred at one of the properties I managed. Apparently, a new tenant was getting help from *six-pack movers* — friends who assist with a move in exchange for a six-pack of their favorite beverage. The fire started when one of the tenant's friends negligently placed a box of paper goods right on top of the gas stove pilot light.

Luckily, no one was seriously injured, but 12 of 16 rental units in the building were completely destroyed. None of the tenants had renter's insurance, and even the innocent neighbors lost everything they owned. I was covered legally because all the tenants had initialed the rental contract clause indicating they should have renter's insurance. But facing tenants who'd just lost everything because they didn't get around to buying renter's insurance was still difficult.

Handling potential claims

Immediately document all facts when an incident occurs on your property, particularly if it involves injury. Use an Incident Report (like the one available on the CD and via the link in the table of contents) to record all the facts. Be sure to immediately get in touch with your insurance company or your insurance agent. Follow up with a written letter to ensure your contact was notified and has the information on file. Failure to do so in a timely manner could result in the denial of a claim.

The Tax Man Cometh: Knowing Which Taxes You're Responsible for Paying

Taxation laws regarding investment real estate are unique and far more complex than those regarding homeownership. If you're just starting out in property management and you're confused by tax laws, you're not alone. Because tax laws can work for or against real estate investors, you need to have a general understanding of the basic concepts, which is why the following sections paint a clear picture of some tax-related issues you're likely to face.

Tax laws change frequently, and the call for a new federal taxation system seems to become louder every election cycle. And most states have their own income tax system that may or may not mirror the federal laws for income-producing rental properties. So be sure to check with your tax advisor before taking any action. I strongly suggest that you use a Certified Public Accountant (CPA) or tax specialist to prepare your tax returns if you own investment real estate.

Making sense of income taxes

To get a firm grasp on paying Uncle Sam, you first need to understand all about income taxes. Taxpayers generally have two types of income:

- **Ordinary income:** This type includes wages, bonuses and commissions, rents, dividends, and interest. It's taxed at various rates, depending on your net taxable income. The higher the reportable net income, the higher the *marginal tax rate* (the amount of additional tax paid by the taxpayer on each dollar of additional reportable income), with the top rate currently at 35 percent.

- **Capital gains:** You generate this type of income when you sell possessions, including real estate and stock, for a profit. Capital gains are classified as

    - **Short-term:** Currently, short-term gains (applies to investments that are sold within 12 months of acquisition) are taxed at the same rate as ordinary income.

    - **Long-term:** Currently, long-term gains are taxed at lower rates than ordinary income, with a maximum of 15 percent.

The income you receive from your rental property is subject to taxation as ordinary income. The positive cash flow is determined by deducting all operating expenses, including the following:

- Advertising costs
- Auto and travel expenses
- Cleaning and janitorial
- Damages
- Debt service interest
- Depreciation from rental income
- Equipment rental
- Gardening or landscape maintenance
- Homeowner association dues
- Insurance premiums

- Interest paid on mortgage debt
- Leasing commissions
- Maintenance and repair costs
- Management fees
- Payroll
- Professional fees
- Property taxes
- Supplies
- Theft
- Utilities and waste removal

You don't have to pay taxes on security deposits until they become income. When you receive them, security deposits are a liability that you must pay back to tenants at a later time. However, after a tenant vacates and you withhold a portion of the security deposit, it may become classified as income. Essentially, the deposit isn't taxable as long as you have an expense for the same amount as the deduction. For example, if you deduct $300 from a tenant's security deposit to paint and you actually hire a painter for $300, then you don't owe any taxes on that $300 you retained. But if you deduct $300 and then do the work yourself for $100, you owe taxes on the $200 difference, which is classified as income.

Understanding passive and active activity

Rental property owners often start out with their real estate activities serving as a second income. They typically generate the majority of their income from professions and sources unrelated to real estate. The taxation rules that apply to these part-time real estate investors are different from the ones that apply to real estate pros. Unless you qualify as a real estate professional, the IRS classifies all real estate activities as *passive* and limits your ability to claim real estate loss deductions.

The IRS defines a *real estate professional* as a person who performs at least 50 percent of her personal services in businesses related to real estate or spends at least 750 hours per year in these endeavors. These individuals are considered *active investors* and are allowed to claim all their real estate loss deductions in the year incurred. All others are considered *passive investors,* and they're subject to limitations on the real estate losses they can deduct. However, if you're a passive investor, you may still be able to use rental property losses to shelter ordinary income if own a minimum of 10 percent and you're actively involved in the management of your property.

This allowance doesn't mean, however, that you can't hire a property management company to handle the day-to-day activities while you oversee its efforts. According to the IRS, you're *actively involved* if you oversee or approve the setting of rent, approval of tenants, and decisions about repairs and capital improvements.

If you meet the IRS standard of being actively involved, you can take a rental property loss deduction of up to $25,000 against other income in the current tax year, as long as your adjusted gross income doesn't exceed $100,000. If it does, you'll be denied 50 cents of the loss allowance for every dollar over $100,000, which means the entire $25,000 loss allowance disappears at an adjusted gross income of $150,000. You can save any losses disallowed in one year and apply them to reduce rental or other passive income in future years. If you can't use the losses in this manner, you can use them when you sell your property to effectively reduce the taxable gain. Thus, the losses ultimately benefit you.

Taking advantage of depreciation

Depreciation is one expense that allows you to shelter positive cash flow from taxation. *Depreciation* is an accounting concept that allows you the right to claim as a deduction a certain portion of the value of a rental property just because you own it, with no relationship to whether it's actually wearing out or losing value. Depreciation lowers your income taxes in the current year by essentially providing a governmental, interest-free loan until the property sells.

Before 1993, you could accelerate depreciation in the early years of rental property ownership, but under current tax laws, recently acquired rental properties can only use *straight-line depreciation,* which reduces the property's value by set equal amounts each year over its established economic life. The period during which depreciation is taken is called the *recovery period.* Currently, the IRS mandates that residential rental property has a recovery period of 27.5 years, and owners are required to use straight-line depreciation and deduct a depreciation loss of 127.5, or about 3.64 percent each year. Depreciation is prorated for the first or last year of ownership.

Depreciation is only allowed for the value of the buildings; land isn't depreciable. Often, you can use the property tax assessor's allocation ratio between the value of your buildings and land to determine the appropriate basis amount for calculating depreciation.

Using tax-deferred exchanges to your benefit

A *tax-deferred exchange* is an important tool if you're looking to increase the size of your real estate holdings. You can defer taxation of capital gains by effectively exchanging one property for another. Therefore, you can keep exchanging upward in value, adding to your assets without ever having to pay any capital gains tax.

Section 1031 of the Internal Revenue Code allows exchanges, sometimes called *Starker exchanges,* that permit the postponement of a capital gains tax payment when you purchase another property of like kind within a specified period. The tax is deferred, not eliminated. For real estate purposes, the IRS defines *like-kind property* as any property held for business, trade, or investment purposes. This broad definition allows real estate investors to use a Section 1031 exchange to defer taxes when they sell an apartment building and buy raw land, or vice versa. Check out www.irs.gov for the basic rules for the Section 1031 exchange.

The IRS also allows a reverse Section 1031 exchange. This regulation permits a real estate investor to purchase a new investment property first, before following the 1031 guidelines to close on the sale property within the 180-day limitation while deferring any capital gains taxes.

Grasping (and appealing) property taxes

Local municipal and governmental agencies generally receive a major portion of their operating funds by taxing real estate within their jurisdictions. Typically, property taxes are an *ad valorem* (based on the property's value) tax, but sometimes, other factors or mathematical formulas are used to reach the final value upon which the tax rate is applied. Contact your local county tax assessor to find out exactly how your county determines your property taxes.

In certain areas of the country, improvement districts have been established with special assessments in addition to the property tax obligations. These taxes are usually flat fees or amounts based on square footage, as opposed to the property's value.

Naturally, problems can arise in determining the value to place on a property. Real estate is valued, or *assessed,* for real estate taxation purposes by governmental tax assessors or appraisers. These public employees are responsible for determining a market value for each property in a jurisdiction. The *market value* of a property is the price the property would most likely sell for in a competitive market.

The building and land are appraised separately, and most states have laws that require the property to be periodically reassessed or revalued. A tax or mill rate is then applied to the assessed value to determine the actual tax billed to the property owner. The higher the assessed value of your property, the higher your property tax bill. Property taxes are typically due in two semiannual installments, and unpaid taxes or special assessments become liens on the property. A *lien* is a claim or attachment against property as security for payment of an obligation.

You may feel helpless against the property tax bureaucracy in your area, but remember that tax assessors have been known to make clerical errors or fail to take all pertinent factors into account when placing a value on your property. If you feel that your property assessment is too high, contact your local tax assessor. The assessor may be willing to make an adjustment if you can back up your opinion with careful research and a good presentation. Or you may need to make a formal property tax protest. Tax protests are often first heard within the tax assessor's office or a local board of appeal. If a dispute still exists, appeals may be taken to court in many states.

Contact your assessor and inquire about a reassessment if real estate values decline in your area. A lower assessment leads to a direct reduction in your property tax bill and a corresponding increase in your cash flow. Some jurisdictions even temporarily lower the valuation based on broad declines in real estate, but most of these programs call for an annual reassessment, and your value can quickly increase to the previous or even higher assessed valuation.

Many municipalities have implemented business license or rental unit taxes for rental property owners. Sometimes these resources are used to finance code enforcement or mandatory inspections of some or all rental properties. But these special taxes may just generate revenue for the general fund. Contact your local government to ensure you're meeting all its specific requirements. The licensing or rental taxes are high enough, but the fines and penalties can be extreme.

Chapter 20

Financial Management and Record-Keeping

*I*f you ask several rental property owners what their least favorite part of the job is, you'll probably hear "paperwork" more than any other response. Most owners don't mind the hands-on aspects of managing their properties, such as cleaning or painting the rental unit; many of them even enjoy that. And meeting rental prospects and showing the property is fun compared to recording rents, sending out late notices, and writing checks to pay the bills. But the financial management aspects of accounting for all the funds you receive and expend are critical elements of running your rental housing venture. In this chapter, I show you how to get a handle on good financial record-keeping.

Organizing Your Files

If you have an aversion to keeping track of documents, then managing your own rental properties may not be for you. If you own rental property, you need to prepare many important written records and keep them ready for prompt retrieval. Every rental property owner must be organized, which includes having a basic filing system with separate records for each property.

Scanning and storing documents electronically is easier today than ever, so you may opt to keep many of these files and copies of all important documents on your computer. Of course, be sure to regularly back up your files on a flash drive or to a reliable cloud server so you don't lose your critical data. If you're not computer-savvy or you own only a few rental units, a manual system works just fine. If you own a few more units, your filing system can be a simple accordion filing box with dividers, available at any office supply store. If you outgrow the filing box, moving up to a filing cabinet (preferably one that's fireproof and lockable) makes sense.

From the moment you take your first steps toward purchasing an investment property, begin storing your paperwork in a property ownership file. Keep all the important documents of this transaction together, including

- ✔ Appraisals
- ✔ Closing statement
- ✔ Correspondence
- ✔ Due diligence inspection and pest control reports
- ✔ Insurance policies and any product warranties
- ✔ Loan documents
- ✔ Photocopy of your deed (store the original in a fireproof safe or safety deposit box)
- ✔ Purchase offers and contracts

To help you keep track of everything you need, I suggest you use separate file folders on the following topics for each rental property:

- ✔ **Income and expense categories:** Set up a file section for each of your properties with separate folders for income items and expense categories. Keep copies of all receipts in the expense folders so that you can easily locate the information you need when tax time rolls around.

- ✔ **Insurance:** Hang on to a copy of the insurance policy for each property. Make sure you ask each tenant to give you a copy of her renter's insurance. Furthermore, keep a master insurance file that contains current policies for all types of insurance coverage on all your properties. This file should also have a calendar so you can track the expiration or renewal dates for each policy and ensure that you request competitive bids well in advance of the policy expiration date. Keeping accurate records of any incident reports or claims against your insurance coverage is also critical.

- ✔ **Maintenance:** Keep a master maintenance file for storing records and receipts from all maintenance and capital improvements at each rental unit. Doing so gives you a history of the physical condition of each unit throughout your ownership.

- ✔ **Service contracts and supplier information:** Keep all your contracts in one place so you know what each vendor should be doing and what the cost is for said service. You also want to have quick access to all the sources for the supplies and materials you regularly use. It's especially helpful to standardize the purchase of capital items — such as appliances, flooring, and window coverings — to be able to operate efficiently and get the best values.

✔ **Tenant complaints and maintenance requests:** Store this info all in one place to provide a valuable paper trail if a dispute ever arises regarding your conduct as an owner in properly maintaining the premises. Failing to have good records can result in a court dispute that's your word against your tenant's — and your odds aren't as good under such circumstances.

✔ **Tenant information:** For each rental unit, create a tenant file that contains all the important documents for each tenant, including the rental application, rental contract, other legal notices, move-in/move-out checklists, tenant maintenance requests, and correspondence. Always keep the original and provide the tenant with a photocopy.

When a tenant vacates, attach a copy of her Security Deposit Itemization Form (see Chapter 15 for details) and bind the entire tenant file together. Transfer it to a separate file for all former tenants, filed alphabetically by property. You should always retain these records as required by your state real estate commission or other legal authority, which generally means saving them for three or four years. Of course, keeping documents a year or two longer than the minimum is always a safe bet.

Although many people use electronic calendars to track their schedules, you can also use what's called a *tickler file.* Any office supply company sells accordion files for this purpose. You keep one with 12 slots for each month of the year and one with 31 slots for each day of the month. This system allows you to track any number of things manually. For example, if an insurance contract is due in November, you can place a copy of the contract in the September slot to remind you to start the bidding process. If the lease on your only investment property runs through June, you can write the renewal letter far in advance and place it in the April slot, all ready for mailing.

Maintaining Property Records

Maintaining complete and accurate records of all transactions is extremely important in the world of property management. Courts typically take the stance that tenants are merely consumers, so the burden is primarily on the owner to provide any documents outlining the relationship or understanding between the parties. If the owner can't provide the required records, the tenant almost always prevails.

But you also want to keep proper records because you have to report your income and expenses for each rental property on IRS Schedule E to determine whether you made a profit. The IRS requires rental property owners to substantiate all income and expenses by maintaining proper records, including detailed receipts of all transactions. Don't put yourself in a situation where you can't support the accuracy of your tax returns.

Document your profits in income journals and keep all bank deposit slips. Rental property expenses, even if you write business checks, must be accompanied by written receipts that fully document the expenditures. The IRS may not accept a check as proof of a deductible property expense unless you have a detailed receipt as well.

If you own or manage multiple properties, you can assign a one- or two-character code to each property and mark each receipt accordingly. (Indicate the unit number, if appropriate.) When you have info for multiple properties on a single receipt, make photocopies and store the receipts in the respective properties' folders. This way, you can provide evidence of the expense for each property instead of having to wade through all your folders looking for the info you need.

You can also get small scanners and even phone applications that simplify the receipt-storage process. For example, you can scan the receipt when you buy paint or office supplies and have it readily available when you do your rental property accounting later.

If you use your vehicle for your rental property activities, be sure to keep a detailed, written log of all your mileage. Your mileage is a deductible business expense, as long as it's directly related to your property and you have accurate documentation. This simple log should indicate the date, destination, purpose, and total number of miles traveled. You may be surprised at the number of miles you travel each year in your rental activities; the deductible expense can be substantial.

Keep all records pertaining to your rental property for a minimum of three to five years. (The time period usually depends on the legal requirements of the state regulatory commission or department of real estate where you live and/ or own property.) I suggest keeping documents at least a full year past the minimum requirement. For taxation purposes, most certified public accountants advise keeping records regarding the purchase and capital improvements made during your ownership for as long as you own the property, plus another six years in case the IRS wants to review your tax return.

You should maintain certain rental property records, such as those concerning injuries to minors, forever. There's no *statute of limitations* (the law restricting the time frame during which a specific legal action can be taken) for injuries to minors. For example, if a young child is hurt on your property, the statute of limitations doesn't begin until that child has reached 18. In these cases, the tenancy records and maintenance records can be subpoenaed and become critical for defending your actions of 20 years ago.

Taking Care of Business: Accounting

The IRS doesn't require you to keep a separate checking account for each rental property you own, but you do need to keep your rental property activities separate from your personal transactions.

If you own or manage just a few rentals, you may think you can track your tenants' rent payments in your head, but don't rely on your memory. Always track each rental payment in writing. If your tenant pays by check, the canceled check can serve as the tenant's receipt, but the best policy is to provide a receipt whenever possible, regardless of the payment method. *Note:* Make sure you record all other income you receive from your rental property, including dollars from laundry, vending, parking, or furniture rental, just to name a few.

Pop in the CD or click the link in the table of contents to access a sample Receipt for Rent and Other Payments.

Be sure you accurately record the payment of a tenant's security deposit. These funds aren't typically considered income; instead, they're a future liability that's owed back to the tenant if he honors the rental contract's terms. The security deposit may become income at a later date, such as if you apply any portion of it to cover delinquent rent, cleaning, repairs, or other charges. Also, you may be in a state that requires landlords to pay interest on security deposits, with the terms set by statutes that can change frequently, so it's important to keep good records.

Although rental property accounting is fairly straightforward, you may not have the time or inclination to do it. If you aren't prepared to handle your own accounting and record-keeping, hire an accountant or a property management company to handle it for you. Some property management firms will solely perform rental property accounting services for a fee. However, if you want to try your hand at rental property accounting, the following sections can help you with the basics.

Creating a budget and managing your cash flow

Every rental property needs a budget. A *budget* is a detailed estimate of a property's future income and expenses for a certain period, usually one year. A budget allows you to anticipate and track each property's expected income and expenses. Many rental owners neglect to allocate enough money for projected expenses, so when it comes time to make a repair, for example, they don't have the money set aside to cover it. But if you set up a budget, you're better able to anticipate your expenses.

Doing your accounting manually

Most rental property owners begin their real estate investing with a single rental home or condo. Although more and more people are using computer programs to do their accounting, the math is extremely simple at this level. So if you choose to do your accounting manually with pencil and paper in a simple spiral notebook or on an accountant's columnar pad, that's okay. But as you expand your real estate empire, you need to look for better and more efficient systems geared to the specific needs of rental property accounting.

The classic manual accounting system for rental property is the pegboard that allows for a *one-write system,* in which you enter each transaction once using stacked, carbonized documents. A single entry records information needed for a consecutively numbered rental receipt, the tenant's individual ledger card, a bank deposit ticket, and the daily journal that provides a master record of all transactions. Some rental property owners and managers still use this popular rental accounting system, which is available from Peachtree Business Products (800-241-4623 or www.pbp1.com).

Although the budget for a single-family home or rental condo is fairly simple, a proper budget for a newly acquired, multi-unit apartment building can require some careful planning. That planning includes a thorough review of past expenses and the property's current condition. Trends in such expenses as maintenance repairs, utilities, insurance rates, and property taxes can also be important when estimating the future cash flow of a rental property, so don't overlook them.

Many owners rely on cash flow from their rental properties not only to cover their expenses but also to supplement their personal income. Particularly if you're a small rental property owner, you need to have a built-in reserve fund set aside before you start taking out any rental income funds for personal reasons. Maintain a reserve balance large enough to pay your mortgage, cover the full security deposit refund, and cover all the basic property expenses for *at least* one month, without relying on any rental income.

Set aside money for anticipated major capital improvements in a bank account. For instance, you may own a property that will need a new roof in the next five years. Rather than seeing your cash flow wiped out for several months when it comes time to pay for that roof, you can set aside small amounts of money into a capital reserve account over several years. This is the same way that homeowners and community associations reserve funds for major capital items.

Don't forget to allocate and reserve funds to cover semiannual and annual expenses, such as property taxes and potential income tax due on your rental property net income.

Using computers for financial management

Unless you really enjoy manual accounting, I strongly recommend you use your computer and specialized property management software to simplify one of the most mundane yet essential tasks for rental property owners and managers.

Not that long ago, using your computer to properly handle the accounting for rental properties required the use of a spreadsheet program customized to track different rental units, along with a general accounting software program. As is often the case when you're dealing with two different software systems, obtaining needed results could be extremely difficult, and you could spend a lot of time wishing you'd stuck with manual accounting.

A number of today's property management software companies feature everything you need in a single, seamless package. Wading through the myriad choices to make a decision can be difficult unless you really know what you're seeking in specific features. The next two sections help demystify the software selection process.

Evaluating and comparing software solutions

With so many property management software packages on the market, knowing some of the different choices and options available to you is important. Your challenge is to find one that serves all your needs, is cost-effective, and can expand and adapt to your future growth.

The software programs you need typically offer the following:

- ✔ Complete accounting (general ledger, accounts receivable, and accounts payable with check-writing, budgeting, and financial reporting)

- ✔ Tenant and lease management, including many standard rental management forms

- ✔ Tenant service requests, maintenance scheduling, and reminder notes

- ✔ Additional services such as electronic payments, tenant screening, payroll, and utility billing

Many property management accounting packages are available for a nominal investment, but as always, you get what you pay for. Many of the less expensive systems may work in the short run, but if something goes wrong, you may be left stranded without technical support or help. If a software firm has only a few systems in place, you're in for a much higher risk of program errors or incorrect results. The company may not even update or support the software years down the road. Your financial investment, and all the timesaving and other significant benefits of computerized accounting, may be lost if the software package isn't backed by a solid company.

Another advantage of using most computerized rental property accounting software packages is the ability to have your mortgage and bill payments deducted electronically. And you can work with these software packages to pay your bills online. If your tenants pay their rent electronically as well, you can decrease the time you spend handling rent collection and accounting.

You can also customize the financial reporting offered by software programs to meet your needs. Monthly reports often contain income and expense information compared to the monthly budget, as well as year-to-date numbers. Figure 20-1 shows an example of a very basic monthly financial statement for a single-family rental home.

437 Grand View Street (gvs)
Income Statement
For The Period Ending May 2008
Books = Cash

	Month to Date	%	Year to Date	%
Rental Income				
Rent	2,250.00	100.00	11,250.00	100.00
Net Rental Income	2,250.00	100.00	11,250.00	100.00
Other Income				
Effective Gross Income	2,250.00	100.00	11,250.00	100.00
Operating Expenses				
Payroll				
Administrative Expense				
HOA Dues	125.00	5.56	625.00	5.56
Total Administrative	125.00	5.56	625.00	5.56
Utilities				
Water and Sewer	94.87	4.22	405.77	3.61
Total Utilities	94.87	4.22	405.77	3.61
Repairs and Maintenance				
General Repairs	114.22	5.08	126.83	1.13
Total Repairs and Maintenance	114.22	5.08	126.83	1.13
Management Fees				
Management Fees	180.00	8.00	900.00	8.00
Total Management Fees	180.00	8.00	900.00	8.00
Total Operating Expense	514.09	22.85	2,057.60	18.29
Total Operating Income	1,735.91	77.15	9,192.40	81.71
Net Income Before Interest	1,735.91	77.15	9,192.40	81.71
Mortgage Expense				
Mortgage	1,043.50	46.38	5,217.50	46.38
Total Mortgage Payments	1,043.50	46.38	5,217.50	46.38
Net Profit	692.41	30.77	3,975.90	35.33
Total Net	692.41	30.77	3,975.90	35.33
Net After Depreciation	692.41	30.77	3,975.90	35.33

Figure 20-1: A monthly financial statement for a single-family rental home.

Courtesy of Robert S. Griswold

When you use a management company, you typically receive several important accounting reports within a couple of weeks after the end of each accounting month. If you review these reports regularly, they can provide you with a good understanding of your rental investments and give you the opportunity to inquire about or suggest operational changes. But if you manage your own property and do your own accounting, you need to actually review and analyze the financial reports in the same manner as if you'd entrusted your investment to a property manager. You may think you know everything you need to know about your property, and setting aside those monthly reports until tax time may seem harmless, but they're great tools to improve your management results if you use them properly.

Identifying some of the better programs

The property management accounting software industry is very dynamic, with the mergers and buyouts over the past several years resulting in a consolidation of many of the most well-known products into a handful of competitors. Although in this section I offer my thoughts on some of the most popular and useful rental housing accounting software packages, make sure you assess your own needs and do your homework before buying. For example, if you have 12 rental homes with long-term tenants who pay their rent in a timely manner in a single check or electronically, certain software options are just right for you. But if you have a 16-unit student housing building for which you don't receive all the rent at the same time or even from the same tenants each month, then you'll likely find that other software packages can better handle such situations.

Following are a few programs that I highly recommend:

- **Quicken Rental Property Manager (RPM):** If you have a modest real estate empire of fewer than ten separate properties, you'll find this software package a very affordable and acceptable option that's superior to manual systems or user-customized computer spreadsheet software. Unlike prior versions, the more recent editions of RPM don't require you to have the basic Quicken software to cover everything you need to prepare your own reports. These days, RPM is essentially an upgraded or specialized software built on the foundation of Quicken Home & Business and is fully integrated. You can even prepare your federal 1040 Schedule E to hand to your accountant or import directly into TurboTax if you prepare your own tax return.

  On the downside, RPM is still primarily an accounting program that has been modified to handle some basic rental housing needs. It lets you write checks and even uses accrual (rather than cash basis) accounting, but it doesn't include work orders, assist in preparing tenant notices, or have any of the other important features that can simplify your life as a property manager — features that are found in the more robust software packages that I recommend.

Additionally, RPM users report that even though the program has improved significantly in the past few years, it still has many blind spots when it comes to partial rent payments, coded expenses among various categories, and some of the other day-to-day issues faced by landlords. I suggest you carefully follow the user reviews as subsequent versions are released and see whether the concerns about the product are issues that you find troubling. Clearly, if you own only a couple of single-family or condo units, you won't have any problems. But if you have more units, if your income sources are complicated (such as miscellaneous income, or if you accept rent from multiple roommates), or if detailed breakdowns of your expenses are important, then this entry-level product will frustrate you.

One aspect of RPM I particularly like is that parent company Intuit seems to have made a commitment to this product and is introducing frequent updates that allow users to easily decide when the new features are worth the investment in the latest edition. But if you decide that changes aren't really that important, the company continues to support its Quicken family of products for several years. For information on RPM and other Quicken products, go to `http://quicken.intuit.com`.

Rent Manager: One of the most popular software programs for landlords with small- to medium-sized portfolios who've outgrown RPM (see the preceding bullet) or simply need a more comprehensive software package than RPM is Rent Manager, by London Computer Systems (LCS). LCS offers a Small Business Edition of Rent Manager that's perfect for owners and managers with up to 175 units.

Rent Manager has everything you need, starting with a strong financial accounting package that includes a general ledger with accounts receivable and accounts payable, budget management payroll import, and financial reporting. The property management tools include rent collection (even preparing the bank deposit slips), tenant lease management, contact management and word processing (for correspondence and all types of notices), as well as a work order module. I really like the built-in marketing features that allow you to monitor the results of your advertising, track your prospects, and even quickly post ads on Craigslist or to your own website.

Rent Manager is offered in an online version and a stand-alone version; I recommend the online version because you get automatic updates and LCS handles all data backup and technical support. Visit `www.rentmanager.com` for more details.

✔ **Yardi Systems:** Yardi has been in the rental housing software business since 1982, and its reputation has steadily improved and solidified its position as the industry leader. Though it has always been a top choice for the largest property management firms in the country, its product offerings have grown to cover all segments of the market, which is good news for landlords with more modest portfolios. Here's a description of some recommended Yardi products:

- **Yardi Voyager:** For rental property owners or property management companies with portfolios of 250 or more rental units, I recommend the Yardi Voyager asset and property management software suite. My property management company uses this industry-leading, browser-based software, and I've been very impressed with its ability to provide real-time daily and weekly reporting to effectively manage properties. Yardi Voyager also offers detailed monthly financial reports, which allow my company to provide a greater level of service to clients and outperform the competition.

  Yardi Genesis: For smaller property owners and managers, Yardi Systems also offers a fully integrated, Windows-based product called Yardi Genesis that has much of the same basic functionality as Yardi Voyager but with less sophisticated reporting capabilities and fewer features and configuration options. Yardi Voyager is accessible anywhere via the Internet, whereas Yardi Genesis is accessible only through a local network. Like Yardi Voyager, Yardi Genesis includes all the basic features of prospect and tenant management, fully integrated accounts receivable and accounts payable, a general ledger, and cash management. It also allows ready access to information, elimination of duplicate entries, and spontaneous delivery of reporting. The downside is that it's accessible only through a local network.

- **Point2 Property Manager (P2PM):** P2PM, another Yardi Systems creation, is geared specifically toward the small multifamily manager and is an easy-to-use property management and accounting software-as-a-service option. P2PM is easy to implement as well. Simply go to the P2PM website at www.point2property manager.com, sign up for a monthly or annual option, and begin using.

  Yardi has a variety of pricing and hosting options for its software available on either a monthly or annual basis, which can be based either on total program users or units. It also offers a variety of optional modules to enhance internal operations, streamline processes, and increase service level to residents and clients. Find out more at www.yardi.com.

When evaluating different software packages, gather as much info as possible. Be sure to talk to actual product users, preferably people in your area with comparable rental properties and similar accounting needs. Determine what features a program offers, how easy it is to operate, its computer hardware requirements, the availability and cost of technical support, and the strength and reputation of the company backing the product. Obtain a demo or trial version of the software that you can use before you buy, just to make sure it's truly what you want.

Storing data in the cloud

Yardi Systems is also a leader in the *Software as a Service* (*SaaS*) arena, where it hosts and maintains your database on redundant servers and performs all IT functions, including automatic software upgrades. This offering can save any size organization tremendous costs on both staffing and hardware, and it's becoming an increasingly popular option, now being the deployment of choice for the vast majority of the marketplace. Increasing numbers of owners and managers of all sizes are implementing this technology for competitive and cost-saving reasons.

Just like with any technology product, another factor to keep in mind is not just whether the product meets the current standards but whether it incorporates or has the ability to upgrade and include the latest trends. The current trends in the rental housing industry software that you should look for include web-based Software as a Service (SaaS); subscription-based software; automatic posting of vacancies on Craigslist and other sites; integrated hosting and management of websites; electronic maintenance work order requests; electronic rent collection and bill payment; and integrated credit checks and applicant screening.

Chapter 21

Finding New Ways to Increase Your Cash Flow

The goal of owning and managing rental housing is to maximize your *net operating income,* which means the more money you bring in and the lower your expenses while properly maintaining your property, the higher your actual income. Achieving that goal is easier said than done because you have to be willing to think outside the box. So in this chapter, I offer you some new ideas about revenue opportunities outside of base rent.

As a rental property owner, you need to be aware that the government can assist you and your tenants if their limitations and requirements are met and you're interested in participating in certain federal programs. So I explore the ins and outs of government programs that can subsidize your tenants' rent or allow you to rehabilitate your property. I also look at niche opportunities to expand your target market to include tenants who traditionally don't have as many rental options. Catering to these folks can lead to profitable real estate investing through long-term, stable tenancies and reduced turnover.

Considering Non-Rent Revenue

Savvy rental property owners are always looking for additional ways to increase their buildings' incomes. *Non-rent revenue* is income from sources other than basic rent, such as from laundry machines, storage, parking, Internet access, and furnished rentals, all of which I cover in the following sections. These services not only earn you extra money but can also give your rental property the competitive advantage to attract and retain tenants long term.

You can earn non-rent revenue regardless of whether you have a condo, rental home, small apartment property, or large, multifamily apartment building. Every property is different, so you need to evaluate what services or features you can put to work for you. The best way to do this is by looking at your property from the perspective of your current and prospective tenants. Although you should always focus on ways to maximize rent, if you have a single-family home or condo rental, you're more restricted on options for non-rent revenue, such as charging for parking and storage, which are almost always included in the base rent in your case. If you own a multifamily rental property, you may be able to take advantage of other opportunities to generate income.

You can charge your tenants for these non-rent services and amenities separately from the rent or you can bundle them together as rent. The method you choose may depend on what's common practice in your area.

Earning some cash with the wash: Laundry machines

Providing your tenants with laundry equipment is one of the best ways to increase your non-rent revenue. But your ability to meet this need probably depends on the size of your property.

If you own a single-family rental home, including a washer and dryer allows you to charge an extra $50 to $75 in monthly rent. The plumbing and connections are probably already installed (or, if they aren't, they can be added easily).

Unless you want to see all your potential profits go down the drain, make sure your tenants pay for the utilities, including the water and sewer charges. If they don't, then see if you can change that through a process called *submetering;* refer to Chapter 17 for the scoop on submetering.

Rental property owners with 2 to 12 rental units have the toughest time offering laundry equipment because they often lack appropriate locations. If you can't install washers and dryers directly in the rental units, look for a place to build a common area laundry facility. You may be able to convert a portion of the garage or build an enclosure in a carport space, but be sure the location is safe and secure. Always use a licensed and bonded general contractor and get the proper permits.

Larger rental properties are ideally suited for common area laundry facilities with coin-operated or coinless smart-card washers and dryers. Typically, one washer and dryer for every eight to ten units is sufficient, but check first with other owners in your area to see what they offer. If you purchase your own equipment, you'll have an initial cash investment and the burden of ongoing equipment maintenance, but you'll add to your net income. You can also negotiate competitive contracts with laundry service contractors who install, maintain, and collect the revenue from the machines. They often pay upfront bonuses and send you a monthly check for your share of the gross proceeds to cover your utility costs and generate a profit. Some laundry service companies are willing to lease or sell you laundry equipment with a service contract. You then handle your own collections.

Stowing some dough: Storage

If your rental property doesn't have proper storage, you may be faced with the challenge of tenants who regularly leave items on their patios, balconies, or yards. If that's the case, your property can begin to look unsightly in very little time. Instead of getting upset with your tenants, keep in mind that they don't have much choice. New rental units are becoming smaller and smaller, and they often don't include adequate storage. At the same time, many renters are acquiring more and more possessions, and their need for storage is increasing.

Consider adding secure, weatherproof, lockable storage units. Ideally, your storage units should be at ground level, be at least 5-x-5-feet square and 6 feet tall or taller, have a solid door and a heavy-duty locking mechanism, and be constructed out of solid material so that no one can see the contents. The money spent in obtaining quality storage units is a great investment because the price per square foot of storage in many urban rental markets rivals or even exceeds the cost of the rental unit itself. Plus, if you offer storage facilities with your unit, you'll have a competitive advantage that helps keep your property occupied and allows you to charge a higher rent.

Selling your space: Parking

At many properties, parking is a real problem. A good solution — like the carports and garages in high demand in many areas of the country — can be an excellent source of additional revenue. Look around and you may be surprised to see what the going rates for parking are at other properties in your area.

If your property doesn't have extra parking, check to see whether you can add a parking area. Parking is very important to many tenants who gladly pay for the convenience of a reserved space. Even if you have limited parking, consider charging separately for rent and parking. Some tenants may not have vehicles, so instead of including a fee in their rent for a parking space they won't use, you can keep their rent lower while generating additional income by renting parking spaces to tenants who need them.

If you charge for parking, be sure to implement detailed parking rules and have reserved parking stickers or permits. Also, put up proper signage (in keeping with local code, of course) that allows you to enforce your parking regulations through fines or towing.

Converting the World Wide Web to cash: Internet access

Almost everyone has a computer, and Internet access is a must for virtually all rental properties. The days of dial-up connections are gone, and the demand for access to high-speed broadband Internet is rising. Currently, owners of small rental properties in urban areas can usually only offer their tenants Internet access through a local cable television, traditional phone, or Internet Service Provider (ISP) company. But some owners of larger rental properties have been able to negotiate master contracts with ISPs that provide revenue to the landlord when tenants sign up for service with the ISP.

High-speed Internet technology is improving all the time, and the costs to provide this service are dropping. Currently, these five basic types of high-speed Internet connections are available:

- ✔ Cable Internet
- ✔ Digital subscriber lines (DSL and various related enhancements)
- ✔ Satellite Internet
- ✔ WiMax (Worldwide Interoperability for Microwave Access)
- ✔ Wireless Internet Service Providers (WISP)

Don't underestimate the importance of the availability of Internet access. You may not be Bill Gates, but you need to understand technology enough that you can answer your tenant's and prospective tenant's questions. If you have trouble with the terminology, contact service providers in your area and request written information on the services they offer and the cost; certain technologies are better suited and more cost-effective for certain properties and locations.

Cashing in on the ol' dining room set: Furnished rentals

The majority of rental properties are unfurnished because most tenants have their own furnishings. In urban areas, short-term renters may need furnished units, but this group is a specific market that's usually addressed by one or more major apartment owners or hospitality companies. However, in some suburban or rural areas, you can find a demand for furnished rental units for short- or long-term rentals.

Your target market and location often have a bearing on whether you want to consider offering your units partially or fully furnished. Furnishing your rental is a major investment, but if your property is adjacent to a major employer who regularly relocates employees into the area, you can often generate significantly higher rents for a furnished unit.

 Consider using a company that specializes in this market (such as CORT, www.cort.com) if you're looking to competitively offer furnished rental units. This type of company can supply all the furnishings, housewares, and accessories, plus provide corporate relocation referral services that can assist you in locating tenants. High demand for furnished, single-family homes or condos can be common in urban areas with major corporations, so be sure to do some research and see whether offering your property as a corporate rental is a good opportunity. The length of tenancy may be shorter with corporate rentals, but you can usually charge a higher rent to compensate for the increased turnover and higher vacancies.

Putting Lease Options to Work for You

Offering short-term lease options is another way to generate additional cash. A *lease option agreement* generally consists of a standard lease, plus a separate contract that gives the tenant the right to purchase the property at a later fixed date or within a mutually agreed time frame. Lease option agreements typically require an upfront payment and/or monthly payments to secure the purchase option, which is often credited toward the down payment or the purchase price.

Although every lease option is unique, here's an example of how a deal may be structured for a rental home with a current market rent of $1,000 per month and a current market value of $120,000. Real estate forecasts indicate that appreciation will be 4 percent, or approximately $5,000, in the next 12 months. The tenant signs a 12-month standard lease and agrees to pay $1,200 per month, with $1,000 as rent and $200 as a nonrefundable option fee that will be applied to the down payment. At the same time, you and the tenant enter into a lease option agreement that offers the tenant the right to buy the property within 12 months of the lease for $125,000. This amount is the mutually agreed, estimated fair market value of the property by the end of the option period.

In this situation, you receive an additional cash flow of $200 per month, and the tenant treats the property with care because he may very well be the new owner soon. If the tenant exercises the option, he receives a credit toward the down payment of $200 per month for each month he paid the option fee. On the other hand — because you used your standard lease form and guaranteed the lease option documents were drafted properly — you still have the right to evict the tenant for nonpayment of rent or any other material lease default.

In most instances, the tenant isn't able to exercise the purchase option because he doesn't have the money for the down payment and closing costs. In the meantime, you increase your monthly rental income by $200 and have a good tenant. Of course, at the end of the option, the tenant is well aware that he has paid an additional $2,400 in rent that would've been applied to the down payment or purchase price if he had exercised his purchase option. Depending on the circumstances, you can renegotiate an extension of the purchase option or negotiate a new lease without the purchase option.

Lease options are a strategy to consider as a way to increase cash flow from your rental under the right circumstances. They can work very well or be a complete disaster if you don't have the right agreement in place. Both you and the tenant must have a thorough understanding of the unique benefits and challenges of lease options for them to benefit you both. Table 21-1 lists some pros and cons of lease options for your consideration.

Table 21-1	Pros and Cons of Lease Options
Pros	**Cons**
The lease-option tenant is usually better financially qualified.	The lease-option tenant may not be willing or able to buy the property at the end of the lease.
The lease-option tenant pays a nonrefundable option fee upfront or with his rent that's applicable to the down payment or purchase price.	Lease options have income tax ramifications and can trigger due-on-sale clauses in your financing or a reassessment of your property under certain circumstances.
Strong demand for lease options exists; the tenant typically stays longer and often treats the property better.	The agreed option purchase price may be much lower than actual fair market value of rental property if the property appreciates significantly during the option period.
A lease-option tenant may be willing to pay a top-dollar option price.	The lease-option tenant may not exercise the option and instead insist on the return of the extra rent paid or demand a renegotiation of the option terms.
You continue to receive the tax benefits of owning rental property.	A lease-option tenant who doesn't exercise the option after paying a large nonrefundable fee may get even by damaging your rental property.

The availability of lease options often fluctuates with the strength of the rental market. When you're having difficulty finding qualified tenants, a lease option may make good sense. If you have an abundance of qualified tenants, however, a lease option offers you fewer advantages.

Avoid long-term lease options of more than two years because real estate appreciation can be very unpredictable. Don't provide a set option purchase price for any longer than one or two years or else be sure to include a clause that the purchase price will increase by an amount equal to the increase in the average median home price in your area. Consider setting the option purchase price slightly *higher* than the current market rent in your area to account for potential significant appreciation in the property's value.

If you do decide to go with this option, hire a real estate attorney with extensive experience in lease options to review your contract in advance. Lease options can have very serious business and ethical problems if they aren't drafted properly. An improperly structured lease option can be considered a sale and can trigger the due-on-sale clause with your lender, causing you to lose the tax benefits of depreciation and deductible expenses. Your property may be reassessed for property taxes, you may be liable for failure to comply with seller disclosure laws, or you may be prevented from evicting the tenant, even if he has defaulted on the lease. Keep the nonrefundable option fee reasonable so that if the value of the property declines or your tenant doesn't exercise his option for any reason, you can feel comfortable that you've treated the tenant fairly. Or you may want to renegotiate or consider offering an extension.

Taking Advantage of Government Programs

Housing is generally the largest single expense for many families, and the United States is facing a very severe affordable housing crisis. According to the federal government's definition, housing is *affordable* as long as the rent and utility costs don't exceed 30 percent of household gross income. But housing costs often exceed 40 percent of household income, and the lower the income, the more difficult it is to make ends meet. So people who receive Supplemental Security Income (SSI) or who work in low-wage jobs often have trouble finding affordable housing.

Although the recent economic cycle has decreased demand, there is still a need for new rental units in most areas of the country, yet construction of new rental housing is at all-time lows. When the demand for rental housing exceeds the supply, a shortage of available rental units occurs, which leads to increased rents. In this situation, many tenants are forced to pay a large share of their incomes in rent. Rents have declined or held stable for the past few years but are beginning to increase in many urban areas as the economy improves or demand increases with larger populations.

With such a shortage of decent, affordable rental units, low-income tenants have a difficult time finding rental housing. To make matters worse, many rental property owners have a firm policy of not accepting applicants who rely on subsidies to assist with their rent payments. Owners' most common complaints about subsidy programs are that the rent limitations are too low, program administrators fail to cooperate, and some property inspectors are unreasonable in their required repairs and extensive paperwork.

In the following sections, I review some of the benefits and concerns of rent subsidy programs for rental property owners. If you're not sure whether participating in rent subsidy programs is for you, read on.

The scoop on rental subsidy programs

A *rental subsidy* is a payment of some or all of the rent by a governmental or nonprofit agency for the use and occupancy of a rental unit for qualified individuals. These individuals may receive subsidies as a result of insufficient income, disability, relocation assistance, or other similar programs. Most aspects of the tenancy relationship with participants in rental subsidy programs are usually the same as with other tenants.

In some areas, the public housing agency will scrutinize any attempt to terminate the tenancy of subsidized tenants or encourage the tenants to seek legal representation to protect their rights. But landlords who are fair and reasonable and document legitimate concerns about the tenancy shouldn't have any unreasonable hurdles in terminating a subsidized tenancy.

Local housing agencies, religious organizations, and charitable groups offer many types of rental subsidy programs. The majority of the local rent subsidy programs only offer short-term assistance, whereas the *Housing Choice Voucher program* (HCV, also known as Section 8) — a federal U.S. Department of Housing and Urban Development (HUD) program — offers rental subsidies on an ongoing basis.

Be careful with local rental subsidy programs that only offer short-term financial assistance to your tenant. Some programs provide payment of the security deposit, moving costs, and a few months' rent. But you need to be sure that the tenant meets your tenant screening criteria, including possession of sufficient income to meet the full rent and utility costs on an indefinite basis, so that when the short-term assistance runs out, the tenant can still pay you.

Some rental subsidy programs have their limitations. But the need is significant, and many lower-income families and other needy tenants receive important assistance from them. Rental subsidy programs are targeted in their approach and allow you to retain control over tenant selection and all other aspects of the rental relationship.

The lowdown on the Housing Choice Voucher program (also known as Section 8)

HUD established the Section 8 program (or HCV) in 1974 as the federal government's major program for assisting very-low-income families, the elderly, and the disabled in renting decent, safe, and sanitary housing in the private market. It remains the largest rental subsidy program, with more than 2 million tenants participating, and is offered and administered through the 2,500 state, regional, and local public housing authorities (PHAs) throughout the country.

HCV helps twice as many families as the next largest nationwide housing program, public housing. It's available to qualified low-income tenants and requires each tenant to pay a percentage of her monthly income toward rent, with the balance paid by the local PHA. You can find complete details of the program in the HCV Guidebook, located at www.hud.gov/offices/pih/programs/hcv/forms/guidebook.cfm. In the meantime, the next few sections give you an overview on what you need to know about the HCV program.

Understanding how HCV works

The HCV program has two goals:

- ✔ To allow low-income households more choice in housing
- ✔ To reduce the concentration of low-income households in particular buildings and neighborhoods

A wide variety of residential rental housing qualifies for HCV certification, including single-family homes, condos, duplexes, apartments, and mobile homes. HUD requirements state that the rental unit must comply with HUD occupancy standards guidelines, which generally allow two occupants for every bedroom.

HUD allows you to establish your own occupancy standards for your property, which can be higher or lower than the federal standards. But be cautious about establishing standards that are more restrictive (fewer tenants in your rental unit) because they must be based on legitimate business reasons or be required to protect your tenants' health and safety. Of course, you must abide by more stringent state or local restrictions if they exist.

The HCV program provides tenant-based Housing Assistance Payments (HAP), which are rental subsidies or vouchers that tenants can use to rent privately owned rental housing. Tenants with household incomes that are less than the published PHA maximum annual income by family size for a local area are eligible for HCV assistance. The overall income caps for families admitted to the HCV program are usually set between 50 percent and 80 percent of the local median income.

After qualifying, tenants receive HCV vouchers or certificates and have up to 60 days to locate rental units. In certain tight rental markets, tenants have up to 120 days to find suitable rental units. The local PHA makes inspections to ensure that the rental unit meets the HUD Minimum Housing Quality Standards (HQS) at the beginning of the tenancy, upon annual renewal, and upon request if the tenant believes the condition of the unit is unacceptable.

The PHA pays the rental subsidy directly to the rental property on behalf of the program participant. Under this program, the tenant must pay whichever amount is greater — the PHA minimum rent (usually $25 to $50) or the Total Tenant Payment (TTP), which is based on either 30 percent of a tenant family's monthly adjusted income or 10 percent of a tenant family's monthly gross income. Another possibility is if the family receives payments for welfare assistance from a public agency and part of the payments are specifically designated to meet housing costs. Usually the calculation — based on 30 percent of the adjusted monthly income — is the basis for setting the minimum tenant portion of the rent. If the tenant selects a unit with rent higher than the PHA limits, the program also provides for a maximum initial rental burden limit so that the tenant's share of the rent doesn't exceed 40 percent of her monthly adjusted household income.

The HCV rental subsidy is based on the HUD Fair Market Rent, available from local PHAs. At least annually, the PHA surveys the local rental housing market and determines the median rents and utility allowance for each unit type based on the number of bedrooms. The amount of rent that owners can charge is limited to amounts set by the local PHA that don't exceed a maximum of the HUD Fair Market Rent level for the particular county. HCV tenants may choose rental units with higher rents than the PHA maximums and then pay the difference or choose lower-cost units and keep the difference for themselves.

In some areas of the country, the maximum allowable rents are reasonable. But in a lot of areas, the maximum rents set by the local PHA rule out many of the local rental units because they're too low. In these locations, HCV participants and rental property owners are effectively unable to work together to achieve decent affordable housing. The PHAs have been allowed to adjust the maximum HCV rents up to 10 percent higher than the HUD Fair Market Rent to be consistent with actual rents in the area and allow tenants more alternatives.

The maximum rents vary based on whether the owner or the tenants pay the utilities. In general, you're better off having the tenants pay their own utilities because the HUD utility allowances are typically insufficient, and owner-paid utilities don't encourage your tenants to conserve energy.

Knowing what to do if you rent to HCV tenants

If you take part in HCV, you're required to enter into a one-year lease with a participating tenant using a standardized, HUD-approved lease form or a combination of your lease with a HUD addendum. You're locked into the one-year lease agreement except for nonpayment of rent or another serious breach. You must also sign a Housing Assistance Payments (HAP) contract with the local public housing authority authorizing the payment of rent, which can be deposited directly into your bank account.

Use your own standard rental application, rental contract, and all other forms and procedures. Attach the PHA lease and HAP contract to your paperwork. If your HCV tenant doesn't pay her share of the rent or you have another problem, immediately notify your contact person at the local PHA. Although the PHA is limited in what it can do, it *can* be helpful in resolving issues.

The greatest benefit to rental owners is that the local PHA pays the majority of the tenant's monthly rent like clockwork, and the tenant's portion is low enough that she usually doesn't have any problem meeting this financial obligation. Also, if the tenant fails to pay her portion of the rent, you have the right to evict her and apply the security deposit to any unpaid rent or rental unit damage. Some PHAs may have formal or informal requirements to contact them to resolve any issues before beginning an eviction action.

Process an HCV tenant's move-out just like any other tenant, but be sure to notify the local PHA. The availability of HCV assistance is limited, with long waiting lists. This fact can be very helpful in motivating your tenants to be responsible because the termination of their leases for nonpayment or other breaches often results in a loss of their rental assistance.

For most rental property owners, participating in the HCV program is very easy. Contact the PHA in your city or county for more info or to be sure your rental rates are within their maximum guidelines. If they are, your local PHA will refer eligible applicants to you and prepare the necessary documents should you decide to rent to an eligible applicant. Make sure you obtain a copy of the HCV rules and procedures from HUD before determining whether the HCV rental program will work for you.

You can't charge higher rent for an HCV rental unit than you would if you were renting the same unit to a private, unassisted tenant. Make sure you regularly conduct market surveys of rents for comparable properties in your area so that you know your rents are reasonable. Most PHAs conduct periodic audits, so be prepared to provide your local PHA with documentation that supports the fact that you're collecting the same or a higher rental rate for a comparable non-HCV unit.

Summarizing the pros and cons of HCV

The HCV rental subsidy program can be a great resource for rental property owners in certain areas of the country. The key is to ensure that the PHA-determined maximum rental rates for your area are competitive and that the PHA's inspection requirements are reasonable. If these criteria are sound, then HCV can provide you with additional rental prospects. Screen the tenants carefully (just like any other applicant) and work with the local PHA representative to avoid problems. (I provide pointers on tenant screening in Chapter 10.)

Participating in HCV may provide you with stable, long-term tenants at market rents, where the majority of the rent is paid by a government agency, and the tenants are highly motivated to pay their share of the rent and abide by your rules and guidelines. But weighing the pros and cons is still worthwhile.

Here are some advantages to participating in the HCV program:

- ✓ You encounter less competition because many rental property owners refuse to participate.
- ✓ A portion of the rent is guaranteed by the local PHA and backed by the federal government.
- ✓ You retain full control over the screening and selection process, with the PHA providing the names and addresses of the current and one prior landlord for verification and reference checking.
- ✓ You may collect a full security deposit up to the maximum allowed under state and local laws, and you may adjust rent annually, subject to PHA maximum rents for comparable rental units in the area.
- ✓ You gain a stable tenant profile with competitive rents and property that's inspected regularly.

And here are some disadvantages to participating in the HCV program:

- ✓ Additional paperwork leads to a delay in initial occupancy.
- ✓ The first payment is delayed, and you may have difficulty stopping payment when the tenant leaves.
- ✓ You must meet HUD Minimum Housing Quality Standards through regular inspections by your local PHA and make all required repairs.
- ✓ Rents and utility costs can't exceed HUD's Fair Market Rent determination.

The 411 on rehabilitation loans

A large percentage of rental housing in the United States is old and in need of renovation and modernization. According to National Multi Housing Council tabulations from the latest U.S. Census Bureau's American Housing Survey, less than 25 percent of the apartments in the country have been built since 1990. Clearly, great opportunities exist for property owners to renovate rental units.

With the difficulty in providing new low-income rental housing, HUD encourages the rehabilitation of existing rental units through state and local governmental agencies, including the HOME program; community development block grants; and rural housing programs. Most programs are administrated by local PHAs. They allow owners of qualified rental units to obtain improvement grants or borrow money to upgrade and rehabilitate their properties. The grants cover weatherproofing and other health and safety issues, and the low- or even no-interest loans allow owners to make capital improvements.

As with most governmental programs, you can expect to fill out numerous forms and wait for processing, inspections, and approvals when you apply for a rehabilitation loan. However, besides offering below-market interest rates, these loans are often *assumable,* which means a purchaser is allowed to take over the below-market interest rate loan as part of her financing upon acquisition.

Some programs offer owners of larger rental properties rehabilitation funds if they provide housing for specific targeted groups. For example, people with physical and mental disabilities find it difficult to locate private and affordable rental housing, so if you rent to them, you may qualify for rehabilitation funds.

Demand for special housing for the aging population, as well as for people struggling with HIV/AIDS and substance abuse, is growing. Because of the lack of new rental housing construction, the federal government is developing programs to encourage the renovation and conversion of existing rental units, particularly single-family houses, targeted for these particular groups.

Contact your local PHA or visit the HUD website at www.hud.gov for more information on funding programs and qualification standards.

Working in Niche Markets

Sometimes thinking outside the box and looking for angles, like niche rental markets that other rental property owners overlook or aren't willing to pursue, makes sense. You may own property in a soft rental market or just want to find a market niche where your rental units can outperform others.

The following sections explore several of the niche rental markets — ranging from students and senior citizens to nonsmokers and tenants with pets — that you can use to your benefit. These niche markets may or may not be right for you. But be sure to at least consider whether you can dip into one or more of them and increase your cash flow in the process.

Taking another look at your pet policy

In today's rental market, one of the most effective strategies to keep your rental units occupied with stable, paying tenants is to allow pets. According to the 2011/2012 American Pet Products Association (APPA) National Pet Owners Survey, 62 percent of American households have at least one pet. That includes 46.3 million households with one or more dogs and 38.9 million households with one or more cats — a huge target market!

Although many rental property owners immediately reject the idea of allowing pets, the reality is that rental options are extremely limited for pet owners — meaning if you're one of the few landlords who accept pets, you immediately increase the demand for your rental unit.

Allowing pets under certain conditions can result in much higher rental income and fewer vacancies. Accepting pets can be successful if you

- ✔ **Have a rental property that's suitable for pets:** Some rental properties are particularly well suited for tenants with pets. An older rental property or one with certain features such as a fenced yard, hard-surface flooring (rather than carpeting), and vertical blinds (as opposed to curtains) is a good candidate for tenants with pets.

- ✔ **Verify through references and an interview that your tenant is a responsible pet owner:** Be sure to confirm all references and ask specific questions about the pet. Actually meeting and spending a little time with the pet to determine its demeanor is a good idea. Be sure to properly complete the pet or animal agreement addendum to your rental contract and have the tenant agree to your terms. Restrict any animal with dangerous or potentially dangerous tendencies, and take a photo of the pet for your tenant file.

✔ **Implement and enforce stringent pet policies and rules:** For your pet policy to run smoothly, you need detailed rules, including a limit on the number of animals allowed. You also need to have clear policies about pet and tenant behavior outlined in a pet or animal addendum. For example, you want to forbid tenants from flushing cat litter down the toilet (otherwise you'll end up with clogged pipes) or allowing large birds to roam free all day in the rental unit. Put limits on what you consider to be an acceptable pet; think about making exotic animals off-limits. Be sure your addendum provides that any violation of your pet rules can result in your right to unilaterally revoke the permission to keep a pet, or, in severe cases, in an Unconditional Quit Notice (a notice that requires the tenant to vacate without the opportunity to cure the lease violation).

✔ **Require an extra deposit for tenants with pets:** Because so few rental properties accept pet owners, those that do are able to charge higher rental rates and collect much larger security deposits. Most responsible pet owners don't balk at a reasonable monthly rental rate premium or an increased security deposit of several hundred dollars.

Avoid using the label *pet deposit;* instead, just include the additional amount in your total security deposit. But check state statutes for language and limitations (many states have specific dog breeds that can be denied by landlords). If you were to use the label *pet deposit,* a savvy tenant or court could possibly limit your use of those funds to damage you can prove was caused by the pet. Your goal is to ensure that the rental rate and larger security deposit provide adequate compensation and protection against any or *all* damage to the unit that results in increased cleaning or repair costs.

Even "no pet" properties must accommodate renters who have companion or service animals if they're prescribed under the HUD and DOJ guidelines. For more on this topic, flip to Chapter 10.

Renting to students

A large number of rental properties are located near colleges and universities; yours may be one of them. But many property owners have the same strong feelings against renting to students as they do about accepting pets. The major problem, however, is that (except for the ADA exemption) you can legally have a "no pet" policy, but you can't unlawfully discriminate against students if they meet your tenant screening criteria. Though students aren't a federally protected class, there's a trend among more progressive local municipalities with a large student population (such as Madison, WI; Austin, TX; and Washington, D.C.) to establish students, or "matriculation" in general, as a protected class in their jurisdictions.

Deciding which dog breeds to allow

A landlord is virtually guaranteed to be sued if a dog bite occurs on his property and the issue is whether the landlord acted reasonably in allowing the animal to reside on-site. Unless state or local laws prohibit a certain dog breed, the decision to accept or reject a specific dog or breed of dog as a pet remains with the landlord. Prior to accepting a dog of a breed that you're not familiar with, I suggest you have the prospective tenant offer a written note from a veterinarian indicating the dog's breed and that it's suitable for your rental unit. This may not completely protect you in case of an incident and you're sued, but it will certainly show that you made a reasonable effort to make a prudent decision.

Your decision may be affected by the fact that some insurance companies don't extend coverage to certain animals and certain breeds of dogs. Note that if the animal isn't a pet but an assistive animal necessary because of a disability, you should work with your insurance company to attempt to extend coverage for this purpose, and if you're unsuccessful, you should seek alternate coverage so that you can reasonably allow the disabled resident the animal he needs. Landlords have the right on a case-by-case basis to assess the reasonableness of the size and type of assistive animals. In other words, a companion elephant or rattlesnake wouldn't be acceptable.

Note that the Humane Society of the United States is among the many pet advocacy and rescue organizations becoming increasingly involved in addressing the issue of pets in rental housing. The Humane Society offers advice and tips for both tenants and rental owners at its website, www.rentwithpets.org. This resource (and others like it) can provide great information. As an added bonus, following the Humane Society's guidelines can show that you were reasonable in your decision to accept a dog.

The National Multi Housing Council has researched the nationwide student housing market and points out that many of the 75 million people born between 1981 and 1995 will be entering college in the next decade. The Council studied 64 college towns across the country and found that the demand for off-campus, privately owned student housing is very high.

One of the most common problems with renting to students is the fact that students have special needs regarding the lengths of their leases. Many schools are in session for only 4 or 5 months in the fall and spring and 2 or 3 months in the summer. If you only offer a 12-month lease, you may end up with student tenants who default on their leases and leave right after the end of the quarter or semester.

If your rental properties attract prospective student tenants, be sure to adopt policies and leases that allow you to take advantage of this large target market while minimizing its downside. One strategy is to offer 3-month and 9-month leases at a premium rental rate rather than the 12-month leases available at competitive rental properties. Students attending the fall and spring sessions will be delighted with the 9-month term, and summer students will go for the 3-month term.

The other primary concern with renting to students is their behavior. Mitigate this risk by implementing strict policies concerning noise and, ideally, having an on-site manager to enforce them. Be sure to consistently require a larger security deposit and/or cosigner or guarantor of the lease at properties where you rent to students. Also, you should insist on receiving the full rent each month in a single check (as explained in Chapter 14).

Catering to senior citizens

The need for rental housing for active seniors is increasing as America's rapidly expanding population of older adults chooses to maintain and prolong its independent living status. The U.S. Census Bureau estimates that the number of seniors (age 65 or older) will swell from the present 40 million to a projected 88.5 million by the year 2050. As a result, many rental property owners are finding the demand for senior housing a great investment opportunity.

Senior rental housing is no longer required to offer "significant facilities and services" designed for the elderly, but it must show that one person who's 55 or older lives in at least 80 percent of the occupied rental units. Federal law also requires that rental property owners follow policies and procedures that demonstrate intent to provide housing for persons age 55 or older. This requirement typically means that you must post a sign outside and that all literature you provide to the public must include a statement indicating that housing for older persons is available.

Before designating your multifamily rental property as housing for older persons, be sure to check with an attorney about discrimination laws in your area. (Note, however, that qualified seniors rental properties can exclude families with children without violating the Fair Housing Act.) Many state and local fair housing laws may still be modeled after the former federal law requiring owners to provide "significant facilities and services."

Seniors are typically excellent long-term tenants; however, do some advance research to determine whether your property is ideally suited for seniors. Evaluate your units to consider their proximity to local transportation, shopping, medical facilities, special senior centers or activities, and places of worship.

If your property has services and facilities for seniors, prepare to attract a senior target market. Be sure to advise local agencies catering to seniors about the availability of your rental units.

Designating your rental units smoke-free

One of the most controversial issues in rental housing management in the past decade concerns the ability of a property owner to restrict the use of the rental unit to nonsmoking status. The growing trend in the United States is to restrict smoking in almost all public areas, and the elimination of smoking on airplanes has even become widely accepted internationally. Although the hotel industry successfully implemented policies offering both smoking and nonsmoking rooms for years, rental property owners are just starting to seriously embrace this issue.

I've found that a strong demand exists for properties where smoking is partially or completely restricted. One frequent complaint I receive from tenants who write in to my nationally syndicated "Rental Forum" newspaper column is about secondhand smoke from a neighbor. Unfortunately, in some properties, tobacco smoke can drift from one rental unit directly into another. The smoke can enter from hallways, stairs, balconies, and patios, usually through windows and doors, but sometimes also from the building's common ventilation system.

The majority of Americans are nonsmokers. Smoking is considered a controllable behavior, not a disease, so people who smoke aren't categorized as a protected class under federal and state fair housing or antidiscrimination laws. Although tenants who smoke need places to live, so do nonsmoking tenants who want to avoid drifting secondhand smoke.

The best practice to control behavior and reduce the risk that you'll be accused of arbitrary discrimination or unfair business practices is to focus on the behavior rather than the person. So you need not inquire as to whether an applicant smokes; just have enforceable policies regarding smoking.

However, currently no federal or state laws prohibit you from adopting a policy that requires all or part of a building to be smoke-free, including individual rental units. Some states are beginning to pass laws protecting tenants. Because the rights of individuals who smoke and those opposed to secondhand smoke are constantly changing, be sure to check local and state laws in your area before deciding to implement a smoke-free rental program.

Following are some good business reasons to consider offering smoke-free rental units:

- Lack of damage from cigarette burns
- No need to thoroughly clean carpets, drapes, and other surfaces or completely repaint the unit just to remove a permeating smoke smell
- Potential for reduced insurance premiums

Some groups promote rental properties that don't allow smoking on the premises. For example, in southern California, the Smokefree Apartment House Registry (www.smokefreeapartments.org) offers a free listing service to rental property owners with total or partial smoke-free policies. I believe that this concept is finally reaching widespread acceptance and will be increasingly popular throughout many areas of the country in the next few years.

Although you can simply put a "no smoking allowed" clause in your rental contract, I recommend surveying your current tenants before doing so. You may find that prohibiting smoking in common areas, rental units, balconies, and patios is a popular idea — or you may meet with more resistance than anticipated. Knowing where your tenants stand on this issue should be an important part of your decision.

As with any major policy change, be sure to implement a conversion to a smoke-free property upon tenant turnover or only after giving proper legal notice to current tenants. If you want to implement a smoke-free policy at a larger property, start by prohibiting smoking in all common areas, such as the rental office, laundry room, and recreational facilities. Then you can expand the smoke-free policy to individual units if the program is positively received by your tenants.

To see a sample Smoking Policy Addendum from the California Apartment Association, pop in the CD or click the link in the table of contents.

Part VI
The Part of Tens

In this part . . .

This wouldn't be a *For Dummies* book without the Part of Tens. Here you can find short bursts of information on why you should buy rental property in the first place and how to rent a vacancy. So if you're looking for a lot of information but you don't have much time, you've come to the right part.

Chapter 22

Ten Reasons to Become a Rental Property Owner

● ●

In This Chapter

▶ Investing in real estate to diversify, generate income, and get tax advantages

▶ Understanding the benefits of holding real estate properties over the long term

● ●

*O*wning rental property isn't for everyone. So if you're just starting to think about investing in real estate through rental property, check out these ten great reasons to take the plunge. (Disclaimer: I should point out that I believe so strongly in real estate investing that I wrote *Real Estate Investing For Dummies* with Eric Tyson [Wiley].)

You Can Diversify Your Investments

Buying rental property helps vary your investments. Owning your own home is a first step toward diversification, but owning rental real estate is a prudent strategy to protect your assets from volatility in certain areas of the economy. Unlike owning your own home, owning rental property that someone *else* calls home is an investment because it gives you a tangible asset and allows you to use other people's money to build your wealth.

You Don't Need Much Money to Start

A lack of money is often cited as the number one factor that keeps people from investing in real estate. But you can typically purchase real estate for a down payment of 20 percent or less, with the balance provided by others. After a few years of restructuring in the lending community, real estate loans are again becoming readily available at very competitive terms throughout the United States. Some sellers are willing to assist the buyer by financing a portion of the purchase price.

If you're a first-time home buyer, you may qualify for up to 100 percent financing. So basically, you can take advantage of a first-time home buyer program, build up equity in your home, and then refinance it to generate additional capital, which you can use as the down payment to buy rental property.

It Can Be a Second Income

Real estate values may have dropped in most areas of the country in recent years, but a look through the list of the 400 richest Americans, published annually by *Forbes* magazine, shows that real estate has played a key role in making many of the world's great fortunes.

The majority of residential rental real estate in the United States is owned by working middle-class individuals of all backgrounds and ages who sought viable opportunities to augment their current incomes or careers. Real estate investing can truly begin as a part-time job and supply a second income.

You Gain Tax Advantages

The federal tax code has many unique advantages for real estate. Property owners can benefit from expense deductions, depreciation write-offs, tax-deferred exchanges, and favorable capital gains tax rates. Owning and operating rental property is a business, and the tax laws allow deductions against your rental income for the cost of payroll, property management, advertising, maintenance and repairs, utilities, insurance, and property taxes.

You can depreciate your rental property, giving you another tax break. Current federal tax laws allow you to depreciate your property improvements over a 27½-year life span. The depreciation loss can reduce your taxable income or give you a taxable loss on the property, even if you have a positive cash flow. After depleting your depreciation on income-producing real estate, you can take advantage of IRS code 1031 (also known as a tax-deferred Starker exchange) to postpone taxation on any gain by rolling over your equity into a new and often larger rental property.

Tax codes change from year to year, so discuss your personal tax situation with your accountant, tax attorney, or tax preparer.

Real Estate Holds Its Value

Real estate is one of the most popular investments available because income-producing rental properties have held their value through many economic cycles over the decades. Throughout history, the tangible nature of real estate has been extremely important to both people and the economy.

Real estate is cyclical. Many businesses have their ups and downs, and real estate is no exception. However, real estate usually rebounds and grows in value after a slump. Historically, many solid real estate investments have declined for a period but then grown again in value. Think of market downturns as a buying opportunity. Real estate appreciates because its quantity is limited. Over the long run, real estate is an established performer and offers a solid foundation for your financial future.

You Get Leverage

Real estate *leverage* is the use of mortgage financing to purchase an investment property with only a small cash outlay, with the expectation that appreciation and inflation will create a disproportionately high return on the original cash investment upon sale. The key to successfully using leverage is having a mortgage interest rate *lower* than the return on your real estate investment. Here's an oversimplified example: A buyer purchases a $150,000 rental home for $30,000 cash down and a $120,000 loan at a 5 percent interest rate. If the property appreciates and sells in three years for a net of $180,000, the owner will have earned $30,000, or a 100 percent return on his money. This is called *positive leverage.* Conversely, high interest rates and flat real estate values with no increases in cash flow result in *negative leverage,* and undercapitalized investors may lose their properties.

It Beats Inflation

Inflation is the loss of buying power as prices rise. Most investments — such as money market accounts, bonds, stocks, and mutual funds — have trouble keeping up with the inflation rate. Thus, investors in these assets often find that they lose purchasing power over time. Real estate, however, is a formidable tool in the battle against inflation. When you purchase rental property with fixed-rate financing, the property's price and financing cost are set. Other operating costs, such as property taxes and utilities, are bound to increase, but rental property owners can typically increase the amount of rent they charge to offset these heightened costs. Of course, temporary softness or downturns in the rental market may delay rent increases in the short run, but historically, real estate cash flows have been able to maintain an owner's purchasing power in the long run.

You Can Shelter Your Income

Currently, the tax laws affecting real estate offer tax advantages to individuals actively involved in managing their rental properties. If you're an active investor and you don't exceed the adjusted gross income limits, you may qualify for substantial deductions for rental property losses to reduce your taxable earned income from other sources, a process known as *sheltering other income.* Using a property management firm doesn't preclude you from taking advantage of these tax write-offs as long as you're involved in setting the rents and policies for your rental property.

Qualified real estate professionals are allowed to claim all real estate loss deductions in the year they incur them. However, the requirements to achieve the status of a *real estate professional* are strict; consult your tax advisor.

You Get a Positive Cash Flow

Rental property owners know that the right investment property generates sufficient rental income to cover the property's mortgage and operating expenses. And after the tax advantages of depreciation, real estate generally provides positive cash flow. This pattern may not always hold true in the first few years of ownership, but positive cash flow is a real benefit for many investors. Of course, after the mortgage has been paid, the positive cash flow can be very significant.

It Can Help You Retire

Real estate investment is one of the best methods to fulfill the dream of retiring wealthy. This worthy goal requires a diversified investment strategy, with assets that are purchasable with leverage, generate cash flow, appreciate consistently over time, and maintain their purchasing power in an inflationary environment. Like most investments, the earlier you begin your real estate investment career, the better your results. Buying and holding the right rental properties for 20 to 30 years is an ideal way to hedge inflation, take advantage of unique tax benefits, and build wealth for retirement.

Chapter 23

Ten Ways to Rent Your Vacancy

In This Chapter

▶ Keeping your property appealing and rent-ready

▶ Offering new tenants various incentives to move in

▶ Making use of corporate relocation services and housing choice vouchers

*E*very day that a rental unit sits vacant is a loss of revenue you can never fully recover, regardless of whether you eventually secure a higher rent. In this chapter, I give you ten tips to help you rent your vacancy right away.

Maintain Curb Appeal

Your rental prospect forms his first impression of your property as soon as he approaches it. If the property doesn't look clean and attractive on the outside, he often doesn't wait to see the inside! Your chances of leasing your rental unit at a competitive market rent to a stable and financially solid prospect are about nil if your property doesn't have good curb appeal. You can't always dramatically improve the property's architectural look, but you can usually control the appearance of its grounds. Buy annuals when they're in season and on sale, keep the lawn mowed and watered, and trim and fertilize the trees and shrubs. A great-looking yard can be your best marketing tool.

Familiarity is the enemy of rental property owners; when you're familiar with your property, you may have trouble looking at it with an independent and critical eye. Drive up to your property and continually ask yourself what looks tacky or poorly maintained. You may really have to focus, but you'll find several items that need immediate attention. Take care of them now.

Keep the Unit in Rent-Ready Condition

Distinguish your rental unit from the others by keeping up its professionally maintained, clean, bright, and airy appearance. This noticeable difference will appeal to the best rental prospects.

Although you may eventually find a tenant willing to accept your rental unit before it's in rent-ready condition, you can almost guarantee that the unit will be in worse condition when that tenant vacates. Naturally, the tenant will argue if you try to take any deductions from her security deposit, and the courts will probably side with her because the unit wasn't clean originally. Spare yourself this agony and make having a rent-ready unit that's clean and defect-free your goal.

Establish a Competitive Rent

If you don't have vacancies on a regular basis and you're in a market where rents are fluctuating, setting the rental rate at the right amount can be a real challenge. Be sure to do your homework and carefully review the local market for rental properties that are truly comparable to yours. If you set your rent too low, you'll have multiple qualified applicants and you can select the best one, but you won't maximize your rental income. If the rent is too high, you'll suffer lost rental income. The key is to set your rent at or slightly below the market rent for your area.

This isn't magic, and your competitors don't know all the answers. So don't just pick a number out of thin air or charge what the guy down the block is asking. Be confident enough to ask a solid rent in your market, one at the top of the range in which your property fits. If you sign a lease at a lower rent than you could have gotten, you'll never recover that lost income.

Offer Prospects a Rate Guarantee

Prospective tenants may feel comfortable with your current rent, but virtually all rental prospects are concerned about your ability to unilaterally raise their rent, unless you offer a lease. Of course, a long-term lease isn't in your best interest because you can't increase rent and may have trouble evicting a problem tenant.

If you know that you don't intend to raise your new tenant's rent in the near future, offer him a rental rate guarantee for a set period. This move allays his fears of being hit with an unreasonable rent increase soon after moving in. It also helps you avoid getting locked into a long-term lease that may one day lead to expensive and aggravating court action.

Provide Wireless Internet Access

High speed Internet connections have become critical to rental property owners seeking to remain competitive, but the options vary depending on where your property is located. One thing's for sure, though: Tenants like having wireless Internet access. Partner with local Internet service providers to see what kind of a deal you can work out to supply wireless Internet access across your property. If you have a larger rental property, the provider may well cover the installation costs and offer to share in the revenue. If you own a single-family or small property, you may be able to arrange free installation with a tenant commitment to subscribe to the service for a minimum time period.

Offer Referral Fees

Your current tenants or your rental property neighbors can be the best sources for finding your next tenant. They may work with, go to school with, or participate in activities with someone who's looking for a new rental. So let them know that you have an upcoming vacancy and that you want to reward them for taking the time to refer a rental prospect to you. Referral fees can be an extremely cost-effective source of qualified renters. You need to determine what a motivating referral fee is in your area, but I commonly see fees of $100 to $300, with an extra $100 offered during the holidays or slow rental traffic times of the year. Another benefit is that most people don't personally refer a potential tenant whom they don't respect and trust. Referral fees thus allow tenants to make some money and have a hand in picking their own neighbors!

Accept Pets

Rental property owners who don't accept pets eliminate nearly 50 percent of the country's potential renters, according to the Humane Society of the United States. With the requirement to accept certain animals for tenants qualified under the Americans with Disabilities Act (see Chapter 10), many owners already find their ability to keep animals out of their buildings diminished.

So if you can't beat 'em, why not join 'em? Good pet owners and their pets can make wonderful renters. If you establish sound pet policies, collect a larger security deposit, and meet both the tenant and the pet, you'll often find that you have an excellent, stable tenant for many years to come.

For safety and insurance reasons, avoid dangerous animals or potentially dangerous breeds of dogs, such as pit bulls (often called various types of "terriers"). See Chapter 21 for a more thorough discussion of the breeds that a prudent landlord should carefully evaluate before accepting.

Offer Move-In Gifts or Upgrades

The word *free* is one of my favorite words — and one of the most powerful sales tools ever! The word *new* is also very persuasive. If you want to rent your vacancy today, seriously consider offering your prospect a move-in gift or an upgrade to the rental unit. Every day your unit sits vacant, you're losing money you'll never see again, so you may as well sweeten the pot.

You have a choice: You can offer a move-in gift that immediately belongs to the tenant or an upgrade to the unit that stays when she leaves. For example, countertop microwave ovens make great move-in gifts, whereas a built-in microwave range hood or ceiling fan is an excellent unit upgrade. If you're planning to replace the carpet, consider giving your incoming tenant the option to choose from her favorite neutral carpet colors.

Contact Corporate Relocation Services

Many areas of the United States have a high demand for rental units for corporate employees relocating to the area. In particular, corporate relocation services have an extremely difficult time finding rental properties for families of executives requiring single-family homes with yards and plenty of storage. These services are often willing to pay above-market rents for rental units or homes on short-term leases of 6 to 12 months. From your perspective, the additional turnover can be worth it if the rent is enough. From the services' perspective, your rent is much cheaper than placing their clients in extended-stay lodging.

Some corporate relocation pros may want to lease your property for multiple years with the provision that they can move in different occupants. Make sure you have very firm house rules, set a reasonable limit on the frequency of tenant turnover, collect complete information on the occupants, and require a detailed inspection upon each move.

Accept HUD's Housing Choice Vouchers

The U.S. Department of Housing and Urban Development's Housing Choice Voucher (HCV) program (also known as Section 8; see Chapter 21) is administered by 3,000 local public housing authorities located throughout the country. Some of those agencies aren't easy to work with, and some have maximum allowable rents that are well below market value. If these factors aren't a problem in your area, you may find some tangible benefits in participating in the HCV program, such as

- Your vacancy won't last long because of the severe shortage of rental units available for HCV tenants in many areas.
- The government typically pays the majority of the rent promptly each month, so you at least have that guarantee.

Appendix

About the CD

*T*he accompanying CD has everything you need to make your life as a property manager much easier, and this appendix gives you the information you need to navigate the CD. *Note:* If you're reading this in an electronic format, go to http://booksupport.wiley.com for access to the additional content.

System Requirements

Make sure that your computer meets the minimum system requirements shown in the following list. If your computer doesn't match up to most of these requirements, you may have problems using the software and files on the CD. For the latest and greatest information, refer to the ReadMe file located at the root of the CD-ROM.

- A PC running Microsoft Windows
- A Macintosh running Apple OS X or later
- An Internet connection
- A CD-ROM drive
- Microsoft Word
- Microsoft Excel
- Adobe Reader 7.0 or later

If you need more information on the basics, check out these books published by John Wiley & Sons, Inc.: *PCs For Dummies,* by Dan Gookin; *Macs For Dummies,* by Edward C. Baig; *iMacs For Dummies,* by Mark L. Chambers; and *Windows XP For Dummies* and *Windows Vista For Dummies,* both by Andy Rathbone.

Using the CD

To install the items from the CD to your hard drive, follow these steps.

1. **Insert the CD into your computer's CD-ROM drive.**

   The license agreement appears.

   Note to Windows users: The interface won't launch if you have autorun disabled. In that case, choose Start⇨Run. (For Windows Vista, choose Start⇨All Programs⇨Accessories⇨Run.) In the dialog box that appears, type ***D:\Start.exe***. (Replace *D* with the proper letter if your CD drive uses a different letter. If you don't know the letter, see how your CD drive is listed under My Computer.) Click OK.

   Note to Mac users: When the CD icon appears on your desktop, double-click the icon to open the CD and then double-click the Start icon. Also, note that the content menus may not function as expected in newer versions of Safari and Firefox; however, the documents are available by navigating to the Contents folder.

2. **Read through the license agreement and then click the Accept button if you want to use the CD.**

   The CD interface appears. The interface allows you to browse the contents and install the programs with just a click of a button (or two).

Software

The files on the CD are in Adobe PDF, Microsoft Word, and Microsoft Excel formats. In case you don't have Adobe Reader, Microsoft Word, or Microsoft Excel on your computer, I've added links to the following software so that you can access everything:

- ✓ **Adobe Reader:** This is a freeware application for viewing files in the Adobe portable document format.

✔ **OpenOffice.org:** This is a multiplatform office productivity suite that's similar to Microsoft Office or Lotus SmartSuite, but it's absolutely free. It includes word processing, spreadsheet, presentation, and drawing applications that allow you to create professional documents, newsletters, reports, and presentations. OpenOffice.org supports most file formats of other office software, so you should be able to edit and view any files created with other office solutions.

What You'll Find on the CD

The CD includes all the great forms you see in this book, plus a whole lot of extra forms that are useful for effectively managing rental properties. Many of these forms are ones I either use in my company or created for this book. The CD also has nearly 150 forms from the Institute of Real Estate Management (IREM), plus additional resources and information on professional organizations and designations.

Landlord-tenant laws vary from state to state. Although I encourage you to use the CD forms at your properties, be sure to have them reviewed by a local landlord-tenant legal expert before using them.

The following sections summarize the forms and other valuable legal info and resources you find on the CD. If you need help accessing the items on the CD, see the instructions in the earlier "Using the CD" section.

Forms

All the forms in this book, as well as the more than 60 additional forms I developed to make your job as a property manager much easier, are on the accompanying CD. Following is a breakdown of the categories of forms I've included to help you tackle any and every property management scenario you may encounter, from the mundane to the challenging:

✔ **Chapter forms:** In most chapters, I reference forms that are helpful, including everything from an Animal Agreement to the Tenant ACH Debit Authorization Form. Most of the forms I reference in the book are in this folder.

✔ **Rental contract forms:** The CD includes a sample Month-to-Month Rental Agreement and a sample Lease Agreement. Use them as starting points for crafting your own rental contracts that comply with your local landlord-tenant laws. The CD also features various rental contract addendums, such as the following:

• Extension of Lease Addendum

• Military Addendum

- Pool Rules and Regulations Addendum
- Radiant Ceiling Heat Addendum
- Smoke-Free Addendum

✔ **Rent collection forms:** Some of the rent collection–related items I've included are Courtesy Rent Reminder Cards, a Rent Adjustment Notice, and a Notice of Cash Payments Only for three months for tenants whose checks are returned.

✔ **Association-related forms:** Because so many rental units are located within homeowners' or community associations, the CD contains forms to help you notify the association that you're renting your unit. It also features a form that advises your tenant that she must comply with the association's governing documents and rules and warns your tenant that she's responsible for assessed charges or fines for violations.

✔ **Vendor- or employee-related forms:** Some of the documents found in this folder include a sample Landscape Maintenance Contract, an Employee Warning Notice, and a Vendor Contract for Services Addendum.

✔ **Institute of Real Estate Management forms:** IREM (www.irem.org) has generously permitted me to share nearly 150 forms from its residential form database, including a basic Residential Management Agreement. Included on the CD are forms in the following categories:

- Business Development and Management
- Finance and Asset Analysis
- Human Resources
- Maintenance
- Marketing and Leasing
- Risk Management

✔ **California Apartment Association material:** The CAA (www.caanet.org) is a great resource for rental property owners and managers in California. It offers a comprehensive database of forms for all situations, and its members can purchase unlimited access to this material for a nominal annual fee. I strongly encourage you to look into joining if you live in California. As a preview of what you can find in the database, the CAA has graciously allowed me to give you a small sample with these six forms:

- Bedbug Addendum
- Mold Notification Addendum
- Move-In/Move-Out Itemized Statement
- Renters Insurance Addendum
- Satellite Dish and Antenna Addendum
- Smoking Policy Addendum

Legal information

Throughout this book, you see references to the importance of verifying state, and sometimes even local, landlord-tenant laws. On the CD, I share the web links and specific code sections for the most common landlord-tenant statutes by state. These regulations are constantly in flux, so making sure you have the latest information is essential. Routinely confirm that you fully understand and are complying with the pertinent landlord-tenant law that applies to your specific situation.

I also share several tables that summarize some of the most important and commonly used landlord-tenant legal information, including the states that permit rent control and those that either prohibit or preempt it, the time permitted for tenants to pay rent after a nonpayment notice is served, and security deposit limits by state.

The CD also features required addendums for residential tenancies in the states of California and Washington and the city of Chicago.

Bonus Part of Tens chapter

This fun chapter covers ten of the biggest mistakes landlords commonly make and what you can do to avoid them. Reading this chapter can save you plenty of headaches — and money!

Educational opportunities and professional designations

Ongoing education is important for all rental property managers. Aside from this book, one particularly valuable source of education on leasing and management skills is the My Leasing Coach online video program taught by Kathy Harmon. To find out more about this great educational tool, simply call 612-850-3123.

Professional organizations are also fabulous resources for furthering your property management education. I encourage you to get involved with your local rental groups and seek out professional designations. Both IREM and the National Apartment Association (NAA) have local affiliates you can contact to attend their educational courses and regular meetings. They can also be extremely valuable resources for current and pending landlord-tenant laws, forms, legal referrals, tenant screening, and up-to-date market conditions. They're also your best source for local vendors, suppliers, and contractors that specifically cater to the residential rental housing market; many of these firms offer discounts to members of the local IREM chapter or NAA affiliate.

IREM has 80 chapters located in most major metropolitan areas in the United States and is expanding internationally as well. Go to www.irem.org and search for your local chapter to find out about its regular meetings, seminars, and educational courses. IREM holds two major national meetings each year that attract members from all parts of the country. One meeting is typically held in Washington, D.C., and the other meeting is held in varying locations.

The NAA (www.naahq.org) has nearly 200 local affiliates, and many are quite active, with monthly meetings and educational offerings, including seminars and workshops on new developments and legal updates. Some local NAA affiliates have annual education and trade shows.

Both organizations provide a range of professional designations and certifications, which I highly recommend you look into. Specific information on each of these is included on the CD, but here's a quick overview:

✔ **IREM certifications and designations:** IREM is the premier professional real estate management organization and is affiliated with the National Association of Realtors (NAR). Individuals who combine a prescribed curriculum of course work, experience, and ethics can attain the prestigious Certified Property Manager (CPM) designation or the Accredited Residential Manager (ARM) certification. If you're just starting out as a rental property owner or manager, I suggest you consider the entry-level ARM certification, which is geared strictly toward managers of residential property. After you have the ARM, you can consider the more advanced CPM designation, which is for managers of all types of properties — including residential, commercial, retail, and industrial.

IREM also offers the Accredited Management Organization (AMO) accreditation for property management companies. This requires additional educational and minimum experience requirements, plus references, strict ethics, and minimum insurance coverage standards. The premier property management firms hold this accreditation.

✔ **NAA certifications and designations:** NAA is the premier national trade association for the residential rental housing industry. It offers several national certifications and designations, including the following:

- Certified Apartment Maintenance Technician (CAMT) and Certified Apartment Maintenance Technician II (CAMT II)

- Certified Apartment Manager (CAM)

- Certified Apartment Property Supervisor (CAPS)

- Independent Rental Owner Professional (IROP)

- National Apartment Leasing Professional (NALP)

✔ **National Association of Residential Property Managers (NARPM) designations:** NARPM is a national organization of real estate professionals who focus on the management of single-family and small residential properties. NARPM offers the following designations:

- Certified Residential Management Company (CRMC)
- Certified Support Specialist (CSS)
- Master Property Manager (MPM)
- Residential Management Professional (RMP)

Resources

Although this book has a lot of great information, you need to know much more as a rental property owner or manager, so I've developed a comprehensive resource database with details on

✔ **Professional and trade organizations:** These groups are each actively involved with a different segment of the residential rental housing market, from development and management to affordable and public housing. In addition to providing contact information for IREM, NAA, and NARPM, the CD tells you how to get in touch with the National Multi Housing Council (NMHC), National Association of Home Builders (NAHB), National Leased Housing Association (NLHA), National Affordable Housing Management Association (NAHMA), Urban Land Institute (ULI), and National Council of State Housing Agencies (NCSHA).

✔ **Governmental agencies:** Important federal agencies to know include the Department of Housing and Urban Development (HUD) and the Environmental Protection Agency (EPA).

✔ **Media and newsletters:** Media regarding rental real estate can be very informative. That's why I provide details on the CD about Inman News Features; Mr. Landlord; *Multi-Housing News; Professional Apartment Management, Fair Housing Coach,* and other publications from Vendome Group, LLC; my "Rental Roundtable" column; and the Tenants Legal Center of San Diego.

✔ **Rental housing industry vendors/suppliers:** The list of national firms catering to the rental industry that I share on the CD is a great resource for researching products and services you need for your property or for simply finding out more about what's available. Contact information and websites are included.

Troubleshooting

I tried my best to compile programs that work on most computers with the minimum system requirements. Alas, your computer may differ, and some programs may not work properly for some reason.

The two likeliest problems are that you don't have enough memory (RAM) for the programs you want to use or that you have other programs running that are affecting installation or running of a program. If you get an error message such as Not enough memory or Setup cannot continue, try one or more of the following suggestions and then try using the software again:

- ✔ **Turn off any antivirus software running on your computer.** Installation programs sometimes mimic virus activity and may make your computer incorrectly believe that it's being infected by a virus.

- ✔ **Close all running programs.** The more programs you have running, the less memory is available to other programs. Installation programs typically update files and programs, so if you keep other programs running, installation may not work properly.

- ✔ **Have your local computer store add more RAM to your computer.** This is, admittedly, a somewhat expensive step. However, adding more memory can really help your computer's speed and allow more programs to run at the same time.

Customer Care

If you have trouble with the CD-ROM, call Wiley Product Technical Support at 800-762-2974. Outside the United States, call 317-572-3993. You can also contact Wiley Product Technical Support at http://support.wiley.com. John Wiley & Sons will provide technical support only for installation and other general quality control items. For technical support on the applications themselves, consult the program's vendor or author.

To place additional orders or to request information about other Wiley products, call 877-762-2974.

Index

John Wiley & Sons, Inc.
End-User License Agreement

READ THIS. You should carefully read these terms and conditions before opening the software packet(s) included with this book "Book". This is a license agreement "Agreement" between you and John Wiley & Sons, Inc. "WILEY". By opening the accompanying software packet(s), you acknowledge that you have read and accept the following terms and conditions. If you do not agree and do not want to be bound by such terms and conditions, promptly return the Book and the unopened software packet(s) to the place you obtained them for a full refund.

1. **License Grant.** WILEY grants to you (either an individual or entity) a nonexclusive license to use one copy of the enclosed software program(s) (collectively, the "Software") solely for your own personal or business purposes on a single computer (whether a standard computer or a workstation component of a multi-user network). The Software is in use on a computer when it is loaded into temporary memory (RAM) or installed into permanent memory (hard disk, CD-ROM, or other storage device). WILEY reserves all rights not expressly granted herein.

2. **Ownership.** WILEY is the owner of all right, title, and interest, including copyright, in and to the compilation of the Software recorded on the physical packet included with this Book "Software Media". Copyright to the individual programs recorded on the Software Media is owned by the author or other authorized copyright owner of each program. Ownership of the Software and all proprietary rights relating thereto remain with WILEY and its licensers.

3. **Restrictions on Use and Transfer.**

    (a) You may only (i) make one copy of the Software for backup or archival purposes, or (ii) transfer the Software to a single hard disk, provided that you keep the original for backup or archival purposes. You may not (i) rent or lease the Software, (ii) copy or reproduce the Software through a LAN or other network system or through any computer subscriber system or bulletin-board system, or (iii) modify, adapt, or create derivative works based on the Software.

    (b) You may not reverse engineer, decompile, or disassemble the Software. You may transfer the Software and user documentation on a permanent basis, provided that the transferee agrees to accept the terms and conditions of this Agreement and you retain no copies. If the Software is an update or has been updated, any transfer must include the most recent update and all prior versions.

4. **Restrictions on Use of Individual Programs.** You must follow the individual requirements and restrictions detailed for each individual program in the "About the CD" appendix of this Book or on the Software Media. These limitations are also contained in the individual license agreements recorded on the Software Media. These limitations may include a requirement that after using the program for a specified period of time, the user must pay a registration fee or discontinue use. By opening the Software packet(s), you agree to abide by the licenses and restrictions for these individual programs that are detailed in the "About the CD" appendix and/or on the Software Media. None of the material on this Software Media or listed in this Book may ever be redistributed, in original or modified form, for commercial purposes.

Apple & Mac

iPad 2 For Dummies,
3rd Edition
978-1-118-17679-5

iPhone 4S For Dummies,
5th Edition
978-1-118-03671-6

iPod touch For Dummies,
3rd Edition
978-1-118-12960-9

Mac OS X Lion
For Dummies
978-1-118-02205-4

Blogging & Social Media

CityVille For Dummies
978-1-118-08337-6

Facebook For Dummies,
4th Edition
978-1-118-09562-1

Mom Blogging
For Dummies
978-1-118-03843-7

Twitter For Dummies,
2nd Edition
978-0-470-76879-2

WordPress For Dummies,
4th Edition
978-1-118-07342-1

Business

Cash Flow For Dummies
978-1-118-01850-7

Investing For Dummies,
6th Edition
978-0-470-90545-6

Job Searching with Social
Media For Dummies
978-0-470-93072-4

QuickBooks 2012
For Dummies
978-1-118-09120-3

Resumes For Dummies,
6th Edition
978-0-470-87361-8

Starting an Etsy Business
For Dummies
978-0-470-93067-0

Cooking & Entertaining

Cooking Basics
For Dummies, 4th Edition
978-0-470-91388-8

Wine For Dummies,
4th Edition
978-0-470-04579-4

Diet & Nutrition

Kettlebells For Dummies
978-0-470-59929-7

Nutrition For Dummies,
5th Edition
978-0-470-93231-5

Restaurant Calorie Counter
For Dummies,
2nd Edition
978-0-470-64405-8

Digital Photography

Digital SLR Cameras &
Photography For Dummies,
4th Edition
978-1-118-14489-3

Digital SLR Settings
& Shortcuts
For Dummies
978-0-470-91763-3

Photoshop Elements 10
For Dummies
978-1-118-10742-3

Gardening

Gardening Basics
For Dummies
978-0-470-03749-2

Vegetable Gardening
For Dummies,
2nd Edition
978-0-470-49870-5

Green/Sustainable

Raising Chickens
For Dummies
978-0-470-46544-8

Green Cleaning
For Dummies
978-0-470-39106-8

Health

Diabetes For Dummies,
3rd Edition
978-0-470-27086-8

Food Allergies
For Dummies
978-0-470-09584-3

Living Gluten-Free
For Dummies,
2nd Edition
978-0-470-58589-4

Hobbies

Beekeeping
For Dummies,
2nd Edition
978-0-470-43065-1

Chess For Dummies,
3rd Edition
978-1-118-01695-4

Drawing For Dummies,
2nd Edition
978-0-470-61842-4

eBay For Dummies,
7th Edition
978-1-118-09806-6

Knitting For Dummies,
2nd Edition
978-0-470-28747-7

Language & Foreign Language

English Grammar
For Dummies,
2nd Edition
978-0-470-54664-2

French For Dummies,
2nd Edition
978-1-118-00464-7

German For Dummies,
2nd Edition
978-0-470-90101-4

Spanish Essentials
For Dummies
978-0-470-63751-7

Spanish For Dummies,
2nd Edition
978-0-470-87855-2

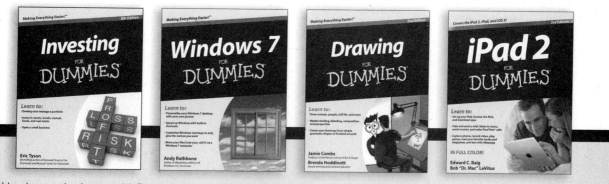

Available wherever books are sold. For more information or to order direct: U.S. customers visit www.dummies.com or call 1-877-762-2974.
U.K. customers visit www.wileyeurope.com or call (0) 1243 843291. Canadian customers visit www.wiley.ca or call 1-800-567-4797.

Connect with us online at www.facebook.com/fordummies or @fordummies

Math & Science

Algebra I For Dummies,
2nd Edition
978-0-470-55964-2

Biology For Dummies,
2nd Edition
978-0-470-59875-7

Chemistry For Dummies,
2nd Edition
978-1-1180-0730-3

Geometry For Dummies,
2nd Edition
978-0-470-08946-0

Pre-Algebra Essentials
For Dummies
978-0-470-61838-7

Microsoft Office

Excel 2010 For Dummies
978-0-470-48953-6

Office 2010 All-in-One
For Dummies
978-0-470-49748-7

Office 2011 for Mac
For Dummies
978-0-470-87869-9

Word 2010
For Dummies
978-0-470-48772-3

Music

Guitar For Dummies,
2nd Edition
978-0-7645-9904-0

Clarinet For Dummies
978-0-470-58477-4

iPod & iTunes
For Dummies,
9th Edition
978-1-118-13060-5

Pets

Cats For Dummies,
2nd Edition
978-0-7645-5275-5

Dogs All-in One
For Dummies
978-0470-52978-2

Saltwater Aquariums
For Dummies
978-0-470-06805-2

Religion & Inspiration

The Bible For Dummies
978-0-7645-5296-0

Catholicism For Dummies,
2nd Edition
978-1-118-07778-8

Spirituality For Dummies,
2nd Edition
978-0-470-19142-2

Self-Help & Relationships

Happiness For Dummies
978-0-470-28171-0

Overcoming Anxiety
For Dummies,
2nd Edition
978-0-470-57441-6

Seniors

Crosswords For Seniors
For Dummies
978-0-470-49157-7

iPad 2 For Seniors
For Dummies, 3rd Edition
978-1-118-17678-8

Laptops & Tablets
For Seniors For Dummies,
2nd Edition
978-1-118-09596-6

Smartphones & Tablets

BlackBerry For Dummies,
5th Edition
978-1-118-10035-6

Droid X2 For Dummies
978-1-118-14864-8

HTC ThunderBolt
For Dummies
978-1-118-07601-9

MOTOROLA XOOM
For Dummies
978-1-118-08835-7

Sports

Basketball For Dummies,
3rd Edition
978-1-118-07374-2

Football For Dummies,
2nd Edition
978-1-118-01261-1

Golf For Dummies,
4th Edition
978-0-470-88279-5

Test Prep

ACT For Dummies,
5th Edition
978-1-118-01259-8

ASVAB For Dummies,
3rd Edition
978-0-470-63760-9

The GRE Test For
Dummies, 7th Edition
978-0-470-00919-2

Police Officer Exam
For Dummies
978-0-470-88724-0

Series 7 Exam
For Dummies
978-0-470-09932-2

Web Development

HTML, CSS, & XHTML
For Dummies, 7th Edition
978-0-470-91659-9

Drupal For Dummies,
2nd Edition
978-1-118-08348-2

Windows 7

Windows 7
For Dummies
978-0-470-49743-2

Windows 7
For Dummies,
Book + DVD Bundle
978-0-470-52398-8

Windows 7 All-in-One
For Dummies
978-0-470-48763-1

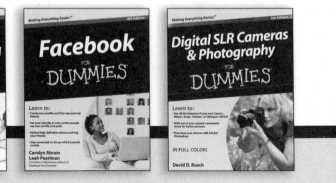